Parents and Children
with Society

This volume opens a new frontier in family communication research as it brings together veteran researchers and younger scholars to explore the communication of parents and children as they create relationships outside the family. The work breaks new ground in family communication in three key areas:

- Communication between parents, children, and significant societal agents (childcare workers, teachers, coaches, healthcare workers)
- The role of media (Instant Messaging, hotlines) in parent-child-societal relationships
- Parent-child-societal communication and evolving parental and caregiver roles (step-parents, foster parents, gay/lesbian parents)

Families today raise children in complex relationships with society, and this volume reflects the significance of this condition in the studies of unique parent-child communication. This volume will be an indispensable tool for scholars, researchers, and students in communication, as well as psychologists and sociologists. It will help all readers achieve a better understanding of how parents, children, and key members of their societal sphere communicate.

Thomas J. Socha is ODU University Professor and Associate Professor of Communication at Old Dominion University. He is the founding editor of the *Journal of Family Communication,* and received the NCA's Bernard J. Brommel Award for Outstanding Scholarship and Distinguished Service in Family Communication. His publications include books, chapters, and articles about various facets of family communication.

Glen H. Stamp is a Professor, Department Chair, and Director of Graduate Studies in the Department of Communication Studies at Ball State University. He has previously published one book (with Thomas J. Socha) on parent-child communication, as well as authoring numerous articles and chapters in interpersonal communication and family communication.

COMMUNICATION SERIES
Jennings Bryant / Dolf Zillman, General Editors

Selected Titles in Applied Communications
(Teresa L. Thompson, Advisory Editor) include:

Parents and Children Communicating with Society
Managing Relationships Outside of Home

Edited by

Thomas J. Socha
Glen H. Stamp

NEW YORK AND LONDON

First published 2009
by Routledge
711 Third Ave, New York, NY 10017

Simultaneously published in the UK
by Routledge
2 Park Square, Milton Park, Abingdon, Oxon OX14 4RN

Routledge is an imprint of the Taylor & Francis Group, an informa business

© 2009 Taylor and Francis

Typeset in Goudy by EvS Communication Networx, Inc.

Library of Congress Cataloging in Publication Data
Parents & children communicating with society : managing relationships outside of home / editors, Thomas J. Socha and Glen H. Stamp. -- 1st ed.
p. cm.
Includes bibliographical references and index.
1. Communication in the family. 2. Intergroup relations. 3. Social interaction. I. Socha, Thomas J. II. Stamp, Glen H. III. Title: Parents and children communicating with society.
HQ515.P37 2009
306.87—dc22
2008055157

ISBN10: 0-415-96487-3 (hbk)
ISBN 10: 0-415-96488-1 (pbk)
ISBN 10: 0-203-93860-7 (ebk)

ISBN 13: 978-0-415-96487-6 (hbk)
ISBN 13: 978-0-415-96488-3 (pbk)
ISBN 13: 978-0-203-93860-7 (ebk)

To our parents...
Mary & Jim Socha
Nell & Fred Stamp

Contents

Figures and Tables

Figures

Tables

Foreword

Anita Vangelisti

In 1995, Socha and Stamp published *Parents, Children, and Communication: Frontiers of Theory and Research*. The volume represented a milestone for communication researchers. Scholars in other fields had done extensive studies of parent-child interaction, looking at issues such as communication between infants and their mothers (Barratt, Roach, & Leavitt, 1992; Field, Healy, Goldstein, & Guthertz, 1990), the association between parent-child interaction and marital change (Belsky, Youngblade, Rovine, & Volling, 1991), and conflicts between adolescents and their parents (Silverberg & Steinberg, 1987; Smetana & Gaines, 1999). But, with the exception of some excellent work done in the late 1970s and early 1980s (e.g., Delia & Clark, 1977; Haslett, 1983), communication researchers had left interactions between parents and their children largely unexamined. The Socha and Stamp volume served as an impetus, for many communication scholars, to study the various ways that parents and children relate to each other.

Now, more than 10 years later, Socha and Stamp have turned their attention to a different frontier. In *Parents and Children Communicating with Society: Managing Relationships Outside of Home*, they examine the communicative interface between parents, their children, and the outside world. Socha and Stamp have compiled a collection of chapters that address the links between families and a number of societal entities ranging from schools, to healthcare systems, to the media. In some cases, the entities under study are easily identifiable institutions (hospitals, childcare centers); in others, they are more abstract and difficult to identify (cyberspace, the public sphere). Although the societal entities examined vary from chapter to chapter, they all point to two common themes: first, that the interactions parents and their children have with society affect, and are affected by, their interactions with each other; and second, that communication researchers have a great deal to learn from, and about, the ways each of the relevant entities interacts with parent-child dyads. In short, this volume, like its predecessor, maps out territory for research on parent-child communication that is both influential and mostly unexplored by those who study communication.

The willingness of the volume's authors to examine interactions between parents, children, and society is timely. Today, many of the constraints that once prevented family members from communicating with a broad range of societal entities have been eliminated by technology. People travel now more than they used to, they have immediate access to news and information via the internet and, in many instances, they have more contact with the individuals who represent social entities. Parents who are concerned about their child's performance in school can email the child's teacher or the school principal. Grown children who want information about an elderly parent's health can seek out that information on the internet, email the parent's physician, or go to an on-line forum to discuss the parent's symptoms.

Although many of the constraints on communication between parents, children, and society have been lifted, researchers and theorists know relatively little about whether, and under what circumstances, the increased opportunity for communication is beneficial. Having greater access to information can be helpful in some situations and harmful in others (Brashers, 2001). Further, increases in the frequency of communication may not be indicative of high quality interaction or highly satisfying relationships. Indeed, some scholars have argued that the constant accessibility individuals are afforded by certain technologies has actually led to greater isolation and less satisfying, less intimate relationships (Putnam, 1995). It also is important to note that there are forces—both within and outside families—that shape the degree to which parents and children communicate with societal entities and the extent to which societal entities interact with parents and children. Family rules, cultural norms, and economic forces all can serve to encourage or discourage interaction between family members and society. The restrictions that some individuals face in their communication with society can shape their lives, and their relationships, as much as the access enjoyed by others.

Clearly, as noted by Socha and Stamp, the interactions that take place between parents, their children, and society are complex. Perhaps the most obvious source of their complexity lies in the fact that they involve multiple constituencies that operate on different levels. Thus, for example, each instance of parent-child-societal communication involves the simultaneous engagement of individuals (e.g., a parent, a child, a teacher), dyads (e.g., parent-child, parent-teacher, child-teacher), and groups (e.g., parent groups, classrooms of children, teachers in a school). Another source of their complexity lies in the process of communication itself (Sillars & Vangelisti, 2006). Communication conveys multiple meanings simultaneously. More specifically, researchers typically distinguish between the content of messages and the "command" (Ruesch & Bateson, 1951) or "relationship" (Watzlawick, Beavin, & Jackson, 1967) aspect of messages, suggesting that the former is literal and relatively explicit whereas the latter is implied and involves social or relational evaluations. Communication also is complex because it serves multiple functions. Whenever individuals, dyads, and groups interact, they simultaneously seek to fulfill multiple goals (e.g., coherence, impression management, persuasion; see Street & Cappella, 1985). In addition, each act of communication is interpreted in the context of the messages that precede and follow it. So, for instance, when a parent, a child, and a school administrator interact, their communication is influenced by any prior interactions they may have had with each other as well as by interactions they may have had with others in their social environment. Even after they conclude their interaction, the way that each of them interprets the other's communication is affected by subsequent interactions.

The studies and commentaries included in the current volume take on the challenge of exploring the complex interactions that occur between parents, children, and society. In doing so, they not only offer a rationale for studying parent-child-societal communication, they also provide grounds for conducting additional work on the subsystems that compose various parent-child-societal systems. For instance, understanding the different ways that parents, children, and teachers view schoolwork raises questions about how parents and children talk together about the work that children do at school, how parents and teachers communicate about homework assignments, and how teachers and children discuss the roles and responsibilities associated with schoolwork. Similarly, looking at interactions between nontraditional parents (e.g., stepparents, gay and lesbian parents), their children, and the larger community points to issues about how these parents communicate with their children about their parental role, how nontraditional parents cope with the challenges they face when interacting with the surrounding community, and how various members of the community interact with the children of nontraditional parents.

By highlighting questions that can be asked about the subsystems associated with parent-child-societal communication, the chapters in the current volume present researchers with the opportunity to further explore, and understand, each of the subsystems and their components. If, as suggested by this volume, researchers start their work by situating each subsystem within a larger system, they are likely to uncover information about the subsystems and their components that might not otherwise be uncovered. For instance, in examining conversations between healthcare professionals, children who are chronically ill, and the parents of these children, researchers are likely to find variables that predict the quality of the relationship between the parents and their children (DiMatteo, 2004). It may be that parents who involve their children in the interaction or who translate complex words or phrases for their children have higher quality relationships with their children than those who do not. Inasmuch as this is the case, researchers might then go on to examine the scope conditions that define the degree to which, and the circumstances in which, this sort of inclusion is functional for children (e.g., being included may be more important for older children than for younger children whereas being reassured may be more important for younger children). Similarly, interactions between parents and their children concerning the children's use of various media may provide a telling indicator of their relationship (Jennings & Wartella, 2004). For example, the tendency of parents and children to approach (as opposed to avoid) discussions of this sort may predict the degree of trust and openness that characterizes their association with each other. It also may be that the link between parents' and children's tendency to engage in these discussions and the quality of their relationship is moderated by such variables as the parents' beliefs about the use of particular media and the parents' willingness to explain those beliefs to their children.

Describing and explaining the various subsystems associated with parent-child-societal communication certainly will provide researchers and theorists with information they can use to better understand parent-child-societal interactions. However, as noted by systems theorists, larger systems cannot be understood solely on the basis of their subsystems or their parts. The chapters that make up the present volume not only provide a motivation for researchers to look at various parent-child-societal subsystems, they also underline the importance of examining the system as a whole.

Researchers have long argued that families are open systems and that, as a consequence, they should be studied in context. In bringing together the chapters written for this book, Socha and Stamp take this argument one step further. *Parents and Children Communicating with Society: Managing Relationships Outside of Home* suggests not only that we need to study families in context, but also that what we conceive as context can become an integral part of family interactions. Socha and Stamp are being modest in noting that this volume represents a first step in "navigating the terrain of communication for parents, children, and society" (chapter 1). The book does more than that. It reconceptualizes parent-child communication by defining societal contexts as interactive. This reconceptualization really does represent a new frontier.

References

Barratt, M. S., Roach, M. A., & Leavitt, L. A. (1992). Early channels of mother-infant communication: Preterm and term infants. *Journal of Child Psychology and Psychiatry, 33,* 1193–1204.

Belsky, J., Youngblade, L., Rovine, M., & Volling, B. (1991). Patterns of marital change and parent-child interaction. *Journal of Marriage and the Family, 53,* 487–498.

Brashers, D. E. (2001). Communication and uncertainty management. *Journal of Communication, 51,* 477–497.

Delia, J. G., & Clark, R. A. (1977). Cognitive complexity, social perception and the development of listener-adapted communication in six-, eight-, ten-and twelve-year-old boys. *Communication Monographs, 44,* 326–345.

DiMatteo, M. R. (2004). The role of effective communication with children and their families in fostering adherence to pediatric regimens. *Patient Education and Counseling, 55,* 339–344.

Field, T. M., Healy, B., Goldstein, S., & Guthertz, M. (1990). Behavior state matching in mother-infant interactions of nondepressed versus depressed mother-infant dyads. *Developmental Psychology, 26,* 7–14.

Haslett, B. J. (1983). Communicative functions and strategies in children's conversations. *Human Communication Research, 9,* 114–129.

Jennings, N., & Wartella, E. (2004). Technology and the family. In A. L. Vangelisti (Ed.), *Handbook of family communication* (pp. 593–608). Mahwah, NJ: Erlbaum.

Putnam, R. D. (1995). Bowling alone: America's declining social capital. *Journal of Democracy, 6*, 65–78.

Ruesch, J., & Bateson, G. (1951). *The social matrix of psychiatry.* New York: W.W. Norton.

Sillars, A. L., & Vangelisti, A. L. (2006). Communication: Basic properties and their relevance to relationship research. In A. L. Vangelisti & D. Perlman (Eds.), *The Cambridge handbook of personal relationships* (pp. 331–351). New York: Cambridge University Press.

Silverberg, S. B., & Steinberg, L. (1987). Adolescent autonomy, parent-adolescent conflict, and parental well-being. *Journal of Youth and Adolescence, 16*, 293–312.

Smetana, J., & Gaines, C. (1999). Adolescent-parent conflict in middle-class African American families. *Child Development, 70*, 1447–1463.

Street, R. L., & Cappella, N. (1985). Sequence and pattern in communicative behavior: A model and commentary. In R. L. Street & J. N. Cappella (Eds.), *Sequence and patter in communicative behavior* (pp. 243–276). London: Edward Arnold.

Watzlawick, P., Beavin, J., & Jackson, D. D. (1967). *Pragmatics of human communication: A study of interactional patterns, pathologies, and paradoxes.* New York: Norton.

About the Contributors

Erica Weintraub Austin (PhD, Stanford University) is Professor of Communication and Interim Director of the Edward R. Murrow School of Communication at Washington State University. She has published dozens of peer-reviewed studies and a variety of book chapters focusing on children's and young adults' uses of the media in decision making. She also has served as a consultant to evaluate young peoples' responses to media and media literacy curricula nationwide, including as a panelist for the development of the National Youth Anti-Drug Campaign's statement advocating media literacy as a strategy for substance abuse prevention and suggesting best practices. She was the recipient of the 2001 Krieghbaum Under-40 Award from the Association for Education in Journalism and Mass Communication. She recently was named the Greater Spokane Public Relations Society of America Educator of the Year.

Raymond D. Baus is an Associate Professor in the Communication Department at the University of Wisconsin, Whitewater. His research publications have included college students as caregivers, couples' condom use scripts, and dialectic tension management strategies.

Dawn O. Braithwaite (PhD, University of Minnesota) is a Willa Cather Professor of Communication at the University of Nebraska-Lincoln. Her research focuses on communication in times of family transition. She has authored 70 articles and four books. She received the National Communication Association's Brommel Award in Family Communication and will be the Association's President in 2010.

Jennings Bryant is CIS Distinguished Research Professor, holder of the Reagan Endowed Chair of Broadcasting, and Associate Dean for Graduate Studies and Research at the University of Alabama. He was President of the International Communication Association in 2002–2003. His primary research interests are in entertainment theory, mass communication theory, media effects, and media, children, and families.

Elizabeth A. Craig (PhD, 2008, The University of Oklahoma) is an Assistant Professor in the Department of Communication at North Carolina State University. Her research interests include relational maintenance processes, social support within stigmatized groups, friendships, stepfamily communication, and relational aggression. She has co-authored articles in *Communication Quarterly* and *Communication Studies*.

Christine S. Davis (PhD) is Assistant Professor in the Department of Communication Studies at the University of North Carolina at Charlotte. Her research is in the intersection of health, family, interpersonal, and group communication. She is currently studying issues of communication and discourse in children's mental health, aging, end-of-life, and disability.

Brett Dobesh is a graduate student in the Communication Studies Department at the University of Northern Iowa. He is currently completing his last semester of coursework toward the completion of an MA degree.

Norín Dollard (PhD) is Assistant Professor in the Department of Child and Family Studies at the Louis de la Parte Florida Mental Health Institute, University of South Florida. Dr. Dollard has over 15 years of services research and evaluation experience in the area of behavioral health needs of children and families.

Ashley Duggan (PhD, 2003, University of California, Santa Barbara) is an assistant professor in the Communication Department at Boston College. Her research examines the intersection of nonverbal, relational, and health communication. Current project include analysis of interpersonal control over health, emotional expression in provider-patient relationships, and family disclosure about illness.

Kathleen M. Galvin is Professor of Communication at Northwestern University. A communication pioneer and one of the founders of the field of family communication, her text in family communication was the first and is the field's longest running. Her recent research examines family communication and varied forms of adoptions.

Eileen S. Gilchrist (MA, 1997, University of Houston) is an Assistant Professor in the Department of Communication at the University of Wyoming. Her research interests include social support, relational maintenance strategies, and risk processes across selected health, family, and organizational contexts. She has published three book chapters, a *Communication Monographs* article, and has received two top paper awards.

Michel M. Haigh (PhD, 2006, University of Oklahoma) is an Assistant Professor in the College of Communications at the Pennsylvania State University.

Her research interests include mass media influence and strategic communications. She has co-authored 19 journal articles in such venues as *Journalism & Mass Communication Quarterly, Communication Research, Journal of Broadcasting & Electronic Media,* and *Harvard International Journal of Press/Politics.*

Stacey J. T. Hust (PhD, University of North Carolina at Chapel Hill) is Assistant Professor of Communication in the Edward R. Murrow School of Communication at Washington State University. She has published articles about health communication in several journals including *Women & Health* and the *Journal of Health Communication.* She has also authored encyclopedia entries and book chapters in the area of media's effects on gender identity. Hust's research has also investigated how parents manage their children's access to the mass media

Amy Janan Johnson (PhD, 1999, Michigan State University) is an Associate Professor in the Department of Communication at the University of Oklahoma. Her research interests include stepfamilies, friendships, long distance relationships, and interpersonal argument. She has published 15 journal articles and four book chapters in such venues as *Communication Monographs, Journal of Communication, Communication Studies,* and *Journal of Social and Personal Relationships.*

Peggy Kendall received an MA in Secondary Education from the University of St. Thomas in St. Paul, MN, an MA in Counseling Psychology from St. Mary's University in Winona, MN, and a PhD from the University of Minnesota in Communication Studies in 2004. She is an Associate Professor in the Communication Studies' Department at Bethel University in St. Paul, MN, where she has taught for the past 7 years. She is also the mother of two teenage IM'ers.

Michelle E. Kistler (MA in Human Development, Washington State University) is currently a PhD student in the Edward R. Murrow School of Communication at Washington State University. She has published entries in the *Encyclopedia of Children, Adolescents, and the Media,* and has co-authored a media literacy article for the *Academic Exchange Journal.* Kistler has been an invited speaker on the subject of media literacy at 4-H conventions and parenting conferences within Washington State. Her research interests include health communication and media effects, with emphasis on parent-child media literacy efforts.

Gary Kreps is Eileen and Steve Mandell Professor of Health Communication, Director of the Center for Health and Risk Communication, Professor and Chair, Department of Communication, George Mason University. Considered the father of health communication, extensively published in health and organizational communication, that includes many funded projects, as well as a former Director at the NIH-National Cancer Institute.

Lindsay T. Lane (MS, 2005, Radford University) is a PhD student in the Department of Communication at the University of Oklahoma. Her research interests include resistance to influence, threat, motivation, health campaign messages, and interpersonal relationships.

Cindy Larson-Casselton, a doctoral candidate at North Dakota State University, is an assistant professor at Concordia College, Moorhead, MN. Her interest in parent/child communication stems from her dual role as coach and mother of two children in competitive activities. She has directed forensic programs at the high school and collegiate levels.

Robert S. Littlefield (PhD 1983, University of Minnesota) is a Professor of Communication at North Dakota State University, Fargo, ND. His interest in parent/child communication in the competitive context began as he successfully coached his children's high school forensic teams for 12 years.

Sally S. Martin (PhD, Oregon State University, 1992) is a Professor and State Extension Specialist in the Department of Human Development and Family Studies at the University of Nevada, Reno. Her current research interests include literacy development in very young children, helping parents choose child care, identifying and understanding risk and protective factors, and cultural issues. Recent publications appear in *Early Childhood Research Quarterly, Reading Research Quarterly, Early Care and Development, Child Care Centre Connections*, and *Journal of Family & Economic Issues*. She began her professional career as a preschool teacher and continues to train early childhood teachers and parents on quality child care.

Tara G. McManus (PhD, Pennsylvania State University, 2008) is an Assistant Professor of Communication Studies at University of Nevada, Las Vegas. She teaches family and interpersonal communication. Her research focuses on stress, coping, and information regulation in families.

John C. Meyer (PhD, University of Kansas, 1991) is Professor of Speech Communication at the University of Southern Mississippi, Hattiesburg. Recently editor of the *Southern Journal of Communication*, he is the author of *Kids Talking: Learning Relationships and Culture with Children* (2003, Rowan & Littlefield). Along with children's communication, his research and teaching interests include humor in communication, values in organizational narratives, and conflict management.

Michelle Miller-Day (PhD, Arizona State University, 1995) is an Associate Professor of Communication Arts and Sciences at Pennsylvania State

University, where she teaches family communication, interpersonal communication, and qualitative research methods. Her research examines communication in personal relationships, and she is the author of three books and numerous scholarly articles.

Carol B. Mills (PhD, Purdue University, 2001) is an Assistant Professor in Communication Studies at the University of Alabama. Her primary research interests include communication skill development in children, and examinations of teasing, humor, and social support. Her secondary line of inquiry is in health and disability communication. She has published in the *Journal of Health Communication* and the *Southern Communication Journal.*

John Palladino (PhD) is Associate Professor of Special Education at Eastern Michigan University, and specializes in emotional-behavioral disorders and special education administration. His research agenda addresses the provision of educational services for youth in foster care, especially for students with disabilities. He and his partner are foster-adoptive parents.

Dennis Patrick (PhD) is a Professor of Family and Interpersonal Communication in the Communication, Media, and Theatre Arts Department at Eastern Michigan University. His research focuses on gay parents and communication in foster and adoptive families. He and his partner, Tom, have adopted five boys and fostered 15 other children.

Barbara A. Penington is an Associate Professor in the Communication Department of the University of Wisconsin-Whitewater where she currently serves as chair. Her previous work in the area of family communication has focused on the mother-adolescent daughter relationship in both African-American and European-American families and listening behavior.

Sandra Petronio (PhD) is a Professor in the Department of Communication Studies, Core Faculty, Indiana University School of Medicine at Indiana University-Purdue University, Indianapolis, Senior Affiliate Faculty, Fairbanks Center for Medical Ethics, Clarian Health Partners. She developed an evidenced-base theory of how people manage private information and also focuses on health and family communication.

Thomas J. Socha (PhD, University of Iowa, 1988) is University Professor (for distinguished teaching) and Associate Professor of Communication at Old Dominion University, Norfolk, Virginia. Dr. Socha's publications include two books, numerous book chapters, articles, and conference papers that report his research focusing on family communication and children's communication. Dr. Socha was the Founding Editor of the *Journal of Family Communication*, a national research journal. He continues to be a member of the Editorial Board of the *Southern Communication Journal*. Dr. Socha received the *Bernard J.*

Brommel Award for Outstanding Scholarship and Distinguished Service in Family Communication (from NCA) as well as numerous teaching awards. Dr. Socha has taught three courses in family communication as well as communication research methods at the National Communication Association's Hope Faculty Development Institute.

Jordan Soliz (PhD, University of Kansas) is an Assistant Professor in the Department of Communication Studies at the University of Nebraska-Lincoln. His research focuses on communication and intergroup processes in family and personal relationships with an emphasis on grandparent-grandchild relationships, multiethnic families, stepfamilies, gay and lesbian families, and in-law relationships.

Glen H. Stamp (PhD, University of Texas at Austin, 1991) is Professor of Communication and Department Chair in Communication Studies at Ball State University, Muncie, Indiana. Interests include interpersonal and family communication, the transition to parenthood, computer-mediated communication, and communication and conflict. Along with the co-edited book (with Tom Socha), *Parents, Children and Communication* (1995, Lawrence Erlbaum) are chapters in the *Handbook of Family Communication* (2004), the *International Encyclopedia of Marriage and Family Relationships* (2003), as well as articles in *Communication Studies, Communication Quarterly, Communication Monographs, Journal of Applied Communication Research*, and *Human Communication Research*. He was a founding member of the editorial board of the *Journal of Family Communication* and also serves on the editorial board of *Communication Studies*.

Paul D. Turman (PhD, University of Nebraska, Lincoln 2000) is Director of Academic Assessment, South Dakota Board of Regents. His research interests focus on the examination of communication and sport across a variety of coaching and family context. He has published a number of manuscripts in journals such as *Communication Education, Small Group Research*, and *The Journal of Applied Communication Research*.

Anita Vangelisti (PhD, University of Texas at Austin) is a Professor of Communication Studies at the University of Texas at Austin. Her research focuses on the associations between communication and emotion in the context of close, personal relationships. Dr. Vangelisti has published numerous articles and chapters as well as several books.

Keren S. Vergon (PhD) is Assistant Professor in the Department of Child and Family Studies at the Louis de la Parte Florida Mental Health Institute, University of South Florida. She conducts program evaluation and services research in the areas of children's mental health, child welfare, substance abuse, and older adult mental health.

Sally Vogl-Bauer (PhD, 1994, University of Kentucky) is Professor of Communication at the University of Wisconsin-Whitewater. Her research interests include parent-child communication, emphasizing parent-adolescent and parent-adult child relationships as well as family maintenance behaviors. She has published work in these areas as well as in relational development and instructional communication.

Kasey L. Walker (PhD, Purdue University, 2003) is a Visiting Assistant Professor in the Department of Communication at the University of Arkansas. Her primary research interests are within organizational and small group communication, focusing on issues such as interorganizational collaboration, power relationships, and semantic networks. She has published in *Management Communication Quarterly* and in an edited volume on small group communication

Daniel J. Weigel (PhD, University of Nevada, Reno, 2002) is a Professor in Human Development and Family Studies and Cooperative Extension at the University of Nevada, Reno. He has published in the areas of family communication, child development, and parenting. Recent publications appear in *Early Childhood Research Quarterly*, *Reading Research Quarterly*, *Early Care and Development*, *Journal of Family Communication*, *Personal Relationships*, and *Journal of Social and Personal Relationships*. He began his professional career as a preschool teacher and continues to train early childhood teachers and parents on quality child care.

Nakia S. Welch (MA, 2005, Stephen F. Austin State University) is a PhD student in the Department of Communication at the University of Oklahoma. His research interests include instructional communication and interpersonal communication.

Leah Wingard (PhD, Applied linguistics at University of California, Los Angeles) is a faculty member in the communication studies department at San Francisco State University. For the last 5 years, she has been a graduate student researcher in the Center for the Everyday Lives of Families at UCLA and a primary data collector and organizer of the data collected for this project. Her primary interests are family communication, in particular parent-child communication.

Julie Yingling has studied communication development since her dissertation on infant speech. Later topics included infant-parent interaction, children's friendships, and the communication needs of children treated for cancer. Recent books include *A Lifetime of Communication*, on lifespan communication development, and *Final Conversations* (with Keeley), about interactions with dying loved ones.

Angela Zimmerman is a Graduate Student in the Communication Studies Department at the University of Northern Iowa. She is currently completing her last semester of coursework toward the completion of an MA degree.

1 A New Frontier for Family Communication Studies
Parent-Child-Societal Communication

Thomas J. Socha and Glen H. Stamp

Over a decade ago within the field of communication studies, *Parents, Children, and Communication: Frontiers of Theory and Research* (Socha & Stamp, 1995) helped to launch research explorations of communication in parent-child relationships. That volume charted new theoretical and methodological terrain and built a platform for subsequent parent-child communication studies. This volume widens the platform of parent-child communication scholarship by bringing together veteran family communication researchers and newcomers to collectively explore the frontier of parents' and children's communication with the world outside of home. Specifically, the volume explores: communication processes and problems of parents, children, and society in the contexts of childcare, education, healthcare, and youth sports; how parents, children and societal agents use electronic media in their interactions; and communication challenges facing stepfamilies and gay/lesbian families in their interactions outside of home. Paraphrasing the thesis of a popular book that focused on children, *It Takes a Village* (Clinton, 1996), this volume examines communication between and among parents, children, and some of the villagers entrusted with children's welfare.

A Rationale for Studying Parent-Child-Societal Communication

Family communication scholars have perennially regarded families as open social systems, that is, families both affect, and are affected by, interactions with society. Parents, children, and society connect in various communication contexts as interorganizations (e.g., family units and childcare centers), intergroups (e.g., groups comprised of family members and childcare-center members such as parent/child/childcare-center administrator, parent/child/childcare worker, child/childcare worker/childcare administrator, etc.), and in interpersonal relationships (e.g., relationships between a family member and a childcare center member, such as parent/childcare worker, child/childcare worker, parent/childcare administrator, child/childcare administrator, child/classmate, etc). The media of parent-child-societal communication can include face-to-face communication, print (e.g., parents' letters, childcare center newsletters, etc.), and electronic media (e.g., phone calls, e-mail, childcare-center web sites, childcare help-lines, television, etc.).

To date, research in the field of family communication has shed significant light on interorganizational communication between families and society via television (e.g., Bryant & Bryant, 2001), and tremendous strides have been made towards understanding communication within family systems as well as family relationships (e.g., Vangelisti, 2003). However, what is needed is a better understanding of the everyday intergroup and interpersonal interactions between parents, children, and the many societal systems to which families connect. Such an understanding should also include insights into parent-child-societal communication struggles unique to various types of families such as stepfamilies and gay/lesbian families as well as insights into the increasing role played by personal electronic media.

There are at least five reasons that support a warrant for research of communication in the everyday lives of parents, children, and societal agents/agencies: managing family-society boundaries and privacy, better handling of family-society communication problems and conflicts, managing family-society status inequalities, dealing with differences in communication standards and styles between families and society, and coordinating systems of shared care by families and society.

Boundaries and Privacy

First, in light of the many significant interdependencies between contemporary families and societal agencies (e. g., childcare, education, healthcare, organized sports, etc.), it is important to better understand how parents, children, and society use communication to manage the many boundaries between families and society as well as protect privacy (see Petronio, 1991, 2002). As with all groups, as parents, children, and society communicate they create and manage boundaries (Putnam & Stohl, 1990). These boundaries can sometimes become blurred, potentially creating confusion and misunderstandings in situations such as during a sports practice when a "father" and "son" must communicate as "coach" and "player," or during a homework session when a "parent" and "child" interact as "teacher" and "student," or during a medical consultation when a parent asks a pediatrician for his or her opinion "as a parent." Some family-society boundaries are legal and can determine who can interact with whom about what, such as laws that prevent noncustodial stepparents from gaining medical information or school information about stepchildren.

Boundaries between families and society separate what is considered private or "family business" from what is public and available for display (Petronio, 1991, 2002). Many questions arise concerning, on the one hand, how to maintain family privacy, and, on the other hand, how to provide and secure information needed by systems outside of home, especially with societal agencies upon which families depend for essential services and support (i.e., childcare, education, medical, governmental, etc.). For stepfamilies, foster families, and gay/lesbian/bisexual/transgendered families, managing privacy can be especially difficult due to legalities and clashing familial and societal values.

2 Conflicts and Communication Problems

Second, communication is used to manage the wide array of inevitable conflicts and problematic communication episodes between parents, children, and the outside world. Such situations can include, for example, managing value differences between parents, children, and childcare agencies over ways of directing children's behaviors, managing clashes between parents, children, and healthcare agencies concerning optimal healthcare approaches, managing differences between parents, children, and athletic coaches concerning children's athletic development, managing clashes between gay/lesbian/bisexual/transgendered family units and governmental institutions over childcare rights, and even managing clashes between parents, children and society over the extent to which to include children in conversations that directly affect them (children as full participants, limited participants, or left out).

Well-managed and effective communication between parents, children, and society can be an incredibly positive force, but mismanaged communication can become a catalyst for a host of negative outcomes that has led, in some cases, to physical injury to parents and societal agents (e.g., see Heinzmann, 2008), and although rare, death (e. g., the case of a father who beat another father to death during a hockey practice over a boy's rough play as the team watched, see *Hockey Dad*, 2008).

3 Status Inequalities

Third, as parents and children communicate with the outside world, they are not always on equal footing with societal agencies. Parents turn to many agencies outside of home for assistance, support, and specialized knowledge and expertise. For example, by virtue of their extensive education, specialized training, and experience, medical doctors (relative to parents and children) bring greater relative informational status to parent-child-physician interactions. However, caring for the health of a child is ultimately the parents' responsibility and, although they may lack scientific medical information, parents do bring particularized insights into their children. Thus, children's healthcare is best regarded as a coordinated endeavor between children, parents, and medical practitioners, where coordination failures (sometimes and in part due to status conflicts) can pose significant risks and dangers. Similarly, successfully educating children is a coordinated effort between parents, children, and teachers, where, for example, status clashes between parents and teachers can compromise educational quality and jeopardize educational success.

Interactional Differences

Fourth, rules shaping family interaction at home (backstage) can mirror or be at odds with rules shaping interaction in public (front-stage) (e.g., Goffman, 1959, 1963; Sennett, 1976). For example, adults' occasional use of vulgar language might be acceptable behavior in some homes, but is generally not acceptable behavior for parents (or children) while interacting at school (e.g., see Sennett, 1980). When familial and traditional-societal standards of politeness and decorum are in sync, this can result in positive social attributions during interaction outside of home ("Your children are so polite!"), whereas inconsistencies between familial and societal standards can lead to negative social attributions ("Your children are rude."). Unfortunately, today it is not uncommon for children to hear parents publicly using vulgar language while watching children's sporting events, or for children to hear vulgar language on television shows. In all cases, children are observing and learning about what constitutes effective and appropriate public communication as they view the adults communicating around them.

Shared Care

Fifth and finally, it is of particular importance to begin to understand communication between parents, children, and the primary societal systems upon which parents and children depend: childcare, healthcare, education, and recreation, to name but a few.

With respect to childcare, parents employed outside of home must extend their authority, in loco parentis, to outside care systems (see Sennett, 1980). Parents count on this care to be of high quality, and expect that care will be in concert with their values and styles. To secure this care, parents can turn to family members, and/or childcare systems outside of home. Parents are, of course, the primary participants in initiating and obtaining agreements of care, but children are also participants in this process and their point of view should be considered. Once agreements of care are struck, parents, children, and day-care agents and day-care participants begin to create a network of communication structures that serve communication functions including surveillance, information sharing, social influence, and so on. These structures can be many and varied: "daycare relationships," (e.g., with daycare workers, other parents, etc.), "daycare groups" (e.g., advisory boards) as well as in "daycare organizational communication" (e.g., reading daycare-center handbooks). Parents communicating with a daycare center may also interact with organizations affiliated with the center (e.g., parks and recreation systems that sponsor programs, museums, governmental and professional agencies that regulate and monitor operations, etc.).

Since we know that children's well-being is dependent on the effectiveness of parent-child interaction in the home, when daycare outside of home is utilized, by extension, children's well-being also relies in large part on the effectiveness of interaction within a given childcare system. However, since parents and daycare providers share childcare, it is important to better understand the contribution that parent-child-daycare center interactions have on children's well-being.

New Directions in Parent-Child-Societal Communication

The volume seeks to open research in these five areas as well as offer a research agenda for future studies. The chapters in the volume represent work selected from proposals received in response to a national competitive call as well as invited research commentaries written by leading communication experts having expertise in the contexts of childcare and education, health communication, family media, and stepfamilies. The volume is not intended to be an exhaustive treatment of parent-child-societal communication, rather the volume seeks to introduce communication scholars, students, and interested parties to parent-child-societal communication, draw attention to various significant lines of inquiry, and, similar to Socha and Stamp (1995), begin to build a platform for future inquiry. The volume is divided into four sections: childcare and education; health and recreation; families, society and electronic media, and evolving family-societal relationships.

Childcare and Education

Families depend on societal agencies outside of home for the daily care and education of children. Section one of the volume is comprised of five chapters that focus on parent-child-societal communication in the contexts of childcare and elementary education. Weigel and Martin (chapter 2: *Connecting Two Worlds of Childhood: How Do Parents, Childcare Providers, and Children Communicate?*) open the section with an overview that seeks to begin to address some fundamental questions: What is the nature of the communication between parents and child-care providers (e.g., frequency, content, behaviour, channels, affect, etc.)? What factors enable and hinder parent childcare-provider communication? What questions remain in understanding parent childcare-provider communication? Weigel and Martin report the results of a survey study of parents and childcare providers. Results suggest that parent childcare-provider communication is regular but brief (e.g., 3–5 minute conversations during pickup time). The content of these conversations include information about the child's day, the child's behaviors during the day, and supportive miniparenting lessons. They also found that parents reported the most frequently used means of communication included newsletters, parent-provider meetings, and notes from the provider. Providers, on the other hand, reported that parents were more likely to read newsletters than any other form of home-childcare program interaction. The chapter concludes by offering an important, preliminary conceptual model for future studies.

Meyer (chapter 3: *Kids, Parents, and Organization: Cooperation and Conflict in a Child Development Center Culture*) reports on his continuing and extensive research of everyday communication in a daycare center. In this chapter he focuses attention on how individuals use communication to manage the variety of intersecting relationships in the context of a child-care center. Framing children as boundary spanners (liaisons), Meyer used interviews with parents and childcare workers, and engaged in participation observation with children to gather qualitative data to address how parents, children, and childcare workers managed these multi-layered connections and understandings. A variety of themes emerged from each point of view. From the point of view of children, it is clear that they have to manage a great deal of relational work with the many adults at the center, their parents, as well as the many children at the center. Across the 12 child themes identified by Meyer, children are indeed moving back and forth between the world of adults and the world of children, as when, for example, they have to decide to "tell a teacher" about another child's behavior, or to ask for assistance in managing childhood relational struggles. Caregiver themes included trying to keep everyone happy (parents, children, and supervisors), managing boundaries between caregivers, children, and parents, as well as having to code-switch, or adapt their interaction to dramatically different audiences. Parents indicated they desired child-centered communication from the staff, wanted staff to be open, preferred staff to create a safe, community-feeling at the center, and wanted staff to model competent communication as they helped guide children. Meyer concludes:

> Venues like child development centers may be viewed as communication crossroads, where norms and values from family and child cultures meet, blend, and clash. On the whole, preschool children seem to profit from becoming boundary spanners at such a young age, learning to adapt their communication strategies to varying organizational cultures. Future research could richly explore such crossroads and the recurring issues that emerge there, such as how power differences affect dominant norms in each culture and in their blending, how the family culture affects children interacting in child care cultures, and how extensive divergences in communication norms really may be between child care centers and family cultures. (Meyer, this volume)

Miller-Day and McManus (chapter 4: *The Interface of HOME-work and Low-Wage Maternal Employment*) examine home-school-work communication among working poor families trying to juggle homework along with long hours at work. The increasing number of mothers in the workforce has created work-family-school conflicts for many families. Families are trying to find creative ways to balance daily work-family-school responsibilities, with some relying on other family members for assistance and other families outsourcing this help (e.g., childcare). This chapter focuses on work and family interactions, specifically maternal low-wage work and mother-adolescent relationships. Their chapter reviews research literature addressing work-family balance in working poor families, reviews the research literature intersecting maternal work and mother-adolescent relations, specifically focusing on mother-adolescent communication, and then reports on an original research study examining low-wage maternal employment, parenting, and mother-adolescent communication in a sample of 94 mother-youth pairs (with a qualitative follow-up with 10 families). The chapter highlights new problems such as the role of communication in parentification (assigning adult care-giving duties to children) and reminds us that families vary economically, socially, and educationally and that such differences make a difference in interaction among parents, children, and society.

Wingard's chapter (chapter 5: *Communicating About Homework at Home and School*) takes a closer look at the discourse of homework. The accomplishment of children's homework is one aspect of the relationship between the institutions of children's schooling and everyday lived family life. The chapter documents the day to day impact of children's homework in the everyday lives of dual-earner families. The chapter is based on three main sources of ethnographic data collected from 32 dual-earner families in the broader Los Angeles area. First, the corpus includes naturally occurring video-recorded interactions of parents and children negotiating and accomplishing homework on 2 weekday afternoons and on 2 weekend days. This data allows for examination of the face-to-face interaction that homework entails, including the ways in which papers from school and online assignments guide, as parents and children interpret and negotiate about them together. Second, the corpus includes separate open-ended interviews of parents and children about family education practices including their views of homework in family life. The data paint a varied picture of homework from the vantage points of teachers, parents, and children, showing how this task is perceived differently from each point of view. For example, parents look to teachers for guidance about their role in homework, but also want to shape their child's habits in their own ways, that is, they want predictability, consistency, and reasonableness.

Julie Yingling, Professor Emeritus (Humboldt State University), a nationally well-known children's communication scholar and leading developmental theorist, concludes section one with a commentary. Yingling is encouraged that communication is taking an important step by studying children and communication development. Theoretically, she reminds us that the section's studies only begin to examine the bandwidth of ages that are needed to create developmental theory and that studies need to follow the lead of these scholars and systematically include the point of view of children. Using Weigel and Martin's model, Yingling then points out that future parent-child-societal research can benefit from looking at both proximal and distal factors, and the need to widen outcome variables asking, for example, "what leads to an effective teacher, satisfied parent, and socially adept child?" Together, these chapters and Yingling's commentary suggest that it is important for future studies to understand that outcomes of childcare and education are shared among many stakeholders.

Further, these outcomes are also subject to developmental processes. We need to examine the interactions of parents, children, childcare providers, and educators across time and across the wide variety of contexts they share in order to better understand how these shared goals might be better realized. In the next section we turn our attention to connections between parents, children, and societal relationships pertaining to health and wellness.

Health and Wellness

Families also depend on societal agencies outside of home for their health-care and wellness. This necessitates that families communicate with health-care systems at interorganizational (e.g., a parent choosing a pediatrician using information on the internet), intergroup (e.g., a parent participating in a weight-management exercise group at a local hospital), and interpersonal levels (e.g., parents and children forming relationships with healthcare professionals—physicians, nurses, therapists, pharmacists, etc.). Receiving quality, routine healthcare is undoubtedly important for the well-being of families, and providing quality care is, of course, an important criterion used to assess healthcare systems. However, for families and healthcare systems, communication has become increasingly complex, costly, and fraught with many obstacles. For example, families with children facing special healthcare needs (e.g., particular medical conditions, developmental obstacles, etc.) encounter many layers of complexity as they coordinate a child's healthcare with a team of professionals representing diverse medical specialties. All parties involved must coordinate their lines of communication, if health management is to be positive and effective. In section two, five chapters focus on some of the increasing complexities of parent-child-societal communication in the contexts of health, wellness, and recreation.

Duggan and Petronio (chapter 7: *When Your Child is in Crisis: Navigating Medical Needs with Issues of Privacy Management*) examine circumstances surrounding the way that parents of children with unexpected, serious medical conditions, the care team, and child manage privacy boundaries within the context of navigating their health-driven relationship parameters. Their chapter uses Communication Privacy Management Theory (CPM; e.g., Petronio, 1991, 2002) to examine conversations between physicians and parents of children who have recently been admitted to neonatal intensive care and conversations between parents and family members after meeting with the physicians. In addition to the need to use communication to manage parental anxieties and fears, issues of privacy loom large. On the one hand, medical participants require information upon which to base decisions of care, yet, on the other hand, as Duggan and Petronio point out, parents expect to manage the flow of information so as to protect family privacy among various goals. This process also involves governmental regulation (the Health Insurance Portability and Accountability Act of 1996, United States Department of Health & Human Services, 2008).

Communication Privacy Management Theory poses implications for the ways in which families play a role in advancing the health of their children as illustrated during high crisis times of medical need (Petronio, 2002). The application of CPM theory provides a map for ways physicians and the medical staff can involve parents, child, and family members as allies in the child's health by recognizing the significance of learning the family's rules that regulate privacy. Doing so eases the availability of having families grant or deny access to important private information that bears on the medical condition of their child.

Davis, Dollard, and Vergon (chapter 8: *The Role of Communication in Child-Parent-Provider Interaction in a Children's Mental Health System of Care*) look at how the team planning process in general, and the wraparound and system of care processes specifically, affect child-family-provider interaction. In particular, their chapter examines system of care principles in practice in child-parent-provider interactions among children with severe emotional disturbances, their families, and mental healthcare providers with a preliminary goal of shedding light on how team communication address questions of how communication facilitates and inhibits care. Systems of care principles feature the acknowledgement that care (emotional, physical, spiritual) is a coordinated effort of families and various societal systems of care of varying specialties. As Davis et al. outline, successful care is dependent on coordinated case management. Relying on analysis of observations and field-notes, they highlight that stakeholders bring varied and often divergent framings to meetings, taking on ambiguous roles, but also share a desire to provide quality care. The chapter points to the work on bona fide groups (Stohl & Putnam, 1994, 2003) as a useful framework for future studies and inquiry.

Mills and Walker's chapter (chapter 9: *Early Intervention or Early Imposition: A Bona Fide Group Perspective Analysis of the Parent-Child-Early Intervention Relationship*) also examines family-medical team communication in the context of early intervention teams by means of examples drawn from a variety of public sources (e.g., training manuals, guidebooks, examples drawn from online discussion postings, etc.). Early Intervention is a collection of services designed to support the development of children with disabilities under 36 months of age and to provide support for family growth and stability as they learn more about the child's diagnosis. Ideally, providers and families work together to help maximize the child's development and identify the family's strengths, as well as provide assistance for potentially problematic areas. Their chapter offers a new perspective from the lens of the work on bona fide groups that highlights difficulties in coordinating care with severely disabled children where parents simultaneously stand-in for their children as well as function as parents in complex interactions with numerous medical members of the healthcare team.

In addition to healthcare, children and parents also depend on societal agencies to help meet their needs for wellness and fitness by means of participation in organized sports and recreational activities. In order to fulfill their wellness/fitness needs, families can: connect with various kinds of organizations (e.g., YMCA's, community-centers, schools, parks, etc.), join and/or form groups within these organizations (e.g., teams, exercise/fitness groups, etc.), as well as form relationships in these organizations and groups (e.g., with coaches, sports officials, league officials, team parents, player parents, etc.).

Communication between families and recreational sports systems are important to study in part because of the many shared benefits that families and society can derive from such interactions (e. g., increasing well-being, happiness, etc.), but, also in part, to shed light on increasingly common instances of negative communication, including violence, in interactions between parents, children, sports officials, and coaches. For example, the National Association of Sports Officials (NASO, 2006) reported that it receives more than 100 reports annually of violence against sports officials perpetrated by parents and/or children.

Turman, Zimmerman, and Dobesh (chapter 10: *Parent-Talk and Sport Participation: Interaction Between Parents, Children, and Coaches Regarding Level of Play in Sports*) interviewed parents of children involved in organized junior/ high school sports to uncover how communication is used to manage boundaries with coaches as well as to manage children's participation. By means of interviews, the chapter reports a study that examines topics of sport-talk within families and parents, children, and coaches as they negotiate boundaries and form relationships regarding sports participation. Parents identified a variety of sport-related topics (i.e., playing time, sport politics, inappropriate coaching behaviors, sports competitiveness) they typically discussed with coaches regarding their child's sport. Despite coaches' attempts to limit interaction with parents, parents employed a combination of direct and indirect methods to form three kinds of role relationships: spectator (high coach-parent distance), enthusiast (moderate coach-parent distance), and fanatic (low parent-coach distance). The study suggests that shared goals (e.g., physical fitness, sportspersonship, team values, etc.) not be lost in parent-child-coach interaction and that openness needs to be cultivated by coaches, parents, and players as they discuss topics that often prompt conflict such as playing time, negative coaching behaviors, and more. Applications for coaches and parents are discussed.

Littlefield and Larson-Casselton (chapter 11: *Coaching Your Own Child: An Exploration of Dominance and Affiliation in Parent-Child Communication in the Public Sphere*) examine the tenuous balance of coaching/parenting. Specifically, their chapter focuses on how parents and children in a coaching relationship described their communication in various settings. Their research contributes to a better understanding of communication between parents and children when they become coaches and members of the team; how parent/ coaches and children communicate outside of the home in competitive contexts; and how the parent/coach and child communicate in public contexts with each other, as well as with other parents, coaches, and members of the team. Based on an analysis of interviews with parents/coaches and children/ players the chapter reports a study that examined communication and the management of relational control and support structures. Results highlight difficulties in negotiating parental/coaching authority, managing the public-private sides of coaching/parenting, the role of other family members, as well as managing information and privacy. The chapter highlights the need for research into instructional communication in the context of parents/coaches-children/players.

Section two concludes with a commentary by Gary Kreps, professor and chair of communication at George Mason University, regarded by many as the father of health communication. In particular, Professor Kreps calls attention to the lack of research about the role of family communication in health and wellness and highlights areas ripe for future research such as health information, patient support, care giving, role models for the management of health, as well as support for managing the complexities of navigating relationships with health agencies. His comments about the section's chapters highlight many new avenues for collaboration between family communication researchers and health communication researchers especially in the new areas opened by the chapters such as team healthcare management and the role of athletic coaches, trainers, and health consultants and professionals in supporting the health and wellness of families.

Parent-Child-Society Relationships and Media

This section features three chapters that begin to consider the increasing role of various media in creating and maintaining family relationships outside of home. In the 21st century, media connect families and society in a wide array of commercial relationship. This not only includes television but an increasing presence of various forms of personal electronic media such as text messaging, instant messaging, hotlines, and more.

Weintraub Austin, Hust, and Kistler, (chapter 13, *Powerful Media Tools: Arming Parents with Strategies to Affect Children's Interactions with Commercial Interests*) liken using media to using power tools, that is, power tools can be useful when individuals are trained how to use them and their use is supervised, but also present dangers when they are misused, or used without supervision. Because mass media is driven by commercial interests, parents and children's participation with media affects their consumer relationships outside of home. Children, in particular, are learning about how to form and interact in commercial relationships as they consume television and have become a large audience for sellers. Before media, children learned how to communicate in commercial relationships outside of home by watching parents interact and negotiate with shop-keepers, tailors, butchers, and a wide variety of individuals selling, door-to-door, everything from ice to elixirs of youth. Today, television mediates and shapes family-societal commercial relationships virtually, sometimes with little or no face-to-face interactions. Weintraub Austin, et al.

offer a new perspective of parental intervention of children's media use that is intended to moderate the effects of viewing television on family-societal commercial relationships. As they conclude:

> Neither parents nor children are defenseless in this situation. Armed with developmentally-appropriate active parenting strategies with child-centered goals in mind, such as active coviewing and parental mediation, parents can socialize their children to become critical thinkers toward media content. With media literacy as a family value, parents and children alike can learn to think reflectively about media content and to operate the powerful media tools in a way that benefit them as much as or more than the professionals targeting children for their own benefit. (Weintraub Austin, et al. this volume)

Kendall (chapter 14: *Finding Adolescents through Cyberspace: Youth Workers, Teenagers, and Instant Messaging*) examines adolescents who often have a strong desire to connect with caring adults outside of the home. How this connection occurs, however, has changed as adolescents are becoming increasingly technologically savvy, turning to cyberspace to establish and maintain friendships. The study reported in this chapter looks specifically at the role of youth pastors and how Instant Messaging (IM) is being used in their work with young people. The first study surveyed 72 IM'ing youth pastors asking them to identify the strengths and weaknesses of using IM. The second study surveys 138 college students who used IM in high school, asking them how they would feel about a youth pastor being an IM buddy. Most adolescents were positive about IM as a form of communicating with pastors, but others expressed discomfort about the presence of youth pastors in IM space. In spite of what was perceived as extensive investments of time, pastors, on the other hand, viewed these interactions as positive, with most recommending this as a means to communicate with adolescents. Kendall raises important questions about both the horizons and dangers of this new form of technology.

Penington and Baus (chapter 15: *Response to Family Crisis: Mood Disorders, Supportive Listening, and the Telephone Helpline Volunteer*) look at the central role of listening both inside and outside of home as playing a significant role in general family welfare but, in particular, in situations where family members are struggling with mood disorders. After reviewing the literature on therapeutic listening, Penington and Baus consider the training of telephone hotline volunteers by taking a close look at training manuals and sessions, as well as conducting a review of a recorded call. They conclude that active listening is a highly significant, but relatively understudied aspect of family communication, and that family members will turn to outside sources to fulfill their unmet needs to be heard. However, in doing so, additional problems can be created that concern the role of parental involvement, as well as untrained operators.

This section closes with a commentary by the renowned media scholar, Jennings Bryant (University of Alabama). Professor Bryant highlights the pioneering efforts of these chapters as they begin to move the field beyond existing normative data and into new worlds that he refers to as digital childhood, or digital family life. He points out that these studies raise heretofore unasked questions about complex interactions between parents-children-society-media interactions, and suggest new directions. He also points out that more work is needed on fuller explications of digital childhood, mobile and personal technologies, as well as the need to refine some of our basic models of family communication given work on this new frontier. Future researchers will benefit from these comments as well as the work of the authors in this section.

Evolving Caregiving Roles and Relationships

Given the variety of family forms today, coupled with ongoing redefinition of parental roles, we can also expect to find variety in the qualities of parent-child-societal relationships, especially for those families where definitions of parental authority are grounded in shifting legal and social ground. These kinds of relationships can pose unique challenges that can include reaching agreements about how to define a family member's status, determining authority lines, managing divergent values, and so on. How well these communication obstacles are managed can affect the desired quality of a variety of outcomes, and worse, can also pose additional harm to struggling families.

Vogl-Bauer (chapter 17: *When the World Comes Home: Examining Internal and External Influences on Communication Exchanges Between Parents and Their Boomerang Children*) examines the communication of adult-children who return home to live (with or without their children). Her chapter explores how parents and boomerang children process messages that could rapidly and strongly impact their relationships. First, based on a review of literature, three primary communication issues faced by boomerang children and their parents are examined. Then four different theoretical perspectives: systems theory, relational dialectics theory, social exchange theory, and communication privacy management theory, are invoked to assess the role each could play when trying to understand how parents and their adult children cope with outside influences when adult children return home. Vogl-Bauer argues for the need for more research into boomerang child-parent communication as well as for the impact that such relationships have on young children returning to live in mom's or dad's childhood home.

Sixty-five percent of households contain children from a prior relationship, making them a stepfamily (Marano, 2000). Current estimates suggest that one third of children will live with a stepparent before they turn 18; however, this figure does not include children who may interact with stepparents while visiting a noncustodial parent (Visher, Visher, & Pasley, 2003). Even though many stepparents act as parental figures to their stepchildren, there are legal and social barriers that hamper their ability to enact this role. One setting where these barriers are particularly apparent is the communication process between stepparents, stepchildren, and social entities outside of the household, such as educational, medical, and legal personnel.

Johnson, Craig, Haigh, Gilchrist, Lane, and Welch (chapter 18, *Stepfamilies Interacting Outside the Home: Barriers to Stepparent/Stepchild Communication with Educational, Medical, and Legal Personnel*) offer an overview of the many communication obstacles faced by stepparents as they and their children attempt to communicate outside of home. They argue that through stigmatization and failure to define stepfamily roles, on the one hand, society encourages the stepfamily to interact and present themselves as a nuclear family with the stepparent playing a parental role; however, on the other hand, the stepparent is a "legal stranger" to his or her stepchildren. This dilemma creates numerous communication issues when parents and children attempt to interact with teachers, lawyers, and doctors on behalf of stepchildren. As an incompletely institutionalized form, stepfamily-society interactions, for example, need to include ongoing negotiation of basic legal and care-giving statuses of the participants. This can lead to numerous conflicts, hurt feelings, and potential relational damage. Given the ubiquity of stepfamilies in the United States, there is an urgent need for more attention to parent-child-societal communication for stepfamilies.

Patrick and Palladino (chapter 19: *The Community Interactions of Gay and Lesbian Foster Parents*) close the section with a look at communication between societal agencies of childcare, foster children, and gay/lesbian foster parents. With a shortage of foster homes, some sectors of society are gradually moving towards more inclusive policies that afford gay and lesbian citizens the opportunity to participate in foster care. Somewhat similar to stepfamilies, the incomplete institutionalization of gay, lesbian, bisexual, transgendered, and transsexual family systems, coupled with societal bias against gays/lesbians as parents, and discriminatory practices, lead to unique communication circumstances that can be very difficult to navigate for all concerned. This includes having to demonstrate higher levels of parental ability to qualify for licensing, struggling to manage childcare workers' preconceived notions about the effects of sexual orientation on parenting practices, and managing communication with birth parents. The chapter makes an important contribution to the family communication literature, reminding us that family life is experienced across the wide span of human sexual orientations, and of the unique qualities that gay/lesbian foster parents bring to this important parent-child-societal relational context.

The section and volume conclude with a commentary by Dawn Braithwaite, a well-known family scholar and President of the National Communication Association (2010), and her colleague Jordan Soliz, whose research focuses on communication in grandparental relationships, multi-ethnic families and more. Their commentary supports the call for the need for more work in this area of family communication and they add that parent-child-societal communication work is also needed in the contexts of custodial grandparents, fictive kin, extended family relationships, and multi-ethnic families. Most importantly, they also call for development of communication programs that can educate agencies outside of home to help make parent-child interactions outside of home productive for all families.

Conclusion

In sum, navigating the terrain of communication for parents, children, and society is indeed complex, but this volume takes an important first step by offering a preliminary map for students, researchers, and families of this new and significant family communication frontier.

References

Bryant, J., & Bryant, J. A. (Eds.). (2001). *Television and the American family*. Mahwah, NJ: Erlbaum.

Clinton, H. R. (1996). *It takes a village: And other lessons children teach us.* New York: Simon & Schuster.

Goffman, E. (1959). *The presentation of self in everyday life.* Woodstock, NY: Overlook Press.

Goffman, E. (1963). *Behavior in public places: Notes on the social organization* New York: Free Press.

Heinzmann, G. S. (2008). *Parental violence in youth sports: Facts, myths, and videotape.* Retrieved on August 21, 2008, from Rutgers University Youth Sports Research Council, http://youthsports.rutgers.edu/resources/general-interest/parental-violence-in-youth-sports-facts-myths-and-videotape

Hockey Dad. (2002). *Hockey dad gets 6 to 10 years for fatal beating.* CNN.com LawCenter. Retrieved September 1, 2008, from http://archives.cnn.com/2002/LAW/01/25/hockey.death.verdict/index.html

Marano, H. E. (2000, Mar/Apr). Divorced? Don't even think of remarrying until you read this. *Psychology Today, 33,* 56 61.

NASO. (2006). *National Association of Sports Officials website.* Retrieved September 1, 2008, from http://www.naso.org/sportsmanship/badsports.html

Petronio, S. (1991). Communication boundary perspective: A model of managing the boundaries of private information between couples. *Communication Theory, 4,* 311–332.

Petronio, S. (2002). *Boundaries of privacy: Dialectics of disclosure.* Albany: State University of New York Press.

Putnam, L. L., & Stohl, C. (1990). Bona fide groups: A reconceptualization of groups in context. *Communication Studies, 41,* 258–265.

Sennett, R. (1976). *The fall of public man.* New York: Knopf.

Sennett, R. (1980). *Authority.* New York: Knopf.

Socha, T. J., & Stamp, G. H. (Eds.). (1995). *Parents, children, and communication: Frontiers of theory and research.* Mahwah, NJ: Erlbaum.

Stohl, C., & Putnam, L. L. (1994). Group communication in context: Implications for the study of bona fide groups. In L. R. Frey (Ed.), *Group communication in context: Studies of natural groups* (pp. 285–292). Hillsdale, NJ: Erlbaum.

Stohl, C., & Putnam, L. L. (2003). Communication in bona fide groups: A retrospective and prospective account. In L. R. Frey (Ed.), *Group communication in context: Studies of bona fide groups* (pp. 399–414). Mahwah, NJ: Erlbaum.

United States Department of Health & Human Services. (2008). *Summary of the HIPAA Privacy Rule.* Retrieved August 26, 2008, from http://www.hhs.gov/ocr/privacysummary.pdf

Vangelisti, A. (Ed.). (2003). *Handbook of family communication.* Mahwah, NJ: Erlbaum.

Visher, E. B., Visher, J. S., & Pasley, K. (2003). Remarriage families and stepparenting. In F. Walsh (Ed.), *Normal family processes* (pp. 153–175). New York: Guilford.

Section I
Childcare & Education

2 Connecting Two Worlds of Childhood

How Do Parents, Childcare Providers, and Children Communicate?

Daniel J. Weigel and Sally S. Martin

One of the most significant changes in American family life in recent decades is the increasing numbers of mothers in the workforce (Perry-Jenkins, Repetti, & Crouter, 2000). In 2006, 63% of mothers with children ages 6 and under were in the labor force (U.S. Department of Labor, 2007). Because of this, a majority of young children in the United States are cared for regularly by someone other than their parents (Dickinson & Sprague, 2001). The Federal Interagency Forum on Child and Family Statistics reports that as many as 80% of all children in families surveyed in 2005 were in some type of nonparental care before they entered first grade (Federal Interagency Forum on Child and Family Statistics, 2007).

Family communication researchers are interested not only in how members communicate within families, but also in how the families communicate with systems and in relationships outside the home. With the importance of childcare in the lives of so many families, creating a better understanding of the communication between and among parents, childcare providers, and children is critical. Yet, despite the prominent role childcare plays in the lives of so many families with young children, we know surprisingly little about the quality of the communication between parents, childcare providers, and children. Researchers have examined parent-child communication (e.g., Socha & Stamp, 1995; Stafford & Bayer, 1993; Wingard, 2007), stepparent-stepchild communication (e.g., Braithwaite & Baxter, 2006), and to a lesser extent, communication in the childcare center (e.g., Kontos, 1999; Meyer, 2003; Meyer & Driskill, 1997; Powell, Burchinal, File, & Kontos, 2008). However, very little research has explored parent-provider-child communication, and almost none of this research comes from the communication studies field.

This chapter characterizes what we know about the nature and quality of parent-childcare provider-child communication, and identifies factors that encourage and hinder that communication. We also present some of our research on the topic and discuss questions that remain in order to create a better understanding of parent-provider-child communication. The chapter is organized into five sections. The first explores the ecological context of parent-provider-child communication; the second briefly summarizes the results of both our own research and the research of others around the nature of communication between parents and childcare providers (e.g., frequency, content, behaviors, channels, affect, etc.) as well as the factors that enable and hinder parent-provider communication; the third focuses on children's communication experiences in childcare settings; the fourth presents a descriptive model designed to bring together the research on parent-provider-child communication; and the last section concludes with thoughts for future directions.

The Context of Parent-Childcare Provider-Child Communication

Research has shown that effective parent-provider and provider-child communication can have positive impacts on parents, providers, and children. For example, strong partnerships, between parents and providers, enhance mother-child interaction as well as caregiver-child interaction (Owen, Ware, & Barfoot, 2000). For parents, active involvement in their children's early education has been linked with improved parental attitudes, understanding, and engagement related to their children's development (Roskos & Neuman, 1993). For providers, parent involvement can improve the overall quality of care in the center (Zellman & Perlman, 2006). For children, a stronger connection between parents and centers has been found to be positively associated with children's social development, greater mastery of early basic school skills, and decreased behavior problems (Bennett, Weigel, & Martin, 2002; Fantuzzo, McWayne, & Perry, 2004; Marcon, 1999; Meyer, 2003; Rimm-Kaufman & Pianta, 1999).

The ecological systems theory of Bronfenbrenner (1992) provides a basis for understanding the connections between parents, childcare providers, and children. Ecological systems theory purports that children's development occurs within a variety of social contexts. The home environment and the childcare environment are two primary contexts that directly influence preschool-aged children's development. The home context(s) can include interactions between the child, his or her parent(s) (or legal guardians), any siblings, or other children or adults who are present in the home or family unit. For some children, multiple home contexts may be experienced as in situations of divorced parents with joint custody. The childcare setting includes interactions between the child, his or her peers and preschool providers, and other adults that are present in the setting. The childcare setting includes day care centers, preschools, and family day care homes.

Rather than just looking separately at the home and childcare settings, however, Bronfenbrenner (1992) recommends that scholars attend to the interactive processes between these two settings. According to this approach, the links between the home and childcare center constitute a "mesosystem." Supportive mesosystem links—embodied by the quality of the connection between parents and providers—facilitate development by enhancing continuity between the contexts, providing a consistent environment conducive to optimal child development (Shpancer, 1997). Therefore, from this perspective, parent-provider-child communication is a primary means of connecting the home and childcare contexts, and takes on added importance in light of effective child development.

The existence of close, supportive ties between parents and providers is a hallmark of quality childcare programs (Bredekamp & Copple, 1997). Parent-provider communication is "best viewed as a means of integrating children's childcare experiences with family life" (Zellman & Perlman, 2006, p. 526). Shimoni (1992) identified three broad goals of efforts to improve connections between the home and childcare: enhanced parent education and support, improvement of the childcare program through parent involvement, and increased continuity for the child between the program and the home. In this way, positive parent-provider-child communication can help parents and providers gather valuable information about children and can help children make a smoother transition between the home and childcare (Zellman & Perlman, 2006).

The interactions between parents, childcare providers, and children can occur along a number of dimensions and take a variety of forms. For example, the interaction can be direct (e.g., face-to-face conversations) or indirect (e.g., newsletters). It can also be formal (e.g., parent-provider conference) or informal (e.g., chatting about a child's or parent's day). Communication can be supportive (e.g., relaying positive feedback) or conflictual (e.g., discussing policy violations, behavior problems, removal, etc.). Lastly, the interaction can be parent initiated (e.g., parent offering to bring snacks to the center), provider initiated (e.g., sending a note home in child's back pack), or child initiated (e.g., asking a teacher for help with an activity).

An Exploration of the Nature of Parent-Childcare Provider Communication

Given this backdrop, underscoring the importance of the communication between parents and childcare providers, we conducted a study to more closely examine how parents and providers view their communication with each other. We asked parents and providers how often they interacted, what media they used to communicate, and their feelings about their interactions. This research was part of a larger study examining the contributions of the home and childcare settings to young children's language and literacy development.

Methods and Data

Participants

We surveyed 151 parents and 58 childcare providers (providing care for these parents' children). Parents ranged in age from 20 to 46 with a mean of 34 years. The average annual family income was in the $40,000 to $49,999 range, with responses ranging from "less than $9,999" to "more than $60,000." A vast majority (88.1%) of the participating parents was Caucasian and most were married or living with partners (77.6%). A majority of participating parents was employed either full-time (65.7%) or part-time (18.9%). Although there was a range of educational attainment, overall, the sample of participating parents was well-educated: 42.0% had completed high school and some college, 18.9% had completed a 4-year college degree, and 28.0% had completed a graduate degree.

All childcare providers in the sample were women, with an average age of 37.7 years ($SD = 10.9$). A majority (89.3%) of the providers was Caucasian, whereas 7.1% were of Hispanic decent, and 3.6% were multi-ethnic. Most (75.0%) reported completing high school and some college or trade schooling; 7.1% had attended some high school but did not graduate, 7.1% had completed high school or received a GED, and 10.7% had completed a 4-year college degree.

Procedures

Parents were recruited through licensed childcare centers in an urban city in a western state. Childcare centers were randomly selected from a list of all licensed facilities in the city. The researchers contacted directors of the randomly selected childcare centers to request consent for participation. Of the 80 directors contacted, a total of 30 (37.5%) gave consent for their centers to participate in the study. Participating childcare centers varied in that many were private, for-profit facilities; several were religiously affiliated; some were targeted for low-income families; and one was a Montessori program. Once permission was granted by the participating directors, researchers contacted childcare providers and 58 providers agreed to participate. Providers then distributed flyers inviting families to participate in the study to the parents of the children in their classrooms. Interested parents either directly contacted researchers or returned slips to their children's providers.

Once direct contact was made with parents, interviews were scheduled. Most interviews took place in family homes, although a few were conducted in university offices and childcare centers. As part of the interviews, the researchers provided parents with self-administered questionnaires. Parents were assured their participation was completely voluntary and that all responses would be kept strictly confidential. Parents were paid $20 for their participation.

Upon initial consent to participate, researchers also scheduled interview times with providers. All provider interviews were conducted in childcare centers and took approximately one hour to complete. At the beginning of each interview, researchers explained the goals and procedures of the study, and providers signed informed consent forms. Providers then completed self-administered questionnaires and were paid $20 for their participation. All procedures were approved and in compliance with IRB (Institutional Review Board) guidelines.

Data

We asked parents to complete several measures to assess their attitudes toward, and contact with, their children's childcare providers and centers. Several of the measures were taken from the Hopkins Survey of School and Family Connections (Becker & Epstein, 1982; Epstein & Becker, 1982). Parents were asked the frequency of verbal contact with childcare centers: 1 = *almost never*, 2 = *1–2 times per week*, 3 = *3–4 times per week*, 4 = *once a day*, and 5 = *2 or more times a day*. Parents also were asked the number of times, from 0 to 10, during the preceding 6 months that childcare providers did the following: sent a memo or notice home, talked to you before or after school, sent you a handwritten note, called you on the telephone, asked for a meeting with you, and invited you to a workshop at school.

To measure type of contact, parents were asked how often they were in contact with the childcare center in a variety of ways using a 12-item scale (Becker & Epstein, 1982; Epstein & Becker, 1982). Helping behaviors included assisting teachers in the classroom or on a field trip, participating in discussions or parent-teacher meetings, and volunteering time in the classroom. Responses were made along a 3-point scale (1 = *never* to 3 = *very often*).

We also asked parents about the types of emotions they experienced following typical conversations with their childcare providers. On a scale from 1 (*never*) to 5 (*very often*) parents rated nine potential emotions—respected, warm, trusting, friendly, helpful, tense, cold, misunderstood, and uninterested (Becker & Epstein, 1982; Epstein & Becker, 1982). Three additional items from Hughes (1985) asked parents how confident they felt after interactions with teachers, how effective they felt they were in addressing concerns raised by teachers, and how satisfied they were after their interactions. Parents responded to these questions on 3-point scales (1 = *not confident, not effective,* and *not satisfied*, respectively, to 3 = *very confident, very effective,* and *very satisfied*, respectively).

Providers completed parallel measures assessing their contact with parents. It should be noted that although parents were providing responses about their child's provider, providers were responding based on all parents whose children were in the classroom, not each individual parent. Thus, the responses cannot be compared directly to see if parent-provider dyads agree, and we do not provide analyses that would determine statistically significant differences.

Results

Our results are organized around six primary questions related to the nature of parent-provider communication. Within each question we both summarize the existing literature and, as appropriate, present data from our study.

How Often Do Parents and Providers Interact?

A starting point in describing parent-provider communication is identifying how often they interact. Research has found a wide range in the frequency of parent-provider interaction. Some studies have found that interactions between parents and providers tend to be infrequent and brief, and that a large percentage of the parents experience few, if any, meaningful exchanges with caregivers (e.g., Ghazvini & Readdick, 1994; Zigler & Turner, 1982). Other studies have uncovered more frequent exchanges between parents and providers (e.g., Hughes, 1985; Marcon, 1999; Owen et al., 2000), typically when the child is being dropped off or picked up (Endsley & Minish, 1991). The length of these interactions is most often less than 5 minutes. However, some interactions are more than 30 minutes, usually as part of a scheduled parent-provider conference or home visit (Rimm-Kaufman & Pianta, 1999).

In our study, we asked parents how often they interacted with providers. Figure 2.1 shows that the largest percentages of parents reported talking with their child's provider either once a day or at least 1–2 times per week. Few parents indicated that they never talked with their providers. Overall, it appears that parents and providers talk regularly, although these conversations are typically brief.

What Do Parents and Providers Communicate About?

Parent-provider communication primarily involves routine exchanges or greetings and small talk (Endsley & Minish, 1991; Hughes, 1985). Such interaction often takes place as a parent is dropping off or picking up their child from the childcare center. However, some exchanges involve sharing child and family

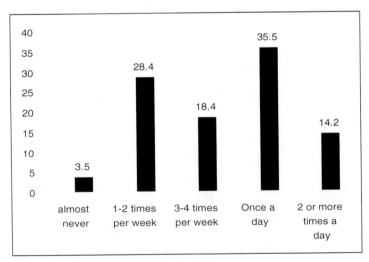

Figure 2.1 Percentage of parents reporting how often they talk with their child care providers.

information involving the child's behavior and special experiences (Endsley & Minish, 1991; Galinsky, Shinn, Phillips, Howes, & Whitebrook, 1992). For example, Rimm-Kaufman and Pianta (1999) identified the topics of conversation as positive comments about children, health, behavior problems, family support issues, and academic problems.

Owen et al. (2000) categorized the content of parent-provider communication into three general types. The first type of communication occurs when the parent or provider seeks information about the child's day. For instance, a parent might ask about the types of things the child did during the day, or a provider might ask about the child's food preferences. They also can tell each other when the child has a difficult day. A second type identified by Owen includes communication about the child's behavior. For example, parents and providers might discuss child problems and what makes the child angry, happy, sad, and so on. The child might be fighting or acting out and the provider may talk to the parent about the behavior. Finally, according to Owen, parent-provider communication can be intended to provide support. For example, they communicate praise to the other for her or his skill in dealing with the child, give child development information to the other, or receive help with activities or materials. Thus, it appears that the majority of parent-provider communication includes the exchange of general information, but can become more in-depth when needed.

What Communication Methods do Parents and Providers Use to Communicate?

Research has found a wide variety of methods through which parents and providers communicate, including: face to face, attending conferences with provider, notes, phone calls, volunteering in classroom, participating in school events, going on class trips, talking with other parents, participating in planning school activities, participating in fundraising activities, and conducting home visits (Fantuzzo et al., 2004; Rimm-Kaufman & Pianta, 1999). In addition, communication between parents and providers tends to be more face-to-face and more informal than when children enter public school (Rimm-Kaufman & Pianta, 1999).

In our study, we asked parents and providers in what ways they were in contact with each other. As illustrated in Table 2.1, parents indicated that their most frequent ways of interacting with their child's provider and classroom were through reading newsletters, participating in parent-provider meetings, receiving a note from the provider, and bringing snacks for all the children in their child's classroom.

Providers, on the other hand, reported that parents were more likely to read newsletters than any other form of home-childcare program interaction (see Table 2.2). They also noted that parents were likely to bring snacks for the children, donate supplies, or call the provider on the phone. Overall, the strategies used to communicate between the home and childcare take a wide

Table 2.1 Parent Reports: Frequency of Parent Contact with Classroom and Provider

Type of Contact	Very often %	Sometimes %	Never %	M
Stayed informed through newsletters	63	26	11	1.5
Participated in parent-provider meetings	30	59	7	1.7
Received a note from provider	39	47	14	3.0
Brought snack for all children	13	51	36	2.2
Donated supplies, toys, or books	17	36	48	2.3
Received phone call from provider	4	34	62	2.6
Volunteered in classroom	9	23	68	2.6
Helped provider in classroom/field trip	6	27	67	2.6
Participated in workshops at school	7	13	80	2.7
Participated in advisory or parent board	9	4	87	2.8
Served as guest speaker	5	6	89	2.8
Helped with newsletters	1	4	94	2.9

variety of forms—direct and indirect, formal and informal, and parent vs. provider initiated.

What Communication Behaviors Do Parents and Providers Use?

An important question for communication researchers concerns the specific types of verbal and non-verbal communication behaviors that are used during parent-provider communication. Unfortunately, the research on those specific types of behaviors is limited. Hughes (1985) asked childcare providers to describe the typical ways in which they responded to the concerns of parents. He found that providers most often ask questions, offer sympathy, share personal experiences, present alternatives, try to be light-hearted, and just listen.

Table 2.2 Provider Reports: Frequency of Parent Contact with Classroom and Provider

Type of Contact	Very often %	Sometimes %	Never %	M
Stayed informed through newsletters	64	26	10	1.3
Brought snack for all children	35	59	7	1.7
Donated supplies, toys, or books	39	47	14	2.0
Called provider on phone	19	59	22	2.0
Participated in parent-provider meetings	23	45	32	2.1
Sent a note to provider	11	60	30	2.2
Helped provider in classroom/field trip	16	47	37	2.2
Volunteered in classroom	7	55	38	2.3
Participated in workshops at school	7	42	51	2.4
Participated in advisory or parent board	14	16	71	2.6
Served as guest speaker	5	33	61	2.6
Helped with newsletters	7	14	79	2.7

Clearly, more research is needed on the specific communication strategies parents and providers use during their interactions.

How Do Parents and Providers Feel About Their Communication?

Communication is more than just frequency and content—it touches people personally. Some research has considered the emotions parents and providers associate with their communication. Hughes (1985) asked providers about their feelings in regards to talking with parents. The five most common feelings were feeling supportive, encouraging, satisfied, sympathetic, and puzzled. Elicker, Noppe, Noppe, and Fortner-Wood (1997) examined perceptions of the perceived quality of the relationship between parents with infants and toddlers in childcare and their providers. They found that both parents and providers think of confidence in the other and willingness to collaborate as a distinct aspect of the relationship.

We asked parents and providers how confident, effective, and satisfied they felt about their conversations with each other, using a scale of one to three (with 3 high). Our data show that parents typically felt confident in talking with their child's provider (M = 2.59), effective in dealing with concerns raised by providers (M = 2.45), and satisfied with their conversations with providers (M = 2.30). Likewise, providers generally felt confident (M = 2.46), effective (M = 2.21), and satisfied (M = 2.26) in their communication with parents.

In addition, we asked how often parents and providers experience positive (e.g., respected, warm, trusting, friendly) and negative (e.g., tense, cold, misunderstood, uninterested) emotions after talking with each other. The findings are presented in Figure 2.2. Overall, the responses suggest that both parents

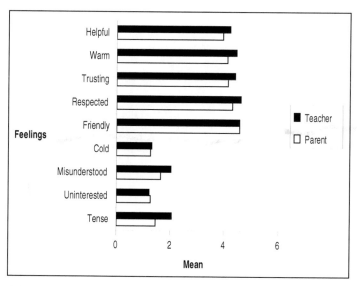

Figure 2.2 Mean levels of parent and teacher feelings after conversations with each other.

and providers are more apt to experience positive than negative feelings after conversations. Nevertheless, some parents and providers do report more frequent negative emotions and less frequent positive emotions. These parents also tend to be less confident and satisfied in their communication with providers, and to be in less frequent contact with childcare centers. However, with some exceptions, most parents and providers feel pretty good about their communication.

What Factors Enhance and Hinder Parent-Childcare Provider Communication?

Communication researchers often want to know what factors enhance or hinder the communication process between people. Some research has investigated factors that seem to impact positive parent-provider communication. This section identifies some of these key factors.

Enabling Factors   Factors that have been found to foster more frequent and positive parent-provider communication include: nonauthoritarian childrearing beliefs on the part of both parent and provider, higher educational attainment of mothers, perceptions of parents and providers that schools are working to involve parents, having an older provider, and the more years providers have taught preschool (Epstein, 1996; Fantuzzo et al., 2004; Hughes, 1985; Marcon, 1999; Owen et al., 2000; Rimm-Kaufman & Pianta, 1999).

We correlated various factors with parents' and providers' perceptions of their communication. Table 2.3 presents findings from our study indicating that parents are more likely to talk with providers, feel confident, effective, and satisfied with the communication, and experience more positive feelings after talking with providers when they feel that they personally play an important role in their child's development, they feel good about the provider and center, and they had good educational experiences themselves. Likewise, providers are more likely to experience more positive emotions after talking with parents when they feel that they have an important role, believe that parents should be involved, and are more experienced in the childcare profession.

Hindering Factors   Other factors have been found to hinder parent-provider communication, such as: parents working or going to school during the day, parents often feeling lack of energy to participate in childcare center activities, differences in language between home and center, lack of training for providers in partnering with parents, lack of effective communication skills for parents and/or providers, and conflict in the perception of parents' roles (Christenson, 2004; Delgado-Gaitan, 1991; Epstein, 1990; Lamb-Parker et al., 2001).

Correlations from our study indicate that parents are less likely to talk with providers, feel confident, effective, and satisfied with the communication, and experience less positive feelings after talking with providers when they are less

Table 2.3 Factors that Enable or Hinder Effective Parent-Child Care Provider Communication

Factors that Enable Effective Communication		Factors that Hinder Effective Communication	
Parents	*Providers*	*Parents*	*Providers*
• feel that they have an important role in their children's learning	• feel that they have an important role in children's learning	• feel that there is little they can do to help their children learn	• feel that they do not know how to help children learn
• have greater expectations for their children's school success	• express feelings of care for the children	• have not felt encouraged to participate	• have more years in the profession
• feel that their child's preschool is very good	• believe that parents should be involved in their children's learning	• have conflicting work schedules,	• have less educational attainment
• feel that the provider cares about their child	• believe that parents see them as partners	• have no transportation	• did not do well in school themselves,
• feel welcome in the center	• work at the center more hours per week		• are younger
• feel like they are a partner with the provider	• have been at their present center longer		
• are satisfied with their child care program			
• have their child attending the center more hours per week			
• have other younger children at home			
• have more education			
• did better themselves in school			
• have a higher income			

confident in their own abilities as parents, do not feel welcome in the center, or have work schedules that make it difficult to interact with providers (see Table 2.3). Similarly, providers are less likely to feel confident, effective, and satisfied in their communication with parents, and experience less positive feelings after talking with parents when they feel ineffective in their role as a provider, are less educated, and were less successful in their school experiences.

The Nature of Communication within Childcare Settings

Although not the primary focus of the study reported in this chapter, another aspect of home-childcare communication is children's communication experiences in childcare settings. In an in-depth study, Meyer and Driskill (1997) observed interactions in one childcare center over a period of 6 months. Much of the communication was children with other children, although some of the observed communication involved teachers. Meyer and Driskill uncovered ten key communication strategies used by children to manage relationships: making statements of friendship, managing proximity, touching, listening, expressing feelings, engaging in conflict, joking or teasing, playing and taking roles, controlling others, and invoking rules. Children used these strategies both positively and negatively to manage their needs for inclusion, affection, and control.

In general, children tend to spend more time in whole groups, where they are twice as likely to be listening and/or watching (passively engaged) than talking and/or acting (actively engaged; Powell et al., 2008). When involved in free play, children spend most of the time playing with or near their peers. The majority of their play, however, is parallel rather than cooperative, and children engage in verbal interactions only about 20% of their play time (Farran & Son-Yarbrough, 2001). Overall, complex interaction with peers is less frequent than cursory interaction (Kontos & Keyes, 1999).

In addition to peer communication, children communicate with teachers, as well. In general, teachers tend to spend the majority of their time (70–75%) involved with children, but because they are outnumbered by them, each individual child spends relatively little time in direct interaction with an adult (Kontos, 1999). Furthermore, teachers spend much of their talk time directed to the class as whole rather than individual children (Hestenes, Cassidy, & Niemeyer, 2004). Interestingly, the frequency of teacher-child talk appears to impact the frequency of peer communication. Harper and McCluskey (2003) report negative correlations between the amounts of time that children spend interacting with peers and the amounts of time they spend interacting with teachers, and once a child interacts with an adult, she or he seems to be more inclined to subsequently seek out adults than children.

Kontos and Wilcox-Herzog (1997) identified several dimensions of teacher-child communication in terms of roles, sensitivity, involvement and talk. Teacher role includes the general types of involvement that teachers have with children such as socializing, encouraging, and monitoring. Teacher sensitivity describes the caring and kindness that is demonstrated toward children in the context of the different roles the teacher assumes. Teacher involvement can be seen as the intensity, engagement and responsiveness that teachers display toward children. Teacher talk refers to the type and frequency of the teacher's verbal interactions with children. Such teacher-child communication typically occurs in the context of setting limits, providing positive guidance, facilitating and supporting play, offering practical or personal assistance, and providing social contacts (Hestenes et al., 2004; Kontos, 1999).

Although the preponderance of research on communication in the child-care setting has examined childcare centers, one can speculate about the nature of communication in family day care homes. On one hand, because family day care homes have fewer children (typically six or less) and a less structured curriculum, communication between children and providers might be more frequent but less formal. On the other hand, children likely use the same communication strategies identified by Meyer and Driskill (1997) to manage their needs for inclusion, affection, and control. Likewise, family day care providers likely engage in the same types of communication strategies around roles, sensitivity, involvement and talk as their center-based colleagues (Kontos & Wilcox-Herzog, 1997).

A Model of Parent-Provider-Child Communication

The literature cited above begins to paint a picture of parent-provider-child communication, albeit a sketchy one. The descriptive model presented in Figure 2.3 presents another way of organizing what we know (and do not know) about parent-provider-child communication. The model organizes parent-provider-child communication into distal context, proximal context, communication context, and communication outcomes.

The distal context includes more stable general context features that provide the broad setting in which the home and childcare center connection exists. These features predate the proximal context and include factors such as: social norms, values, and policies around childcare and parent involvement; childcare philosophy regarding the role of the teacher and children in children's development and learning; children's developmental levels and abilities; cultural aspects of both families and providers; the economic status and perceived power differentials between parents and providers; and historical interactions parents, providers and children have had between themselves and with other parents, providers and children. The distal context provides the broad parameters in which parent-provider-child communication takes place.

The proximal context includes the more immediate communication enhancers and barriers. As noted in Table 2.3, proximal context features include the characteristics, backgrounds, and attitudes of parents, providers and children that can enhance or hinder positive parent-provider-child communication. Features such as personal opinions of parent and provider roles, or perceptions of (in)efficacy can impact the nature of specific parent-provider interactions. In terms of provider-child communication, factors such as group size, the degree of structured curriculum, and provider and child communication goals can enable or hinder quality provider-child communication.

Next, the communication context includes the more specific communication process features. The research to date has identified communication variables such as frequency and duration, content of communication, methods and channels of communication, and the feelings both parents, providers and children experience in conjunction with the communication experience. These

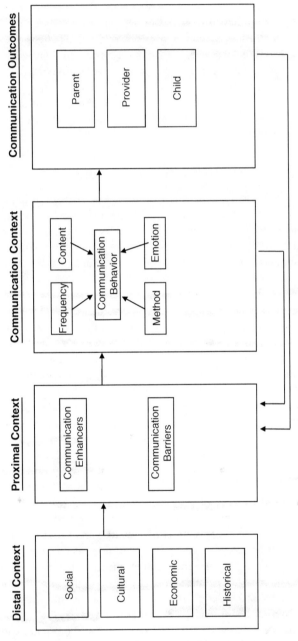

Figure 2.3 Descriptive model of parent-child care provider-child communication.

features will shape the exchange of information and formation of meaning involved in the actual communication process.

Finally, the model identifies the types of outcomes for parents, providers, and children as a result of communication between parents and providers. As noted earlier, some of the outcomes that have been found in the literature include parent support and knowledge gain, provider support and greater childcare program quality, enhanced child social and intellectual development, and greater continuity between home and childcare for children.

Readers will notice various feedback loops in the model, as the communication process and outcomes will inform future communication interactions between parents, providers and children. For example, the emotions experienced in conjunction with a specific communication episode will filter back to either enhance or hinder subsequent interactions. Likewise, outcomes from parent-provider-child interactions will help set the context for future interactions.

We hope that this model can help describe and organize the literature around parent-provider-child communication and provide a basis for more systematic and comprehensive research in the future. The following hypothetical example may help bring life to the model. Consider Maria and Luis, a young, Latino couple who recently had their first child and now need to find day care for their infant. Both Maria and Luis work full-time but still cannot afford expensive care. They have been directed to a program that provides care on a sliding scale fee for lower income families. Maria and Luis go to meet with Roberta, the director of the childcare program. Maria and Luis feel uncomfortable at first because of their limited English and their inexperience interacting with educational agencies. And they worry about leaving their baby with strangers for a good part of the day. However, Roberta, who is an older, African-American woman, is warm and inviting and tells them how important they are to their baby's growth and that they are welcome to visit the center anytime they want. She also gives them print material in Spanish to help them better understand the childcare program. Maria and Luis decide to register their baby at the center and leave the meeting feeling much better about the program and themselves. This communication episode sets the stage for future positive interactions between Maria, Luis, and Roberta. And as their baby settles into the childcare setting, the communication experiences of all will evolve. The example illustrates how features of the distal context (e.g., income, ethnicity, history), proximal context (e.g., language abilities, provider attitudes), communication context (e.g., direct interaction, print material, positive emotions), and communication outcomes (parent confidence) can impact parent-provider interaction.

Future Directions and Conclusions

As the review so far shows, researchers have generated some information about the nature of home-childcare communication. We know that most parents and providers communicate regularly, albeit briefly, that they use a variety of direct and indirect means of communication, and that, in general, they feel positive about their communication. Likewise, children are regularly engaged in some aspect of communication with peers and adults in childcare settings. However, we believe that there is much we still need to know about parent-provider-child communication.

First, most of the research on parent-provider-child interaction has been descriptive and has focused on simple frequency, content, and types of communication. We have a general sense of the frequency and channels used to communicate, but clearly what is lacking is a more systematic examination of direct communication interactions, that is, the sequences of verbal and non-verbal exchanges between parents, providers and children. What communication behaviors do parents and providers use in their conversations? How do aspects such as communication competence, compliance gaining and resistance, or individual communication goals impact the communication process? How do issues such as culture, power, and societal value of early childhood education influence the specific communication processes parents, providers and children use in their conversations? What types of individual and joint meaning do parents, providers and children construct as a result of their communication? And, how do these influence the types and frequency of future exchanges?

Second, even though some progress has been made on understanding parent-provider-child communication, much of the research has come from outside the field of communication studies (an exception is Meyer, 2003, and chapter 3, this volume). Most of the research has emerged from the field of early childhood education either under the theme of parent involvement, typically focusing on impacts and efforts of increasing parent involvement in childcare programs, or under the theme of childcare quality, examining provider characteristics and behaviors that enhance the overall quality of the childcare program. There is a need for the kind of focus on interaction that communication scholars can bring and a closer link to existing theories of interpersonal communication, such as uncertainty reduction (Berger, 1987), information management (Afifi & Weiner, 2004), communication apprehension (Richmond & McCroskey, 1998), or face-negotiation (Ting-Toomey & Kurogi, 1998).

Third, a more integrated approach is needed to study parent-provider-child communication. Previous research has tended to examine either parent-provider or child-center communication. Research that simultaneously integrates the communication experiences of parents, providers and children could more fully describe the integrative links and processes that exist between the home, childcare, and children's development (Bronfenbrenner, 1992). Likewise, there is a need for more action research that examines the design, implementation, and evaluation of efforts intended to improve parent-provider-child communication.

In conclusion, it is important to understand not only how parents and young children communicate within the family, but how families interface with systems outside the home. The childcare center provides one predominant and fundamental system for many families with young children. Although limited, the research gathered to date shows that parents, providers and children communicate in a wide variety of ways, and that when constructive, this communication has positive outcomes for parents, providers, and children. We hope that this chapter will provide both a summary of existing knowledge about parent-provider-child communication, and be a catalyst for increased research and theorizing about the critical connection among parents, childcare providers and children.

Note

Portions of this paper were presented at the National Council on Family Relations, November 2005, Phoenix, Arizona. The research was supported by a grant from the Nevada Agricultural Experiment Station.

References

Afifi, W. A., & Weiner, J. L. (2004). Toward a theory of motivated information management. *Communication Theory, 14,* 167–190.

Becker, H. J., & Epstein, J. L. (1982). Parent involvement: A survey of teacher practices. *Elementary School Journal, 83,* 85–102.

Bennett, K. K., Weigel, D. J., & Martin, S. S. (2002). Children's acquisition of early literacy skills: Examining family contributions. *Early Childhood Research Quarterly, 17,* 295–317.

Berger, C. R. (1987). Communicating under uncertainty. In M. R. Roloff & G.R. Miller (Eds.), *Interpersonal processes: New directions in communication* (pp. 39–62). Beverly Hills, CA: Sage.

Braithwaite, D. O., & Baxter, L. A. (2006). "You're my parent but you're not": Dialectical tensions in stepchildren's perceptions about communicating with the nonresidential parent. *Journal of Applied Communication Research, 34,* 30–48.

Bredekamp, S., & Copple, C. (Eds.). (1997). *Developmentally appropriate practice in early childhood programs.* Washington, DC: National Association for the Education of Young Children.

Bronfenbrenner, U. (1992). Ecological systems theory. In R. Vasta (Ed.), *Six theories of child development: Revised formulations and current issues* (pp. 187–249). London: Jessica Kingsley.

Christenson, S. L., (2004). The family-school partnership: An opportunity to promote the learning competence of all students. *School Psychology Review, 33,* 83–104.

Delgado-Gaitan, E. (1991). Involving parents in the schools: A process of empowerment. *American Journal of Education, 100,* 20–46.

Dickinson, D. K., & Sprague, K. E. (2001). The nature and impact of early childhood care environments on the language and early literacy development of children from low-income families. In S. B. Neuman & D. K. Dickinson (Eds.), *Handbook of early literacy* (pp. 263–280). New York: Gulford.

Elicker, J., Noppe, I. C., Noppe, L. D., & Fortner-Wood, C. (1997). The parent-caregiver relationship scale: Rounding out the relationship system in infant child care. *Early Education and Development, 8*, 83–100.

Endsley, R. C., & Minish, P. A. (1991). Parent-staff communication in day care centers during morning and afternoon transitions. *Early Childhood Research Quarterly, 6,* 119–135.

Epstein, J. L. (1990). School and family connections: Theory, research, and implications for integrating sociologies of education and family. *Marriage & Family Review, 15,* 99–126.

Epstein, J. L. (1996). Advances in family, community, and school partnerships. *New Schools, New Communities, 13*(3), 5–13.

Epstein, J. L., & Becker, H. J. (1982). Teachers' reported practices of parent involvement: Problems and possibilities. *Elementary School Journal, 83,* 103–113.

Fantuzzo, J., McWayne, C., & Perry, M. A. (2004). Multiple dimensions of family involvement and their relations to behavioural and learning competencies for urban, low-income children. *School Psychology Review, 33,* 467–480.

Farran, D. C., & Son-Yarbrough, W. (2001). Title I funded preschools as a developmental context for children's play and verbal behaviors. *Early Childhood Research Quarterly, 16,* 245–262.

Federal Interagency Forum on Child and Family Statistics. (2007). America's *children: Key national indicators of well-being, 2007.* Retrieved March 15, 2008, from http://www.childstats.gov/americaschildren/index.asp

Galinsky, E., Shinn, M., Phillips, D., Howes, C., & Whitebrook, M. (1992). *Parent/provider relationships.* New York: Families and Work Institute.

Ghazvini, A., & Readdick, C. (1994). Parent-caregiver communication and quality of care in diverse child care settings. *Early Childhood Research Quarterly, 9,* 207–222.

Harper, L. V., & McCluskey, K. S. (2003). Teacher-child and child-child interactions in inclusive preschool settings: Do adults inhibit peer interactions? *Early Childhood Research Quarterly, 18,* 163–184.

Hestenes, L. L., Cassidy, D. J., & Niemeyer, J. (2004). A microanalysis of teachers' verbalizations in inclusive classrooms. *Early Education & Development, 15,* 23–38.

Hughes, R. Jr. (1985). The informal help-giving of home and center childcare providers. *Family Relations, 34,* 359–366.

Kontos, S. (1999). Preschool teachers' talk, roles, and activity settings during free play. *Early Childhood Research Quarterly, 14,* 363–382.

Kontos, S., & Keyes, L. (1999). An ecobehavioral analysis of early childhood classrooms. *Early Childhood Research Quarterly, 14,* 35–50.

Kontos, S., & Wilcox-Herzog, A. (1997). Teachers' interactions with children: Why are they so important? *Young Children, 52,* 4–12.

Lamb-Parker, F., Piotrkowski, C. S., Baker, A. J. L., Kessler-Sklar, S., Clark, B., & Peay, L. (2001). Understanding barriers to parent involvement in Head Start: A research-community partnership. *Early Childhood Research Quarterly, 16,* 35–51.

Marcon, R. A. (1999). Positive relationships between parent school involvement and public school inner-city preschoolers' development and academic performance. *School Psychology Review, 28,* 395–412.

Meyer, J. (2003). *Kids talking: Learning relationships and culture with children.* Lanham, MD: Rowman & Littlefield.

Meyer, J., & Driskill, G. (1997). Children and relationship development: Communication strategies in a day care center. *Communication Reports, 10,* 75–85.

Owen, M. T., Ware, A. M., & Barfoot, B. (2000). Caregiver-mother partnership behavior and the quality of caregiver-child and mother-child interactions. *Early Childhood Research Quarterly, 15,* 413–428.

Perry-Jenkins, M., Repetti, R. L., & Crouter, A. C. (2000). Work and family in the 1990s. *Journal of Marriage and the Family, 62,* 981–998.

Powell, D. R., Burchinal, M. R., File, N., & Kontos, S. (2008). An eco-behavioral analysis of children's engagement in urban public school preschool classrooms. *Early Childhood Research Quarterly, 23,* 108–123.

Richmond, V. P., & McCroskey, J. C. (1998). *Communication apprehension, avoidance, and effectiveness* (5th ed.). Boston, MA: Allyn & Bacon.

Rimm-Kaufman, S. E., & Pianta, R. C. (1999). Patterns of family-school contact in preschool and kindergarten. *School Psychology Review, 28,* 426–438.

Roskos, K., & Neuman, S. (1993). Enhancing Head Start parents' conceptions of literacy development and their confidence as literacy teachers: A study of parental involvement. *Early Child Development and Care, 89,* 57–73.

Shimoni, R. (1992). Parent involvement in early childhood education and day care. *Sociological Studies of Child Development, 5,* 73–95.

Shpancer, N. (1997). The link between caregiver-parent relations and children's experiences in daycare and at home: What does the research tell us? *Early Child Development and Care, 135,* 7–20.

Socha, T. J., & Stamp, G. H. (Eds.). (1995). *Parents, children, and communication: Frontiers of theory and research.* Mahwah, NJ: Erlbaum.

Stafford, L., & Bayer, C. L. (1993). *Interaction between parents and children.* Newbury Park, CA: Sage.

Ting-Toomey, S., & Kurogi, A. (1998). Facework competence in intercultural conflict: An updated face-negotiation theory. *International Journal of Intercultural Relations, 22,* 187–225.

U.S. Department of Labor. (2007). Employment characteristics of families. Retrieved on August 20, 2007, from http://www.bls.gov/news.release/famee.t05.htm

Wingard, L. (2007). Constructing time and prioritizing activities in parent-child interaction. *Discourse and Society, 18,* 75–91.

Zellman, G. L., & Perlman, M. (2006). Parent involvement in child care settings: Conceptual and measurement issues. *Early Child Development and Care, 176,* 521–538.

Zigler, E., & Turner, P. (1982). Parents and day care workers: A failed partnership? In E. Zigler & E. Gordon (Eds.), *Day care: Scientific and social policy issues* (pp. 174–182). Boston: Auburn House.

3   Kids, Parents, and Organization
Cooperation and Conflict in a Child Development Center Culture

John C. Meyer

Interactions involving children are fraught with emotions and questions that add a layer of concern above and beyond communication processes between adults. The extra care, concern, and complications faced in adult communication with children give pause to many adults engaging in such as well as to scholars studying children's communication. Today, adults may view children as "incomplete" and highly vulnerable communicators, to be treated with special care. Yet, clearly children's communication is key to the development of adult communication, so studying the former involves seeking out potential origins of communication development, specifically communication between parents and children in key areas such as mutual influence (Dunn, 1997), cultural socialization (Clancy, 1989), knowledge growth (Goodwin, 2007), sports participation (Kremer-Sadlik & Kim, 2007), and use of time (Wingard, 2007).

A central focus, especially of psychological studies of children, is the bonding that grows through children's communication with their parents. Such bonds serve as a crucial basis for communication, development, and handling stress in later life (Luecken, Appelhans, Kraft, & Brown, 2006). Parent-child bonds also strongly influence how children perceive and engage in conflict (Zhang, 2007). As children grow older, family communication patterns about topics such as sexuality and alcohol use definitively influence how they act on those issues—the children seek to "balance independence needs with ties to family values" (Booth-Butterfield & Sidelinger, 1998, p. 296). Communication development starts in the family, but then extends outward to additional social groups. Family communication patterns set the stage for how individuals negotiate communication in new social settings (e.g., see Dixson, 1995). For instance, family communication patterns and personal communication apprehension relate to both what and how individuals self-disclose to friends in later life (Bradac, Tardy, & Hosman, 1980), along with risky behavior enacted later (Koesten, Miller, & Hummert, 2002). Rich possibilities continue to exist for research involving connections between children's family communication and later organizational communication outside the home.

As both children and parents communicate with a variety of third parties (e.g., members of organizations they may be affiliated with), communication patterns quickly become complicated. For young children, a child care center could be the key organization outside of the family in which both children and parents develop important relationships (see Weigel & Martin, this volume). The child-parent bond will then inevitably be supplemented by multiple communication bonds with staff members and child peers at the child care organization. Each party develops communication strategies with organization members that are unique to such varying organizational relationships, while maintaining the family relationship as well. Here is a point where the basic family communication patterns may be enacted, supplemented, and altered, especially by the child, as new people and settings present themselves for communication.

To explore particular instances of developing communication among children and adults, mutual interactions relating to a child care center presented a promising venue. Here was a place where children regularly interacted with adults on staff, as well as with parents as they were dropped off and picked up. Here, also, adults interacted with one another about teaching and care for the children, while certainly children communicated with one another as peer relationships developed. All such interactions, while diverse, were necessarily focused and bounded by the organization of which all participants were a part. Making some sense of such complex communication adjustments and characterizing strategies used by all parties, but especially the children involved, was the overall goal of this study.

Key Questions

This study asked the question: How do individuals manage the intersecting relationships involved in being part of a child care center? Follow-up questions included how do children and parents develop and maintain relationships with a child's peers and teachers, and how do those relationships affect one another as they incorporate the child development center's workplace culture? Both at homes and at child care centers, communication "creates and constitutes the taken-for-granted reality of the world" (Pacanowsky & O'Donnell-Trujillo, 1982, p. 121). Through recurring, shared patterns of communication, participants create a sense of shared reality. Understanding the management, integration, and differentiation of relationships in the contexts of family and center cultures through communication were among the goals of this study. Children, their parents, and center staff members may "act differently" depending on who is present and the context of the communication, and such varying communication adaptations can shed light on how people manage changing communication contexts involving family, work, and school.

Creating understanding in organizational contexts occurs through communication in developing relationships where patterns are recognized and adapted. Weick (1979) discussed retrospective sense-making by organization members as the primary way for them to reduce uncertainty in evolving interactions. Rather than rationally developing a strategic plan for communication and then following it, members try to enact varied roles within their mutual interaction. Later, through pondering their actions and creating narratives about them, they make sense of their actions as fitting some retroactively rational plan or motivation (Weick, 1989). In the specific child care context studied here, the question followed: How do children, parents, and organization staff members make sense of their relationships? The comfortable parent-child relationship (perhaps) will be complicated when children spend long periods of time in child care settings. In turn, communication norms between parent and child may be radically different from expectations in the child care group.

Three points of view on communicating needed to be explored to fully understand the management of the intersecting relationships: the children's, the parents', and the child care staff members'. Each of these parties has unique perspectives on these relationships not only as individuals, but as persons playing social roles. Children, parents, and child care workers are expected to conform to unique norms of communication associated with their social positions. At the same time, they must interact with people in varying contexts—home and child care center—as well as in alternating roles—child or classmate, parent or teacher. Such a challenge likely will "stretch" anyone's communication and relationship strategies, especially children's, whose communication skills are newly emerging and developing.

Children as Boundary Spanners

Placement in a child care setting requires that children learn boundary spanning, as they simultaneously navigate the culture of their child care class while continuing to communicate effectively within the family. The ability to manage such links among organizations benefits members (Albrecht, 1984), and thus may be rewarding for children who learn early. Children bring expected communication patterns from home to child care, modify those interactions based on communication patterns encountered at a care center, and in turn alter further interaction patterns back at home (Dixson, 1995; Howes, 1987). Some researchers argue that home or family patterns will outweigh alternate communication patterns encountered at a child care center every time: "If the norms of family, peer group, and school are roughly similar, the child will have communication reinforced at every turn. If the family and peer group norms are in conflict with those of the school, however, there is very little chance that the education system will prevail, either in or out of the classroom" (Allen & Brown, 1976, p. 31). Yet, parenting and family interactions evolve with extrafamilial communication to lead to a child's development of communication competence with peers (Hart, Olsen, Robinson, & Mandleco, 1997).

Family communication patterns affect children's communication at child care centers, and research has shown that family patterns lead to complementary or clashing integration for children into new organizational cultures. For example, parents of unpopular 5-year-olds at one center were found to be more controlling, directive, and intrusive in their interactions (Foot, Chapman, & Smith, 1995). Children found to be securely attached to caregivers showed higher levels of peer confidence than those with more anxious attachments (Kerns, 1994; Shulman, Elicker, & Sroufe, 1994). Integrating children's communication at home and school may occur smoothly, roughly, or chaotically in rare fits and starts (Bradbard, Endsley, & Mize, 1992). Children may communicate using certain familiar patterns with parents, but need new patterns for interactions with teachers and peers at the child care center. Although staff members come to know the children as they interact during the day, parents or caregivers know the children from birth (usually) and through their at-home communication habits.

Children thus learn to function in different communication contexts, or organizational cultures, very young. How do they adapt? How do parents react to such adaptation? They may encourage or discourage aspects of the child care culture, thus reinforcing or contradicting communication norms the child encounters at the child care center. All parties communicate to achieve degrees of influence or control within the differing contexts encountered. Children seek to influence peers, teachers, and parents, while parents seek to influence those parties as well. Teachers may feel the least able to influence parents directly, while having a clear and direct venue for affecting children through their communication in the classroom. The patterns each party develops to engage in communication with the others blend, merge, and clash where communication venues intersect. The child's interactions at school may alter or cast doubt on home interactions, and staff members may attribute children's communication problems in school to home-life problems (as well as successes).

Communication Perspectives as Narratives

Narratives told by observers and participants in organizational cultures allow for sense-making and understanding of their patterns (Brown & McMillan, 1991) and how participants manage relationships through communication (Meyer, 2003). Brown (1990) found that organizational stories helped members learn about roles, rules, and desired values to enact in an organization. When members must adapt their communication as they cross family and organizational boundaries, communication and relationship management become even more complex. Such rich adaptations, and how children learn to handle them, will reward close study, as one key to communication competence involves how we adjust to our changing audiences in varied venues. This study sought to closely examine narratives of all three parties involved at a child care center, enhancing understanding of the development of shared and contrasting meanings and norms at a rich boundary-spanning opportunity.

Method

This study gathered accounts of interaction to show how children, parents, and child care center staff members related to each other as they spanned family and organizational boundaries. Exploring such interactions showed how the varied organizational cultures blended and clashed. By choosing to start with what participants said, the approach elicited details of regular daily communication from the points of view of those involved (Van Maanen, 1988). A grounded theory approach allowed for a systematic emergence of themes by comparing elements of data gathered to one another and later to existing theories (Strauss & Corbin, 1990). Stories of interactions among children were obtained through participant observation (Meyer, 2003; Meyer & Driskill, 1997) and interviews with parents, teachers, and staff members (Meyer, 1995). Interviews have recurrently proven to be an effective way to gather organizational narratives (Canary & Canary, 2007). Relationship strategies were revealed (Meyer, 2003) through cataloguing of narratives used to make sense of communication or relational events (Bochner & Ellis, 1992).

Observational Approach

Obtaining data for the study began with participant observation of children and staff members interacting at a child development center, as well as children and parents interacting during the brief times parents were at the center for pick-up. The child development center was on the edge of the campus of a mid-size southern university, with a street filled with fraternity houses behind it and intramural sports playing fields to one side. Residences and a house converted to a Family Treatment Center surrounded the center on its other side. One entered the center through a hallway past a reception office where the hallway branched off toward classrooms; infants and toddlers to the left, 3- through 5-year-olds to the right. Two classrooms enrolled children at each preschool age level, except for one larger classroom each of 4-year-olds and 5-year-olds, respectively. Each classroom had one lead teacher and two or three teacher aides who worked varying hours and days, along with regular student observers or volunteers from the university. The researcher served as a classroom volunteer for 2 afternoons a week, for 2 hours each day. Volunteers interacted with the children, monitored them, and helped guide them in following center activities and rules. Thus, as a researcher, I was part of and easily able to observe children's interactions, recording in a journal during breaks and immediately afterward events and dialogue. I could also observe interactions of parents picking up their children, although these usually only lasted for a couple of minutes. For all consenting participants, records of their interactions were detailed in journal entries to serve as part of the data set. Observations took place over the course of 6 months, leading to 68 pages of typed notes describing interactions and dialogue. Additionally, staff members including teachers, along with parents, were interviewed about patterns of communication with children in their usual setting as well as perceptions of how the alternative setting (i.e., home or the center) affected communication with the children. Interviews lasted an average of 45 minutes and took place in locations selected by interviewees, whether their office, my office, or mostly in a private conference room at the child development center. Four staff members and 10 parents were interviewed (leading to 47 pages of typed transcripts), while 15 children were approved participants out of two classes totaling 28.

Data Analysis

Each data set was analyzed for themes involving strategies of communication in the child development center culture, and how they compared and contrasted with strategies in other cultures (especially at homes or alternative workplaces). Key words were noted from a close reading of all transcribed text, and through constant comparison themes based upon those key words were compared and categorized through multiple readings of the text (Glaser & Strauss, 1967; Miles & Huberman, 1994). Each event, or narrative, was reviewed and labeled with a theme, often based on the most common key word associated with that theme, and new events were grouped with new themes or similar themes until all seemed most aptly categorized. Then, the list of emerging themes were compared to see if there was overlap, similarity, or some ambiguity with several themes seemingly merged into one. Because of a different focus of communication for each and methods of data-gathering varying for each, children, parents and staff narratives were analyzed separately.

Results

Key Intersecting Themes

Themes emerged from three sets of data that were then compared and contrasted: child interactions, staff member interviews, and parent interviews.

Child Interaction Themes   Twelve themes indicating communication strategies emerged from the preserved interactions among children. Many were similar to earlier research (Meyer & Driskill, 1997), yet all emerged as a new, unique cluster of communication behaviors or re-emerged with a similar clear focus.

Roles   Playing or taking roles with one another remained a primary and most used strategy for the children to manage relationships with one another. Often, one child would say, "I'm Batman." Then another would chime in, "I'm Spiderman." A third might take the role of another superhero or a villain, and off they would run enacting their roles. Or, they would manipulate or construct blocks to house their superheroes. Not only would such identifications of roles start a game, they would also define and engage a relationship, providing a pattern to structure messages. Once, two boys approached me when I was sitting with another child on a step. "You're on the airplane's driveway, and an airplane is gonna land. It's coming." The other boy chimed in, "You're on the driveway! Look out." "Should we move, Nick?" I asked the boy who was sitting beside me. "No," said Nick. "You're on the driveway! An airplane's coming!

Move." "Oh, look out!" I said, playing along. The two boys eventually "flew on," leaving Nick and me sitting on the step, but they had clearly used their game and roles taken within it as a method for approaching me and Nick and initiating interaction with us. If we had played along further, as other children often would, the relationship would likely have continued through several interactions.

Control and Influence   Seeking control or influence was another common strategy. Children would order, bargain, or make requests to get another child to do something. Two boys were interacting together in the classroom one morning, and over the course of an hour one boy would tell the other, "Come over here," or "Let's go play there." The second boy valued the relationship enough to continue to follow these commands. When the second boy went into the block area and lost interest in the first boy, he came over and said, "Adam, come over here; I need your help with these puzzle pieces." Adam shook his head and continued playing with blocks. That was the end of their active friendship, at least for that morning. For preschool children, gaining verbal control over another child was a rewarding relationship strategy, as was submitting to control for the sake of an ongoing secure or fun relationship with the controlling child. At times, though, "controlled" children would rebel by moving away or refusing to do what was asked; that would endanger the relationship for a time or force the controlling child to try another strategy. In a way, the children in seeking to control one another were mirroring the operation of the power hierarchy they could observe constantly in the form of adult control being enacted over them.

Rules   Appealing to rules or to the power hierarchy helped children to structure and understand relationships in the context of the center. "Telling a teacher" or letting a peer know that there were already the maximum number of children allowed in an area could prevent undesirable interaction and preserve another ongoing desirable one. Often a child would come tell an adult what another child had done, and seemed satisfied when that child got "talked to" or chastised by the adult. In one example, 4-year-old Adam came over to the table where the lead teacher was sitting one day, and said, "Teacher, David and Brandon have their shoes off." The teacher responded, "Tell them to put their shoes back on." Possessing this extra authority, Adam walked back over to the living play area and said, "Ms. Sarah said to put your shoes back on!" Eventually, after a few short delays, they did. Perhaps one of the more memorable times I saw a child appeal to the rules of the classroom to manage relationships was when a boy was coming into the block area that the boys already there did not want to play with. "But I'm your friend," said the boy trying to gain entry. "We'll be your friend if you get out of here," responded one of the boys in the block area. Realizing he was exceeding the allowed number in the block area, the boy moved away. Rules could be broken, of course, if a child was happily engaging in communication; but they could also be invoked knowing that adults would enforce the rules to temporarily end or curtail a relationship.

Repeated Patterns   Repeated patterns of interaction often served to reinitiate and reinforce relationships. A strategy that a child found to "work" will be repeated again as a comfortable and familiar pattern. One child said, "You think I'm a worm but I'm a snake, and I come out from under there [the table] and bite you." The response was "Ow! Call a doctor." Another child, seeing this, approached and said, "Say I'm a worm; you think I'm a worm but I'm a snake, and I come out and poison you." He hoped to elicit the same reaction, and so tried the same pattern. I often found a child trying to repeat a fun game with me by repeating a phrase as a greeting that had been a key to our game even days earlier. Such familiar patterns would be repeated by children to immediately return relationships to a comfortable place that could then be managed from that point.

Response to Adults   Choosing to stay quiet with adults or seek their attention and support was a fifth key dynamic of the children's relationships. Some children would quietly stay involved with their own play or become involved with peers, but be less talkative or involved with adults, merely following along with their peers or responding only when directly spoken to (if then). Other children would purposefully engage adults in interaction to actively develop relationships. I noticed that children who had a conflict with peers or found no available child for play got more interested in adults and would initiate interaction more readily with them. Some children were more insistent on developing relationships with adults than others. Almost all children would tell an adult about an infraction by another child, hoping for support and/ or consequences for the offending child. Others would come over and seek a hug from an adult coming into the classroom or playground, along with telling them about a previous event going on at home or earlier at the center. All children would seek adult support at times, but some did so much more regularly than others.

Humor   Joking or teasing served as a sign of clear unity in a relationship, or alternatively as an attack emphasizing a potential negative relationship. Once Nick was pulling out a box of toys and it fell onto the floor, spilling some of the toys out. I looked at him and he looked at me, and we both laughed, emphasizing the relational tie between us and reassurance that things were fine in spite of the spill. A few seconds later, when Ryan started laughing, Nick turned, upset, and said, "It's not funny!" He turned and said, "They're laughing at me." I responded, "You're picking them up just fine." He got busy playing with the toys, and played contentedly after a short interval with the boys he thought had been laughing at him. Strikingly, laughing together had further unified us, while Ryan's laughter had been taken as a putdown. I often observed shared humor as a unifying communication, but also saw laughing *at* another as a sign of division.

Conflicts   Engaging in conflicts was a common strategy to obtain or defend a child's own wants. All kinds of conflict styles were enacted by the children; from one accommodating the other to actual negotiations to even violent competition. Relationships between children that "survived" conflicts often became stronger. One typical incident had Brian joining Carlos at a table to play with LEGOs®. Soon, I heard Carlos say, "Hey, stop taking those! He's taking my LEGOs." Brian dropped Carlos' LEGOs on the floor. "Don't break them," Carlos said. "I won't play with you if you keep taking my LEGOs."

"I don't care," responded Brian. "I'll just play with one of the teachers," he added, seemingly reassuring himself as much as telling Carlos. Soon, their conversation continued, and they happily built with LEGOs and interacted together as friends. Conflicts often seemed to be a "testing" process—if it could be gotten through children often could stay together and act as friends for a longer time.

Direct Expression of Feelings   This was often evident among the children, especially of anger and aggression, but also of happiness and friendship. I was once quite thrown when Tamara, a quiet 3-year-old, initiated a conversation with "Hey, John." I responded absent-mindedly, "Hey Tamara." Her next words were "I love you," and she moved away grinning as I realized what she had said and remained speechless with surprise. Of course, some children brought to the center the idea that crying and hollering would get what they want, and they would try that strategy, too, usually unsuccessfully. Staff members would say, "Use words" the most frequently with such children. If another child hit or kicked or pushed, a dramatic cry in response simply expressed that child's feelings. Staff members often balanced comforting communication (hugging, sympathetic words) with encouraging the child's use of words to describe the event or her feelings.

Listening   This conveyed a clear sign to others that relating to them through communication was valued. Being listened-to indicated a valued relationship. At lunch one day, Brian called out to all the children at his table: "Everybody be quiet! Everybody listen. I have something to tell you." After all the children gave him attention, he said, "Do you know how to do magic? You have to study hard." Sarah responded, "I *have* studied hard." Brian responded, "Well, I've studied *harder.*" Brian liked the attention he received and such attention showed the positive relationship he had with other children. On the other hand, being ignored indicated a distancing or poor relationship at that moment. One day I noted Tiffany calling across the classroom to Arianna: "Arianna! … Arianna! … Arianna!" A nearby staff member said, "Tiffany is calling you, Arianna." Yet Arianna stayed very occupied with building blocks. So Tiffany tried again: "Jamie! … Jamie!" "I don't wanna come over!" responded Jamie, also busy in the block area. "I don't wanna come over," echoed Arianna, following Jamie's lead. Both girls' determination not to listen at that moment signaled no closer relationship wanted at that moment, either.

Touching   Touch behaviors showed a strong positive or negative relationship— hugs, or tackles, showed liking and affection; hitting or kicking was an ultimate display of anger or wanting to dramatically distance a relationship. As the children got to know me, I would have some ask me to "pick me up," or run over for a hug or to sit in my lap. Many children also liked to hug other children they liked upon their arrival for the day or just before their departure with a parent. The negative touch behaviors were also enacted, unfortunately, as anger often led to hitting or kicking. Sometimes such touches started as part of a game but were then taken seriously and negatively by another child who responded in kind. At times children would hit or kick me in a playful way, only to be reprimanded for it by a nearby adult—or, at times by me: "That's hitting, [or kicking,] I don't play that way," or "Please keep your hands [feet] to yourself." Preschool children certainly valued touch as a key indicator of relationship status, and used it frequently.

Proximity   Proximity was a clear indicator of friendship for the children— sitting or playing near another indicated friendship, and vice versa. As Laurel went to a table for snack, she saw Jamie sit at a different table. "OK," said Laurel, "I'll move this chair over by *you*." Jamie responded, "OK," and they interacted happily during snack. "Sit by me," was often heard from a child wanting to show friendship to another. The act of sitting near or next to another was taken as a token of friendship. Certainly, the converse was true, also; as when Yolanda was inadvertently kicked by another girl sitting down next to her, she said "Ow! That hurt! I'm not sitting by you!" Yolanda moved to another spot to sit, clearly indicating there would be no developing relationship at that point. Literal closeness was taken as a direct indicator of the figurative relationship between the parties.

Friendship Statements   Such statements were made regularly, and confirmed often by questions like, "Are you my friend?" or "Will you be my friend?" One boy wanted to play with a toy jeep with another, and so he said, "Roll it to me." "No," responded the second boy. "I won't be your friend *anymore*," said the first boy, and dramatically moved elsewhere. Ongoing relationships were often checked up on verbally by concerned children, as when Jeremy approached Carlos and said, "Hey, buddy; are you my buddy, my very best buddy?" Carlos did not reply, but did climb up on a climber near to Jeremy, who took that as a "yes," and both boys played together outside for a while.

Staff Member Interaction Themes

Staff members evidenced five key themes as they reflected on their communication strategies at the child development center. First, a positive, supportive communication climate was highly valued. "Some I'll approach," explained one staff member. "'Hello, whatever,' with the staff members, but others I'm more careful. It's hard walking both sides of the fence. Trying to keep everybody happy." Another pointed out that "some days a teacher has had a very hard day and even is about to cry. I try to be a little more comforting to them. Communicate to 'hang in there, there's always tomorrow.'" Second, open communication was prized and regularly sought; protests or negative narratives followed preventions or violations of open communication. "Staff members are open," noted one. "Teachers need to talk to the parents more," pointed out another. "If it's good they're happy to talk to the parent, but if it's bad they come to us." Third, assertions of control through communication were evident. Staff members communicated their territoriality surrounding certain work spaces, classrooms, and children. "We're territorial here—'don't touch my stuff,'" noted one staff member. "And people don't want to deal with stuff that is not theirs." Another teacher pointed out, "sometimes I get frustrated. These are adults. I ask them with something specific to do, and it's half done, or brushed off, or done just once and that's it." They also stressed the need to guide the children for the sake of their learning, maturing, and safety. Children were encouraged to express desires and emotions in words rather than loud shouts or cries.

Fourth, adaptive communication was prized—staff members described adjusting their communication to a more formal or informal teasing style depending on the individual, their situation, or their mood. "Sometimes no communication is best," noted one staff member. "I've had to kind of learn to either communicate or not communicate, depending on who the person is." The center director noted that "most problem conversations involve my pointing out something that has not been done properly.... I'm not confrontational. I just happen to say that we need this done again." Fifth and finally, an encouragement of independence was evident—to the children and other staff members. None wanted to be in another's "face" about work that needed to be done, and most phrased desired tasks as requests or suggestions rather than directives or orders. Although some noted that such requests were not complied with as consistently or long-term as desired, none wanted to move to more direct "commands" or "orders." Children were also encouraged to make choices without constantly being told by teachers what the next activity would be or what the rules were.

An event that took place during my observations illustrated these key staff values in action when they were violated by a child's caretaker. One universally accepted rule at the center had children cleaning up an area they had played in before leaving it. This rule applied when changing activities as well as when going home for the day. Parents, on the whole, appreciated this rule and liked to reinforce it before taking their child home. "Do you have anything to clean up?"—this was often asked by parents before leaving with their child. One day after all the other children had left for the day, Jawon's grandmother came in and found Jawon playing with blocks in the block area. Mr. Duane, the classroom teacher, had told Jawon he would need to clean up the blocks he got out, and Jawon seemed fine with that, knowing it was a pervasive classroom rule. Without talking directly to Mr. Duane, Ms. Tina, or myself, who were sitting nearby, she told Jawon it was time to go. "Clean up the blocks first, Jawon," said Mr. Duane. As Jawon started to clean up the blocks, his grandmother said, after a pause, "No, this is too much. He's only 4." "The children know that they clean up toys that they get out," said Ms. Tina. "This is not right," said the grandmother. "You are ganging up on him. Who is his teacher?" "I am," said Mr. Duane. "They are just in here," he added, referring to Ms. Tina and myself. "You're his teacher?" said the grandmother, in a surprised tone. Mr. Duane was African American as she was herself, while Ms. Tina and I were not. She seemed surprised that Mr. Duane was actually the teacher.

Meanwhile, Ms. Tina had asked Ms. Grace, the center's assistant director, to come in the room after seeing her passing in the hallway. "Ms. Grace, could you come in here for a second, please.... We have a conflict about cleaning up." "Jawon should not have to clean all of this up," said the grandmother. "We do encourage the children to clean up toys they have taken out," said Ms. Grace. "Well, if he could have some help, then maybe he could; he's only 4. He should not have to do all these," said the grandmother. "Well, OK; Mr. Duane can help him get the blocks cleaned up," said Ms. Grace.

Mr. Duane reluctantly helped Jawon clean up the blocks, as the latter looked uncomfortable about this scene as he had willingly begun to clean the blocks up before his grandmother had stopped him. Without a word other than a "Thank you, Jawon" from me and a "See you tomorrow, Jawon," from Ms. Tina and Mr. Duane, the grandmother observed Jawon help clean up the blocks and led him out of the room. "How rude," said Ms. Tina, under her breath, even before they had left the building. A conversation ensued as the staff members made final preparations to close and leave the center. "That's one reason Jawon has so much trouble (with expressing his feelings in words and complying with staff members)," it was noted.

Parent Interaction Themes

Parents, too, discussed five key themes that for them typified communication in the child development center culture, although they naturally differed from the staff in some. First, they valued the child-centered education found at the center. There were many staff members and observers available to monitor and interact with the children, they thought the staff knew and loved the children, and there were regular, structured developmental activities for them. "They show caring" when communicating with the children, noted one parent. Second, open communication was valued by parents just as much as by staff. In fact, parents were impressed with the availability and willingness of staff members to communicate, but many still felt a hunger for more daily reports or discussions about their children, especially as the latter got older. One mother explained: "I could always call there. I like that open and comfortable sense that communication is welcome. Nobody says, 'Why are you calling?'" Another cautioned that "communication varies depending on age—infants you get daily written communication, but with 5-year-olds communication is not as consistent." Another noted that "they do not sit down to talk to you at all; there are no sit-down conferences about how your child is doing or progressing.... If something happens, they'll tell you, but not on a day-to-day basis." Third, a sense of community was clearly felt by parents at the center. Daily greetings of other parents were often seen as kind and friendly even if superficial, but several noted that their children becoming friends caused them to talk and arrange activities together. Child birthday parties were nearly universally cited as times when parents would plan together and interact with one another for a longer period of time, leading to a sense of community. "I remember a lively conversation at a birthday party at the center about a variety of topics," noted one father. Fourth, safety was mentioned by most as a key reason for their child being at the center—the surroundings were safe, the building and grounds were seen as safe, and all the attention their children got enhanced their sense of safety. Fifth and finally, encouragement of talk was appreciated by parents, as staff members would calmly disengage apprehensive children from parents in the morning, and children would come home talking about their feelings rather than screaming or yelling. At times, when appropriate, parents and teachers included a child in conference about behavior or other issues. One parent explained, "We asked J.R. to come in and we brought it down to his level. I said that it was very important to me that I know he is being taken care of and is happy, because I can't do a good job and concentrate on my work if he is not. I said it's like a team, and everyone has responsibilities for the team to work better." Children were encouraged to use their words and make choices as much as possible.

All parents had some sense that communication characteristics enacted by their child had some similarity with those they saw at home or regularly in other communication settings. Children, who were creative and imaginative, or headstrong and obstinate, were often reported acting similarly at home and at the center. Other children wanted full attention when talking to someone, used words to describe emotions, and were polite in both venues. One mother noted that her son "likes to talk about what he did throughout the day. Sometimes I may be looking another way, and he gets impatient. 'Look at my eyes!' he'll say." That child would enact similar behavior at the center. Children who parents saw as happy and playing well with others, talking a lot, playing hard, or alternatively reading and concentrating well, enacted such behaviors at home and at the center setting too. Some children would try to be a bossy leader or lash out when frustrated in both settings.

All parents also, however, noted clear and striking differences between their children's communication at the center as reported to them or rarely surreptitiously observed by them. Children would take naps at school regularly, for instance, when they almost never did at home. Most often, children would be viewed as much better behaved at the center, with more compliance and less complaining. Similarly, children kept clean or cleaned up much more readily at the center than at home with parents and family. "She actually listens, and sits still," noted one parent about her daughter at school, suggesting she wanted some of that behavior at home as well. Some children, however, would test boundaries at the center much more than at home; some took aggressive actions such as throwing rocks, pulling a toy away from another child, or stomping in a tantrum that surprised parents who did not usually see those behaviors from their children. One mother noted that when they were really surprised by a negative behavior, they would ask their son, "'Who is it in your class that does this and gets their way?' It's a phrase, not what we use, or a certain kind of whine." At the center, surrounded by teachers and peers, parents and staff noted that some children would engage in unusual behaviors from a family perspective: using a sarcastic tone, learning mean names or sayings, sneakily breaking clear home as well as school rules, or acting more independently with less whining, and less demanding attention. Some children were more affectionate toward their parents at school than at home, and other children were viewed as following the group more by yielding to peer pressure more at school than at home where peers were usually absent.

The child care center culture gave preschool children a chance to try out alternative communication behaviors. Those children who were content with their communication strategies and had them reinforced at home would consistently use the same ones at the child care center. Other children, though, found the center a place to be either more reticent or bolder in trying alternative communication styles. Those communication strategies that were reinforced at the center might then appear at home with parents and siblings.

Conclusions: Cross-Organizational Sense-Making

Family relationships set the tone for children developing relationships outside the family, as the child-parent relationship naturally continued while outside relationships developed, and children and adults found ways of adapting to increasingly varied relationships (see Dixson, 1995). Staff members definitely attributed much communication by children to home and family norms, and parents were often surprised by new communication strategies enacted by their children taking place at the center or imported back into the family relationship. One finds that as children grow they turn more to peers for emotional support, and this clearly began to happen during the preschool years for children at the center. They do not completely leave family norms behind, though. Studies reveal that comforting skills of both mothers and peers increasingly and independently contribute to a child's social acceptance, as the child learns to create sensitive or comforting messages that lead to such acceptance (Burleson & Kunkel, 2002). Family resources for learning communication strategies may be usefully supplemented by learning from center communication norms.

Three Cultural Perspectives

Studies of organizational cultures suggest three lenses for potential findings on communication perspectives, as culture may be approached from integrative, differentiated, and fragmented perspectives (Frost, Moore, Louis, Lundberg, & Martin, 1991). One may expect some integration among the relationships as certain meanings and values were widely shared, and helped to integrate all relationships consistently with the child care center culture, perhaps complemented by the family culture. Alternatively, some contradictions were likely to be found as parties must differentiate between "school" and "home," or interaction with a child instead of with a parent. Fragmentations or ambiguities were evident with some strategies variously tried and avoided, accepted and not accepted, by others in different settings. Consistencies in communicating with children, for instance, may be comfortable and beneficial with both parents and teachers conveying similar expectations. However, differences may be necessary in strikingly varied contexts (like at home with siblings as opposed to at school with at least 15 other children) and beneficially enhance communication adaptability in children. Discomfort may result, however, from the need to communicate one way with one party while using a contrasting communication strategy to fulfill different expectations with another. Children must learn to adapt and alter their communication given the context, as do adults. The adaptations shown as parties made transitions from child care center to home proved to be fertile ground for viewing such integrated, differentiated, and fragmented communications.

As new communication strategies were tried, consistencies and contrasts between settings became evident, and parties grew used to adapting to them. For some issues, "at school is at school and at home is at home," and those differences were accepted and reinforced. With others, communicators adapted by approving or disapproving messages tried in either setting. Through such interactions, retrospectively, uncertainty was reduced by new patterns becoming accepted in any context or as narrowly applying to just one (Weick, 1979). Roles in the different settings were enacted through parties changing and elaborating mutual interactions. Recurring patterns created socially constructed realities constituted in communication that became organizational cultures (Weick, 1989). Children are socialized into such cultures in both the family and child care environments, and children, parents, and staff members tried to make sense of and integrate communication expectations.

Culture enactments clashed with discontinuities in the flow of experience when sudden differences emerged as "imported" from the child care or home context into the other. Such "ecological change" may be said to spur reorganizing and adaptation by all parties in their settings (Everett, 1994). Routines would then be reformed through communication to once again reduce uncertainty or equivocality. Differences may be integrated and accepted by communicators as they adapt, or they may be foregrounded as conflict sparks. At times, parents may outwardly disagree with organization members about how their children communicate. McHoul and Rapley (2005) extensively analyzed text of a doctor and principal pushing a mother to accept a drug solution to her son's diagnosed Attention Deficit/Hyperactivity Disorder diagnosis. The mother preferred a communicative solution, while the organizational authorities sought the standard medication prescription. At the center, most such family/center disagreements were downplayed, and people simply adapted their communication to others.

Venues like child development centers may be viewed as communication crossroads, where norms and values from family and child cultures meet, blend, and clash. On the whole, preschool children seem to profit from becoming boundary spanners at such a young age, learning to adapt their communication strategies to varying organizational cultures. Future research could richly explore such crossroads and the recurring issues that emerge there, such as how power differences affect dominant norms in each culture and in their blending, how the family culture affects children interacting in child care cultures, and how extensive divergences in communication norms really may be between child care centers and family cultures. At the center studied here, parents, staff, and children on the whole found a communication crossroads that they liked and appreciated as a venue for learning.

References

Albrecht, T. L. (1984). Managerial communication and work perception. In R. N. Bostrom (Ed.), *Communication yearbook 8* (pp. 538–557). Beverly Hills, CA: Sage.

Allen, R. R., & Brown, K. L. (1976). *Developing communication competence in children.* Skokie, IL: National Textbook Company.

Bochner, A. P., & Ellis, C. (1992). Personal narrative as a social approach to interpersonal communication. *Communication Theory, 2,* 165–172.

Booth-Butterfield, M., & Sidelinger, R. (1998). The influence of family communication on the college-aged child: Openness, attitudes and actions about sex and alcohol. *Communication Quarterly, 46,* 295–308.

Bradac, J. J., Tardy, C. H., & Hosman, L. A. (1980). Disclosure styles and a hint at their genesis. *Human Communication Research, 6,* 228–238.

Bradbard, M. R., Endsley, M. R., & Mize, J. (1992). The ecology of parent-child communications about daily experiences in preschool and day care. *Journal of Research in Childhood Education, 6*(2), 13–23.

Brown, M. H. (1990). "Reading" an organization's culture: An examination of stories in nursing homes. *Journal of Applied Communication Research, 18,* 64–75.

Brown, M. H., & McMillan, J. J. (1991). Culture as text: The development of an organizational narrative. *Southern Communication Journal, 57,* 49–60.

Burleson, B. R., & Kunkel, A. (2002). Parental and peer contributions to the emotional support skills of the child: From whom do children learn to express support? *Journal of Family Communication, 2,* 79–97.

Canary, H. E., & Canary, D. J. (2007). Making sense of one's career: An analysis and typology of supervisor career stories. *Communication Quarterly, 55,* 225–246.

Clancy, P. M. (1989). A case study in language socialization: Korean wh-questions. *Discourse Processes, 12,* 169–191.

Dixson, M. (1995). Models and perspectives of parent-child communication. In T. J. Socha & G. H. Stamp (Eds.), *Parents, children, and communication: Frontiers of theory and research* (pp. 43–62). Mahwah, NJ: Erlbaum.

Dunn, J. (1997). Lessons from the study of bidirectional effects. *Journal of Social and Personal Relationships, 14*, 565–573.

Everett, J. L. (1994). Communication and sociocultural evolution in organizations and organizational populations. *Communication Theory, 4*, 93–110.

Foot, H. C., Chapman, A. J., & Smith, J. R. (1995). *Friendship and social relations in children.* New Brunswick, NJ: Transaction.

Frost, P. J., Moore, L. F., Louis, M. R., Lundberg, C. C., & Martin, J. (1991). *Reframing organizational culture.* Newbury Park, CA: Sage.

Glaser, B. G., & Strauss, A. L. (1967). *The discovery of grounded theory: Strategies for qualitative research.* New York: Aldine de Gruyter.

Goodwin, M. H. (2007). Occasioned knowledge exploration in family interaction. *Discourse and Society, 18*, 93–110.

Hart, C. H. Olsen, S. F., Robinson, C. C., & Mandleco, B. L. (1997). The development of social and communicative competence in childhood: Review and a model of personal, familial, and extrafamilial processes. *Communication Yearbook, 20*, 305–373.

Howes, C. (1987). Social competency with peers: Contributions from child care. *Early Childhood Research Quarterly, 2*, 155–167.

Kerns, K. A. (1994). A longitudinal examination of links between mother-child attachment and children's friendships in early childhood. *Journal of Social and Personal Relationships, 11*, 379–381.

Koesten, J., Miller, K. I., & Hummert, M. L. (2002). Family communication, self-esteem, and white female adolescents' risk behavior. *Journal of Family Communication, 2*, 7–27.

Kremer-Sadlik, T., & Kim, J. L. (2007). Lessons from sports: Children's socialization to values through family interaction during sports activities. *Discourse and Society, 18*: 35–52.

Luecken, L. J., Appelhans, B. M., Kraft, A., & Brown, A. (2006). Never far from home: A cognitive-affective model of the impact of early-life family relationships on physiological stress responses in adulthood. *Journal of Social and Personal Relationships, 23*, 189–203.

Meyer, J. (1995). Tell me a story: Eliciting organizational values from narratives. *Communication Quarterly, 43*, 210–224.

Meyer, J. (2003). *Kids talking: Learning relationships and culture with children.* Lanham, MD: Rowman & Littlefield.

Meyer, J., & Driskill, G. (1997). Children and relationship development: Communication strategies in a day care center. *Communication Reports, 10*, 75–85.

McHoul, A. & Rapley, M. (2005). A case of attention-deficit/hyperactivity disorder diagnosis: Sir Karl and Francis B. slug it out on the consulting room floor. *Discourse and Society, 16*, 419–449.

Miles, M. B., & Huberman, A. M. (1994). *Qualitative data analysis* (2nd ed.). Thousand Oaks, CA: Sage.

Pacanowsky, M. E., & O'Donnell-Trujillo, N. (1982). Communication and organizational cultures. *Western Journal of Speech Communication, 46*, 115–130.

Shulman, S., Elicker, J., & Sroufe, L. A. (1994). Stages of friendship growth in preadolescence as related to attachment history. *Journal of Social and Personal Relationships, 11*, 341–361.

Strauss, A., & Corbin, J. (1990). *Basics of qualitative research: Grounded theory procedures and techniques.* Newbury Park, CA: Sage.

Van Maanen, J. (1988). *Tales of the field: On writing ethnography.* Chicago: University of Chicago Press.

Weick, K. (1979). *The social psychology of organizing* (2nd ed.). Reading, MA: Addison-Wesley.

Weick, K. (1989). Organized improvisation: 20 years of organizing. *Communication Studies, 40,* 241–248.

Wingard, L. (2007). Constructing time and prioritizing activities in parent-child interaction. *Discourse and Society, 18,* 75–91.

Zhang, Q. (2007). Family communication patterns and conflict styles in Chinese parent-child relationships. *Communication Quarterly, 55,* 113–128.

4   The Interface of HOME-Work and Low-Wage Maternal Employment

Michelle Miller-Day and Tara G. McManus

> Kids see their parents as being stuck, having no hope. So why should we even try? It's really not that 'I won't', it's more like 'I can't even see it ... ya know, what's the point? (Interview excerpt)

The above quote is from a 13-year-old girl living in poverty and being interviewed about her own efficacy, goals, and aspirations. This girl is not alone in her feelings of hopelessness; research has consistently found that youth living in low-income households may be at higher risk for a number of troubling outcomes, including low levels of efficacy and academic underachievement, than other youth (Gennetian, Duncan, Knox, Vargas, Clark-Kauffman, & London, 2004). This finding is neither pejorative nor stereotypical of all low-income families. Having worked for the past 5 years with mothers and youth who live in poverty and having lived in poverty stricken neighborhoods during my young adulthood, I[1] have seen firsthand how poverty can impact one's sense of general efficacy. Yet, poverty can also provide a powerful motivating force; a desire to move out of poverty into self sufficiency to provide a better life for your children.

Not surprisingly, the impact of poverty on contemporary families is multilayered and complex. To understand the development of efficacy in children of poverty, ecological systems theory posits that scholars need to address the many "layers" of influence on a child's development (Bronfenbrenner, 1979). The ecological perspective stresses the importance of examining not only the child, but his or her family and their interaction with the larger environment (Bronfenbrenner). An aim of this chapter is to do just that—to explore the triadic relationship of work-parenting-adolescents; specifically, the intersection of maternal low-wage employment, mother-adolescent relations, and adolescent efficacy.

Background

Mothers and Low-Wage Work

In an effort to address poverty in America, the passage of the Personal Responsibility and Work Opportunity Reconciliation Act (PRWOR) changed the ecology of many families by creating incentives for welfare recipients to influence them to enter the workforce as quickly as possible (PRWOR, 1996). The impact has been marked, with welfare recipients decreasing by 51% at the end of the 20th century, but ultimately increasing the ranks of low-income and working poor families (Fremstad, 2003). As Hastings, Taylor, and Austin (2005) noted, the general tendency to "constrain public welfare programs has forced poor families into a continuous survival mode involving temporary jobs and time-limited public benefits" (p. 56).

Currently, the types of low paying jobs many of these mothers hold are often stressful and demanding, with very low levels of employment security. Indeed, families who make up the "working poor"—those living just above or below the poverty line—are most likely to be headed by women who work in low-paying service-sector jobs, are less educated, and have health constraints (O'Neill & Hill, 2003). According to Morris, Huston, Duncan, Crosby, and Bos (2001), in the 2 years following the 1996 welfare reforms, labor force participation among single mothers increased by 10%. This dramatic change has fueled concern about the effects of poverty on children.

Qualitative data from a study conducted by the Manpower Demonstration Research Corporation (MDRC) shows those women who are able to become upwardly mobile and increase their income and benefits by moving off welfare, improve in terms of mental and physical health (Morris et al., 2001). Yet, when the move is lateral (merely moving to a different job) or downward, mother and children tend to suffer. During her 2-year transition period, a 25-year-old mother in the Morris et al. study moved from one low-paying job to the next, subsidizing income with under the table cash payments. She reported that the principal of her daughter's school told her that her daughter was acting out in school and chided her for not giving the child enough attention. In exasperation, the mother responded, "How do you expect me to spend time with my kid when welfare's telling me to go to work all the time?" Morris and colleagues found this same sense of wearied frustration in many of the mothers in their study. Although many welfare-to-work programs increased mothers' employment opportunities, the programs had some negative effects on both the mothers and their adolescents. Several studies have been conducted in the past 5 years seeking to understand why this is so (see, for example, Brooks, Hair, & Zaslow, 2001).

To understand the affects of a maternal transition from welfare into the workforce for low-income adolescents, some researchers have turned to ecological systems theory. Ecological systems theory (Bronfenbrenner, 1979, 1986; Bronfenbrenner & Morris, 1998) casts the individual family as a microsystem nested within a larger framework of social systems, where parents and children are members of multiple systems (e.g., families, places of employment, communities, and government agencies). These multiple systems may enhance or impede healthy family interactions and individuals' well-being (Grzywacz & Marks, 2000). When involved in one subsystem (e.g., work), individuals are unavailable in other systems (e.g., family). Parents who work outside the household likely spend much of their time in systems outside the family. In fact, one of the major trends observed in the 1990s was the significant increase of women's contributions to the family income (White & Rogers, 2000). However, national data reveal that low-income mothers tend to invest a greater portion of their time at work compared to the time spent with the family (Deitch & Huffman, 2001). Occupational factors such as more work hours, lack of job security, poor benefits, and working nonstandard shifts are more likely to be found among low-income workers and lead to more time at work, and subsequently, to work-family conflict (Cox & Presser, 2000; Deitch & Huffman, 2001; Johnson & Corcoran, 2003).

The basic tenets of ecological systems theory argue that parent-child interactions and the well-being of offspring may be affected profoundly by a parent's experiences outside the family (Bronfenbrenner, 1979, 1986; Bronfenbrenner & Morris, 1998). Therefore, the more investment a parent has in another subsystem, the less available they are to their family (Voydanoff, 2004), and the greater impact it could have on offspring. However, as many working parents will attest, time spent on the job is not universally negative. Recent research on welfare leavers has found that many women experience improvements in psychological wellbeing when they are employed, reporting increased self-esteem, greater self efficacy, and feeling like a better role model for their children (London, Scott, Edin, & Hunter, 2004). Yet, for some women who make the transition from welfare to the workforce, the shift is fraught with negative work experiences such as employment instability (multiple jobs, unstable shift work) and negative job opinions (Crouter & McHale, 1993) often leading to increased stress, depression, and less time and inclination to address family management (Grzywacz, Almeida, & McDonald, 2002; Mayseless, Bartholomew, Henderson, & Trinke, 2004). As Hays (2003) pointed out, relative to middle-class parents, "welfare mothers must face these demanding dual commitments [to work and family care] with many fewer financial assets, marketable skills, and familial resources backing them up, and under much more powerful economic and logistical constraints" (p. 53).

As we embark on the 21st century, little is known about the impacts of low paying, unstable, maternal work on family functioning and adolescent well-being. This is especially important since youth are undergoing significant challenges of their own as they transition into adolescence.

Most research on work-family tensions has focused on young children because they are viewed as particularly vulnerable to the potential costs or benefits of maternal employment (Morris et al., 2001). However, using data from eight random assignment studies and employing meta-analytic techniques, Gennetian et al. (2004) provide evidence that low-wage work and welfare-to-work policies targeted at low-income parents have many deleterious effects on adolescents—particularly those with younger siblings. Morris et al. (2001) noted that merely moving mothers into the workforce does not appear sufficient to foster the healthy development of children who are living in poverty. Children living in poverty are at risk of low achievement, problem behaviors, and health problems; as a result, it is critical that policies affecting families enhance children's well-being rather than leaving them at the same level of deprivation and risk that they experienced under the welfare system (Gennetian et al., 2004).

The concern is not that low-income mothers are working outside the home; indeed, mothers may ultimately benefit from policies easing a transition into the workforce. Rather, it is that managing the nature and quality of the work (e.g., low-paying, stressful jobs of limited security) with few social and personal resources may significantly affect mother-youth relations and adolescent well-being. Once they are working, the difficult work situations and job instability may weaken mother-youth communication (Huston, 1991; Orthner, Jones-Sanpei, & Williamson, 2004), and increase the likelihood that youth will experience negative outcomes (Brooks et al., 2001; Gennetian et al., 2004).

In contrast to the picture painted above, some policy makers argue that all work is good work for the poor and receiving welfare is what is linked to poorer well-being and psychological distress in mothers and higher drop-out rates in youth (Ensminger, 1995). Research on general (primarily Caucasian) samples suggests that women who are employed outside the home are generally more satisfied and report less psychological distress than women who are not employed (Jackson, Gyamfi, Brooks-Gunn, & Blake, 1998). Ross and Mirowsky (1988) suggested that employment reduces a woman's multiple role distress because she has access to two potential sources of gratification, both job and home, instead of the singular source available to full-time homemakers. In addition, Barnett, Marshall, and Singer (1992) posited that women benefit from employment because of the additional opportunities to enjoy work-related rewards, which can positively influence women's overall well-being. This is good news since, as we enter into the 21st century, a large majority of mothers in the United States are employed outside the home (Bond, Thompson, Galinsky, & Prottas, 2003). In terms of the family as a whole, maternal employment can bring additional economic resources, which often may mean the difference between dependence on government financial assistance and self-sufficiency (Jackson et al., 1998)

There is mounting evidence, however, that "working poor" mothers may have a different work-family experience than do other classes of women (Voydanoff, 2004), and that the types of low-paying jobs for which many welfare-to-work mothers qualify are more harmful than helpful to psychosocial functioning (Loprest, 2001). Frequent transitions from welfare to work, moving from one low paying job to the next, and subsidizing income with "cash pay" from under-the-table jobs may lead to increased maternal stress, less time and inclination to address family matters, and fewer positive interactions between mothers and children (Seccombe, James, & Battle-Walters, 1998). Living in poverty relates to a number of negative outcomes, including aggravation with parenting, mental health problems, more harsh parenting, and child depression (e.g., McLoyd, 1998). Furthermore, these negative outcomes may be exacerbated by remaining in poverty while attempting to balance stressful work-family interactions

(Halpern & Murphy, 2005). In fact, it is often the case that welfare losses are not matched by earnings gains; parents' employment is increased, but not their income (Gennetian et al., 2004). Thus, the impact of welfare reform on mothers and youth may vary widely, depending upon the types of jobs that mothers secure (Gennetian et al., 2004; Grzywacz & Marks, 2000).

Given the impact of mothers' work experience on low-income families, it is important to understand how maternal work relates to family interaction and youth outcomes. Rather than being uniformly positive or negative, the impact of work on the family depends upon the characteristics the work experience (Crouter, 1994; Parcel & Menaghan, 1994). Previous research suggests several aspects of the work experience are important, including wages and benefits of the job, the degree to which family income alleviates financial stress on the family, and job stability, including time in job, perceived security, and transitions on and off welfare support. When mothers work for minimal wages or at part-time jobs, their job earnings and benefits may not be sufficient to meet the financial needs of the family. Chronic financial stress may contribute to maternal distress and depression and increase conflict between mother and children, and therefore may threaten positive family relations (Crouter & McHale, 1993; McLoyd, 1998). In addition, job stability may also affect maternal and child well-being. Previous longitudinal research has demonstrated that work instability, particularly when combined with family instability, can have deleterious effects on child development (Parcel & Menaghan, 1994). Consequently, for the study reported in this chapter, we were interested in examining the relationships among job stability, mother-adolescent relations, and adolescent efficacy.

Mother-Adolescent Relations

Mother-youth relations are central to adolescent adjustment and the prevention of problem behaviors (Brody et al., 2006). All youth, regardless of socioeconomic status (SES), are challenged with the normative development of independence from parents during the early adolescent years, as they move toward becoming autonomous, self-sufficient, productive, and competent adults (Allen & Land, 1999). During these years, parent-adolescent relations including parental monitoring, effective communication, and competent family management, foster youth self esteem (Brody et al., 2004).

Maternal monitoring takes on a critical function during the early adolescent years, particularly for youth living in high-risk urban areas (Brody et al., 2004; Brody et al., 2006). Young adolescents who spend unsupervised time affiliating with deviant peers are at increased risk for school dropout, problem behaviors, early substance use, and criminal activity (Romer, 2003). Effective parental monitoring has the direct effect of reducing adolescent problem behavior and the indirect benefit of protecting youth from associations with deviant peer influences (Brody et al., 2004; Griffin et al., 2000). Parental monitoring has been found to relate to adolescent delinquency, antisocial behavior, sexual activity, drug use, depression, and academic achievement (Jacobson & Crockett, 2000; Brody et al., 2004). Importantly, parental monitoring seems to be particularly important for adolescent outcomes when mothers work full time, particularly for mothers who are single-parents (Jacobson & Crockett, 2000). Parents who are employed outside the home may have less time to monitor their child's schooling or outside activities and may be under more stress which, in turn, affects their ability to involve themselves in their children's lives (Chase-Lansdale et al., 2003).

Mother-adolescent communication is also central to predicting adolescent adjustment. Parents affect their sons and daughters, both in the actual messages they communicate and in the manner in which they convey these messages. As Markman and Notarious (1994) pointed out, relationships can tolerate considerable adversity as long as it is offset by positive and constructive communication. Yet, although parent-adolescent communication (PAC) is professed to be important in the adolescent development literature (see, for example, Barnes & Olson, 1985; Jackson, Bijstra, Oostra, & Bosma, 1998; Reisch, Anderson, & Krueger, 2006), there is very little research examining the effects of parental employment on PAC. In fact, as Galinsky (2005) pointed out, there has been a decided lack of emphasis on studying actual family processes in the work-family interaction literature. Ritchie (1997) examined family communication patterns, SES, and parent education and found that lower SES families were likely to express a conformity communication orientation and that parents with more complex jobs communicated with a more open and expressive orientation than those with less complex jobs. However, in most of the sociological, psychological, and even family relations literature, parent-adolescent communication has been subsumed within latent constructs such as family functioning or parent-child communication about sex (see, for example, Brody et al., 2004), with few studies assessing quality of parent-adolescent communicative interaction or assessing specific parent-adolescent communication practices. Consequently, very limited information is available about the impact of maternal work on parent-adolescent communication.

Family Management and Parentification

For low-income families, parents often have multiple jobs and spend much time away from home, posing difficulties for the fulfillment of household tasks. Parents often need to rely on children to assume some adult and household responsibilities and this adoption of instrumental and/or emotional adult responsibilities by a child is referred to as parentification (Chase, 1999). For some low-income families, the household work and caregiving that adolescents provide the family system can aid family functioning and adolescent well-being (e.g., Byng-Hall, 2002). On the other hand, young adolescents who offer assistance to family members may be involved in dimensions of care that are developmentally inappropriate, which may jeopardize their mental health (Burton, 2007; Mortimer, Finch, Ryu, Shanahan, & Call, 1996).

Parentification comprises a variety of processes in which youth are, often inappropriately, participating in adult roles and responsibilities within their family networks, with little or no supervision, restricting their recreational activities with their same-age peers and exposing them to adult knowledge (Jurkovic, Thirkield, & Morrell, 2001). In Western cultures, a child's assumption of "adult roles"—such as being the household financial manager or primary care provider for one's siblings—is considered nonnormative (Burton, 2007). Moreover, access to restricted, adult information may be developmentally or relationally inappropriate (e.g., Boszormenyi-Nagy & Spark, 1973; Chase, 1999).

Parentified children can occur across all socioeconomic classes when there is stress placed upon a family by divorce, chronic illness, alcoholism, or poverty. In these instances, family members need to "pick up the slack" for others in the household due to a particular strain or stressor on the family. Burton (2007) pointed out that economic disadvantage shapes families' everyday lives in ways that may lead to childhood parentification. She reminds us in her research that families may have limited access to formal child care or other social services, requiring older children in the family to provide extensive care for younger ones (Burton, 2007). Burton further argues that children in economically disadvantaged families are more likely to be involved in unguided and unmonitored household labor than their economically better-off peers. In these contexts, parents are required to put more hours into work to improve the family's financial situation, and the children must assume responsibilities that the parents might have attended to if they were not working. When families live in poverty, children often feel the emotional burden and financial strain and may assume the role of comforter to parents and sibling alike.

Although many argue that parentification is fundamentally problematic, others have found this role reversal to have nondetrimental outcomes (Erikson, 1959; Mayseless, Bartholomew, Henderson, & Trinke, 2004). The parentified child may serve a functional purpose in low-wage households because they provide care for siblings in the absence of a primary wage earning parent (Minuchin, 1974). Erikson's (1959) model of psychosocial ego development also accounts for healthy forms of parentification where the parental role contributes to the child's need to be useful and feel competent in family relations. Further, responsiveness (to parents' needs) can be construed as a family strength and may assist a child in developing a sense of reciprocity with others, ultimately contributing to overall positive well-being (Byng-Hall, 2002; Erickson, 1959; Masten & Coatsworth, 1998). For instance, parentification of adolescents from low-income families may aid the offspring's social competence and demonstrate resilience because it exhibits their ability to adjust to environmental difficulties and illustrates independence (Masten & Coatsworth, 1998; Rodgers & Rose, 2002). Indeed, a basic premise of structural family therapy has been that when parents engage their older children to take on sibling supervisory and other parent-helping roles in a manner that supports their role in the sibling hierarchy, and the parent teaches and supervises them, and does not abandon them to figure it all out by themselves, these children can function quite well in these roles and obtain a sense of pride from them. Additional research is needed to clarify the contradictory findings about parentification in low-income households, perhaps gaining some perspective on the practice of parentification from parentified youth themselves.

Adolescent Efficacy

Lim and Loo (2003) found that children of job insecure individuals experienced lower levels of general efficacy. General efficacy is a generalized competence belief reflecting individuals' perception of their ability to perform across a variety of different situations (Judge, Erez, & Bono, 1998). Parents, in general, seek to promote competence and efficacy in their children; however the strain of demanding work and impoverished conditions makes relational maintenance difficult and provides challenges for parents to promote children's efficacy (Murray & Brody, 1999). Mallinckrodt (1992) reported that the quality of parent-child interactions in his study had an impact on youth's general self-efficacy, and Lim and Loo (2003) argued that this might be due to the increased stress associated with job instability leading to more aggressive communication with children, which seemed to negatively impact children's' efficacy. Yet, the results from this study were inconclusive. The body of research discussed above suggests that maternal low-wage work characteristics impact mother-youth relationships and may also affect adolescent's perceptions of their own efficacy; yet this research is suggestive and not conclusive. There is still much to be learned about how low-wage maternal work interfaces with parenting, which may—in turn—affect youth outcomes such as efficacy. What, then, are the relationships among maternal low-wage work, parent-adolescent relations, and adolescent efficacy? This is the question that guided the following study.

The Present Study

For the remainder of this chapter, we will report findings from a study conducted with mothers and at least one of their adolescent children. The study included a sample of 94 mother-adolescent dyads (56 daughters, 38 sons) meeting specific criteria: the mother had transitioned from welfare to work in the past year, annual household income was equal to or less than the Federal Poverty Level guidelines (i.e., less than $18,859 for a family of four; U.S. Bureau of the Census, 2002), and the child was enrolled in the sixth grade at the local school district.

One home visit was completed with each dyad and a two-part interview was conducted (consisting of a structured interview schedule followed by a semi-structured qualitative interview) with each person separately. Two interviewers arrived at the home of the participants and one interviewer was assigned to the mother and another to the child, then the interviews occurred simultaneously in private locations within the home. Participants were assured confidentiality and Certificates of Confidentiality were issued by the National Institutes of Health to protect identifiable research information from use in any civil, criminal, administrative, legislative, or other proceeding at the federal, state, or local level (National Institutes of Health, 2006).

As part of a larger study, maternal interviews addressed demographics, employment and work experiences, social and instrumental support, maternal well-being, mother-adolescent relations, and perceptions of the child. Youth interviews collected information regarding demographic characteristics, school experiences, youth well-being, mother-adolescent relations, and perceptions of self. To accommodate varying reading levels, interviewers read the questions to participants and recorded their responses on the interview form. Participants earned $25 compensation for their involvement.

Although there were many constructs examined in this research project, in this chapter we will address three primary domains: maternal work situations, mother-adolescent relations, and adolescent efficacy. Mothers reported on their own maternal work situations, and adolescents reported on their perceptions of mother-adolescent relations and their own efficacy.

Measures

Maternal Work Situation   Based on the review of literature in the area, two aspects of maternal-work were assessed—job stability and financial support/strain. To assess these, subscales from the Work and Economic Conditions Scale (Crouter & Manke, 1997) were used. Job stability was assessed by five yes/no questions assessing the stability of the mother's employment in the past year (e.g., "During the past year have you changed jobs?"; "During the past year have you been laid off or fired from a job?"; "During the past year have you experienced a demotion or cut back in hours?") and higher values reflect greater employment instability. Financial support/strain consisted of ten questions asking if the family did or did not have enough money for certain items (e.g., "My family has had enough money for clothing") and these assessments were rated on a 5-point scale (1 = "had enough money for"; 5 = "did not have enough money for") ($a = .85$). Higher scores reflect more financial strain.

Mother-Adolescent Relations   Based on our review, we were interested in exploring the impact of low-wage maternal work situations on mother-adolescent relations. Mother-adolescent relations were conceptualized using four specific quality indices: maternal monitoring, mother-adolescent communication, maternal aggressive conflict communication, and parentification. Youth reports were used for all measures. Maternal monitoring was assessed by an adapted version of the Parental Monitoring scale used in the Pittsburgh Youth Study (Loeber, Stouthamer-Loeber, Van Kammen, & Farrington, 1991). This measure assessed the adolescent's report of his or her parent's knowledge of the youth's whereabouts, the amount of time that the youth is unsupervised, and the parent's knowledge of the youth's friends. Monitoring was assessed on a 3-point scale (1 = "doesn't know"; 2 = "knows a little"; 3 = "knows a lot") ($a = .70$)

The Parent-Adolescent Communication scale (PAC, Barnes & Olson, 1982) was used to assess PAC. The 20-item adolescent-report version of the measure assessed open family communication and problems in communication with mother (*a* = .78). The Open Family Communication subscale reflected feelings of free expression and understanding in parent-adolescent interactions (e.g., "When I ask questions, I get honest answers from my mother"). The Problems in Family Communication (PFC) subscale measured negative interaction patterns with the adolescent's mother (e.g., "My mother insults me when he/she is angry with me.") Agreement was assessed on a four-point scale (1 = "agree a lot", 2 = "agree a little", 3 = "disagree a little", and 4 = "disagree a lot"). For the entire PAC scale, higher scores represent higher quality parent–adolescent communication.

Adolescents' perceptions of their maternal verbal aggression were assessed using the 20-item aggression subscale of Kerig's (1996) Conflicts and Problem-Solving Scale. Each adolescent was provided the prompt "I'm going to present you with a list of ways people handle disagreements, for each tell me how often your mother uses each to handle disagreements" and then responded to each strategy (e.g., becomes sarcastic) on a scale from 1 to 4 (1 = "never" to 4 = "often") (*a* = .83). Higher scores indicate more aggressive problem solving strategies.

To assess parentification, we utilized adolescent reports on a modified version of Mika, Bergner, and Baum's (1987) Parentification scale. Six questions were included (e.g., "My mother has been away for more than 24 hours and I was the main person responsible for taking care of my siblings") with four response options (1 = "never", 2 = "sometimes", 3 = "often", and 4 = "very often") (*a* = .67). Higher scores indicated higher levels of parentification.

Adolescent Efficacy   Adolescents' perceptions of efficacy were assessed using the 38-item Efficacy Scale (Sherer, Maddux, & Mercandante, 1982) including questions about competence (e.g., "I believe I can become whatever I want to become"; "failure makes me try harder"), with each item reported on a 4-point scale (1 = "totally", 2 = "pretty much", 3 = "a little", and 4 = "not at all") (*a* = .84). Positively valenced items were reverse scored so that higher scores indicated higher levels of efficacy.

What We Learned

One Family

Dena[2] is a home health aide in Pennsylvania who struggles to provide food, shelter, and clothing for herself and her two children on a $560 monthly income. She also receives $160 in food stamps and a housing subsidy each month. For Dena and her family, this income barely meets with monthly needs. Expenses such as car payments and prescription medicine for the children eat up much of the income and, recently, her child care subsidy was cut in half. This was typical. For the majority of participants, there was difficulty bridging the gap between the family's needs and available resources.

A Profile of the Families

As indicated in Table 4.1, the families in this study faced many challenges. Twenty-nine percent of mothers had not completed high school, 44.2% com-

Table 4.1 Maternal Demographics

(Average age mothers, 35.8 years; N = 94)	Total (%)
Race and Ethnicity	
Black	67.2%
Hispanic	13.8%
White	11.7%
Other	7.3%
Educational Attainment	
No high school diploma	29%
High school diploma or GED	44.1%
More than high school	12.9%
Did not report	14%
Households with 2 or more Children Marital Status	
Not married, not cohabiting	50.5%
Married or cohabiting	28.5%
Separated, divorced, or widowed	21%
Employment Status	
Unemployed	18%
Employed with one job	73.6%
Employed with two or more jobs	8.4%
Gross Family Income	
Less than $20,000	58.5%
$20,000–$35,000	30.7%
More than $35,000	10.8%
Shift work of Employed Mothers (N = 77)	
Day shift (approx. 8am–5pm)	53%
Afternoon shift (approx. 3pm–11pm)	13%
Evening shift (approx. 11pm–7am)	10%
Variable, uncertain shift	26%
Economic Supplements	
Free school lunches	91.5%
Free health insurance for child	69.9%
Food stamps	61.7%
Medicaid	22.5%
Temporary assistance to needy families	19.1%
Child-care subsidy	10.6

pleted high school only, 4.3% attained associate degrees, 8.6% completed some college, and 14% did not report on their educational attainment. Eighteen percent of mothers were unemployed, 73.6% were employed with one job, and 8.4% employed with two or more jobs. The median household income was $13,000 per year.

The ethnic composition of the mothers was primarily Black: 67.2% were Black or Black and other, 13.8% were Hispanic, 11.7% were White, and the remaining 7.4% of participating mothers reported multiple ethnic backgrounds. Adolescent's ethnicity was similar: 69.2 % were Black or Black and other, 11.7 % were Hispanic, 10.6% reported multiple ethnicities, 7.4% were White, and 1.1% did not report ethnicity. Mothers' marital status was: 28.5% married or cohabiting, 21% divorced/separated, and 50.5% single or never married. The mean age was 12.03 years (SD = 0.69) for adolescents and 35.77 years (SD = 6.03) for mothers. In the school district serving this community, 26% of children lived in poverty (U.S. Bureau of the Census, 2002).

Maternal Low-Wage Work and Family

A summary of the means, standard deviations, and correlations of the study variables is presented in Table 4.2. From these descriptive data, pictures emerge that highlights the important relationship of mother-adolescent communication to adolescents' efficacy.

In terms of maternal low-wage employment, all participants in this study were recruited based on their poverty level status and although the mean and

Table 4.2 Intercorrelations, Means, Standard Deviations for all Study Variables

Study Variable	1	2	3	4	5	6	7
1. Job instability	—						
2. Financial strain	.10	—					
3. Maternal monitoring	.02	.01	—				
4. Parent-adolescent communication	−.16	.12	.36**	—			
5. Maternal verbal aggression	.13	−.07	−.30**	−.43**	—		
6. Parentification of adolescent	−.10	−.21	.09	.12	.07	—	
7. Efficacy of child	−.28*	−.09	.23*	.51**	−.37**	.20	—
M	.22	2.61	2.50	3.07	2.21	2.18	3.25
SD	.25	1.02	.38	.43	.65	.68	.35

* $p < .05$
** $p < .01$

standard deviation for financial strain indicated variation in the sample (M = 2.61, SD = 1.02), financial strain was not significantly associated with any study variable. Employment stability, however, was related to adolescent's sense of efficacy, with less stable employment significantly associated with less youth efficacy ($r = -.28$, $p < .05$).

The most striking relationships uncovered in this research were in the area of mother-adolescent relations and adolescent efficacy. Surprisingly, parentification of the adolescent had no significant relationship with any of the study variables. This may have been due to the few adolescents who perceived themselves as parentified. Yet, the strong associations between parent-adolescent communication and maternal verbal aggression ($r = -.43$, $p < .01$), maternal monitoring ($r = .36$, $p < .01$), and adolescent efficacy ($r = .51$, $p < .01$) are noteworthy. The strength of the associations between PAC and adolescent efficacy ($r = .51$, $p < .01$), as well as between maternal verbal aggression and adolescent efficacy ($r = -.37$, $p < .01$) provides support for the claim that effective (open and unproblematic) mother-adolescent communication is associated with enhancing adolescent self efficacy. Additionally, although most research to date suggests that maternal monitoring is more important than communication in promoting adolescent well-being, the findings from this study suggest that both are important factors, with parent-adolescent communication having a stronger association to adolescent efficacy than monitoring. Given these findings, a post-hoc regression analysis was computed to examine if employment stability predicted lower adolescent efficacy when controlling for PAC, maternal verbal aggression, and maternal monitoring. Results for the logistic regression model indicate that work stability along with effective (open and unproblematic) mother-adolescent communication are statistically significant predictors of adolescent efficacy ($F = 8.35$, $p < .001$). However, neither maternal verbal aggression nor maternal monitoring was significant predictors of efficacy in this model. The proportion of variance explained by the model ($R^2 = .32$) indicates that, taken together, maternal work stability, along with open and unproblematic parent-adolescent communication demonstrate moderate power when predicting adolescents' perceptions of efficacy.

But what does all this mean in the context of a mother's work experiences and her interactions at home? The qualitative information gathered during the interviews added some depth to our understanding of the statistical relationships reported above. Moreover, the findings from the qualitative interviews provided a context in which to understand the multiple layers of influence that maternal low-wage employment had on mother-adolescent relations and adolescent efficacy in this study.

Mothers' Talk of the Challenges of Managing Low-Wage Employment and Parenting

The challenges low-wage workers face in parenting are many. Echoing the findings from the quantitative data, few mothers articulated that financial strain was one of their biggest challenges. Instead, many discussed the nature of low-wage work (multiple jobs, insecure job status, and shift work) as providing the most significant demands. Some of these challenges are similar to those faced by middle-class parents, but more often, the nature of low-wage work feels very different to these mothers. For example, as Sheila a young mother of three children pointed out the following, "Do you know what the difference is between most parents and working poor parents? Most parents work one job with steady hours and can plan their lives. It's not uncertain every day; every darn month. If their child gets sidetracked while finding his way, there are usually others around to catch him. For us, we work 2–3 jobs just to put food on the table and our children … well, if *our* children lose their way they fall. They just fall."

Debra, a mother of four children, also provides some insight about particular challenges of parenting adolescent children while managing work outside the home, "Because of the added financial responsibilities, I was working my full-time job and also two part-time jobs. It was really hard because I wasn't home very much. When children become teenagers, they need to be watched over even more. There are so many more things that can happen. But they don't think they [need watched over] and they push you away. It's just easier when you're working so much to just stay away." Kim, also a mother of four, agrees. She pointed out that, "The [kids are] stuck. They're too old for daycare; they're not really old enough to stay home alone, not old enough for jobs, no parental supervision, and no space in after school programs. The Boys and Girls Clubs do not provide enough supervision, so the kids end up leaving and getting into trouble." Kitahna who is a mother of two children concurred, adding, "This is the time in the children's lives that they need their parents the most. But when the kids start rebelling, parents tend to stay away, and not want to deal with it. This is the time the kids get into more trouble."

Cathy, an older mother who was employed part-time in social services for the community, expressed her belief in the futility of "the system," as she pointed out that:

There really is little choice. The working class must work—often in uncomfortable or repetitive jobs. They must be away from their homes and it's virtually impossible to try and look for a new job with time at such a premium. 'Temporary assistance to needy families' has created a whole other class of working poor. See, it's not really an opportunity while it's disguised to be one. Because there have been so many strings attached. So, even though it's said that the best programs focus on getting training and getting placed in a job with equal emphasis; in [our city] what I am aware of is that virtually *no one* gets training. It's all about getting a job and as fast as possible. They have no skills so they're relegated to unskilled labor. I mean, that's what most people got into, you know, they're very limited at what they can do. But, a lot is expected of you.

The expectations of single working mothers, at times, seemed insurmountable to many of the mothers. Rachel (mother of two children) explained her frustration with her situation in the following excerpt.

> The principal, the counselor, and the teachers at my son's school, I mean they don't have a clue. The teachers and principal bashed me really bad. You know, they were like, well, you need to spend more time with your kid. And here's like four people against me and all I could say was, "Well, I'll sit home all day if you pay my bills, and I will take care of him and I'll spend all the time in the world that you want me to spend with him if you pay my bills." I am a single mom. I have no family around. Working is not a choice, it is what I have to do. [People at] school want you to be this super mom and then again it's reality. You have to work for a living.

As with many middle-class households, for single working mothers, the option to just stay at home is neither a viable nor a preferred solution. Working for most of these women was not a burden, and for many it was desirable. Diana, a mother of five children exclaimed, "I go to work for my mental health!" Kitahna added, "Going to work makes me feel like I am providing something for my family. Not just money—although God knows we need that—but, well, hope for my kids. Hope that they don't have to stay stuck in the projects." Christy, a mother of three children, reminded us that stay-at-home mothering is not always the preferred situation, "If someone stays at home, it doesn't mean they're necessarily providing good parenting. Just like, if someone works it's not necessary to assume kids are neglected!"

Any ray of hope in the talk of these women was often quashed, however, with further discussion of the realities of moving from welfare to work. Kim articulated the following common scenario:

> Welfare tells you that you gotta go to work. Get a job and work. Cool. You get into public housing great. This helps you get back on your feet. Then you get a good job. You work and you're payin' cheap rent. You're getting pulled out from under the wet blanket of hopelessness. Then once you have work, you're rent goes sky-high in a few months. They even want to know what gifts you get at Christmas time from who, and they use that as income. This leaves you back where you left off at. Nowhere to go. Can't afford your rent. Gotta take care of the kids. Tryin' to keep this job. Don't have no transportation ... You're back at the shelter. You feel stuck. I ... it feels safer sticking with what you know.

Fostering hope or just giving up, keeping your jobs or losing a hold on your family ... these are just a few of the dialectical tensions inherent in low-wage employment and parenting. Wanda, the mother of one teen, shared the following example of this precarious balancing act.

I was working two shifts at work and at my wits end. I left for my first job before [my son] got up and I had to trust him to get up and get to school on his own. Well, he wasn't. He was so depressed and just stayed in bed all day long. I can request one day off a month and so I did and I went to the school for help. They said they wouldn't fine me for his truancy because I came in. But, then the principal sent these two BIG guys over to [my] house, banged open the door, dragged him out of bed and said to him, 'Get dressed. Do whatever you need to do in 15 minutes, because whatever you have on in 15 minutes is what you'll be wearing in school all day. We're leaving and you are going to school.' He went to school that day and has been going since. At least I think so.

Diana admitted that she didn't have an answer to the question of how to balance work and family, but lamented, "You can't imagine how many young people that I know of personally that are basically raising themselves." Robin, mother of three children, reiterated Diana's sentiments about the lack of adult care in young people's lives today when she shared the following, "In the old days, you had a greater extended family situation. Like … my grandmother raised me while my mom was working. Okay? And my grandmother took care of me. Or when she wasn't there, one of my aunts took the place, her place. It was like an extended family situation. And grandmothers don't want to do that no more. Yeah. They do it, and a large percentage of them are still doing it, but still have to provide for themselves as well. When moms are out working, her mom's out working, too."

For many women, getting additional education was one of the ways they hoped to inspire their children and better their lives. However, as Cathy outlined in the following excerpt, this is not always the path of least resistance.

We're left with minimum wage jobs, you know, maybe a dollar or two above minimum wage, but we can't make a living; it's not a real life-sustaining wage. It's a big setup. Most people need specific skill training so they can go out and get decent jobs at decent pay. But welfare workers have this assumption … So, you want to go to school? You're too good to get a job?

Almost 13% of the participants in this study reported they had a post-secondary education, and those who sought this road after having children were often presented with additional obstacles. Maria, mother of two, explained:

I thought the only way to get out and not just hop from job to job is to go to [the local community college] to get more education. The case workers in the welfare office didn't like that. They asked me, 'You don't wanna get a job?' The one case worker actually asked me if I thought I was too good to get a job that I wanted to go to "*college*" instead of getting a job. They didn't like that I wanted to do things differently.

But I stuck to my guns, I went to [the local community college] and graduated with a 4.0 grade point average, then got some scholarships from [a local 4-year university] to continue. It wasn't easy cause I was what they call a 'nontraditional student,' sometimes having to haul my kids to class with me, taking public transportation to school and to the medical center cause my little guy was sick pretty often. Public assistance would pay for vouchers to take me to class, but I couldn't bring my children on those vouchers. It was tempting to leave my youngest with my oldest [while I went to class] … but I didn't do that very much. I took the bus whenever I could. And guess what? [*Huge smile*] I graduated with highest honors.

The women in the study shared with us stories of misfortune and frustration amidst their challenges to rise above poverty and care for their children. But more often than not, we heard an honest desire to be the best parent as possible to their children given the resources they had at hand. The interactions they had with their children were typically the highlights of their day; that is, if those interactions were not tainted by the stress of daily life.

Perceptions of Low-Wage Work and Mother-Adolescent Relations

Adolescents in this study did not perceive maternal work to be that deleterious to mother-adolescent relations. In fact, the majority of the boys in the sample were in agreement that they enjoyed being at home alone with no adults around. The boys reported that it was "relaxing" and they liked that their mothers worked because, then, they "didn't have to hear mom nagging." But, as Denise pointed out, "Nagging is what mothers do best!"

Both mothers and youth reported that the most common topics of interpersonal conflict in their relationship were *getting along with siblings* followed by *chores*. Many of the adolescents in this study expressed feelings of pride in being responsible for certain instrumental tasks in the household. In fact, when asked what others might do to assist them in feeling "more valued," the majority of the adolescents replied they wished parents and teachers would trust them with more adult responsibility. This reflects findings by Csikszentmihalyi, Rathunde, and Whalen (1993) that suggest a key formula for adolescent success is a balance between experiencing sufficient challenges and adequate support. Additionally, this finding provides some additional insight into why, perhaps, the parentification findings in this study were not statistically significant.

Those youth who reported significant responsibility in the household, however, also tended to have some concerns about adults adequately acknowledging that responsibility. As one 12-year-old girl, Arlene, illustrated in the following excerpt:

I do the floors, vacuuming carpets and scrubbing and sweeping floors, do the dishes, and wipe up the appliances. My (younger) sister and I both scrub our areas and equally clean out the refrigerator. Umm, on laundry days, which fall on Fridays and Saturdays, we alternate washing, ironing, folding clothes, and then hang our own clothes up. That's basically what we have to do. I like that we have a chore chart that my mom makes. We go over the chart on Sundays before the week and talk about what we need to do. I like it when it is clear and get mad when she expects stuff of me when I don't know she wants me to do it.

When Arlene was asked what kinds of rewards she gets for doing her chores she responded, "Sometimes she takes us out, and sometimes gives us money. Most of the time it's, 'Good job. Good job.' I'm like, 'Is that all we get? A good job?' But sometimes after that good job, she will take us to the mall or something or to the movies." While being told that she did a "good job" is nice, Arlene proceeded to remind us that "a good job doesn't really make me feel appreciated. A good job's nothing. It ain't nothing. Just a word. Good job."

The frustration with not being acknowledged was articulated by many of the adolescents. Along with the typical challenges most young people face during the transition to adulthood, parentified adolescents experienced the additional challenge of taking on adult responsibilities without the adult rewards. For example, 13-year-old Chris said, "At home, you have to take care of your siblings, you have to cook dinner, you have to do the chores, you have to do this, but you're not allowed to make your own decisions about relationships, stuff you do in the community, and things like that." Additionally, Tom complained, "Over here [pointing in one direction?] you can be an adult. Over here [pointing in another direction?] you have to do what I say and be a kid." These excerpts illustrate some of the frustrations with being an adolescent— one who often needs to take on adult responsibilities of family management in some contexts but be treated like a child in other contexts. What seemed important to many of these youth was for mothers to be "clear about what they expect," and to "praise me," "recognize me," "reward me for effort, not just accomplishment," "point out what we do that is good, not just bad," "don't yell," "listen," and "ask questions."

For youth living in conditions where schedules were often erratic and sometimes stressful, the ways that mothers and adolescents communicated and managed conflict seemed very important to the participants. Those families who seem to be functioning well appear to have a communication system that worked well for them. For example, 13-year-old Sharon informed us that "my mom makes us have a family meeting every week. We can talk about what is bugging us and what is going on that week. No matter what, we try and have that meeting." Similarly, 12-year-old Josh reported that his mom makes a point of setting a one hour period of the day for homework and about a half hour for just talking about the day. He said, "She doesn't really help me with my homework, but she's around if I have questions. It's kind of annoying that she makes me do schoolwork even if I don't have it due the next day. Anyway, I like being able to talk with her each day."

Conversely, some adolescents such as 12-year-old Marty are resigned to fending for themselves without parental guidance or support. He said, "I can't get math. My parents don't know math. My father is out somewhere and my mom is working two jobs. You see what I'm saying? So when I run into the math problem, which is harder for me than my brother. I'm trying to help my brother. He picks it up better than me because he has the mental support from me. You see what I'm saying? But I don't have any support cause I'm the oldest kid." Thirteen-year-old Flavio added, "When I come home from school … I have no one to do homework with, so if I am confused about something, I just don't do my homework. Basically, that's what I do. I am like, 'Okay, my mom can't help me out. She doesn't know English. She's working anyway. My little brother can't help me out. So, hey, I'm not doing homework." A lack of parental monitoring of homework is especially concerning to educators, according to one high school teacher we interviewed. He shared the following concern, "Many kids whose parents aren't well educated or don't feel adequate in mathematics get lost when it comes to middle school math and everything else in math is based on that. I've found that to be true among the kids who have behavioral problems, it often stems from difficulty learning math. Usually, they get stumped at 6 or 7 times tables [and] they fall behind. The kids get frustrated and give up, sometimes giving up on school entirely" (see Wingard, this volume).

In the end, the focus of this study was to explore two potential layers of influence on adolescent efficacy—maternal low-wage work and mother-youth relations. This study added additional support to Lim and Loo's (2003) finding that children of job insecure individuals experienced lower levels of general efficacy. Although the findings from the current study provide important validation of this relationship, the possible reasons for this association are not yet clear. However, if general efficacy is a belief of one's competence across a variety of different situations, and maternal job stability impacts that sense of efficacy in some way, it seems important to understand more about the mechanisms involved in this process. This study validates an association between maternal job instability and low adolescent efficacy; but, the results of this investigation did uncover the underlying processes.

Future Directions

Future research efforts might commence by listening to the adolescents affected by their parents' low-wage employment, such as April—the 13-year-old whose voice introduced this chapter. April expressed a sense of hopelessness with her words, "kids see their parents as being stuck, having no hope. So why should we even try?" Her feelings, in chorus with many other adolescents from this study, imply a need for greater understanding of how the daily lived experience of low-wage work shapes youth's perceptions of competence. Longitudinal and perhaps ethnographic approaches to capturing the youth perspective of maternal low-wage work might provide more detailed descriptions of the dimensions of communication that most impact their worlds. These descriptions, furthermore, would benefit from including the positive characteristics, strengths, and resilience of youth living in economically stressed conditions. To guide programs and policies for these youth, knowledge of challenges must be complimented by knowledge of strengths.

Additionally, as this study suggests, more information is necessary to fully understand the particular role of parent-child communication in the successful management of low-wage work and parenting. There is very little work in the field of communication that addresses the communicative practices involved in parentification. Additional research attention seems warranted in the communication field to provide more descriptive studies of parental practices that serve to contribute to the parentification of children, but also what communication variables are predictive of parentification in the context of low-income families. For example, how do variables such as conflict management, information management, and privacy management function in low-income families to contribute toward parentification and adolescents' perceptions of efficacy? When adolescent assistance is needed to manage everyday family routines, what might constitute a healthy "balance" of challenges and support for the adolescent and how might those be communicated?

We would like to end this chapter with an excerpt from Monica, a mother of four children, who sums up much of what we heard from mothers in this study. With conviction, Monica stated that it is HOMEwork—the work of family— that is most important in her life, "What's important" she said, "is that mothers are warm, firm, and responsive and—most of all—convey to their children that they are the mother's priority. No matter what the struggle, always let the kids know that they are what matter more than anything else."

Notes

1. Whenever the first person is used in this chapter, it is the voice of the first author.
2. The names of the participants are fictional to protect confidentiality.

References

Allen, J. P., & Land, D. (1999). Attachment in adolescence. In J. Cassidy & P. R. Shaver (Eds.), *Handbook of attachment: Theory, research, and clinical applications* (pp. 319–335). New York: Guilford.

Barnes, H., & Olson, D. H. (1982). Parent-adolescent communication. In D. H. Olson, H. I. McCubbin, H. Barnes, A. Larson, M. Muxen, & M. Wilson (Eds.), *Family inventories* (pp. 33–38). St. Paul: Family Social Science, University of Minnesota.

Barnes, H. L., & Olson, D. H. (1985). Parent-adolescent communication and the circumplex model. *Child Development, 56,* 438–447.

Barnett, R. C., Marshall, N. L., & Singer, J. D. (1992). Job experiences over time, multiple roles, and women's mental health: A longitudinal study. *Journal of Personal and Social Psychology, 62,* 634–644.

Bond, J. T., Thompson, C., Galinsky, E., & Prottas, D. (2003). *Highlights of the 2002 National Study of the Changing Workforce.* New York: Families and Work Institute.

76   Michelle Miller-Day and Tara G. McManus

Boszormenyi-Nagy, I., & Spark, G. M. (1973). *Invisible loyalties: Reciprocity in intergenerational family therapy*. New York: Harper & Row.

Brody, G. H., Murry, V. M., Gerrard, M., Gibbons, F. X., McNair, L., Brown, A. C., Wills, T. A. Molgaard, V., Spoth, R. L., Luo, Z., & Chen, Y. F. (2006). The strong African American families program: Prevention of youths' high-risk behavior and a test of a model of change. *Journal of Family Psychology, 20* (1), 1–11.

Brody, G. H., Murry, V. M., Gerrard, M., Gibbons, F. X., Molgaard, V., & McNair, L., et al. (2004). The strong African American families program: Translating research into prevention programming. *Child Development, 75*(3), 900–917.

Bronfenbrenner, U. (1979). *The ecology of human development: Experiments by nature and design*. Cambridge, MA: Harvard University Press.

Bronfenbrenner, U. (1986). Ecology of the family as a context for human development: Research perspectives. *Developmental Psychology, 22*, 723–742.

Bronfenbrenner, U., & Morris, P. A. (1998). The ecology of developmental processes. In R. M. Lerner (Ed.), *Handbook of child psychology: Vol. 1. Theoretical models of human development* (5 ed., pp. 993–1028). New York: Wiley.

Brooks, J. L., Hair, E. C., & Zaslow, M. J. (2001). *Welfare reform's impacts on adolescents: Early warning signs*. [Child Trends Research Brief]. Washington, DC: Child Trends.

Burton, L. (2007). Childhood adultification in economically disadvantaged families: A conceptual model. *Family Relations, 56*(4), 329–345.

Byng-Hall, J. (2002). Relieving parentified children's burdens in families with insecure attachment patterns. *Family Process, 41*, 375–388.

Chase, N. D. (1999). *Burdened children: Theory, research and treatment of parentification*. Thousand Oaks, CA: Sage.

Chase-Lansdale, L., Moffitt, R., Lohman, B., Cherlin, A., Coley, R., Pittman, L., et al. (2003). Mothers' transitions from welfare to work and the well-being of preschoolers and adolescents, *Science, 299*, 1548–1552.

Cox, A. G., & Presser, H. B. (2000). Nonstandard employment schedules among American mothers: The relevance of marital status. In T. L. Parcel & D. B. Cornfield (Eds.), *Work & family: Research informing policy* (pp. 97–130). Thousand Oaks, CA: Sage.

Crouter, A. C. (1994). Processes linking families and work: Implications for behavior and development in both settings. In R. Parke & S. Kellam (Eds.), *Exploring family relationships with other social contexts (Advances in family research)* (pp. 9–28). Mahwah, NJ: Erlbaum.

Crouter, A. C., & Manke, B. (1997). Development of a typology of dual-earner families: A window into differences between and within families in relationships, roles, and activities. *Journal of Family Psychology, 11*, 62–75.

Crouter, A. C., & McHale, S. M. (1993). Temporal rhythms in family life: Seasonal relations between parental work and family processes. *Developmental Psychology, 29*, 198–205.

Csikszentmihalyi, M., Rathunde, K., & Whalen, S. (1993). *Talented teenagers*. Cambridge, UK: Cambridge University Press.

Deitch, C. H., & Huffman, M. L. (2001). Family-responsive benefits and the two-tiered labor market. In R. Hertz & N. L. Marshall (Eds.), *Working families: The transformation of the American home* (pp. 103–130). Berkeley: University of California Press.

Ensminger, M. E. (1995). Welfare and psychological distress: a longitudinal study of African American urban mothers. *Journal of Health and Social Behavior, 36*(4), 346–359.

Erickson, E. H. (1959). *Identity and the life cycle.* New York: International University Press.

Fremstad, S. (2003). *Falling TANF caseloads amidst rising poverty should be a cause for concern.* Washington, DC: Center on Budget and Policy Priorities.

Galinsky, E. (2005). Children's perspectives of employed mothers and fathers: Closing the gap between public debates and research findings. In D. F. Halpern, & S. E. Murphy (Eds.), From *work-family balance to work-family interaction* (pp. 219–236). Mahwah, NJ: Erlbaum.

Gennetian, L. A., Duncan, G., Knox, V., Vargas, W., Clark-Kauffman, E., & London, A. S. (2004). How welfare policies affect adolescents' school outcomes: A synthesis of evidence from experimental studies. *Journal of Research on Adolescence, 14*(4), 399–423.

Griffin, K. W., Botvin, G. J., Scheier, L. M., Diaz, T., & Miller, N. L. (2000). Parenting practices as predictors of substance use, delinquency, and aggression among urban minority youth: Moderating effects of family structure and gender. *Psychology of Addictive Behaviors, 14*, 174–184.

Grzywacz, J. G., Almeida, D. M., & McDonald, D. A. (2002). Work-family spillover and daily reports of work and family stressing in the adult labor force. *Family Relations, 51*, 28–36.

Grzywacz, J. G., & Marks, N. F. (2000). Reconceptualizing the work-family interface: An ecological perspective on the correlates of positive and negative spillover between work and family. *Journal of Occupational Health Psychology, 15*(1), 111–126.

Halpern, D. F., & Murphy, S. E. (2005). *From work-family balance to work-family interaction.* Mahwah, NJ: Erlbaum.

Hastings, J., Taylor, S., & Austin, M. J. (2005). The status of low-income families in the post-welfare reform environment: Mapping the relationships between poverty and family. *Journal of Health & Social Policy, 21*(1), 33–63.

Hays, S. (2003). *Flat broke with children: Women in the age of welfare reform.* New York: Oxford University Press.

Huston, A. C. (1991). *Children in poverty.* New York: Cambridge University Press.

Jackson, S., Bijstra, J., Oostra, L., & Bosma, H. (1998). Adolescents' perceptions of communication with parents relative to specific aspects of relationships with parents and personal development. *Journal of Adolescence, 21*, 305–322.

Jackson, A. P., Gyamfi, P., Brooks-Gunn, J., & Blake, M. (1998). Employment status, psychological well-being, social support, and physical discipline practices of single black mothers. *Journal of Marriage and the Family, 60*(4) 894–902.

Jacobson, K. C., & Crockett, L. J. (2000). Parental monitoring and adolescent adjustment: An ecological perspective. *Journal of Research on Adolescence, 10*, 65–97.

Johnson, R. C., & Corcoran, M. E. (2003). The road to economic self-sufficiency: Job quality and job transition patterns after welfare reform. *Journal of Policy Analysis and Management, 22*, 615–622.

Judge, T. A., Erez, A., & Bono, J. A. (1998). The power of being positive: The relation between positive self-concept and job performance. *Human Performance, 11*, 167–187.

Jurkovic, G. J., Thirkield, A., & Morrell, R. (2001). Parentification of adult children of divorce: A multidimensional analysis. *Journal of Youth and Adolescence, 30*(2), 245–257.

Kerig, P. K. (1996). Assessing the links between interparental conflict and child adjustment: The conflicts and problem-solving scales. *Journal of Family Psychology, 10,* 454–473.

Lim, V. K. G., & Loo, G. L. (2003). Effects of parental job insecurity and parenting behaviors on youth's self-efficacy and work attitudes. *Journal of Vocational Behavior, 63,* 86–98.

Loeber, R., Stouthamer-Loeber, M., Van Kammen, W. B., & Farrington, D. P. (1991). Initiation escalation and desistance in juvenile offending and their correlates. *Journal of Criminal Law and Criminology, 82,* 36–82.

London, A. S., Scott, E. K., Edin, K., & Hunter, V. (2004). Welfare reform, work-family tradeoffs, and child well-being. *Family Relations, 53*(2), 148–158.

Loprest, P. (2001). How are families who left welfare doing over time? A comparison of two cohorts of welfare leavers. *Economic Policy Review, 7*(2). Retrieved July 25, 2008, from http://ssrn.com/abstract=844286

Mallinckrodt, B. (1992). Childhood emotional bonds with parents, development of adult social competencies, and availability of social support. *Journal of Counseling Psychology, 39*(4), 453–461.

Markman, H., & Notarious, C. (1994). *We can work it out: Making sense of marital conflict.* San Francisco: Jossey-Bass.

Masten, A. S., & Coatsworth, J. D. (1998). The development of competence in favorable and unfavorable environments: Lessons from research on successful children. *American Psychologist, 2,* 205–220.

Mayseless, O., Bartholomew, K., Henderson, A., & Trinke, S. (2004). "I was more her mom than she was mine": Role reversal in a community sample. *Family Relations, 53*(1), 78–86.

McLoyd, V. C. (1998). Socioeconomic disadvantage and child development. *American Psychologist, 53*(2), 185–204.

Mika, P., Bergner, R. M., & Baum, M.C. (1987). The development of a scale for the assessment of parentification. *Family Therapy, 14* (3), 229–235.

Minuchin, S. (1974). *Families and family therapy.* Cambridge, MA: Harvard University Press.

Morris, P. A., Huston, A. C., Duncan, G. J., Crosby, D. A., & Bos, J. M. (2001). *How welfare and work policies affect children: A synthesis of research.* Report from the Manpower Demonstration Research Corporation. Retrieved July 26, 2008, from http://www.mdrc.org/

Mortimer, J. T., Finch, M. D., Ryu, S., Shanahan, M. J., & Call, K. T. (1996). The effects of work intensity on adolescent mental health, achievement, and behavior adjustment: New evidence from a perspective study. *Child Development, 67,* 1243–1261.

Murry, V. M., & Brody, G. H. (1999). Self-regulation and self-worth of black children reared in economically stressed, rural, single-mother headed households. *Journal of Family Issues, 20,* 458–484.

National Institutes of Health (2006). Certificates of confidentiality: Background information. Retrieved June 13, 2006, from http://grants2.nih.gov/grants/policy/coc/background.htm

O'Neill, J., & Hill, A. M. (2003). *Gaining ground, moving up: The change in the economic status of single mothers under welfare reform.* New York: Manhattan Institute, Center for Civic Innovation.

Orthner, D., Jones-Sanpei, H., & Williamson, S. (2004). The resilience and strengths of low-income families. *Family Relations, 53,* 159–167.

Parcel, T. L., & Menaghan, E. G. (1994). Effects of low-wage employment on family well-being. *The Future of Children: Welfare to Work, 7,* 116–121.

Personal Responsibility and Work Opportunity Reconciliation Act of 1996. (1996). Pub.L. 104-193 110 Stat. 2105.

Reisch, S. K., Anderson, L. S., & Krueger, H.A. (2006). Parent-child communication processes: Preventing children's health risk behaviors. *Journal for Specialists in Pediatric Nursing, 11,* 41–56.

Ritchie, L. (1997). Parents workplace experiences and family communication patterns. *Communication Research, 24*(2), 175–187.

Rodgers, K. B. & Rose, H. A. (2002). Risk and resiliency factors among adolescents who experience marital transitions. *Journal of Marriage and Family, 64,* 1024–1037.

Romer, D. (2003). (Ed). *Reducing adolescent risk: An integrated approach.* Thousand Oaks, CA: Sage.

Ross, C. E., & Mirowsky, J. (1988). Child care and emotional adjustment to wives' employment. *Journal of Health and Social Behavior, 29,* 127–138.

Seccombe, K., James, D., & Battle-Walters, K. (1998). They think you ain't much of nothing: The social construction of the welfare mother. *Journal of Marriage and the Family, 60,* 849–865.

Sherer, M., Maddux, J. E., & Mercandante, B. (1982). The self-efficacy scale: Construction and validation. *Psychological Reports, 51,* 663–671.

U.S. Bureau of the Census (2002). Retrieved May 2, 2008, from http://www.census.gov.

Voydanoff, P. (2004). The effects of work and community resources and demands on family integration. *Journal of Family and Economic Issues, 25,* 7–23.

White, L., & Rogers, S. J. (2000). Economic circumstance and family outcomes: A review of the 1990's. *Journal of Marriage and the Family, 62,* 1035–1051.

5 Communicating About Homework at Home and School

Leah Wingard

Homework, or "tasks assigned to students by school teachers that are intended to be carried out during non school hours" (Cooper, 2007, p. 4) is widely assumed to be beneficial to children. Homework is seen as beneficial, in part, because completing homework means that children spend more time with academic materials (Bursuck, 1994). Other assumed benefits of homework for the child's development are good work practices including time management, distraction management and self-control (Corno & Xu, 2004). While many researchers are generally positive toward homework and suggest that it is beneficial (Cooper, 1989; Cooper & Nye, 1994; Walberg, Paschal, & Weinstein, 1985), not all agree about its usefulness. A number of authors have recently taken strong stances against homework suggesting the research on its effectiveness for academic achievement and child development are not proven. They maintain that the burden it presents for the families outweigh any possible benefits (Bennett & Kalish, 2006; Kohn, 2006; Kralovec & Buell, 2000). Homework has further been blamed for widening a socioeconomic education gap between students who have the resources at home to support them, and those who do not (Lareau, 1987; Lareau, 1989, Lareau & Shumar, 1996).

This chapter presents data from an ethnographic study that supports the idea that homework can be a problematic aspect of family life. When interviewed, parents and children in the study report that homework is a difficult aspect of everyday life. Ethnographic filming of the everyday lives of the families also reflects that the doing of homework has the potential to be a significant site of tension between the parent and child. When asked a standardized question in an interview about which aspects of their daily lives children didn't like, they often named homework. Parents, too, often named homework as a source of trouble. For example, this mother characterized both her own and her children's feelings toward homework unambiguously:

> I hate it. [laughs] I don't like homework as much as kids don't like homework.

Children often named homework as a part of the routine drudgery of life. When answering an interviewer's question about his daily life, this child inserts homework twice as he explains the routine:

Um: come home, do homework, eat dinner, do homework, and go to bed.

This chapter takes a closer look at what parents and children say about homework in open-ended interviews and considers some of the videotaped interactions where homework was difficult for families. In particular, this chapter focuses on these data with the goal of documenting communication processes involved in the activity of homework both between the institution and the family, and within the family itself. These processes of communication will be considered against the backdrop of current recommended guidelines for homework, and the idealized education guideline of parent involvement.

Background

Guidelines for Homework

While there is no definitive national homework policy in the United States, current recommendations for homework policies and practice are outlined in guides for parents and teachers on the U.S. Department of Education, the National Parent Teacher Association, and the National Education Association Web sites. Furthermore, school districts and schools are also increasingly determining and publishing such guidelines for teachers and parents alike. The U.S. Department of Education Web site suggests, for example, that teachers assign homework as a way to enhance what children have learned in class with further learning at home. Homework is also described as having positive implications for learning study habits, independence, responsibility and self-discipline. While it's not clear where the specifics of recommendations originate, the guidelines for the appropriate amount of homework on these Web sites generally suggest that children in kindergarten through second grade benefit from 10–20 minutes of daily homework, and that children in third through sixth grades benefit from 30–60 minutes of daily homework.

The guidelines on the U.S. Department of Education Web site also provide suggestions for how parents can support homework. In general, guidelines suggest that parents should be interested in homework and set a scheduled time and place for the doing of homework. Parents should also provide the necessary resources for doing homework and remove possible distractions. These Web sites also suggest monitoring assignments, especially to see that they are completed and done correctly, and suggests that the appropriate amount of monitoring will depend on the individual child's needs.

Parent Involvement

Parent involvement (and other similar descriptors such as parent engagement) have been and continue to be important buzzwords in education and school policy and is part of a U.S. dominant paradigm for education policy. Parent involvement was explicitly included in President G. W. Bush's education reform policy, No Child Left Behind, which was signed in 2002. Section 1118 of the act requires that every school district receiving Title 1 support (federal money for schools with economically disadvantaged students) have a written parent involvement policy. Involvement is defined in this code as "the participation of parents in regular, two-way, and meaningful communication involving student academic learning and other school activities" (Sec. 9101 [32] p. 1962). In the code, involvement includes assisting in the child's learning and being actively involved in the child's education at school by serving on advisory boards in the school. While the research emphasis on parental involvement often seems to focus on investigations of parents' involvement at school, for example, by serving on advisory boards such as the Parent Teacher Association and volunteering at the school, some attention to parent involvement in learning at home has also been a focus of research (Clark, 1993; K. Hoover-Dempsey et al., 2001). This research, generally, either presupposes or demonstrates that parental involvement is beneficial for the academic achievement of the student. However, there is also work suggesting that researchers have not adequately ascertained what constitutes effective parental involvement, that there may be threshold or ceiling effects of involvement (Baker & Soden, 1998), and that there may be varying styles of parent involvement with different effects on children (Cooper, Lindsay & Nye 2000). The ideal of parent involvement has also been questioned from the perspective of equal access to education. This research suggests that not all parents can participate equally or be equally effective in their involvement (Crozier, 2001; Lareau, 1987; Lareau, 1989, Lareau & Shumar 1996; Lee & Bowen, 2006; McNeal, 1999; Nakagawa, 2000; Sturges, Cramer, Harry, Klinger, & Borman, 2005; Wong & Hughes, 2006). This may be due to any number of reasons including limitations in parents' educational or language background, nontraditional work schedules, or competing ideologies about the role of the parent in education. Even when there are not issues of culturally different perspectives on involvement, or adequate educational background, all parents who work full time face the same dilemmas of balancing the demands of their full-time work with the needs of their children and families. With respect to homework in particular, when parents pick up their children from school or an after school care program, the involved parent must attend to whether or not homework is done. When homework has been assigned, parents must plan homework into the afternoon's and evening's activities. Most parents also juggle homework as just one of their many activities when they come home from work. They may also need to attend to the multiple needs of different children. For the parent, attending to children's homework often goes hand in hand with other family necessities such as the preparation of dinner. Though mostly discussed in the research literature in terms of children's academic achievement, parent involvement is far from an easily achievable ideal in the context of everyday family life.

Communication about Homework

Communication between school and parent is seen as an important component of parent involvement in general (e.g., see Miller-Day & McManus, this volume, Meyer, this volume; Weigel & Martin, this volume). A few studies have focused specifically on the communication about homework between school and parent, or teacher and parent (Harniss, Epstein, Bursuck, Nelson, & Jayanthi, 2001; Jayanthi, Nelson, Sawyer, Bursuck, & Epstein, 1995; Patton, Jayanthi, & Polloway, 2001). Recommendations for good communication practices are wide ranging. Generally, guidelines suggest that parents should clearly understand what is expected of their involvement (Kay, Fitzgerald, Paradee, & Mellencamp, 1994), and that multiple opportunities for communication between parent and institution should be in place and followed up regularly (Callahan, Rademacher, & Hildreth, 1998; Jayanthi, Nelson, Sawyer, Bursuck, & Epstein, 1995). Suggestions for better communication include having homework policies at the district, school, or classroom level (Cooper, 2007), using assignment books (Bryan & Sullivan-Burstein, 1997; Jenson, Sheridan, Olympia, & Andrews, 1994; Trammel, Schloss, & Alper, 1994), and greater use of technologies such as telephone hotlines for communicating about assignments (Barrett & Neal, 1992; Bauch, 1994). This chapter seeks to better document what parents report about the communication processes that surrounds homework between the educational institution and parents. This chapter also seeks to better understand how this communication might impact the communication about homework between the parent and child within the family itself. While these communication processes are often treated as distinct, the data presented here consider the inter-relatedness of these communication processes.

Methodology

The data used for this chapter are drawn from a large interdisciplinary project of The Center for the Everyday Lives of Families (CELF).[1] The project's mandate is to document the everyday lives of dual-earner families with a particular focus on documenting how working parents manage their paid work on the job with the unpaid work of being a parent at home. The data collection methods generally provide insight into the various demands and contingencies of modern family life.

While families were asked to participate in a number of different research protocols under the umbrella of the larger CELF study, the data analyzed in this chapter include open-ended ethnographic interviews with parents about education practices, open-ended interviews with children about their daily lives, and ethnographic filming of families during the course of their everyday lives.

Video-Ethnography

Families were videotaped by researchers in their homes for 2 weekdays and 2 weekend days, and all filming usually occurred within a 1-week period. Filming started early in the morning as family members were getting ready for school and work and continued through the afternoon and until the children went to bed. Both wireless and camera mounted "shotgun" microphones were used to capture enough detail for later transcription and analysis of the interactions. Videotaping additionally allowed a detailed record of both the activities and the nonverbal behaviors of the participants.

Interviews

While the overall study included a number of interviews with different topics, interviews that focused on education were conducted with each parent from each family individually and typically lasted between 20–40 minutes.[2] Parents were asked a range of questions that concerned their views on education, their goals for their children, and their thoughts on the immediate circumstances of their children's schooling. Most pertinent to this chapter were the range of questions that parents were asked about the homework activities in their home, including what homework time was like, and to what extent the parents were involved in homework. Although these interviews were not focused specifically on the communication between parents and educational institutions, the interview data provides a rich resource to understand how parents understand the impact of communication from teachers about homework and how this may impact how homework is accomplished in the home.

Researchers additionally conducted open-ended interviews with the children. This interview was designed to document the children's perspectives of their own lives and activities. While there were no direct questions asked about homework, there were several questions that often elicited talk about homework. The two questions that seemed to elicit talk about homework the most frequently were: "What are your favorite/least favorite things to do during the week?" and "Are there any things that you would like to do that you don't usually get a chance to do? Children responded often that homework was their least favorite thing to do during the week and homework was mentioned with high frequency as the thing that keeps children from doing the things they would like to do.

Criteria for Participation and Recruitment

Families were recruited through flyers sent home with children in the 8-10 year old range from local public elementary schools. Participants were also later recruited for the study through advertisements in local community newspapers and the Los Angeles Times. Families qualified for the study by having either two or three children, and one of the children in the family had to be between the ages of 8 and 10. This meant that families had a wide range of ages of children in school, but all families had at least one 8- to 10-year-old. Families were headed by two parents who both worked outside of the home at least 30 hours or more each week. Finally, participating families were paying a mortgage on their home and were dependent on the income they earned from working in order to pay the mortgage. While families who participated in the study spanned a range of socioeconomic income levels, they were, broadly speaking, middle class. Aside from meeting these basic standardized criteria, families that participated in the study were diverse in terms of ethnicity, religion, and sexual orientation. Families were paid $1,000 for their full participation in the study.

Education Profiles of Participating Families

Parents who participated in the study had a generally high level of education with two-thirds of the parents earning either a Bachelor's or a graduate degree. Only seven individual parents in the study reported not having completed any college or university level work. Children participating in the study attended both public and private schools with one-fourth of the children enrolled in private school. While some parents opted for private schools, parents who chose the public school system were still making active education choices for their children. Some parents had, for example, researched how public schools in their neighborhood ranked and compared student populations at area schools. Two families chose "charter" or "magnet" schools that are part of a public education system and provide enriched programs that require parents to participate in special applications processes and strategic maneuvering within the public system. In some cases, parents opted for public schools not immediately adjacent to their home that were perceived to have a higher quality of education or were perceived to have a "better" population of students or families. The quality of a school was often referenced vaguely in terms of the ethnic make-up of the student body or perceived violence in the school. In sum, the parents in the families who participated in the study were generally interested and involved in their children's education.

Analyses of Data

Parent and child interview data were qualitatively analyzed to determine how and when the issue of homework was discussed. For the parents' interviews, it was noted when parents mentioned homework and whether they either mentioned homework in a generally positive or negative light. Also, when homework was discussed, it was noted if parents referred to communication about homework with the school or the teacher, and if the parent attributed success or problems with homework to this communication or lack thereof. Interviews were also analyzed to determine what parents reported about the experience of doing homework or communicating with their child about homework. For children's interviews, since homework talk was rarely initiated directly by the researcher, it was noted when and how the child mentioned homework. Using analytical induction, themes were determined based on these analyses and are the primary data source reported here. Given space limitations, the presentation of actual interactions and the analysis of the discourse of that interaction is limited to some brief examples that some of the issues about homework raised in the interviews. Following standard IRB protocols, all names have been changed to protect the identities of the participants in the study.

Communication between School and Parent

Part of involving parents effectively in their children's schooling, regarding homework, is establishing effective communication between the school and the parent. In this section, I present excerpts from interviews where parents discuss and assess their communication with teachers and schools about their children's homework and how it impacts family life.

Communicating Expectations of the Parent Role

Teachers and schools must first and foremost communicate clear expectations about the parents' role in their children's homework. Several parents in the study were able to clearly express their understanding of the expected role they should take in their children's homework, as this father does:

> Well, in second grade—I just got the lecture last night—it's twenty to thirty minutes and the parent basically should not be involved. If the kid can't do it, it's a sign that either the homework's too hard or a problem with the skill level of the child ... basically, it's supposed to be for Jonah to do on his own.

While teachers may communicate to parents that they should not be too involved, parents also find that homework may not get done if they are not involved enough. A few minutes later the father reflects on the fact that he does actually have to get actively involved in the sense that he has to pursue his son to get started on homework:

> Last night, for example, I was at parent-teacher thing. He didn't do his homework until I came home at 8:30. And I just said, I went to this whole thing. This is independent study. Go in your room and do it.

A mother expresses a similar sentiment that although the school encourages the child to complete homework independently, the reality is that the child will not do homework unless she is present. Here she underscores the difference between an ideal presented by the teacher versus the reality at home:

> Even though this year they want him to just do his homework without any parental involvement. So technically he could do it, but he won't.

She further explains how establishing a homework routine, though desirable, is difficult when she is not yet home from work:

Homework routine—homework routine, I would love it to be like when he gets out from school, but it isn't because I'm not home.

Another mother also reports getting clear guidelines from her children's teacher that she should have a limited role in homework, but proceeds to explain in more detail the help that is actually needed to get through the homework. She finds that her two children have different needs and sometimes their needs require her to do more than simply check that they've done it:

> The teachers encourage you not to correct their work, just see that they've done it. Um, Bill, I usually have to help him through it. Read the questions with him, um, help him solve it. Um, point out some of his misspellings. Um, Nell, sometimes she doesn't understand hers. Or she just wants- she just needs a little push with it … her's goes pretty fast. Bill's, I feel like he has like, an hour of homework, or more.

These excerpts suggest that though parents may get the clear message they should be only minimally involved in homework, for example, only checking that it's done, parents find that they must often get involved in more substantial ways both to get homework started and to get it done.

Communicating What is Assigned as Homework

Another central point of communication about homework between teachers and parents is conveying what is assigned for homework. While some parents reported that clear communication mechanisms were in place to communicate what was assigned for homework, other parents reported that they often relied on their children to know and accurately report what was assigned for homework.

Many strategies may be used by teachers and parents to ensure clear communication about homework assignments. When communication between the teacher and the parent about homework is successful, parents can easily and accurately ascertain what the child has for homework. Parents in the study often reported checking homework assignment sheets or homework folders that are carried in the child's backpack. In this family interaction, the father orients to the "whatever you call it thing" as what his daughter should show him to let him know what is for homework. This interaction about homework proceeds unproblematically and shows how such an artifact of communication set in place by the teacher can allow for a routine and straightforward way for a parent to accurately know what the assigned homework is:

Father: You're going to start your homework, right?
Child: Yeah.
Father: Can you show me, when you have a chance, your little, whatever you call it thing? That you're supposed to show me everyday? Okay, thank you.

Some parents in the study also reported calling into a centralized homework hotline by telephone or checking a designated online homework assignment log on the Internet. In this interaction, the mother reminds her son that she has the ability to check the homework Web site to verify what he has for homework:

Mother: Mikey?
Mikey: Yes?
Mother: You have to finish social studies?
Mikey: Yes.
Mother: Okay, Mark?
Mark: Spanish.
Mother: And then you're going to show us the rest of your work right?
Mark: Yeah.
Mother: Cause I'll look on the computer and we'll make sure that we've got it all done.

Of course, this "reminder" may also serve as a warning to the child to be forthcoming about what he has for homework since the parent has the ability to check up on the assignments.

If no specific system is set up for the teacher to communicate with the parent independently of the child, the parent must rely on the child to know what is for homework. More importantly, the parent must rely on the willingness of the child to be honest about what he or she has for homework. Some parents in this study reported that getting an honest answer was in fact a problem. When asked about the usual homework routine, this father says that he doesn't always trust that his son is honest about the status of his homework:

He'll say he did it on the bus but I might have to go check. He'll really have some homework he may not even tell us about it.

One mother reports that she has had to develop a specific strategy of calling other parents in order to know what the homework assignment is:

We used to let them play and we used to just take their word for it that they didn't have any homework or anything to study for. But now I call other kids parents to get the scoop on what there is.

Such a strategy would not be necessary if an effective system of communication about homework had been put in place by the child's teacher. The father in this family also mirrored the mother's sentiment that they, as parents, were taking more responsibility for knowing what the assignments are than the children:

And they tend to slide a little bit when it comes to good documentation
for what the assignments are … they don't take it off the board because
they're always there. And, "Oh God I've got a science test tomorrow I for-
got about." Oh great, so we stay up until ten o'clock and he's falling asleep
on the table and we're halfway there and what else can we do about it at
that time? So Mary and I are both focusing on getting the required stuff
uh clearly specified each day so we can keep on top of it.

Even when printed materials are available that specify what is for homework and the child has these materials in his backpack, parents may still find
that there is trouble keeping assignments straight if they trust that the child
remembers the assignment correctly. In this videotaped excerpted interaction,
a mother has discovered only too late that she and her son have spent a good
deal of time doing the wrong homework assignment. She reports this to her
husband when he comes into the kitchen. The interaction grows tense as the
father assesses the son as not taking enough responsibility for knowing what
his homework is:

Mother: Jake and I just wasted about 45 minutes on the wrong chapter.
Father: Ouch. How'd you find out it was—what was the right chapter?
Mother: Because I got his binder out to find the essay (short pause) answers
and there was the new study guide in there.
Father: Whew.
Jake: You didn't hafta to tell him that. (2 second pause)
Father: Doesn't seem like he's really uh (short pause) on top uh his
assignments.
Mother: No. [shaking her head]
Father: in knowing what to do (short pause) even.

Upon hearing what has happened, the father's immediate response "Ouch"
displays his stance toward the reported situation as negative or even a painful
one. The father continues to display his negative assessment with an extended
sigh, "whew." Jake displays his own unhappiness with the fact that his mother
told his father what happened with the reproachful, "You didn't hafta to tell
him that" toward his mother. The father orients to Jake as being the one who
should be held primarily responsible for doing the wrong assignment when
he says, "Doesn't seem like he's really uh (micro pause) on top uh his assignments." After a display of agreement by the mother, Dad adds "in knowing
what to do (micro pause) even". In the (3 second) pause that follows, the emotional impact that this interaction has on Jake becomes clear as tears become
visible on his face. The fact that the wrong homework was done was just the
first step in a homework interaction that became increasingly difficult and
more emotionally charged on that day. Lacking the direct forms of communication between a teacher and parents about homework assignments, or not

having routine ways of communicating about or checking assignments can, as exemplified here, cause parent distrust of children, or further cause homework time to be an emotionally painful part of family communication. This interaction suggests that parent teacher communication about homework can have implications as well for parent child interaction about homework.

Assigning Homework that is Consistent, Predictable and Realistic

Teachers vary with respect to how much homework they assign and how they assign it. Some teachers create a weekly schedule that is the same for each week and follows a predictable and recurrent schedule for homework whereas other teachers assign homework more inconsistently. Several parents in the study report in their interviews that having the same assignment types repeated each week makes managing homework more predictable, and therefore makes homework an easier task to schedule. Again, when teachers do not have a predictable or recurrent schedule for homework each week, it becomes even more important, as explained above, that parents have reliable communication mechanisms in place that allow them to access clear information. Some parents in the study reported wide variation in the amount of homework assigned from day to day as this parent does:

> Um it can be anywhere from an hour up to three to hours depending on what they need to study for….Um Darrin sometimes will work up to three or four hours a night on homework.

Children as well mentioned the inconsistencies in homework in their interviews. Referring to her teacher, this child says:

> Sometimes she just gives us like a worksheet or something, and a math page, or other times she just piles it on.

Variation can occur not only from day to day, but also from year to year. While it is within recommendations and guidelines to expect that amounts of homework might increase gradually as a child advances in grade level, some parents in the study complain that variation does not always correspond to advancing a grade. When talking about the variation from year to year, one mother discusses the prior year when her child was in kindergarten and contrasts it with this year:

> [Last year] it was, like, really, like, oh my god, he can't even write and we're just having to do so much homework. You know, practicing letters and really, it was a lot. Just pages and pages and this year, for some reason, it's not a lot so I don't know.

Another parent also raised objections to having homework for her pre-schooler at all:

> The preschoolers have homework which I'm slightly against because I don't really want him to hate homework at such an early age so sometimes when Mandy's doing homework-it's just coloring and counting so I mean so stuff you can do, but I try not to force it. As a matter of fact we haven't turned in homework for two weeks because if he doesn't want to do it I'm not going to force him.

Parents sometimes report that children with heavy homework loads are kept from doing other activities parents consider valuable. Here, a mother complains that her daughter who is particularly enthusiastic about "Lizzy McGuire" (a popular female TV character in her early teens) doesn't have as much time to read the Lizzy McGuire books for pleasure because of her homework:

> So you know she wants the Lizzy McGuire book I mean we have the Lizzy McGuire CD, we have the Lizzy McGuire movie, I mean she's totally into Lizzy McGuire right now.... Generally we haven't had time to read because it seems like she has so much homework.

This next mother, a teacher in a private school, discussed the vast differences in the amount of homework her two daughters had the previous year. She characterizes the amount of homework one daughter had been assigned as a "joke" and the other as unreasonable to the extent that she ended up actively doing the homework with her daughter to help her to get through it:

> Bess last year had like ten minutes worth of homework and it was totally a joke it was like you know, dittos that she would fill out or color, just a joke. And then Sonya was on the other spectrum she would have three hours sometimes of homework, um way too much for her grade level. Um, so it's a struggle a lot of times, she would throw temper tantrums because she had too much, she'd be tired.... When Sonya has spelling words she was supposed to look up the words and she had so much homework that last year. I would look up the words and I would read her the definitions and she would write them down. I'm not that hands on, but I just thought it was an atrocious amount of homework.

In this case, the mother reported having to be more "hands on" than she would usually be because of the amount being assigned to her daughter. The mother goes on to report that she tried to discuss the amount of homework with the teacher but felt she had no impact on the situation:

> I spoke to the teacher about it and I wrote her notes you know, and I told her Sonya was going to bed way past her bedtime and she said if that ever

happened I could write a note and then Sonya didn't have to finish it but she would always make Sonya finish it the next day at school.

One reason why homework may at times feel unrealistic for the children to do is that homework may not always be used in a way that is pedagogically sound. Whereas homework guidelines often suggest that children should be given homework as a way to enhance what they have learned in school, this mother expressed the concern that homework (and in turn parents) were being used more to teach students what teachers did not have time to cover in class:

> There's so much that the teachers have to teach the kids that they don't have enough time in the day to do it. And if they're going to get all the material in that they're required to get in they have to send it home.

Extreme variations in the amount of homework given by different teachers, as well as high variability day by day make it seem that amounts of homework are random and are not necessarily grounded in pedagogical goals. These variations in homework frustrate both parents and children and suggest that not all teachers follow pedagogical guidelines for homework. Alternatively, teachers may be unaware that children are spending more time on homework than they think. In terms of communication between parents and teachers, it is important that parents communicate with teachers about the amount of time that is spent on homework especially if it does not fall within a realistic range. It is also important that the teacher "hear" parents concerns about time spent on homework and respond accordingly.

Conclusion

These excerpts from family interactions and interviews suggest several things about the communication between teachers and parents about children's homework. First, the teacher (and schools in general) must clearly communicate to the parents what the intended role of the parent should be in homework completion. Many schools have homework guidelines that help parents know how actively they should help their children. This is an important step to ensuring that parents don't take an overly zealous role in homework completion. Second, parents must rely on the teacher to a great extent to institute a mechanism by which the parent may verify what is being assigned for homework on a daily basis. Finally, families report that they can more easily plan for, and manage, homework when it is assigned in ways that are predictable, consistent, and within guidelines for reasonable amounts of homework for a target grade level. In the following section, the process of communication between the parent and the child is considered. Even while some teachers and parents communicate clearly about homework and parents understand their intended or ideal role in the accomplishment of homework, it is not always the case that the situation at home mirrors the ideal for parent participation that a policy of parent involvement suggests.

Communication between Parent and Child about Homework

In general, parent's voices are the voices of the teacher and the educational institution at home. Thus the institution of the school and education meld into parent-child communication and family life at large. In their capacity as "teacher at home," parents report problems with communicating with their children about homework in several ways. Parents report this communication difficulty in terms of getting their children to start homework, keeping them going with the homework projects until completed, and helping them when necessary. I conclude this section with a discussing of one strategy that some parents use to remove the burden of homework from the home and the parent-child relationship.

The Homework Struggle—Getting it Started and Keeping it Going

Parents in this study instituted a number of strategies to schedule homework time that facilitates smooth homework start. Some of these strategies reported by parents and seen in the video are also recommended by guidelines advocated for parents and include establishing a set time and place for when homework starts, removing possible distractions, and having rules about delaying other activities, such as television, until homework is complete. Even when rules for homework start are clearly laid out in the family routine and guidelines are established, video-data suggest that homework start is often a site for extensive parent-child bargaining and negotiation.

Several parents reported difficulty with homework because they are not home to prompt homework start. This mother discusses the relationship between getting home from work late and trying to get the homework project started and underway. She reports that it is harder to get homework started if her child has gotten involved in videogames. She also discusses how she faces the difficulty of tending to both the dinner making task and the homework task at once:

> If I come home at five, I might be able to get him to do his homework before we have dinner. But if I come home at six, they're hungry and they want dinner, I'll try to sneak in the homework while I'm cooking dinner … that's really, not my ideal routine … because I would like him to do homework before he starts getting involved in games.… At 6:00 when you're hungry, your mind's tired. You're not that alert. It's better when you get home from school.

One documented discursive strategy parents use when communicating with children about homework reported by Wingard, 2006 is that parents often topicalized or mention homework early in the afternoon after greeting their children when the school day is over. An important effect of mentioning homework early in the afternoon is that a parent can ensure that there is an opportunity to both gauge what is for homework and to plan the homework time into the rest of the days' activities. Mentioning homework, followed by parent-child planning talk about how and when homework will get done, facilitates the homework enterprise. Even when a parent mentions homework early in an attempt to achieve agreement with a child about when homework needs to be started, children may still resist parent attempts to start homework.

Another kind of difficulty parents often face in getting homework done includes managing the time available for the various activities. Wingard (2007) shows that this can be seen specifically in interactions that constitute negotiation and conflict between parents and children about time and activities. In these interactions, time slots are discursively constructed and negotiated.

Although any number of activities can compete with homework, it was apparent that two of the main activities that were specifically desired by children and that often became a source of negotiation with parents were watching television and playing video games. The mother in this interview excerpt discusses her own strategy of instituting a policy of no videogames and only limited television during the work week as a way to manage the homework conflict:

Mother: Now it's more strict. I took away all their game controls the boy's game controls for the whole week…. Darrin likes to go on the computer and play a computer game through the internet. Uhm Diablo. So that's going to be very limited to the weekend.
Interviewer: So during the week no video games.
Mother: No nothing. No TV unless I see that um their work is all done and they've studied for everything. They do get to choose uh one program for half an hour before bedtime. Whether it be as soon as they get home or right before bed. One half-hour program.

In another excerpt, another mother explains that she does not allow the TV to be turned on until she gets home from work. Also in this family, a nanny picks up the children and is with the children until the mother gets home from work and this prevents problems with conflicts between TV and homework.

The television cannot go on until I come home. So there's not even any reason to rush through the homework … because you can't watch TV until 5:30 anyway and then all of it would have to be done. Including your half-hour of reading whether you feel like it or not.

Problems When Helping Children with Homework

Aside from getting homework started a number of issues arise when parents are actually needed to help their children with homework. Even when guidelines from the teacher or school suggest that children should accomplish homework independently, some parents report that they have to actively help their children in order to do the homework. One assumption of parent involvement in children's homework is that parents are competent to help. In contrast to this ideal, parents expressed in the interview data that they sometimes have difficulty actually understanding the homework instructions and/or actually doing the work assigned to their children and this problematic aspect of parent involvement has been noted in the literature as well (K. V. Hoover-Dempsey, Bassler, & Burow, 1995). When parents feel incompetent, or their children feel that their parents are incompetent to help, it creates frustration during the homework process for everyone in the family. This was discussed both in interviews and was seen in the videos of the everyday interaction. This father, for example, expressed such difficulty and characterized himself as "screwing it up" and then characterizes the kinds of things his children say about his homework help:

> I usually screw it up because I don't usually understand the instructions well, you know? It's one of those things ... you know "Daddy doesn't do it the same way." And it's true Daddy doesn't. Sorry, you know?

Certain subjects like math may be particularly vulnerable to this problem since parents were often taught to do math differently than their children are being taught today. This difference results in problems about how to both do and talk about doing the homework as this mother explains:

> They teach things different now so I've to try to get on track with how they're teaching it. For instance with math, when I was in school, when you're adding you "carry over" with addition, and you, "borrow" with subtraction. Well now you do something else and I can't remember what it is ... we get into this battle when I say well "borrow" this and they say we don't do that. We do it this way and it's the same way but it's just worded different. So "re-grouping" is what I think it's called.

Parents with children who may need extra help for any number of reasons may also find that they face particularly problematic homework time, even when a child has a relatively mild learning disability. Several children in the study had been tested for learning disabilities and some were diagnosed with Attention Deficit Disorder (ADD) and Attention Deficit Hyperactivity Disorder (ADHD). For these children, and in these families, homework often constituted a daily issue that resulted in very difficult interactions. This mother describes homework time with her daughter who was tested for a learning disability:

> *Mother:* It's stressful sometimes ... She's tired and it's just-it can't be done when she gets home from school because I'm not home.... So it's a struggle.

Interviewer: And how often does Anna really need supervision or assistance
    with her homework?
Mother: Hundred percent of the time.

This mother explains that she feels that either her or her husband
must be available for homework help because the child is not able to do it
independently:

> I always have to make sure one of us either my husband or myself is avail-
> able because she gets very frustrated when she can't get the problem.

As has also been documented in Wingard and Forsberg (in press), parents
reported feeling a dilemma about how much they should actually help their
children with homework especially when the child recruits the parent to get
the answers. Some parents reported feeling pressure by their children to help
them with homework even if they feel that the child may actually be able to do
the work independently. This father explains that he thinks his children may
insist on homework help simply as a way to get attention:

> Um and I won't say they need help but they want it. They want the atten-
> tion. They ask you- they want you to do it for them. So you fight them,
> then you gotta be like, you gotta point out every little thing to them and
> walk them through it.... I won't say that they can't do, but something that
> they just want you to help them with it.

Reports like this further support the idea that even if parents are given clear
or idealized guidelines for how they should attend to homework at home, the
realities of the parent-child interaction at home may not mirror the ideal.

"Re-institutionalizing" Homework—After School Programs and Paid Help

Because the difficulties that parents face when getting homework done depends
on their own personal involvement, many parents in the study chose after
school care situations for their children where supervised mandatory homework time was a component. Some parents also employed after school tutors
to work with children on homework, or created clear homework guidelines
with paid in-home childcare providers. Parents whose children participated in
after school programs reported largely that the homework was often completed
when they picked up their children from school. In these cases, the parents
reported that they would usually just check to see that homework was done
and/or they might see that it was done correctly and sign off on a homework
sheet. This father reports that although his son doesn't like homework, he is
good at doing it in the aftercare program:

Well, he'd rather play. You know, but he's real good at doing his homework at the after school program.

The fact that parents turn to aftercare situations as an important homework resource was also evident when parents expressed dissatisfaction with an aftercare program because their child was not completing assigned homework. Parents often were dissatisfied because it was perceived that the program did not provide enough structure, guidance, or supervision for homework. This mother expresses that she feels she can't find a good aftercare program where there is enough individualized attention as concerns homework:

I like the teacher I just don't like the structure I suppose. But I can't find any aftercare that would accommodate her as far as maybe a one-on-one type, "here I want you to sit down and do your homework".

This father repeats the sentiment that his daughter's aftercare program has variable success with structuring and supporting homework time:

She's not using her after care program time to do the homework. She's out playing. It's like I come in there and it depends on who's watching them. They can be focusing quietly, doing things together in groups, or they can be bouncing off the walls. It's like you've got to be kidding me.

Parents also turned to private tutors as important resources in the accomplishment of homework. In some cases parents reported hiring a tutor explicitly to remedy what had become a difficult homework situation between parent and child. While discussing his family's homework strategies, this father alludes to the difficulties he and his son have had in the past while working on math before the parents decided to employ a tutor:

I used to work with him. With Abe, I did some math,... Um but he didn't like it after awhile,... Maybe I was too hard on him. I don't know.

Paid after school caregivers were also reported to be important "frontline" support for doing the difficult work of getting kids to start homework. This mother explains how having a paid caregiver with her children after school gave her the additional authoritative leverage she needed early in the afternoon when she isn't there to make sure homework was getting done. She refers to herself as the "homework Nazi", and her paid caregiver as the "big guy" who does the heavy lifting of getting the kids to start homework:

So I am now the homework Nazi.... And my nanny is the big guy. My partner in crime.

The ability to use outsourced services to help with the homework project is dependent however on the financial resources that are available to the parents. Other families that would have perhaps liked to use such services reported that they didn't feel they had the financial resources:

Interview: We talked about this a little bit before about them receiving additional help outside the home. But you said that they didn't have any right now.
Mother: No, for education…. No, not right now. Um it just gets too costly … no, we can't do that.

Any of the solutions mentioned above constitute outsourced help that may make an important difference in both the amount of time spent on homework within family life and may mitigate the possible difficulty that homework presents in family life. A family that can pay an outside source to accomplish homework with the child frees the parent to some extent from having to negotiate and bargain with the child about starting or finishing homework. The ability to outsource homework time may save the family from conflict and struggle related to homework and may mean substantial relief for parents in families where homework has become problematic. I suggest that the strategy of outsourcing homework help may in this sense be considered a strategy that "re-institutionalizes" homework back to a realm that is less directly located within the family and the parent-child relationship.

Also, as mentioned earlier, while outsourcing the task of homework is a strategy some families adopt, such a strategy is often contingent on the availability of monetary resources in the family to pay for such a service. This is clearly a strategy that is class based and therefore not accessible to all families. The difference between families who are able to employ paid homework help and families who do not have this possibility due to lack of resources may be one of the ways in which homework widens the education gap, since families with less means may therefore not be able to solve the difficulties that homework creates in the parent-child relationship and in the home. Alternatively, communication about homework that continues to be problematic between parent and child due to lack of resources to implement other strategies may negatively impact not just the family relationships at home, but may also impact the child's inherent feelings about education and learning.

General Conclusions

Under the auspices of parent involvement, parents are expected to be involved in their children's education and, as part of this involvement, they are expected to be attentive to their children's homework. To be "involved" with respect to homework means that the parents must ensure that homework that is assigned is completed and turned in on time. While this may seem on the surface a straightforward and reasonable task for parents to attend to, as reported in this chapter, parents suggest that there are, in fact, many problematic aspects of this involvement. This chapter considered the communication processes that surround the homework in two main ways. First, the communication from the educational institution to the home was considered with a focus on how expectations are communicated to the parents about their role in homework, as well as how parents access information about the assigned work. Even when parents are given clear guidelines concerning the scope of their intended role, such as being told they should be minimally involved, parents often reported that the reality of their required attention to homework may be very different from the ideal that is communicated by the institution. Parents also face difficulties when they do not have clear and routine ways of knowing what homework is actually assigned. Not having access to independently verifiable information communicated by the teacher about homework assignments can have negative consequences for the parent-child communication relationship at home if the child's own report or documentation of the assigned homework is inaccurate or questionable. The consistency, predictability and amount of homework assigned also emerged as a problematic issue for both parents and children. Parents did not always feel that the amount or type of homework assigned was pedagogically motivated and they did not necessarily feel that their concerns were heard when they questioned the amount that was assigned.

Next, this chapter considered the communication that occurs between the child and the parent at home while doing homework. Getting homework started is often reported to be a struggle especially when working parents are not home to immediately mobilize the homework process. Other activities (e.g., video games and TV) are reported as competing activities that the parent must actively manage. Negotiation about these activities often becomes the basis for family strife that on the surface are instantiated by the need to get homework done. Even when homework is started, keeping the child on task can constitute the basis of problematic parent-child interaction. Some parents report facing the problem that even if they think children may not actually require help to do the homework, they none-the-less want parental attention as they attend to the homework task. The help that may be required by the parent to complete the homework task may not mirror the educational institutions' ideal, and the possible pedagogical and developmental goals associated with children accomplishing homework independently. Even when children legitimately need homework help, and the institution encourages homework help, parents do not always feel they are competent to help their children do the homework. Finally, this chapter points to a strategy that some parents use to remove homework from the home. When parents make after-school care arrangements where mandatory, supervised homework time is a component; parents are essentially removing part of the homework burden from the home and the family and re-institutionalizing homework. This finding here supports previous research that has shown that parents favor the use of after school programs (Harniss, Epstein, Bursuck, Nelson, & Jayanthi, 2001) and tutoring (Greenwood & Delquadri, 1995; Jenkins & Jenkins, 1985) as part of an overall approach for successful homework completion. While economically feasible for some families, this strategy is also problematic as it arguably contributes to the overall inequalities with respect to support in education.

While this chapter reports on the difficulties families face in managing the homework task, the investigation of this issue was not an intentional focus for data collection of the larger ethnographic study. Despite the fact that this study did not seek to focus on homework, both open-ended questions about parents' general views on their children's education, and interviews with children about their daily lives led to a relatively high occurrence of discussion of homework. Family interaction captured on video, attests to the difficulties families face in managing the homework task.[3] This basic empirical and descriptive work can provide the foundation for later research that more specifically and systematically targets deeper understanding of the interrelatedness of the communication processes surrounding the accomplishment of homework.

Future research that focuses on the communication processes implicated in the accomplishment of homework could include a larger sampling of families from geographically diverse areas and incorporate data collection that systematically sets out to investigate the main issues concerning communication that emerged in this study. One specific issue that is rich for further investigation is how or if parents perceive that policies on parent participation in homework are communicated clearly to them by the educational institution at large and their child's teacher in particular. If and when such policies are communicated clearly, research should determine how and when parents feel that those expectations are unreasonable or achievable. A better understanding of the communication artifacts that are used to communicate assignments and a comparison of the effectiveness of those artifacts would also be fruitful for better understanding the communication processes between parents and educational institutions surrounding homework. Reported outcomes of the uses of those artifacts are also best triangulated by documenting the communication that results between parents and children with actual video recordings during homework time. Future research should also focus more effort on better understanding the child's perspective on the task of homework. From children's perspectives, what kinds of communication practices and artifacts concerning homework best enable homework assignments to fulfill their intended functions for reviewing or extending class materials? What practices concerning homework for children are perceived as detrimental to learning and/or communication with their parents? A systematic analysis of the effects of choosing afterschool programs, and paid tutors and caregivers for accomplishing homework also emerges as an important factor to consider. The process of re-institutionalization reported here ultimately sheds light on the issue of homework as something that may reinforce an already existing education gap. As a study of, broadly speaking, middle-class families, these families may also exemplify some of the more privileged circumstances for parent involvement. Families in this study may not be facing the same level of challenge that working-class or immigrant families experience due to nonstandard work schedules, difficulty with language, or difference in educational experience. The support that many middle-class parents can provide their children ultimately re-enforces the cultural capital that benefit the advancement of some children over others (Lareau 1987; Lareau 1989, Lareau & Shumar 1996). With this in mind, if homework is beneficial in the ways it is suggested, it should be beneficial for all. Research on how homework is accomplished and the parents' role in accomplishing homework, should focus on how all children can access equal support for their homework so that it does not end up being a factor that contributes to inequality in education.

A number of different perspectives can be taken on homework to help scholars better frame an understanding of the role that homework plays in family life. On the one hand, homework can be seen as an unwelcome work task that crosses an imagined boundary between the educational institution and family life and causes problems in family life. If seen in this way, homework can be equated with parent's paid work that encroaches into family territory in the same way that "spillover" has been used to describe this problematic permeation (Greenhaus & Beutell, 1985; Small & Riley, 1990). Homework can also be viewed as a necessary and welcome task that furthers the overall goals of both the educational institution and the parent. This joint goal, which might be articulated as the academic and individual development of the child, suggests that the boundary between educational institution and parent are blurred. By being involved, the parent shares the voice of the teacher and the educational institution at large in the home and, in this sense becomes "pedagogicalized" (Popkewitz, 2003). The interrelatedness of the goals and communication of institution and the family might be best viewed through the lens of bona fide group perspective that emphasizes the fluid boundaries and interdependence between groups (Putnam & Stohl, 1990). Especially the interrelationship between the communication between institution and parent about homework and its relationship to the communication between parent and child at home about homework may be best understood from this integrated perspective of group communication. The fluidity of these boundaries is also further exemplified in the process of re-institutionalizing homework.

In documenting these communication processes surrounding homework, this chapter documents the difficulties working parents face in managing the homework process. While homework is a task that is intended to support a child's development and academic achievement, it may also substantially impact everyday family life and may negatively impact the parent-child relationship. The experience of parent-child communication during homework then becomes part of the child's experience of learning and education. The emotional tenor that surrounds homework in the parent-child communication relationship, if negative, likely impact the child's own experience with education and learning at large for years to come. In the course of considering the communication processes that surround homework, I've compared some of the acknowledged guidelines for educational institutions and teachers who communicate with families about homework with the realities that parents and children face that can make homework a difficult task at home. On the one hand, this chapter suggests that when teachers and parents follow the suggested guidelines for assigning and communicating about homework, difficulties surrounding homework have the potential to be minimized. On the other hand, the chapter also lends support to the idea that even when communication about homework between the teacher and parent follows best practices guidelines, it is not clear that all parents are able to be equally supportive, or can provide the idealized involvement that is presupposed to be possible and desirable. Especially if some parents are able to outsource homework by re-institutionalizing it, homework arguably serves to further an already existing education gap.

Notes

1. The project is generously funded by the Alfred P. Sloan foundation at the University of California at Los Angeles where this author was a graduate student at the time of data collection. All methods and procedures used to collect data for this study were approved by the Institutional Review Board at UCLA.
2. Interview questions for the education interview in the study were developed by Kris Gutierrez, Professor in the Graduate School of Education and Information Studies at UCLA.
3. Interactions about homework from this study and a similar study conducted in Sweden have been documented more extensively in Wingard 2006; Wingard 2007; Wingard and Forsberg (in press); and Goodwin, 2007.

References

Baker, A., & Soden, L. (1998). *The challenges of parent involvement research.* ERIC/CUE Digest, 134 (EDOUD984).

Barrett, D. E., & Neal, K. S. (1992). Effects of homework assistance given by telephone on the academic achievement of fifth grade children. *Educational Research Quarterly, 15*(4), 21–28.

Bauch, J. P. (1994). *Voice-based technology for parent involvement: Results and effects.* (ERIC Document Reproduction Service No. ED382325)

Bennett, S., & Kalish, N. (2006). *The case against homework: How homework is hurting our children and what we can do about it.* New York: Crown.

Bryan, T., & Sullivan-Burstein, K. C. (1997). Homework how-to's. *Teaching Exceptional Children, 29*(6), 32–37.

Bursuck, W. D. (1994). Introduction to the special series on homework. *Journal of Learning Disabilities, 27,* 466–469.

Callahan, K., Rademacher, J. A., & Hildreth, B. L. (1998). The effect of parent participation in strategies to improve the homework performance of students who are at risk. *Remedial and Special Education, 19*(3), 131–141.

Clark, R. (1993). Homework-focused parenting practices that positively affect student achievement. In N. F. Chavkin (Ed.), *Families and schools in a pluralistic society* (pp. 367–449). Albany: State University of New York Press.

Cooper, H. (1989). Synthesis of research on homework. *Educational Leadership, 47*(3), 85–91.

Cooper, H. (2007). *The battle over homework: common ground for administrators, teachers, and parents.* Thousand Oaks, CA: Corwin.

Cooper, H., Lindsay, J., & Nye, B. (2000) Homework in the home: How student, family and parenting style differences relate to the homework process. *Contemporary Educational Psychology, 25,* 464–487.

Cooper, H., & Nye, B. (1994). Homework for students with learning disabilities: The implications of research for policy and practice. *Journal of Learning Disabilities, 27,* 470–479.

Corno, L., & Xu, J. (2004). Homework as the job of childhood. *Theory into Practice, 43*(3), 227–233.

Crozier, G. (2001). Excluded parents: The deracialisation of parental involvement. *Race, Ethnicity & Education, 4*(4), 329–341.

Goodwin, C. (2007). Participation stance and affect in the organization of activities. *Discourse and Society, 18,* 53–73.

Greenhaus, J. H., & Beutell, N. J. (1985). Sources of conflict between work and family roles. *Academy of Management Review, 10,* 76– 88.

Greenwood, C. R., & Delquadri, J. (1995). Class wide peer tutoring and the prevention of school failure. *Preventing School Failure, 39*(4), 21–25.

Harniss, M. K., Epstein, M. H., Bursuck, W. D., Nelson, J., & Jayanthi, M. (2001). Resolving homework-related communication problems: Recommendations from parents of children with and without disabilities. *Reading and Writing Quarterly, 17*(3), 205–225.

Hoover-Dempsey, K., Battiato, A., Walker, J., Reed, R., DeJong, J., & Jones, K. (2001). Parental involvement in homework. *Educational Psychologist, 36*(3), 195–209.

Hoover-Dempsey, K. V., Bassler, O. C., & Burow, R. (1995). Parents' reported involvement in students' homework: Strategies and practice. *Elementary School Journal, 95*(5), 435–450.

Jayanthi, M., Nelson, J. S., Sawyer, V., Bursuck, W. D., & Epstein, M. H. (1995). Homework communication problems among parents, classroom teachers, and special education teachers: An exploratory study. *Remedial and Special Education, 16*(2), 102–116.

Jenkins, J., & Jenkins, L. (1985). Peer tutoring in elementary and secondary programs. *Focus on Exceptional Children, 17*(6), 1–12.

Jenson, W. R., Sheridan, S. M., Olympia, D., & Andrews, D. (1994). Homework and students with learning disabilities and behavior disorders: A practice parent-based approach. *Journal of Learning Disabilities, 27*(9), 538–548.

Kay, P. J., Fitzgerald, M., Paradee, C., & Mellencamp, A. (1994). Making homework work at home: The parents' perspective. *Journal of Learning Disabilities, 27*(9), 550–561.

Kohn, A. (2006). *The homework myth: Why our kids get too much of a bad thing.* Cambridge, MA: Da Capo Life Long.

Kralovec, E., & Buell, J. (2000). *The end of homework: How homework disrupts families, overburdens children, and limits learning.* Boston: Beacon Press.

Lareau, A. (1987). Social class differences in family-school relationships: The importance of cultural capital. *Sociology of Education, 60*(2), 73–85.

Lareau, A. (1989). *Home advantage: Social class and parental involvement in elementary education.* Philadelphia: Falmer.

Lareau, A., & Shumar, W. (1996). The problem of individualism in family-school policies. *Sociology of Education, 69,* 24–39.

Lee, J.-S., & Bowen, N. K. (2006). Parent involvement, cultural capital, and the achievement gap among elementary school children. *American Educational Research Journal, 43*(2), 193–218.

McNeal, R. (1999). Parental involvement as social capital: Differential effectiveness on science achievement. *Social Forces, 78*(1), 117–144.

Nakagawa, K. (2000). Unthreading the ties that bind: Questioning the discourse of parent involvement. *Educational Policy, 14*(4), 443–472.

National Education Association. Help your student get the most out of homework. Retrieved June 12, 2008, from http: //www.nea.org/parents/homework.html

Patton, J. R., Jayanthi, M., & Polloway, E. A. (2001). Home-school collaboration about homework: What do we know and what should we do? *Reading & Writing Quarterly, 17*(3), 227–242.

Popkewitz, T. S. (2003). Governing the child and pedagogicalization of the parent: a historical excursus into the present. In M. N. Bloch, K. Holmlund, I. Moqvist, & T. S. Popkewitz (Eds.), *Governing children, families, and education: Restructuring the welfare state* (pp. 35–61). New York: Palgrave MacMillan.

Putnam, L., & Stohl, C. (1990). Bona fide groups: An alternative perspective for communication and small group decision making. In R.Y. Hirokawa & M. S. Poole (Eds.), *Communication and group decision making* (pp. 147–179). Thousand Oaks, CA: Sage. .

Small, S. A., & Riley, D. (1990). Toward a multidimensional assessment of work spillover into family life. *Journal of Marriage and the Family, 52,* 51– 61.

Sturges, K. M., Cramer, E. D., Harry, B., Klinger, J. K., & Borman, K. M. (2005). Desegregated but Unequal: Some Paradoxes of Parent Involvement at Bromden Elementary. *International Journal of Educational Policy, Research & Practice, 6*(1), 79–104.

Trammel, D. L., Schloss, P. J., & Alper, S. (1994). Using self-recording evaluation and graphing to increase completion of homework assignments. *Journal of Learning Disabilities, 27*(2), 75–81.

U.S. Department of Education. Helping your child with homework. Retrieved June 12, 2008, from http://www.ed.gov/parents/academic/help/homework/homework.pdf

Walberg, H. J., Paschal, R. A., & Weinstein, T. (1985). Homework's powerful effects on learning. *Educational Leadership, 42*(7), 76–79.

Wingard, L. (2006). Parent inquiries about homework: The first mention. *Talk and Text, 26*(4/5), 573–596.

Wingard, L. (2007). Constructing time and prioritizing activities in parent-child interactions. *Discourse and Society 18,* 75–91.

Wingard, L., & Forsberg, L. (in press) Parent involvement in children's homework in American and Swedish dual-earner families. *Journal of Pragmatics.*

Wong, S. W., & Hughes, J. N. (2006). Ethnicity and Language Contributions to Dimensions of Parent Involvement. *School Psychology Review, 35*(4), 645–662.

6 Commentary
Childcare and Education Relationships

Julie Yingling

Family communication has come into its own in the past few decades, and with it questions about how children affect the family system and how the family influences their development. However, early childhood interaction has been a shadowy presence in the periphery of the communication literature until very recently. Given that fact, relationships among children, educational professionals and parents were rarely considered, much less examined systematically. With the burgeoning number of studies examining family interaction, plus the existing literature on student-teacher interaction, the link between the two institutions—familial and education—had to be made. Granted, much of the communication education literature is based on college student populations, but the question of how children learn communication skills had been raised long ago by constructionists and continued to emerge sporadically. If we hope to have an impact on social policy and practice, the communicative links between home and school must be clarified. If we are to be responsive to the call for parental involvement in the education of their children, which has become codified in the Bush administration's No Child Left Behind Act, we have to find out what that involvement means. This set of studies on childcare and education relationships begins to unpack the nature of parent-student-provider interaction.

In the past, communication scholars borrowed from education, child development, developmental linguistics, and family studies to cobble together arguments for the importance of family communication and early communication education. Now, in addition to those sources, we have some studies tailored to the concerns of those of us who take symbolic communication as our starting point.

Although the formal study of education has given us a great deal of information about technique, it was a developmental linguist who gave us the grounded discourse analysis of classroom communication (Cazden, 1988). In the process, she supported the theory that communication and influence were bi-directional in the learning process—that students and teachers learned with and from each other. Developmental psychologists offered research supporting the view that relationships develop in bidirectional processes as well. Fogel (1993) proposed that infants and parents begin creative coregulation immediately in developing their relationship, and that same process—of limiting each other's behavioral choices—is at work in all relationship development.

Considering the puzzle of how parents, children, and education/care professionals communicate, we had the parent-child piece, pursued by communication scholars like Dixon (1995). And we had the student-teacher piece, furthered by communication scholars such as Vaughn (2002). Now, how do those two sets of relationships come together as the child enters daycare and educational settings? That is where these scholars pick up the search, examining the intersection of family (parent-child) and institutional (child-professional) relationships.

Coverage of the Theme

The four studies cover a range of topics and ages. Topics include: parent-provider communication characteristics, parental and professional perceptions of interactions among and between them, children's communication behaviors in daycare, parents' and children's reports and behaviors about homework, and the effects of mother's job status, monitoring, verbal aggression and parent-child communication on young teens' perceptions of self-efficacy. That's a lot of territory in four studies, but always there is more to discover.

The first questions that occur to me concern the child's perspective: What do children think of the interface between home and school? Do they think they act the same in both places? If not, why? If they could get their teachers and parents to listen carefully for ten minutes, what would they say?

The next questions are about the effect of the home/school link on the child: How does the quality of connection between home and school affect their educational achievement? How does the quality of connection between home and school affect their social skills? And which communication skills are influenced by that connection?

Finally, there is the issue of institutionalized connections, for example: How does parental involvement in school boards, committees and associations affect the home/school link and thus the child? Is this kind of institutionalized involvement sufficient or necessary to ensure optimal home/school communication?

The studies covered a wide range of ages, but not all. That becomes important as we consider how useful the studies can be. Two studies looked at the daycare setting (approximately 0–5 years), one at the rules and norms of homework (among 8- to 10-year-old students) and one at the effects on self-efficacy of sixth graders (approximately 12–13 years). A few ranges are missing (6–7, 11, and over 14). Nevertheless, they present us a nice variety, as home/school issues do change with development. The daycare children and their parents will not be concerned about homework yet, while parentification is typically not a problem for 4-year-olds. The only problem with such variety is that we cannot easily or legitimately compare results across studies except for the first two. In the next section, the issues of age and development will come up again.

The Effects of Authors' Methodological and Theoretical Choices on Outcomes

The authors take a variety of approaches to their subjects, so some more easily addressed broad questions and others more focused ones. Namely, the ethnography by Wingard and the participant observation by Meyer afforded them the chance to be more open in their expectations and so they found a variety of themes in observing homework communication and daycare interactions respectively. Weigel and Martin as well as Miller-Day and McManus performed fairly focused interviews to describe specifically the perceptions of parents and professionals regarding their interaction, and the links among mother's employment, mother-teen relations, and teens' efficacy. These latter two sets of authors also chose ecological systems theory as their framework.

Systems theory is the preferred theoretical approach to studying families. Families, after all, are the original human communicative system. When Bronfenbrenner first proposed his ecological system theory in 1977, he used it to examine shifts in childrearing practices in the United States. He found that parental values in the lower and middle classes reversed themselves from 1930 to 1950; lower-class parents became more strict and middle-class parents less so. Later studies looked at how beliefs about parenting changed based on parents' own experiences and their perceptions of the degree of influence they had on their children's development (Haslett & Samter, 1997, p. 240). Thus, the ecological context—culture, education, family of origin, and so forth—affects what will happen in setting up the family system dynamic.

Weigel and Martin (chapter 2) specifically acknowledge that families communicate with other systems and are affected by them. They use Bronfenbrenner's concept of "mesosystem" to refer to the set of links between the home and childcare center, assuming that the quality of those links can facilitate development by providing a consistent environment for the child. They note that there is little research to be found that examines parent-provider-child communication. That's true, but unfortunately their study leaves out the child, as have many before them. Nonetheless, they do a nice review of the literature on children's communication in daycare, some of which echoes the findings in Meyer's study (chapter 3). What they do well is to show us how parents and care providers perceive their communication, and then place that information into a system model of parent/childcare provider/child communication. They also propose a very useful set of future directions, some of which will be repeated below.

All of the data Weigel and Martin reported were from questionnaires and interviews with parents and providers about frequency and type of contact and their feelings following interaction with each other. So, the only portion of the model directly informed by these data is that regarding communication context. Informants also gave their impressions of proximal influences—enhancers and barriers—but we are left unsure of the links to actual communication behavior. The rest of the model is sketched from the results of various other studies. The model is sensible, although it seems unlikely that any single study can fill in all the components of the model so it may remain untested. Given that the model is built from the results of various studies, we cannot know whether the components are the same for each study used to support the model. And if we do not have all the elements consistently identified, the model cannot be used in a predictive fashion. This is ever the problem with systems models: They are often complicated and vague at the same time. Do not misunderstand; they are useful theoretically. They give us a way of talking about the layers of influence involved and that alone is a great help to teachers, students and scholars. But does it get us any further toward mapping out the influences that predict outcomes for a particular child or cohort? Well, it's a long hard process of research to get to the complete picture. That said, Weigel and Martin have accomplished a great deal in filling in one section of the map. And more is promised: Note that the larger study, of which this is one part, examines the effects of context on children's language development. Having a clearly defined outcome like this one will make the model useful indeed.

In chapter 3, Meyer also chose to observe communication in a childcare center, using grounded theory to make sense of his observations and the narratives of his subjects. This study echoes one of Meyer's past studies reviewed by Weigel and Martin (this volume). In 1997, Meyer and Driskill observed 10 communication strategies to manage relationships in daycare. This time, Meyer found 12 themes emerging from children's interaction. Of those, 10 appear to be repeats from the 1997 study (what was labeled "joking or teasing" is now "humor," for example). That supports the credibility of his method of exhausting the available data. The additional two themes, "repeated patterns" and "response to adults," represent respectively: a type of repetitive wordplay used by young children to practice language, and appeals to adults to gain support or develop relationships. Possibly these last two were not observed in the first data collection because of the nature of child play in the two care centers or the character of his observations—note that in this one, he also speaks with staff and parents.

When asked about communication in the daycare culture, parents and staff shared only one theme: open communication. That parents and staff value different communication strategies makes sense given their different agendas and responsibilities vis á vis the childcare center. Their sometimes contrasting agendas could (and did, evidently) make for conflict, but generally the adults from both "organizations" seemed to try to cooperate in making the "communication crossroad" a valuable and enjoyable experience for children. Meyer uses the frame of organizational cultures to good advantage in explaining how children adapt to the shifting communication contexts of school and home. Children carried some behaviors across contexts (characteristics like creativity, obstinacy) but changed others (to more independent, less demanding, more yielding to peer pressure). All this is as we might expect for a child learning social skills at a fast rate. What would be interesting to know now is which of the communication strategies available to them are associated with rapid (or slow or no) adaptation. What does successful adaptation look like? Which sort of cultural mix—integrative, differentiated or fragmented—is likely to stimulate the most growth without crushing the child's ability to adapt? The next step, I think, is to move beyond grounded theory to test a few of the assumptions of cultural theory as they play out in home/school.

Miller-Day and McManus (chapter 4) did test specific questions about the various layers of influence affecting the ecological system encompassing home and school. Recall that in the Weigel and Martin study, the influence of the child was unexamined. In this case the effect of education was left out. Instead, these authors took a closer look at the influence of mother's employment status and mother-adolescent relations on teen efficacy. These sixth graders were well beyond the stage of first adapting to school interaction, and living in low-income family units. Not surprisingly, welfare-to-work mothers who work at or below poverty level may lack the time or energy to provide the kind of "parental involvement" and monitoring those middle-class parents may more easily provide. Young teens are often expected to take on adult responsibilities in stressed families like these. Such parentification may not necessarily be detrimental and indeed, it can contribute to a child's sense of efficacy and competence.

Using standardized assessments, Miller-Day and McManus measured mothers' job stability and teens' perceptions of self efficacy and quality of relations with mother. They then described their population's demographics and reported simple correlations for the variables. I claim no expertise with statistics, but their interpretation of the multiple correlations suggests several predictor variables (job instability, financial strain, maternal monitoring, maternal verbal aggression, and parent-adolescent communication) and at least one criterion variable (teen efficacy, and possibly parentification). If their intention truly is to claim a predictive relationship, a more powerful test of multiple correlations may be warranted. That said, the descriptive table displayed enough interesting simple correlations to warrant further attention, and the interview excerpts shed further light on the problems associated with parenting under conditions of low-wage employment. It would appear that adolescents don't mind fulfilling adult responsibilities if they are acknowledged for it. Indeed, their sense of efficacy is positive related to good quality communication with mother and to mother's monitoring of their behavior. Mothers, however, do feel that their employment status affects their parenting and in fact, mother's job instability was associated with low teen efficacy. The only clue from the study as to the nature of that association came from the qualitative data: a teen expressed a sense of hopelessness about her mother's situation which affected her willingness to hope for more than the life she knew.

The final contribution from Wingard (chapter 5) examines a standard of the home-school interface: homework. Homework is assigned in the educational realm but completed in the home environment. For this reason, we might expect communication missteps between the two contexts. Parents approach it as a problematic responsibility, children as drudgery, teachers as necessity. Wingard saw the opportunity to examine this built-in communication issue and chose ethnography to capture naturally occurring parent-child communication as well as parent and child interview data. Again, there was one piece of the system left out of the equation; in this case, it was the teacher. Parents were asked about their general views of educational practices as well as about specific household practices around homework. While children were not asked specifically about homework, many mentioned it as a high frequency activity as well as a least favored one.

Parents expressed an understanding of their roles in the homework routine, as well as the difficulties they had in performing them. They could not always rely on children to communicate the assignments, so appreciated clear communication from school about each day's requirements as well as a system of verifying such. From the teacher's end, they wanted consistent, predictable, and reasonable homework assignments. What they did *not* want were expectations that parents would teach children material that was not covered in class. Because they often viewed homework as onerous, children were less than clear about assignments and few completed them independently. Many parents reported that they had to establish and enforce a time and place to begin homework, and to remove distractions such as TV and video games. Getting the child started could be complicated by stress and exhaustion in either child or parent, or by a child's special learning needs. Parents also had to make judgments calls about how much help to provide. Some decided to "outsource" homework assistance to a tutor to ensure that the work was done whether the parent was working, tired, or otherwise unable or unwilling to perform the role. Note that, in contrast to the working poor who wanted to squeeze out more time with their children, these parents were middle-class and so could afford to use their time with children in a preferred fashion (i.e., more enjoyable than monitoring homework).

These findings are incredibly important to all three parties who must coordinate their efforts to keep the education process on track. One conclusion is that homework, mandated by the educational professionals, "is ... a task and responsibility for both the parent and child." The involved parent then is the linchpin between the parent-child communication system and the teacher-student system. Thus, the communication around homework becomes part of the educational experience; and the quality of that communication is likely to continue to affect the child's learning for a long time. That is one of the questions that begs further study: What effect does parent-child communication about homework have on the child's current and future educational accomplishments? And further, what teacher practices foster positive parent-child interaction about homework?

Now, we will see how these studies interface and reflect upon one another: The intersections among them point to the next steps in the study of the home/school mesosystem. Throughout the next section, we will use Weigel and Martin's model as a tool for comparison.

Suggestions for the Study of Relationships in Childcare and Education

The methodologies used in these studies were appropriate for a relatively new line of inquiry. Description of what is observed, whether qualitative or quantitative, is a good place to begin searching for the most useful questions to test. Before testing hypotheses, though, we need to fill in some of the gaps in the observed system. More real-time interaction between child and teacher, between teacher and parent, would provide a richer data set from which to derive testable questions. Then, the specifics of the home/school system and the interactions among parents, children, and professionals could be mapped more usefully.

Although all the authors acknowledge the importance of multiple layers of influence on the communication in home and school relationships, only one (Meyer) observed all three sets of interactants: parents, children, and education professionals. If we are to flesh out a systems model of these communication links, as Weigel and Martin propose, we will need observations of all relationships at all levels. Then, we can begin to test the direction(s) of influence and the more specific instances that recur in contexts. To that end, we turn now to see what each study contributes to the systems model as it appears in chapter two.

Distal Context

The preconditions which might influence communication are multiple and complex. As Bronfenbrenner found, parenting values in a culture can shift in a generation depending on the changing circumstances of socioeconomic segments of the culture, past parenting practices, and generational experiences. What this says to me is that one feedback loop is missing from the model: from communication outcomes back to distal context. Generational experiences (communication and outcome contexts), of the child, the parent, the teacher, are likely to feedback to the next generation (as distal context) to inform their own processes. For example, if my own parents did not feel the responsibility to monitor my homework, I may recognize that gap as my children bring homework to me. And even if I had believed that children should do independent work, the prevailing mores of parental involvement, pressure for consistently high grades, and demands from the educational institutions will most likely change my attitude about my parenting role.

Two studies included data about distal influence. Miller-Day and McManus tracked mother's job status and socioeconomic level for their relationships on child efficacy. And Wingard's families were uniformly middle class and highly educated. Interestingly, they both were concerned with the emotional tone of the parent-child relationship and how that affects child's learning. These authors tracked at least the parent-child relationship from distal context through communication context. Although the question of outcome on the child's learning process is left unanswered, they raise intriguing questions about equal access to educational achievement. Most parents do want to be involved in their child's learning process, but some have more time and resources to do so. Children wanted to be acknowledged for their achievements and did not mind their work being monitored. However, children in poor homes felt some hopelessness about the promise of achievement, even when the quality of parent-child communication was high. On the other hand, children in more affluent homes resented homework to the point where some parents hired tutors to make sure it was done in order to avoid imposing a negative emotional tone on their relationship with the child. What we still need to know is which is the more critical influence—positive emotional tone or parent-child interaction quality—that affects such outcomes as student achievement, personal efficacy, future socioeconomic status and so forth. The answers may be the same for each outcome: Both positive tone and high involvement could make for high achievement and personal efficacy. Or they could vary on yet other factors, such as socioeconomic level or positive teacher-child relationship. Future research must unpack the elements of the model into testable factors so more accurate prediction can influence policy on education and childcare.

Proximal Context

Again, communication barriers and enhancers can run the gamut. Miller-Day and McManus measured the children's perceptions of mother's verbal aggression as well as of parental monitoring. As we might guess, if a child perceives mother as verbally aggressive, the teen's efficacy suffered. And open communication between teen and mother had a positive effect on teen's efficacy. So far, so good. However, maternal monitoring also influenced efficacy positively. That link was explained by some of the qualitative data: Children want to be seen, especially when they do something good. So, all things equal—if their relationship is good and communication is open—monitoring per se has a good effect. The value for open communication was again noted in Meyer's study as enhancing parent-provider communication. Wingard noted that clear expectations (openness and transparency) are valued by parents who are trying to fulfill their role in the homework contract. She also went the step further to identify what constitutes clear expectations (consistency and predictability of type and amount of homework) and to communication methods for accomplishing it (a homework hotline, homework folders or logs, assignment sheets). So, for at least one link between homes and school, we have proximal and communication context covered, if not a precise outcome.

There are undoubtedly more possible obstacles and enhancers to communication that may be measured, including opinions of others' roles, self-perceptions, types of curriculum followed by professionals, parenting types, and so forth. As scholars continue to explore the communication context, more proximal factors will be questioned and identified.

Communication Context

Ah, here's the crux of the matter. And indeed, it is the layer of influence we cannot afford to neglect. Several authors captured actual communication behavior. Meyer observed children's interaction for common themes of behavior, many of which he found before in daycare interaction. And Wingard filmed parent-child interaction to record emotional tone and content of communication behavior which in turn supported an interpretation of the interview data. Miller-Day and McManus tapped teens' impressions of their preferred communication methods and emotional tone, although actual interaction between parents and teens would reveal more about specific communication behaviors that lead to outcomes like efficacy. Indeed, we might also question what behaviors reflect efficacy. What situated behaviors can we observe that constitute a positive outcome for a child in the home-school mesosystem?

Communication Outcomes

The authors here have questioned what leads to a satisfied parent, an effective teacher, an educated and socially adept child. But the lines of influence are still *dotted* lines. We aren't sure of all the factors that lead to satisfaction, although we have asked parents. We aren't sure of all the factors that allow teachers to feel they are doing a good job in concert with parents. And certainly, we aren't sure of all the factors that promote child learning and communication development, although we now have some ideas. As ever, I encourage scholars to study communication itself as well as measuring distal and proximal contexts and outcomes. What we have now are some elements that fill in the blanks on the parent/care provider/child model, but also many more questions. I trust that we are on our way to filling in more and more of the specifics of the model. As a consequence, we should feel more and more confident in proposing and supporting shifts in educational policy and procedures, and in the legislation that governs the provision of adequate time and resources for fully involved parenting.

References

Bronfenbrenner, U. (1977). Toward an experimental ecology of human development. *American Psychologist, 32*, 513–531.

Cazden, C. B. (1988). *Classroom discourse: The language of teaching and learning.* Portsmouth, NH: Heineman.

Dixon, M. (1995). Models and perspectives of parent-child communication. In T. J. Socha & G. Stamp (Eds.), *Parents, children and communication: Frontiers of theory and research* (pp. 43–62). Hillsdale, NJ: Erlbaum.

Fogel, A. (1993). *Developing through relationships.* Chicago: University of Chicago Press.

Haslett, B. B., & Samter, W. (1997). *Children communicating: The first 5 years.* Mahwah, NJ: Erlbaum.

Vaughn, M. S. (2002). A delicate balance: The praxis of empowerment at a midwestern Montessori school. *Communication Education, 20*(2), 183–201.

Section II
Health & Wellness

7   When Your Child is in Crisis

Navigating Medical Needs with Issues of Privacy Management

Ashley Duggan and Sandra Petronio

Parents faced with a child's unanticipated, serious medical condition such as a life-threatening illness, premature birth, diagnosis of cancer, stoke, leukemia, Huntington's disease, or life-threatening accident, also experience elevated levels of fear and anxiety. The impact of these health crises are recognized as traumatic by the American Psychological Association (1994). As such, the emotional distress that erupts after finding out about a child's serious health condition can shatter previous assumptions about the role of parenting and the healthcare delivery system, and is likely to generate feelings of high uncertainty for the parents. A diagnosis of serious illness for a child is horrifying for parents and often results in a fractured reality where everyday circumstances, sequences, routines, and relationships are shaken (Clarke-Steffen, 1993; Cohen, 1993). Parents tend to feel helpless during these medical crises and frequently do not know how to make decisions or how to protect their children from additional harm (Clarke-Steffen, 1993). The swirl of events often leaves the parents feeling bewildered. Depending on how ill their child is, the constant fear that there might be a possibility of death is never far away (Cohen, 1993).

There are several reasons coping with a child who becomes unexpectedly ill is so traumatic. First, the unanticipated nature of catastrophic childhood illness is a surprise that strikes at the core of parental responsibility, often shattering any feeling of control. In part, this sense of control for parents is contingent on believing they know how best to make decisions on behalf of their ill child. However, during times when there is an unexpected illness, the parents do not have sufficient experience with medical crises to know enough information to make effective decisions. They are also unfamiliar with how to navigate hospitals, how to best gather information from medical personnel, how to interpret the medical condition, make knowledgeable decisions about the course of treatment, or to formulate judgments regarding the prognosis of the illness. Yet, on a number of levels, the parents are expected to make decisions and handle the crisis.

Second, the parents are coping with feelings of fear, and in some cases, guilt regarding whether they have made effective choices about timing in seeking medical attention. Third, parents may be torn between wanting to trust the medical staff's judgments about treatment, yet, also wanting to continue to protect their child from unnecessary pain and suffering. Because the trauma of a child's serious illness may likely extend beyond the initial diagnosis and prognosis to long-term care, in some cases, parents may face coming to grips with sustained levels of anxiety (Stuber, 1995). Underpinning these three issues is the question of how parents, facing decision making about their child's unexpected health crisis, manage interacting with the medical staff to access the medical care their child needs.

As the child is treated, parents communicate with physicians, nurses, and medical staff about circumstances concerning their child's illness that may evoke high levels of fear, anxiety, and uncertainty. At the base of the problem, the medical context for the communicative interaction is often unfamiliar, even alien to parents. Parent-medical staff communication interactions are shaped by constant reminders of the traumas and apprehension about their child's diagnosis and treatment. Layered on top are the days of waiting for the results of tests and procedures that seem endless, changes in medical personnel as doctors, nurses, and staff rotate in and out of service, constant questions from family and friends about the child, and the unpredictable changes in treatment regimen (Clarke-Steffen, 1993). Because interactions with medical staff and medical decisions are foreign to most parents, they enter these relationships with a disadvantage. Complicating this relationship further is the possibility that parents may have had negative experiences with illness in the past, sometimes leading to feelings that they need to be hyper vigilant about the care of their child. Overall, either past experiences or unrealistic expectations about the healthcare system have the potential to interfere with effective communication parents have with the medical staff (Santacroce, 2003).

Given circumstances that the parents' likely face, a salient issue for the medical staff in undertaking care for a critically ill child is the ability of the healthcare team to gather pertinent information about the child's health history and background to effectively treat the child. The parents are the source of this information, yet, as we have identified, parents are coping with a multitude of concerns that are likely to hinder this information gathering effort. In particular, parents facing this medical crisis often are asked for information that may seem private to them, yet, is pertinent to helping the medical team make decisions about medical care for the child. Sometimes, however, the boundary between information that is considered private to the family and information that is important to share with the providers is blurred, particularly if the reason is not obvious to the parents.

To better understand the way parents and health providers make decisions about privacy management, particularly in the kind of volatile and complex situations found when parents encounter unanticipated, serious medical conditions concerning their children, this chapter turns to Communication Privacy Management (CPM) theory (Petronio, 2002). Using this evidenced-based theory, we can better understand the way that parents of children who face serious health concerns make judgments about how best to manage disclosure and privacy relationally with their physician and healthcare team (Petronio,

2002). This chapter examines circumstances surrounding the way that parents of children with serious medical conditions, the care team, and child manage privacy boundaries within the context of navigating their health-driven relationship parameters.

Parent-Provider Communication and Medical Crises

Before we can delve into the nature of privacy management in circumstances where parents must serve as advocates for their child's well-being during medical crises, it is important to frame the nature of communicative interactions between parent and provider within this highly charged state (Petronio, Sargent, Andea, Reganis, & Cichocki, 2004). Parents' communication with health providers about a child's serious, unanticipated health concern is shaped by several critical factors unique to this health context. In particular, there are at least four essential issues that intervene in managing this kind of medical situation.

First, conversations between physicians and parents about children's medical concerns evoke *anxiety* about the seriousness of the medical problem. Parents face tensions between recognizing the value of the care in juxtaposition to frustrations and anxiety they have about the medical situation their child is facing. Frequently, parents do not have a context to evaluate the seriousness of a medical condition their child is confronting. Consequently, they may feel either thankful for the level of biomedical care or anxious about what they perceive are cues to unmet biomedical needs. Further, the parents often have to infer viable information from off-handed opinions made by providers, friends, and acquaintances. For example, new or pregnant parents experiencing a medical crisis, balance expectations for their child's good health tempered by any advance warnings the healthcare team may indicate. Although many people, both strangers and relatives alike, give their opinions and advise, pregnant parents usually test the information against credible sources and measure the veracity against the attributions they make about reasons for receiving the information (Petronio & Jones, 2006).

However, when parents begin to realize a potential problem exists, they are more likely to experience a disconnect between wanting to continue believing they are going to have a healthy child and the inconsistent information being disclosed from the medical world that surrounds them. In very early preterm birth (< 32 weeks), for example, medical procedures and technology have advanced in ways that increase potential for treating the child and results in many more preterm infants surviving every year (Als, 1986). Yet, the parents are often unfamiliar with the ways the procedures and technology address existing problems with their preterm child. The parents may have difficulty coming to grips with how their baby looks and acts, the prospect for a healthy life, and possible long-term complications associated with mechanical intervention of what the medical community labels "fetal neonates," who are critically dependent on technology for survival (Als, 1986). Medical providers may attempt to reassure parents of their child's well-being by continuously describing the child's progress in terms of medical measures, but parents may be much more concerned with family roles, shattered expectations, and heightened emotions. The medical updates, although accurate, may feel like the experience of parenting has turned into a medical procedure.

Second, the *unanticipated* nature of these medical events for parents poses additional challenges. For obvious reasons, parents have no or limited time to emotionally prepare for the medical challenges inherent in a child's unanticipated, serious illness. With an unexpected health crisis, parents and health-care teams meet for the first time. As a consequence, neither have adequate opportunities to develop relationships, especially with the people who depend on medical care for their child. In addition, the unexpected health crisis for parents compromises their sense of control and throws them into a circumstance that taxes every dimension of their ability to cope. For example, parents of children hospitalized for surgery often express feelings of stress related to dramatic changes in home routines, lack of privacy in the hospital, perceiving a lack of attention given to their child by the medical staff, and fears that their child's behavior could reflect negatively on them as parents (Ogilvie, 1990). Similarly, parents may be uncertain about their role during the child's hospitalization (Adams & Parrott, 1994). Health providers, too, are faced with challenges because they do not have a previous relationship with the parents or the child, and are unclear about how to interpret the parents' behavior in light of the health concern. For example, providers may interpret the lack or reluctance of parent's disclosure as hiding information, an inability to describe a full history, or as stifled by uncertainty. While the adults are coping with these many issues, the child is caught in a triangle of trust between the parents and the healthcare team. If the child is old enough to recount his or her own version of events surrounding the illness, the child too may feel torn between multiple explanations of the medical encounter. For the children, these interactions shape health beliefs, and their participation in the visit likely is consequential for how they understand the role of medicine in their lives (Stivers, 2001).

Third, in addition to the anxiety and the unanticipated nature of these health crises, the *time commitment* parents need to make adds stresses and strains. Particularly for parents living outside of the region where their child is receiving medical attention, added burdens exist. For example, many hospitals equipped to treat a child's serious medical condition are often far from the family's place of residence. Parents may have to travel long distances to be with their ill child, have to travel back and forth, and there may be parents who are only able to visit for a short time during the week. There are accompanying economic burdens as well as emotional worries that add to the stress these parents encounter. Even when the hospital treating the child is local, the parents often spend considerable time away from their other children and family members enabling them to have opportunities to talk to the medical team or consistently monitor their child's care. Further, a parent may need to take time off from a job to be with the child, adding to the high level of existing pressure surrounding the illness.

Fourth, because most parents are not knowledgeable about the inner workings of a hospital system, they may find *navigating* the complex world of medical care and privacy management daunting. For example, the ward round, designed to enable detailed discussion by professionals of a patient's condition and care, is central to the care of patients and may be a good opportunity for parents to meet the medical team (Shellabarger & Thompson, 1993). However, research suggests that frequent breaches of confidentiality take place during ward rounds and may increase the tensions parents feel (Rylance, 1999). For example, in one study, about half of parents with children in neonatal units reported they overheard conversations about other babies, and found that discussions about their baby had been overheard (Bramwell & Weindling, 2005). These parents also described concerns about communication, practicalities, and issues of ethics of care (Bramwell & Weindling, 2005).

Coupled with the stress of knowing their child is in need of immediate medical attention, the four critical factors identified here illustrate the complexity of gathering information under these trying circumstances. Consequently, healthcare providers, who need to obtain *critical information* from parents, are often met with resistance or confusion about what is being asked and why the questions are posed. Possibly, the questions parents are asked may be perceived by them as tangential or imposing. Yet, the medical team needs to depend on answers to those questions for essential clues to the illness or medical condition of the child to decipher the appropriate medical directions. Often, to obtain useful information, the parents' private information is needed to understand the illness or condition of the child and the surrounding circumstances pertinent to the medical condition. Thus, parents may find themselves faced with a serious, unanticipated event having to do with their child, dealing with healthcare providers who are strangers, in a hospital they do not know and is not where they live, and asked to disclose private information about their lives that they may not have told anyone else. In all, the critical factors that influence the anxieties a parent feels are many and set the stage for challenges the parent and the medical team face in order to help the child (Mu & Tomlinson, 1997).

Privacy Management in Medical Health Crises

Managing interactions in early medical crisis situations involves two intersecting issues. Healthcare providers need to solicit private information, and parents expect to manage the information flow. Parents attempt to control uncertainty in serious childhood illness primarily through information management (Stewart & Mishel, 2000). Parents' information management often includes intensive pursuit of information about the child's illness, with zealous alertness to cues from the child and healthcare providers about the child's condition (Stewart & Mishel, 2000). Parents may also manage information through careful evasion of social encounters and awareness of information that might draw attention to embarrassing or negative aspects of their lives and their feelings of uncertainty (Clarke-Steffen, 1993). The tension parents face between wanting both a sense of protected privacy and being willing to disclose information to secure treatment for a child is framed by CPM theory (Petronio, 2002). This tension shifts and jogs around a multitude of issues for the parents that includes face-saving, trust, emotional needs, family secrets, and converges around trying to keep the goal of healthcare for their child front and center.

To uncover some of the main considerations, CPM's five evidence-based principles help identify the management of a privacy-disclosure dialectic surrounding the way parents and providers untangle competing needs for information (Petronio, 2002). Structured using a boundary metaphor, CPM theory's five principles include: (a) people believe they own their private information that metaphorically resides within a privacy boundary and they claim the right to control it; (b) they control the information through the use of privacy rules; (c) once information is disclosed to others or they are granted access, the recipients (confidants) become co-owners; (d) as co-owners, synchronous boundary management depends on coordinating privacy rules to effectively regulate collectively held private information; (e) because boundary coordination does not work consistently or seamlessly, there are times when turbulence occurs and privacy violations or breaches take place. Given that these five principles work interactively together, we will discuss how the management of privacy operates when parents are coping with their child's medical crisis.

Navigating Privacy in a Child's Medical Crisis

The nature of the medical situations, such as parents coping with an unexpected childhood illness, often leads to problematic conditions regarding privacy issues (Petronio & Sargent, 2002). Parents of children with serious health concerns expect that they will be told critical information by the physician or other medical personnel. Parents have these expectations because they define the information about their child as belonging to them and under their control (Tates & Meeuwesen, 2001). Likewise, they believe it is within their rights to decide what information they tell the physician. However, the flow of information outward is not always commensurate with the demand for information coming back to them from the healthcare team. Parents often feel it is appropriate to make demands for information from the healthcare team that is greater than the amount of information they give back. These parental assumptions may be contradictory to the beliefs that physicians have about information management and ownership (Helft & Petronio, 2007). Physicians often consider test results, the medical assessment they make, and their observations about the medical condition as under their jurisdiction until they feel confident that they have a clear picture of what course of action they should prescribe. A dilemma can ensue when each party claims exclusive rights over the information unless there is ample conversation that suggests these embedded expectations about privacy rights are negotiated and therefore clearly known to both parties (Petronio, 1991).

If the parents and providers do not negotiate the way they both understand the treatment of information (in CPM terms, privacy rules) leading to a defined level of co-ownership that is mutually identifiable as shared, the emotional impact of this medical situation is likely to override "typical" interaction patterns between parents and providers resulting in challenges to rightful claims over the information (Petronio, 2007). However, the parents and the providers may not realize that they are vying to control the same information. Regardless of whether a parent tells the physician about this information, there is an expectation that any information about their child should remain in the parent's control and any judgment based on the information, biomedical or other, that calls for deciding a course of treatment is seen as proprietary to the parents but may also be defined as such for the providers.

Typically, families develop a set of privacy rules that, through repeated actions and mutually held expectations, define the parameters for how families, as a whole, regulate the flow, ownership, and who knows what about their private information that belongs to all family members (Petronio & Caughlin, 2005; Serewicz, Dickson, Morrison, & Poole, 2007). For providers, the difficulty resides in knowing how these families may react to inquires that are viewed as private (Petronio, Jones, & Morr, 2003). Some families may feel that any information they have might be of benefit to their child and they offer unlimited information to the healthcare team. Other families firmly close their boundaries around the information keeping it private to only the family (Petronio, 2000). Alternatively, other families may withhold only certain information because they feel it is justified because telling may make them look like bad parents, that telling certain kinds of information may make their child's health problem feel too real for them, or that telling may mean that other family members in attendance would know things they have kept secret from them. As CPM states, families develop a set of privacy rules they use to manage the flow of information both internally among themselves and externally to others outside their family (Petronio, 2002; Serewicz et al., 2007). But, because situational needs can function as a catalyst for changing privacy rules, even family members might be surprised at what they are or are not willing to disclose (Petronio, 2002; Petronio, 2006). In addition, whether they disclose may depend on how the providers and healthcare teams ask the questions. For example, parents may only reveal information about their experiences at home if the physicians illustrate why the home life is connected to the medical concern.

What may not be clear for providers is the transformation that takes place once the parents allow them to know the private information they request. When others are given permission to know private information or receive disclosures, CPM argues that the process of knowing makes the recipient a co-owner, shareholder, or stakeholder. Others are privy and therefore they are brought (linked) into the privacy boundary surrounding the information. In making others co-owners, there is a built-in expectation that the regulation of that information will be treated in similar ways as the original owner might handle the information. For physicians and other healthcare professionals, the definition of co-ownership held by them is more likely defined as a guardianship role (Helft & Petronio, 2007). Ideally, the medical team and parents, in the case of ill children, *would* negotiate the privacy rules for the mutually-owned private information. The physician *would* recognize that the family still claims the right to stipulate how, when, where, and who else might know the private medical information. Most importantly, the healthcare team, and particularly the physicians *would* see that where negotiations are needed to achieve the best outcome, conversations *would* take place to come to consensus about privacy management. Once this transformation occurs, that is, the information becomes mutually owned by those linked into a boundary, the privacy rules for regulating the information, theoretically, are negotiated, thereby achieving a measure of rule coordination among the co-owners. Whether the information is solicited, told by the original owner, or they were granted access, once the recipients have been entrusted with the information, they have certain obligations to uphold the way third parties know.

Doing so represents what CPM defines as coordinating the privacy rules for third party dissemination (Petronio, 2002). Petronio identifies three management processes used in achieving privacy rule coordination. Thus, (a) there are negotiations about boundary linkages where those privy mutually agree upon who else is able to know, (b) negotiations about boundary ownership or what rights the co-owners have to control the information, and last, (c) boundary permeability or how much, what kind, and when private information within the boundary flows to third parties (Petronio, 2002). In the circumstance of the provider-parent within the context of a child's health crisis, it is likely that the parents would give permission for other healthcare staff to know medical issues pertinent to the case. Yet, the parents may not stipulate the extent to which others beyond a certain medical group can know, the degree of ownership that is acceptable, or level of permeability that is allowed. From the perspective of providers, they may likely confer with the parents regarding who is privy outside of the medical team members, but they may not consider talking about the limits of their rights to disseminate the information, the extent to which they can make medical decisions without consultation with the parents, or the restrictions on how much information is either withheld or revealed to the parents and others. Because people make assumptions about expectations and the way they handle private information that belongs to others, CPM argues that rule coordination has the potential to breakdown and lead to turbulent interactions among those privy to the information (Petronio, 2002).

Making Assumptions that Result in Privacy Turbulence

As these points suggest, there are many built-in privacy ambiguities on the part of both providers and the parents. For example, a provider may assume that since the grandparents have been in conversations with the medical staff while the parents are present (thereby meeting the rule as set forth under the Health Insurance Portability and Accountability Act, HIPAA) that speaking frankly about the case to the parents in front of the grandparents is acceptable. Yet, the provider might be caught off guard when the parents, in no uncertain terms, reprimand him for talking about something in front of the grandparents (Petronio, Sargent, Andea, Reganis, & Cichocki, 2004). In this example, we see embedded beliefs about the acceptability of linking others into a privacy boundary, the level of ownership accorded, and the extent of permeability. Thus, in this case, there are issues that had not been discussed or negotiated with the provider regarding the disclosure of information but are clearly assumed by the provider. The lack of open discussion about the rules regulating disclosure of patient information can lead to privacy turbulence, as we see in this example, when the provider disclosed certain aspects of the child's medical conditions in front of the grandparents. For the provider in the case, discussing how the parents wanted him to make choices regarding who else could know and what they could know did not take place. If the provider had talked about these issues, he might have discovered that the parents defined that particular information as off-limits to the grandparents. This example illustrates how inconsistencies between the assumptions the provider made and the expectations the parents had about privacy management lead to what CPM calls a turbulent condition of privacy management (Caughlin & Petronio, 2004; Petronio, 2002). The outcome of these inconsistent assumptions, where the treatment of private information does not fit the expectations of the owners, can lead to a potential for distrust and increasing levels of discomfort (Petronio & Durham, 2008). Yet, as we found with the provider in this case, he took an action that was predicated on cues observed in the medical visit and presumed he was doing the right things. However, he did so without checking with the parents. Consequently, the provider encountered negative, angry, and upset reactions to having the grandparents be privy to information.

Turbulence may also occur in situations where specific information is solicited by the healthcare team. If parents feel that they have little control over what happens to information they disclose subsequently, they may feel uneasy or even resentful. However, they may justify revealing the information in terms of helping their child. Yet, these uneasy feelings may only be passing thoughts in the scheme of care for the child but their uneasiness may grow when disclosing private information to one team of specialists starts to raise questions about how much access other healthcare teams might have to their private information. Despite signing a HIPAA form technically stipulating the parameters of disclosure, the covering entities allowed to know by signing the form are wide and vast, perhaps far exceeding the expectations of dissemination (Bassett, 2007). Even if parents understood the parameters, by signing the HIPAA form, they have little opportunity to negotiate the terms of third party disclosures (Bassett, 2007). Moreover, the structure of fellows, residents, interns, nurses, and social workers gathering information that is reported back to an additional group of providers (perhaps specialists) further exacerbates the lack of power for further negotiation in parents' disclosure. For example, in hospital ward rounds parents may be inhibited by the presence of multiple treatment teams, jargonistic discussions, and the possibility of overhearing discussions that relate to other people's children (Bramwell & Weindling, 2005). During these rounds, parents are not in a position to negotiate how the information will be shared. There also may be situations where both families and the healthcare teams encounter unexpected emotional explosions by members that reveal information families may not want others to know. In all, parents' emotions such as guilt, worry, coming face-to-face with their anxieties and their long-term uncertainty increase the likelihood for turbulence because emotional resources are already challenged (Bonner, Hardy, Guill, McLaughlin, Schweitzer, & Carter, 2006).

Adding to the uncertainty and sense of turbulence is the range of information providers and the healthcare team pursue. Because one of the more salient aspects of crisis care is to quickly access needed health information about the patient, in the case where the patient is a child, the parents are viewed as the most valid and credible source. Though there has been a shift away from a biomedical approach to patient care and toward a communicatively based relationship-centered model, in times of acute need for information such as the circumstance of a child's unexpected, serious illness this situation brings many critical issues to bear in understanding the way that providers interact with distressed parents and how best to obtain needed information from the parents (Roter & Hall, 2006; Suchman, Roter, Greene & Lipkin, 1993).

Particularly if providers introduce topics that are perceived by the parents as private family information, the inquiries may not be welcome. When parents are coping with a child's unanticipated, serious medical condition, they may not be prepared to disclose the onslaught of information being requested by the physician and medical teams. Parents often cannot get clear or definitive facts about their child's situation and the ambiguous nature of the situation itself can frequently result in feelings of hopelessness and confusion (Berge & Holm, 2007; Boss, 1999). Furthermore, family members can also experience ambiguity about what is expected of them in the context of the child's care (Boss, 1999). During these medical situations, the healthcare personnel may not have time to fully explain the reasons they are asking certain kinds of information. Additionally, some of the questions may seem unexpected or scary because the team might need to discern whether the medical emergency is accidental or intentional. Parents of a child born with a life-threatening or potentially fatal condition also have unclear perceptions about whether the ill child will become a vital member of their family. Yet, the family may feel that voicing these concerns validates their worst fears (Boss, 1999). Outside of the context of serious illness, parents may be allowed the ability to preserve a tighter privacy boundary around information that they do not want to readily share. However, both within the context of serious illness and particularly for providers ascribing to a relational approach to illness, the boundaries between biomedical information and the effect of the child's illness on roles and relationships become more salient but complicated. In comparison to providers and the care staff, parents may have an inconsistent view of where privacy boundaries begin and end. Parents may reject inquiries from providers, not necessarily out of defensiveness, but because they are fearful of how the information might be interpreted by the healthcare team. Parents may also find that they are asked information that generally violates their privacy expectations, but they may be uncertain whether disclosing the information is essential to their child's care. In the end, parents must judge the validness of inquiries that violate their notion of privacy.

Thus, as we mentioned earlier, children's serious health concerns have the potential to shift privacy rules that are used to make judgments about disclosure or concealing information. Challenges to an otherwise stable family system impacts existing relationships among the members and changes the way that parents may interact with healthcare providers. Depending on a family's experience with privacy turbulence and assumptions that are somehow not met by the medical team when it comes to private information, family members may be reluctant to make complete disclosures. More likely, members might incrementally disclose, checking to see the extent to which the information adds to an understanding or compromises a sense of credibility (Petronio, Reeder, Hecht, & Mon't Ros-Mendoza, 1996).

As seems evident, these kinds of health situations represent complex privacy management experiences for both the family and providers. For the healthcare team to achieve a productive health outcome, one of the issues necessary is to learn how to negotiate privacy boundaries held by families. For families, learning how best to communicate with providers when there is high stress and a concomitant perceived need for protecting private information, parents and particularly physicians need to work out communicative strategies that accomplish the goal of care for the child. We know that physician's ability to be empathic, show concern, and communicate altruism is generally associated with effective communication and quality, we know less about the choices that physicians make negotiating private information they need to care for others, particularly children in the kinds of medical crises we have outlined above (Bertakis et al., 1998).

Provider Privacy Management Skills

Physicians' information management skills can be informed by CPM (Petronio, 2002). Knowing that people believe they have the right to control information they define as belonging to them means that physicians asking parents questions should also seek out parents' privacy rules for third party dissemination. Similarly, if physicians are mindful of those parental privacy rules, they may have an easier time developing and maintaining relationships with their patients and family members. Once privy to the information, the responsibility of regulating telling others may be accomplished more effectively according to the expectations of the patients and family. Doing so may increase the likelihood that a better relationship can be achieved to attain the most productive kind of healthcare. Knowing when to disclose the condition and the best way to find out needed information contributes to a better working relationship between providers and families. Clearly, part of learning privacy management skills includes the understanding of how timing and control become important.

Synchronization of privacy rules is important to avoid breaches in rules, but the level of uncertainty and expectation for privacy on the part of the parents may conflict with the need for critical information on the part of physicians (Petronio, 2002). Timing of disclosures and continued control over dissemination rights of family private information poses implications for boundary coordination. First, the timing of physician and parent disclosures is important. "The patient [and parents] needs information about their disease, but also needs time and space for shaping thoughts about their situation" (Meyskens, Hietanen, & Tannock, 2005). Parents, physicians, and children may disclose information before the other is prepared to hear the information or at an inappropriate time. For example, parents may not disclose enough information in the beginning for physicians to direct care appropriately. Similarly, parents may disclose too much too late, or they may disclose when the physicians cannot act on the information. Physicians too may tell too much after parents make decisions about directions for treatment, and parents then may not be able to act on the information. Likewise, the children may also provide information, disclosing more than the parents want physicians to know about the family.

Control is also related to dissemination or access rights. Parents expect to have control over medical information because they feel that information belongs to the family. But, physicians may feel that the same medical information is the biological basis for diagnosis and understanding, thus assuming the information is within the continued control of the medical team. Further complicating the interactions, older children, for example, may feel they should have ultimate control over how the information is portrayed because it is about them. As a result, we may find a host of untested assumptions that are used to make decisions such as physicians taking for granted that they have control over *how* other physicians and medical staff know the family's information, over how much information other physicians and staff know, and over *whom else* has ownership rights to the information. Similarly, parents may feel they should decide *which* physicians have access to their information, *how* other physicians and family members know, and *who else* can share the story. Thus, parents, physicians, and children may all feel they control rights to third party access or dissemination, though they may not have discussed the issues surrounding those outside of this core who have been privy to the private family information. Only when there is a conflict will the assumptions about control over the information become apparent. As a result, when medical teams are able to learn basic tenets of how people manage their privacy, it is likely that better patient/family member/provider relationships can prevail.

Conclusions

Interpersonal communication that involves a child's illness poses unique challenges for parents, providers, and the children. Negotiations between parents and physicians involve subtle relational, ethical, and professional boundaries that, at times, are not clearly understood by the individual parties. Exploring ways these relationships, and the boundaries that define them, have been coordinated, particularly between a physician or the medical staff, parents of an ill child, and possibly the child with severe health concerns, helps us see that mistakes in assumptions about disclosure and control over private information needed for care of the child can hamper timely and productive treatment. Depending on the circumstances, physicians may be more or less adaptive at fostering the most beneficial relationship with parents of ill children. In addition, there may be situations where one parent disagrees with the other parent lapsing into conflict over the best course of treatment for the child. Similarly, an older child may have a different agenda than the parents. Physicians may find it difficult in navigating the parents' disagreements with one another and with their child and even less well equipped in handling the underlying fear that is possibly the root cause for the dispute. Family history, patterns of dealing with stress, and the current state of family relationships intervene where high pressure situations occur. As a result, these tensions complicate making decisions about the child's health. Physicians are likely to encounter uncertainty regarding the best relational course of action, understanding family roles, and determining how best to plot a course for different family boundaries, particularly those surrounding privacy and disclosure. In addition, the families may find it troublesome to understand the way physicians and the healthcare teams are communicating with them about the best course of action for their child.

Through the lens of Communication Privacy Management (Petronio, 2002), this chapter examined the physician-parent-child relationship in the context of a child's unanticipated, serious illness and the ways psychosocial and emotional concerns are balanced with health concerns. Explaining communication dynamics in terms of privacy management poses implications for who is responsible for revealing or concealing details about family life, about emotions, and about family systems that impact the care of an ill child. CPM theory poses implications for the ways in which families play a role in advancing the health of their children as illustrated during high crisis times of medical need (Petronio, 2002). The application of CPM theory provides a map for ways physicians and the medical staff can involve parents, the child, and family members as allies in the child's health by recognizing the significance of learning the family's rules that regulate privacy. Doing so eases the availability of having families grant or deny access to important private information that bears on the medical condition of their child. Similarly, parent-physician-child interactions illustrate the complexity in creating an environment in which children feel comfortable to participate in their medical treatment but where parents are ultimately responsible for decision making. This chapter illustrates the ways parents face communicative challenges (i.e., emotional concerns that may conflict with health treatment), the importance of physicians and the medical staff negotiating boundaries to build effective interpersonal relationships with parents while addressing issues of privacy surrounding care.

As this chapter illustrates, previous research documents the importance of measuring the ways the patient perceives and engages in the relationship, as well as the ways physicians engage and validate patient participation in decision making. The current chapter expands on that research by identifying the ways earlier research can be expanded to better understand the role of privacy management in communication with parents facing a child's health crisis as they traverse conversations between themselves, their family member, physicians, medical care teams, and even the ill child. The application of Communication Privacy Management illustrates the utility of the theory in explaining how interpersonal communication about health can be shaped by privacy expectations of parents and healthcare providers.

References

Adams, R. J., & Parrott, R. L. (1994). Pediatric nurses' communication of role expectations to parents of hospitalized children. *Journal of Applied Communication Research*, *22*(1), 36–47.

Als, H. (1986). A synactive model of neonatal behavioral organization: Framework for the assessment of neurobehavioral development in the premature infant and for support of infants and parents in the neonatal intensive care environment. *Physical and Occupational Therapy in Pediatrics*, *6*, 3–53.

American Psychological Association. (1994). *Diagnostic and statistical manual of mental disorders: DSM-IV* (4th ed.), Washington, DC: Author.

Bassett, S. D. (2007). Exploring the issue of confidentiality. *Nurse-Educator*, *32*(4), 147–148.

Berge, J. M., & Holm, K. E. (2007). Boundary ambiguity in parents with chronically ill children: Integrating theory and research. *Family Relations*, *56*, 123–134.

Bertakis, K. D., Callahan, E. J., Helms, L. J., Azari, R., Robbins, J. A., & Miller, J. (1998). Physician practice styles and patient outcomes: Difference between family practice and general internal medicine. *Medical Care*, *36*, 879–891.

Bonner, M. J., Hardy, K. K., Guill, A. B., McLaughlin, C., Schweitzer, H., Carter, K. (2006). Development and validation of the parent experience of child illness. *Journal of Pediatric Psychology*, *31*(3), 310–321.

Boss, P. (1999). *Ambiguous loss*. Cambridge, MA: Harvard University Press.

Bramwell, R., & Weindling, M. (2005). Families' views on ward rounds in neonatal units. *Archives of Disease in Childhood, Fetal and Neonatal edition*, *90*(5), F429–431.

Caughlin, J. P., & Petronio, S. (2004). Privacy in families. In A.L. Vangelisti (Ed.), *Handbook of family communication* (pp. 379–412). Mahwah, NJ: Erlbaum.

Clarke-Steffen, L. (1993). Waiting and not knowing: the diagnosis of cancer in a child. *Journal of Pediatric Oncology Nursing*, *10*, 146–153.

Cohen, M. (1993). Diagnostic closure and the spread of uncertainty. *Issues in Comprehensive Pediatric Nursing*, *16*, 135–146.

Helft, P., & Petronio, S. (2007). Communication pitfalls with cancer patients: Hit and run: Deliveries of bad news. *Journal of American College of Surgeons*, *205*, 807–811.

Meyskens, F. L., Hietanen, P., & Tannock, I. F. (2005). Talking to a patient. *Journal of Clinical Oncology, 23*(19), 4463–4465.

Mu, P., & Tomlinson, P. (1997). Parental experience and meaning construction during a pediatric health crisis. *Western Journal of Nursing Research, 19,* 608–636.

Ogilvie, L. (1990). Hospitalization of children for surgery: The parents' view. *Children's Health Care, 19*(1), 49–56.

Petronio, S. (1991). Communication boundary management: A theoretical model of managing disclosure of private information between marital couples. *Communication Theory, 1,* 311–335.

Petronio, S. (2000). The boundaries of privacy: Praxis of everyday life. In S. Petronio (Ed.), *Balancing the secrets of private disclosures.* (pp. 37–49). Mahwah, NJ: Erlbaum.

Petronio, S. (2002). *Boundaries of privacy: Dialectics of disclosure.* Albany: State University of New York Press.

Petronio, S. (2006). Impact of medical mistakes: Negotiating work-family boundaries for physicians. *Communication Monographs, 73,* 462–467.

Petronio, S. (2007). Translational endeavors and the practices of Communication Privacy Management. *Journal of Applied Communication Research, 35,* 218–222.

Petronio, S., & Caughlin, J. P. (2005). Communication Privacy Management theory: Understanding families. In D. O. Braithwaite & L.A. Baxter (Eds.), *Engaging theories in family communication: Multiple perspectives* (pp. 35–49. Thousand Oaks, CA: Sage.

Petronio, S., & Durham, W. (2008). Understanding and applying Communication Privacy Management theory. In L. A. Baxter & D. O. Braithwaite (Eds.), *Engaging theories in interpersonal communication* (pp. 309–322). Thousand Oaks, CA: Sage.

Petronio, S., & Jones, S. M. (2006). When "friendly advice" becomes a privacy dilemma for pregnant couples: Applying Communication Privacy Management theory. In R. West & L. Turner (Eds.), *The Family communication sourcebook* (pp. 201–218). Thousand Oaks, CA: Sage.

Petronio, S., Jones, S. M., & Morr, M. C. (2003). Family privacy dilemmas: Managing communication boundaries within family groups. In L. Frey (Ed.), *Group communication in context: Studies of bona fide groups* (pp. 23–56). Mahwah, NJ: Erlbaum.

Petronio, S., Reeder, H. M., Hecht, M., & Mon't Ros-Mendoza, T. (1996). Disclosure of sexual abuse by children and adolescents. *Journal of Applied Communication Research, 24,* 181–199.

Petronio, S., Sargent, J., Andea, L. Reganis, P., & Cichocki, D. (2004). Family and friends as informal healthcare advocates. *Journal of Social and Personal Relationships, 21,* 33–52.

Petronio, S., & Sargent J. (2002). Disclosure and privacy in marriage and families. *International encyclopedia of marriage and family (2nd ed.)* (Vol. 3, pp. 1414–1418). New York: Macmillan Reference USA.

Roter, D. L., & Hall, J. A. (2006). *Doctors talking with patients / Patients talking with doctors: Improving communication in medical visits.* Westport, CT: Praeger.

Rylance, G. (1999). Privacy, dignity, and confidentiality: Interview study with structured questionnaire. *British Medical Journal, 318,* 301.

Santacroce, S. J. (2003). Parental uncertainty and posttraumatic stress in serious childhood illness. *Journal of Nursing Scholarship, 35*(1), 45–51.

Serewicz, M. C. M., Dickson, F., Morrison, J. H. T. A., & Poole, L. L. (2007). Family privacy orientation, relational maintenance, and family satisfaction in young adults' family relationships. *Journal of Family Communication, 7,* 123–142.

Shellabarger, S. G., & Thompson, T. L. (1993). The critical times: meeting parental communication needs throughout the NICU experience. *Neonatal Network, 12*(2), 39–45.

Stewart, J., & Mishel, M. (2000). Uncertainty in childhood illness: A synthesis of the parent and child literature. *Scholarly Inquiry for Nursing Practice, 14*, 299–319.

Stivers, T. (2001). Negotiating who presents the problem: Next speaker selection in pediatric encounters. *Journal of Communication, 51*(2), 252–282.

Stuber, M. (1995). Stress response to pediatric cancer: A family phenomenon. *Family Systems Medicine, 13*, 163–172.

Suchman, A. L., Roter, D. L., Greene, M., & Lipkin, M., Jr. (1993). Physician's satisfaction with primary care office visits. *Medical Care, 31*, 1083–1092.

Tates, K., & Meeuwesen, L. (2001). Doctor-parent-child communication. A (re)view of the literature. *Social Science and Medicine, 52*, 839–851.

8 The Role of Communication in Child-Parent-Provider Interaction in a Children's Mental Health System of Care

Christine S. Davis, Norín Dollard, and Keren S. Vergon

This chapter examines system of care principles in practice in child-parent-provider interactions among children with Severe Emotional Disturbances[1] (SED), their families, and mental healthcare providers, using systems theory as the overarching metatheory to explore these interactions. Within this metatheoretical perspective, we also investigate these interactions from the concepts of framing and sensemaking, meeting structure and communication networks, and empowerment and social roles.

Mental and emotional disturbances in children are more pervasive than one might think: between 17% and 22% of children under age 18 have been diagnosed with some form of mental illness, mental illness has been recognized as a major cause of childhood disability, and almost 7 million children between 9 and 17 years old have been diagnosed with SED. Nationally, researchers estimate that 5% to 9% of children have a high level of functional impairment, and 21% have minimal impairment, from emotional disturbances (Faenza & Steel, 1999; Halfon & Newacheck, 1999; Lezak & MacBeth, 2002).

In this chapter, we first briefly describe our main metatheory, systems theory. We next explain and describe the children's mental health system of care process and its team-based approach to care. We then describe our research study that observed and explored child-family-provider interactions in children's mental health system of care team meetings. Finally, we discuss our findings—that these systems of care operate within a system orientation that is subject to issues of framing and sensemaking, meeting structure and communication networks, and team member empowerment and social roles. Using these communication theories and concepts, we describe the ways that team communication facilitates and hinders enactment of the system of care principles.

Systems Theory

The systems theory of communication, based on biological General Systems Theory, is a theory of interactional patterns and processes. This theory defines a system as a group of people who are bound together in relationship by their communication behaviors, existing within an environment that affects and is affected by the people in the system. Human systems are open (i.e., they exchange energy or information with their environment), and thus should be studied in their environmental context. Systems overlap other systems (e.g., a family system is a subsystem of a community system). Open systems have several properties: wholeness (they behave not as an aggregate of parts, but as a coherent whole, and they have an emergent quality that arises out of the interrelationship of the elements in the system); feedback (they interact through a process of continuous feedback loops); and equifinality (the same results may come from different conditions and causes). Systems are characterized by homeostasis, a state in which feedback mechanisms create an equilibrium in which change is minimized. When studying communication in a system, the pattern of communication is more important than the actual content of communication, because communicative statements do not occur in isolation. This idea leads to the concept of schismogenesis, which says that communication patterns can be either symmetrical (partners mirror each other's behavior), or complementary (behaviors complement each other). These interchanges are defined within the social or cultural context (Sabourin, 2006; Watzlawick, Beavin, & Jackson, 1967).

The systems approach to family and family therapy is well documented. This approach revolutionized and complexified family therapy by recognizing the interactional and holistic elements in the family, looking at the family as a whole (Sabourin, 2006). Family theorists hypothesized that mental illness in the family was the result of dysfunctional communication in the family system. Mental illness or deviance, in this view, represents a homeostatic mechanism in the family system, and is seen as behavior that serves a function in the context of the family system (Bochner & Eisenberg, 1987; Hoffman, 1981; Laing & Esterson, 1970; Minuchin, 1993; Sieburg, 1985). Systems theory says that each member of the system is significant to its functioning, and change in one part can change the entire system (Minuchin, 1993; Minuchin & Fishman, 1981; Laing & Esterson, 1970). Family-centered healthcare among social work, psychology, psychiatry, and physical rehabilitation practitioners, and in children's mental health systems of care, takes on a system focus in their treatment of the entire family to promote health and well being (Seligman & Darling, 1997), and later systems therapists include themselves as part of the family system (Minuchin, 1993). Systems theorists understand that a family in distress can involve their entire nuclear family and even the larger systems of which they are a part, in their problems (Hoffman, 1981). Systems consist of elements and processes including boundaries, roles, rules, and feedback (Sabourin, 2006), as well as social networks and relationships (Bryant & Bryant, 2006; Schmeeckle & Sprecher, 2004).

Three theories that extend systems theory are relationship chaos theory (Weigel & Murray, 2000), macrosystemic theory (Laveman, 2000), and constructionist family systems theory (Yerby, 1995).

Relationship Chaos Theory focuses on relational change processes in social systems. This theory says that relationships are chaotic, dynamic systems and as such have an imbalance between order and disorder. In these systems, change can be random and unpredictable. Seemingly insignificant events "may cause a ripple of other events that can drastically alter the course of a relationship" (Weigel & Murray, 2000, p. 430), and relationships experience periods of stability and of instability. The system organizes itself through interaction between the parts of the system and between the system and its environment.

The macrosystemic model takes its idea from the concept of a holon, parts within parts, each fully whole yet also part of the larger structure. This perspective builds on systems theory by recognizing the social constructionist nature of interaction within the system (Laveman, 2000).

Constructionist Family Systems Perspective (Yerby, 1995) suggests an incorporation of family systems theory with social construction theory in which family communication would be viewed as evolutionary, contradictory, culturally and socially constrained and linguistically constructed. Yerby points out the benefits of systems theory, which was responsible for shifting the focus from individuals to the interrelationships in the family system, and suggests an update of the theory based on social construction principles and dialectical theory (which recognizes the dialectical contradictions inherent in interpersonal relationships). These three extensions of systems theory point to the importance of studying communication within a system of care to understand how system of care principles are constructed through discourse.

System of Care Principles

The children's mental health system of care, philosophically, is a system-based approach. In this approach, providers view individual children systemically, within the context of their physical, mental, and emotional systems, and within their family system and their community system, including extended family, neighbors, clergy, and other informal supports. In addition, providers also view their healthcare and support services systemically, within the holistic array of multiagency, multidisciplinary services. The system of care approach emphasizes family involvement in which families of children with SED are treated as full participants in the planning and delivery of services, and in which their needs determine the services provided. This approach also emphasizes a comprehensive, coordinated, community-based system of care that brings together all agencies and resources needed to provide services to children with SED and their families. Since children with SED typically have multiple needs, they are frequently served by multiple agencies and organizations, such as education, social service, juvenile justice, physical health, mental health, vocational, recreation, and substance abuse providers. A system of care approach is an interagency approach in which agencies must work together to develop and coordinate services for the individual child and family. Key to the system of care process is case management, intended to coordinate and integrate the service components within the system (Stroul & Friedman, 1994).

Team-Based Approach to Care

Case management in systems of care is accomplished through teams in which children, parents or caregivers, professionals, and informal supports meet regularly to coordinate and plan services with and for the child and his/her family. In general, a team consists of informal supports such as extended family, neighbors, or clergy; and formal supports such as therapists, juvenile probation officers, case managers, family advocates, and school representatives; depending on perceived child, family, and team information needs and agency involvement. Child and family teams meet regularly in planning meetings to discuss, write, plan, and update an individualized service or support plan, also known as a Family Support Plan (FSP).

Researchers (e.g., Cohen & Bailey, 1997; Guzzo & Dickson, 1996; Kayser, 1994; Senge, 1990) suggest many benefits to a team-based approach. When a group makes decisions as a whole, members show great support. A team approach can create cohesion and team building among group members. Members of effective teams respect and trust their fellow team members, demonstrate well-honed group skills, are productive and proactive, are more motivated, feel more responsible for the team's success, have a higher commitment to help each other succeed, and have less stress and more enjoyment of the task (Guzzo & Dickson, 1996; Kayser, 1994; Senge, 1990). In addition, team collaboration increases team cohesion, and group cohesion results in higher team performance (Cohen & Bailey, 1997; Guzzo & Dickson, 1996). However, group approaches to decision making are also subject to negative processes such as groupthink, a tendency toward unquestioned acceptance of poor quality decisions, especially in the face of group cohesion and threat to member esteem (Janis, 1982; Turner, Pratkanis, Probasco, & Leve, 1992). It is not clear, then, whether a team-based approach to children's mental health helps or hinders facilitation of a system of care orientation. This chapter uses systems theory to look at how child-family-provider interaction within team meetings affects the system of care process. Within the lens of systems theory as a metatheory, we also investigate these interactions from the concepts of framing and sensemaking, meeting structure and communication networks, and empowerment and social roles.

Research Objectives

Team meetings provide a rich opportunity to view team processes in a naturalistic setting. Although observing these meetings does not allow for a complete view of family and team communication, it does provide in-depth snapshots of family and team interaction at important moments in the life of the team. Since service coordination is critical to the system of care philosophy, this research observed the mechanisms behind, and the success of, these child and family teams to act as coordinated systems of care. These snapshots allowed us to address the following research questions (RQ):

RQ1: How do child-family-provider interactions and communication patterns within system of care team meetings facilitate or hinder the key system of care principles in which families of children with SED are treated as full participants in the planning and delivery of services?

RQ2: How do child-family-provider interactions and communication patterns within system of care team meetings facilitate or hinder the key system of care principles in which the needs of children and families determine the services provided?

Method

Research Site

The research site is a children's mental health system of care in a medium-sized southeast city. This system of care, funded from 1998–2004 by a grant from the Child and Family Branch of the Center for Mental Health Services (CMHS) in the Federal Substance Abuse and Mental Health Services Administration (SAMHSA), was a community-based initiative intended to integrate mental health, human, and social services to children with serious emotional disturbances and their families. The project served children identified as having SED, either by the school system, or by a mental health practitioner. Children served by this project were under the age of 22 and received services from more than one human service agency.

Study Design

The Child and Family Team Meeting Observation project was a substudy of a longitudinal study measuring children and families' outcomes. The unit of analysis for this project was the child and family team planning meeting. This research involved a combination of a quantitative checklist (Epstein et al., 1998; Epstein et al., 2003), and a qualitative, ethnographic methodology that was suggested by Eber, Nelson, and Miles (1997) to be the best approach to evaluate a dynamic system in process, such as a mental health care system. This multiple case study approach allowed us to look at system of care practices, to describe them in their naturally occurring context, and to capture in-depth, rich data (Hernandez et al., 2001).

Over the course of 3 years, our research team observed 118 child and family team meetings. There were a total of 16 observers. Each observer went through an extensive training session to understand exactly what behaviors they were to notice and write down. The training consisted of two parts: a one-half day training going over research protocols and procedures, then shadowing another observer until inter-observer reliability on objective observations (life domains addressed in the meetings, system of care principles exhibited), reached adequate levels (80%). Overall, inter-observer reliability on meetings attended by two observers was 90% for life domains addressed and 80% for system of care principles exhibited. The latter of these two measures, not the focus of this chapter, will not be discussed. The training used an extensive 80-page protocol manual. For each meeting, one to two observers attended and, in addition to the objective measurements, took detailed field notes. We wrote down observed behaviors; verbal and nonverbal communication; general background comments about the meeting or the family, youth, or team; contextual comments and observations; and summary comments to help frame the meeting in its entirety. All observations were followed by a detailed debriefing session with both observers and the study project director (first author of this chapter). Fifty-three of the meetings were observed by one observer, and 65 of the meetings were observed by two observers. The three authors personally attended 51 of the meetings, either by ourselves (25 meetings) or with another observer (26 meetings), and the first author was involved in the debriefing sessions for all 118 meetings.

Site Background

The meetings observed represented five different agencies within the one system of care site providing case management and team facilitation and leadership, 33 team leaders, and 91 families. Most (63%) of the meetings observed were initial meetings, that is, the first meeting with the team, but over one third of the meetings (35%) were maintenance meetings, and three were discharge team meetings. Most (58%) of the meetings were held at school. Other meetings were held at the family's home, agency office, or residential treatment facility. On average, the meetings had just under 7 attendees, ranging from 3 to 20, although most meetings had between 4 and 10 attendees. The average meeting was 68 minutes long, and the meetings ranged in length from 5 to 225 minutes. Most meetings were between 30 and 120 minutes.

Meetings were most attended by a team leader, caregiver, family advocate, school teacher, and school social worker. Other, less frequent attendees, included extended family (24%), other school representative (23%), an outside therapist (30%), a case manager or social worker (child welfare; 13%), the youth (27%), and other informal supports (8%).

The children enrolled in services had a history of psychiatric hospitalizations, physical abuse, sexual abuse, running away, suicide attempts, and substance abuse. Their biological family histories included family violence, mental illness, psychiatric hospitalization, crime convictions, and substance abuse. Their diagnoses included ADHD, depression, disruptive disorder, adjustment disorder, and other major psychiatric disorders. Children participating in this research were mostly male (82%), age 6 to 16 (mean 12), in the custody of one or two biological parents (68%), with a family household income between $20,000 and $25,000.

Many of the child and family team meetings were called for a specific purpose, that is, to discuss a change in school IEP (Individualized Educational Plan) or to address a crisis situation. Discussions at these meetings were fairly broad and systemically-focused. The meetings tended to look at both the child or youth and his/her parents or caregivers, and focused on many different aspects of their lives. On average, 5.9 life domains were addressed in a child and family team planning meeting. The domains covered in a meeting depended on the needs of that particular child and family at that particular time. In initial meetings, treatment plans tended to address mental health, education, and family domains. In maintenance meetings, plans tended to address those domains, but also more legal, medical, residential, and vocational domains. This likely reflected two matters: As families got to know their team leaders and family advocates better, they may have become open to divulging additional information and additional needs to them; and, as the initial crisis issues were addressed, teams began to work on more long-term empowerment goals such as improving the family's vocational situation. The mental health domain was discussed in 9 out of 10 meetings; the education and family domains were discussed in 8 out of 10 meetings; and the social/recreational domain was discussed in about three fourths of the meetings. The substance abuse domain was rarely discussed. Typically, the cultural domain was not discussed directly, but when cultural issues were specifically included in the plan of care, they tended to concern religious, neighborhood, or extended family issues. Legal issues were typically not discussed unless there was a specific legal problem that needed to be addressed in the meeting, such as an impending court hearing. The medical domain was usually not discussed at length, but may have been brought up briefly, perhaps in a discussion about a parent or caregiver's health, a discussion about medical treatment for a child living in a residential facility, or a concern that the child's problems may be related to a medical problem or condition. The mental health domain was almost always at least mentioned, often in relation to medications. Often, this domain was the focus of the meeting, and much discussion typically centered around problem behaviors, changes toward more positive behaviors, or consequences to problem behaviors.

The residential domain was included in the plan of care in about one third of the meetings. This might have related to a change of placement or a change in restriction for a youth in a residential facility. It might also have related to a change in the family's residence. The safety domain tended to only be mentioned if specific safety issues (emotional or physical, to the child/youth and/or the family) were of concern at the meeting. This domain came up in about one third of the case plans. The social/recreational domain was often mentioned, often in connection with informal supports, strengths, community involvement, or peer influences on the child/youth. Substance abuse was only mentioned if it was a focus of the meeting, and it was only included in treatment plans in about 10% of the meetings. The vocational domain was included in treatment plans in about one third of the meetings, usually in a discussion of the youth's part time job or future vocational plans, and sometimes in a discussion of the parent's job. The financial domain was included in treatment plans in a little over one third of the meetings. Financial issues typically included parental ability to pay for a child's needs (e.g., medical care), or other family financial issues.

Data Analysis

In the coding and analysis of the field notes, we used a constructivist approach to grounded theory (Charmaz, 2000; Glaser & Strauss, 1967; Strauss & Corbin, 1990). Grounded theory is a systematic, multistep, rigorous coding process that yields targeted interpretive themes. The first author studied the field notes, posed questions, and made analytical notations as interacting with the data itself yielded more questions, ideas, and theories. She next conducted open coding, which consists of creating categories as she further studied the field notes, continued to build ideas, and analyzed the data inductively. Her interpretations first shaped and focused her research questions, then continued to shape emerging codes, categories, themes, and theories. The next step in grounded theory is to conduct line-by-line coding, building ideas inductively, using sensitizing concepts—background ideas that inform the overall research problem. It was at this point that she began specifically noticing the application of the five communication concepts discussed in this chapter, especially systems theory (Other sensitizing concepts also emerged that are the subject of other papers; see Davis, 2008; Davis, 2006). Coding at this point typically consists of action codes—codes of what people are doing and what is happening. Line-by-line coding uses the constant comparative method in which the researcher compares people, views, situations, actions, accounts, experiences, data, points in time, incidents, and categories. The next step in grounded theory is axial coding—connecting categories and sub-categories, subsuming many codes in each. This is the point at which she began to further develop the five concepts illustrated in this chapter. To prepare this chapter, once she had decided to focus on the five communication concepts, she used theoretical sampling, focusing on specific examples of that concept to shed light on that emerging theory. As she further coded and analyzed, she continued to refine ideas until she reached the point of saturation—the point at which no new ideas, themes, or categories emerged.

Grounded theory is an extensive processes in which the data analyst seeks intimate familiarity with the data—seeking meanings, views, values, beliefs, and ideologies. In grounded theory, categories are consistent with the studied life, based on patterns observed from the field notes (Bulmer, 1979; Charmaz, 2000; Stake, 1995). Because of the extensive and rigorous nature of grounded theory coding, this method of analysis typically uses only one coder, who, in this case, was the first author. However, as part of the analytical rigor and to insure the reliability of the findings, the concepts in this chapter were discussed in depth during the de-briefing sessions with the co-authors and with the primary members of the research team. In addition, the findings were taken through a member check via discussions with system of care case managers and team leaders and co-authors. In this chapter, we substantiated the categories by illustrations from the field notes.

Discussion

There were many ways in which child-family-provider team meeting interactions affected the ability of the team to allow families to be full partners in the planning and delivery of services and to fully address and meet their needs. This chapter will discuss the five main ways: (a) the extent to which the team actually operates as a system, (b) the way the team frames or makes sense of the meeting, (c) the structure of the meeting and the related communicative networks operating in the meeting, (d) the manner of empowerment of the team members, and (e) the role ambiguity or clarity evident in the meetings. As in any system, these factors are interconnected and interrelated. We suggest that, in order to fully adhere to system of care principles, there is a need for team meetings to be framed into a system orientation. This framing creates specific roles for the individual players in the team, which causes them to interact in a manner that supports or detracts from a system orientation. The meeting frame is influenced by the meeting structure, the communicative networks, and the empowerment and social roles of the team members.

Teams as Systems

A systems orientation is an attitude held by a team and its members. Systems theorists say that, in a system, the whole is greater than the sum of its parts, and the whole is made up of parts that are interconnected and interrelated (Watzlawick et al., 1967). In other words, groups operating as a system recognize that as a group, they can do far more together than they can accomplish separately. According to systems theorists, successful teams recognize that "We're all in this together. Success is team success, rewards are team rewards, and if the team fails, the members share the blame" (Parker, 1994, p. 5). Systems theorists also say that the relationships among the people in a group are what make the group a system (Watzlawick et al., 1967). In theory, child and family teams embrace this concept. In fact, this is why child and family teams are formed, because the involved organizations and policy makers understand the importance of coordination of efforts between organizations. However, in practice, these child and family teams did not always fully take advantage of their systemic nature.

In a system, instead of objects, there are relationships (Watzlawick et al., 1967). The team meetings showed evidence of some form of relationships between some of the participants, but not all of them. For example, some of the team members knew each other professionally outside of the team, and while participants were waiting for meetings to begin, these members might have been seen chatting with each other. The pre-existing relationships between the family and the team leader, and the lack of pre-existing relationships between the family and other team members often affected interactions during the meeting, with some participants talking in dyads, others not talking at all, and others only talking to certain people. Some comments were made during the meetings that indicated that individuals worked together outside the meeting to meet team objectives, but other participants seemed to leave the meetings without continuing team relationships outside of the meetings.

Systems theorists also suggest that instead of fragmentation, there is whole- ness (Watzlawick et al., 1967). The meetings often appeared fragmented, with members talking in dyads and seeming to participate only at certain points of the meeting. Most meetings included one or two members who said virtually nothing and were much more an observer than a participant. We observed a few notable exceptions, in which the team communicated in a way that could be described as "artful," with members seamlessly playing off of one another's comments, questions, strengths, and skills. This type of artful communication was characterized in these meetings by smooth turn taking and transitions, lengthy exchanges between all or most participants, and content indicating deeper levels of knowledge of each other.

Systems theorists suggest that each dimension of reality is interconnected with all other dimensions of reality (Watzlawick et al., 1967). This concept is the key to the system of care philosophy. By design, child and family teams address all of the major life domains of the child and family: cultural/spiri- tual, educational, family, legal, medical, mental health, residential, safety, social/recreational, substance abuse, vocational, and financial. In addition, by design, child and family teams treat the family holistically, within their system of informal supports such as extended families, neighbors, friends, and clergy. Because of this, in theory, child and family teams are made up of individu- als from many of these life domain and support areas. However, in practice, many of the nonprofessional team members, those from some of the less tra- ditional life domains (e.g., clergy, extended family, friends, and neighbors), did not always act in the meetings as full team partners. They spoke less and were spoken to less (they often said nothing and were ignored by the other meeting participants), they tended to only participate when directly invited to do so, and when they did talk in meetings, their topics of conversation were much more limited and of shorter duration.

In a system, the leader generates the environment and climate and creates the mind-set and the vision of the organization. However, systems theorists also say that changes in any part of the system will affect the entire system (Watzlawick et al., 1967). Related to this is the idea that organisms and organi- zations are unpredictable, uncontrollable, and unmanageable, and are always on the edge of chaos. One small event can have totally unforeseeable system- wide consequences. This concept was seen only indirectly in these meetings, with the observation that these meetings were very difficult to facilitate for the team leaders and that any team participant potentially had the power to disrupt the meeting dynamics. Team members not following the system of care principles sometimes derailed meetings by continuing to return the discussion to deficits (from strengths), attempting to make decisions on their own, grand- standing or dominating the conversation, and belittling or ignoring other team members. In meetings in which team leaders did not conduct any form of team or meeting framing or sensemaking, the meetings sometimes tended to be chaotic and confusing as team members attempted to sort out their respective roles and responsibilities. More will be discussed about this point in later sections. In other team meetings, the leaders were intentional in framing the meeting with a system orientation, sometimes using framing devices such as using the "TEAM: Together Everyone Achieves More" acronym, other times introducing specific meeting guidelines framing the team orientation. A later section will discuss framing devices and meeting structure, but it can be noted here that meetings in which a system-oriented frame was intentionally established seemed more likely to follow such an orientation.

Systems operate on the basis on voluntary relationships—each partner in a system negotiates their relationship (Watzlawick et al., 1967). Some evidence of this negotiation occurred in meetings. For example, one meeting member remarked, "I don't know what this team is all about." The team leader responded by explaining, "We are here to make the family be more successful together." This remark was repeated several times as the first speaker attempted to discuss negative behaviors and the leader attempted to deflect a disapproving discussion by repeating that positive (if somewhat vague) meeting objective. This negotiation was rarely explicitly stated in a meeting. Nonverbal behaviors often played a part in this negotiation: for example, lack of direct questions to a stepfather, effectively rendering him a non-member of the team; refusal to make eye contact with the mother, creating a confrontational relationship.

Framing and Sensemaking

The context of framing or sensemaking is one way of approaching the idea of assimilating or socializing team members to their roles and expectations. According to Bateson (1972), frames are the ways that we organize our experiences to help us understand and interpret them. Social frameworks help us understand a group's belief systems, and help us know how to behave in a specific social situation. Since, in any social situation, there is an infinite range of ways we could behave, framing is the way we interactively guide each other's interpretations of a social context (Goffman, 1974, Gumperz, 1997). Therefore, when we assimilate or socialize someone into a group, we are in fact, helping them define their patterns of behavior to fit into our conceptual framework of a specific situation (Luckmann, 1978).

This assimilation or socialization occurs through contextual cues such as verbal or nonverbal signs that hint at or clarify social expectations. Therefore, even if one interpretation was explicitly stated at the outset of a group meeting, nonverbal communication can create a very different interpretation of the meeting frame (Gumperz, 1997).

For example, in one meeting, a team leader stated at the outset of the meeting, "We are focusing on strengths," but then next stated, "The problem is the child's poor attendance." This framing incongruence created a confusing interpretation of the expectations of the meeting. Because of unintended verbal and nonverbal framing, the child and family wraparound meetings sometimes moved from intentional framing of wraparound principles to unintentional framing of traditional hierarchical medical model principles. Often, team leaders did not state the team meeting principles at the outset of a meeting. In some meetings, little overt assimilation attempts were made. Participants were not introduced or reminded of the system of care principles and meeting guidelines were rarely explicitly stated. When the principles were stated, they were not fully explained and were usually offered as an attempt to deflect problem communication during a meeting, such as saying "we want to focus on strengths," after a lengthy discussion of youth deficits, without explaining the differences between the two frames. Letting the deficit discussion continue without interruption gave tacit approval to the deficit frame, reinforcing that orientation throughout the meeting. In comparison, meetings that began with intentionally listing strengths of the team (from all team members) typically were focused more on strengths throughout the entire meeting, because the opening strengths discussion framed the entire meeting.

In fairness to the team leaders, team members had as much opportunity to frame and reframe meetings as did the leader. Reframing, according to Watzlawick, Weakland, and Fisch (1974), consists of changing the viewpoint of the situation to place it in a new frame that is more acceptable to the situation. Since sensemaking can be self-fulfilling, and, as Weick (1995) stated, "people act in such a way that their assumptions of reality become warranted" (p. 36), team members who did not behave in the system of care "frame" were simply reinforcing their own assumptions of reality. However, we suggest that it is the responsibility of the team leader to facilitate the sensemaking process in which team members coordinate their joint actions by creating equivalent meanings to these meetings. Creating equivalent meanings requires being explicit about the meaning from the beginning.

Meeting Structure and Communication Networks

Systems consist of dynamic relationships and relational patterns (Bryant & Bryant, 2006). According to Bryant and Bryant, family systems theory suggests that relational ties between members of a system are important for transference of resources such as social support or socialization, the structure of the social networks influences relationships in the system, and the relational structure in the system represents a longstanding pattern of system relationships. Messages of support, or lack of support, within a social network, can influence system relationships (Schmeeckle & Sprecher, 2004).

These child and family team meetings could be classified into two categories: those that appeared to be more tightly structured, and those that were less structured. The meetings that would fall into the "more structured" category began with the facilitator arriving first, and positioning himself or herself to greet attendees as they arrive. In these meetings, the facilitator typically had an agenda written on a flip chart and the meeting tended to be fairly well organized around that agenda. Since team members often arrived late, the facilitator might have used the waiting time to introduce attendees to each other, clarify their respective roles for the meeting, and explain the purpose of the meeting. Tightly structured meetings tended to begin with a review of the plan, or goals, created by the team up to this point, usually read from notes by the team leader. The team leader would usually ask the attendees (including the family and/or youth) to comment on, or add to, these goals. The team leader would often next facilitate a discussion of family and child strengths, and would typically invite attendees to participate in this discussion by going around the table and asking each attendee to list strengths of the family and youth. The team leader wrote these strengths on a flip chart as they were mentioned. The team leader typically finished the strengths discussion with a listing of team strengths, as each team member gave one or two strengths of him/herself or his/her agency. Up to this point in the meeting, the discussion tended to be downward, with the team leader tightly controlling the meeting dynamics and content. Any upward communication occurred through the leader (although sometimes directed to the family or youth) and upon the leader's invitation. For example, when the leader invited attendees to list family and child strengths, the attendees often spoke directly to the family and child when answering this question, but rarely volunteered information during this portion of the meeting until it was their turn to do so.

After this introductory portion of the meeting, the communication networks shifted and, while the leader was still in charge of the direction of the meeting, it was a much more subtle management, and communication tended to be more horizontal. In the central body of the meeting, the leader directed attendees' attention to the agenda items, such as review of goals, creation of new goals, discussion of family needs, and goal planning. These discussions were much more free flowing, with participants speaking back and forth to one another and often directly addressing the child and family. Interestingly, and inconsistent with system of care principles, the family and child rarely took part in the discussion to the same level, primarily speaking when addressed directly, and rarely initiating comments or questions. During this portion of the meeting, the leader often acted as note taker, writing down comments or concepts on the flipchart, and at moments seemed to be acting behind the scenes.

In the concluding portion of the meeting, the leader again became more directive and the communication again took a more downward direction. The leader summarized the meeting and questioned participants on assignments and agreements. Participants typically spoke only when directly addressed, and typically mediated their comments through the facilitator.

In contrast, in the less structured meetings, the discussion simply emerged. The team leader might have arrived late, and conversation between participants might have begun before the leader arrived. With little structure imposed by the leader, participants may have opened the conversation by mentioning problems they were having with the youth. These discussions typically turned into deficit based discussions in which the meeting centered around the child's weaknesses. In less structured meetings, certain participants tended to dominate the conversation and other participants tended to speak very little. Even in less structured meetings, the group leader might have imposed some direction, but it was much more subtle and was sometimes ineffective in directing or redirecting the group. Leaders in less structured meetings tended to use nondirective language such as "maybe we should ..." or "maybe you might consider ..." or nonverbal cues such as writing on a flip chart to facilitate the meeting. Communication in less structured groups was much more horizontal, with more back and forth conversation and more conversational turns. Participants were more likely to speak directly to one another rather than to the leader and some were more likely to make more comments about a larger number and variety of topics. These meetings appeared to be more chaotic and some group members seemed to retreat from the chaos by not participating.

There seemed to be both advantages and disadvantages to meeting structure. More structured meetings did seem to better reflect the system of care principles, but they may, by their structure, inhibit some team voices and ideas. On the other hand, less structured meetings may also inhibit voices and seemed to be less likely to be oriented toward a system approach. It seems that it is not simply having a structure, but the nature of the structure, that is important in orienting the team toward a systems orientation. Structure that both overtly and covertly frames the meeting within the system of care principles seemed to be the most effective in ensuring adherence to those principles. This can be accomplished by implicitly stating guidelines and rules, and also by modeling those rules verbally and nonverbally.

Team Member Empowerment

An empowered team is one that has the capability, responsibility, and authority to carry out the mission (Parker, 1994). Empowered team members, including family members, must understand that they are both allowed to and capable of carrying out the group's mission. In a child and family team, empowerment of the family might consist of helping them build the skills required to take care of themselves, and, in fact, this is one of the stated goals of the system of care process. Empowerment of other team members might consist of giving them the authority to make decisions and take action. Some team members were clearly empowered in this manner, while others, especially some informal supports, were not always. Adequate framing of the team and meeting principles will go a long way to fully empower the team.

In addition, researchers have found that attention to both perceived membership in a group and the relational aspects of the group contributes to empowerment of the members. They have found that job involvement, the extent to which a person's job contributes to their self-worth, along with communication of timely, accurate, and complete information increases satisfaction and motivation. This suggests that helping team members feel a part of the group will empower them (Ashcraft & Kedrowicz, 2002; Orpen, 1997). Arnold (1996) suggests involving team members in setting meeting guidelines and rules; perhaps inviting the team members to help frame the meeting within the parameters of the system of care principles will help increase empowerment.

In most meetings, the team acted as the youth's advocate, in insuring his/her voice was heard, and in arguing for needed services or resources for the youth and family, and this certainly reinforces family empowerment. The teams usually involved the family in the discussion and appeared to respect them in these meetings by exhibiting good listening behaviors (eye contact, body posture, and paraphrasing, referring back to their comments). However, instances were observed in which the team did not seem to hear the youth, sometimes ignoring his/her comments entirely, looking away, avoiding eye contact, and not responding, as if the youth was invisible. These reactions did not seem to be intentional, but conveyed a powerful meaning nevertheless.

In the meetings, the families were specifically asked for feedback, and were involved in designing the Family Support Plan (FSP), or at least providing feedback to the FSP as it was being developed, which is certainly a form of family empowerment. However, sometimes this request for feedback was superficial and even leading, such as in a meeting when the team leader said to a parent, "Are you okay with the plan? It's good, right?" and not unexpectedly received an affirmative response from the parent. All team members, especially parents and informal supports, must be empowered by being both verbally and nonverbally encouraged to actively add input into the meeting process.

Typically, the leaders also did a good job in encouraging the family and youth to take on specific responsibilities. There appeared to be a great deal of effort to schedule the meetings at a time and place that was convenient to the families. Unfortunately, when meetings involved school personnel, local policies dictated that the meetings be held during the school day. This often required that parents take off work to participate in their child's team meeting. In the meetings, the teams often invited family members to speak up and offer comments and suggestions, and usually made sure that the families and youth had a voice in the meetings by directing questions and comments to them. When appropriate, the team included the entire family system in the discussion. Family members were always treated courteously by the team leaders, but not always, unfortunately, by all team members, such as the habit of many professionals to refer to the youth's mother as "mother" or "mom" instead of by her name, or another professional criticizing or belittling a parent or child during a meeting.

Role Ambiguity

In social life, we all possess many different identities, each with their own rules for behavior and interaction. Social scientists call these our social "roles," and suggest that these multiple identities shift according to the context in which we find ourselves. In fact, we work hard to avoid committing an infraction of the behavior expected of our social identity in any given situation, because breakdowns in expectations lead to embarrassment (Goffman, 1967; Goffman, 1974).

Without adequate framing of the child and family team meetings, team members, both professionals and family members, seemed to be unclear about their roles on the team. These team members had many social roles outside of the team (therapist, teacher, administrator, social worker, parent, aunt, etc.) and did not understand that, in the team, they had a new role, one of team member. In fact, the team member role has very different rules and responsibilities than the other roles. For example, a teacher role may require a focus on lecturing, criticizing, and correcting, while the teacher in team member role may require a focus on listening, praising, and solving. These are very different orientations, and without framing and instruction on the differences, a system orientation cannot succeed.

Several examples of this role ambiguity occurred in the meetings. For example, there was often confusion about who was running the meetings. The team leader attended the meeting with the expectation that their role was the meeting facilitator, but they often ran into other professionals on the team whose other roles (therapist, teacher, and administrator) called on them to take a dominant role. Without role clarification, the meetings often resembled "dueling facilitators" (see Davis, 2008), resulting in confusion and frustration for attendees.

An important part of framing the team and meetings is to clarify roles; to make sure that all attendees understand what it means to be a member of a child and family team, and how this differs from their other roles they already have in their relationship with the child and family. A "shared leadership model," suggested by Arnold (1996), in which each team member (including the family) would assume authority for different parts of the project, would help empower individuals, reduce competition for power and authority, and reduce social vulnerability of the team members. Socializing the attendees to their expected roles prior to the meeting and framing the meeting at the outset will go a long way to reduce frustration and reinforce the system of care principles.

Conclusions and Implications

Child and family team meeting success begins before the meeting starts. Building a team that is a truly systemic, interrelated whole takes more work than simply inviting people to a meeting. The key to using child and family teams in a way that facilitates optimal child-family-provider interactions is to intentionally frame a system orientation to the child and family teams through meeting structure; communication that implicitly states group guidelines, philosophies, and rules; and nonverbal communication (gestures, paralanguage, eye contact) that is inclusive to all team members, including families and informal supports. Socializing the team members to understand their team roles and to empower them to carry out these roles will allow the entire group to negotiate this system pattern.

The research questions asked how child-family-provider team interactions influenced or facilitated system of care activities, namely, to encourage families as full participants in their care and to ensure that they needs were met and addressed. In theory, the systems approach is the backbone of the system of care concept. In practice, team meetings often fell back on the more traditional medical model of mental health and social service and were challenged to change the meeting paradigm to one of a systems approach. If the team leader framed the team meeting according to system of care principles, team members seemed to be more likely to assume roles within that orientation and the meeting was more likely to adhere to those principles. The extent to which the leader intentionally framed the orientation seemed to have a great deal to do with the successful performance of this orientation.

Specifically, when team leaders facilitated the meeting so that system of care principles were adhered to, they directed the team to goals, early in the meeting, and often summarized the meeting content at the end. They also set ground rules for the meeting at the beginning. In these meetings, the agenda was made clear, and the team leader often directed or redirected the team to a strengths orientation, sometimes in the face of a strong deficit orientation from the family or school attendees. When team leaders framed the meeting at the onset to a system orientation, they encouraged and built upon relationships between team members, clarified team roles, and invited all team members to participate. Communication in these meetings was artful and mindful.

Often, meeting facilitation could have been more assertive. Some meetings were chaotic and disorganized, drowning out the family's voice and the strengths approach. Yet, sometimes, meeting structure seemed to inhibit families' voices; it is a fine line between structuring in system of care principles and structuring out voice.

Teams were generally successful in engaging the family's participation. Parents were always "at the table" and included in the discussion. They were usually treated in a courteous fashion, and were always given voice, albeit often by the case manager speaking on their behalf. However, sometimes team members were observed interrupting the parents or refusing eye contact while they were talking. In some meetings, professionals in attendance drowned out or ignored the family's voice in the discussion.

Families often voiced agreement with the plan and with the services. However, sometimes, the family's voice was simply closed-ended acceptance of a case manager's suggestion ("Anything you want to add?" or "Do you agree with this? Would you like to add something?"), and families didn't always speak up in the meetings. We frequently observed information-sharing with the family. In one meeting in particular, the school representative shared personal information which equalized the partnership with the family and provided useful information: "My son is LD [learning disabled]. When my husband worked at night, we had the exact same problem."

It appeared that some treatment planning is happening outside of meetings, but there are advantages and disadvantages to this approach. It may be time efficient, but unfortunately, it can be disempowering for the family who does not learn how to work through goals or plans on their own. In addition, it works against a team-based approach, and likely disempowers other team members who were not included in planning efforts for the family. While it may insure that the family has a voice in the plan, it does not give them a chance to let that voice be heard by the rest of the team, in effect silencing them in the eyes of other team members. For families that may be reluctant to talk during team meetings, coaching them ahead of time on how to speak up for themselves would do them and the team a great service and be a great empowerment tool.

Teams frequently identified child and family strengths, requiring a fair amount of framing and reframing on the part of the team leaders. However, in some meetings, starting the discussion with "concerns" framed a deficit/problem orientation that pervaded the rest of the meeting, and goals and plans often focused more on problem-solving and therefore deficits rather than strengths-based goals and centered around what is not wanted for the child or family rather than what is wanted. This tended to be a deficit-based approach in which strengths became nonrelevant "fluff," rather than serious considerations for helping the child or family better their situation.

Merely assigning people to a team, and inviting them to a meeting, does not create a child and family team, nor a system of care orientation. This chapter adds to the body of knowledge of the study of bona fide teams. The methodology of naturalistic observation gives us the opportunity to observe how groups with prior history and culture interact within a specific environment of larger systems of which they are a part (Poole, 1999; Sykes, 1990). Studying the group processes in action, we were able to look at the shared meaning in child and family service planning teams as the primary site for the construction of meaning, by taking a dynamic, holistic view of the processes by which the systems of care create their reality (Daly, 1992; Hoagwood & Olin, 2002; Mabry, 1999; Poole, 1999). This research illustrates the importance of separating intent from action, and of mindful communication to create intended meaning.

Note

1. SED (Severely Emotionally Disturbed) is an umbrella term that refers to a mental, emotional, or behavioral disorder that results in an impairment that substantially inhibits the child's ability to fully function in the family, school, or community.

References

Arnold, V. (1996). Organizational development: Making teams work. *HR Focus, 73,* 12–14.

Ashcraft, K. L., & Kedrowicz, A. (2002). Self-direction or social support? Nonprofit empowerment and the tacit contract of organizational communication studies. *Communication Monographs, 69,* 88–110.

Bateson, G. (1972). *Steps to an ecology of mind.* Chicago: University of Chicago Press.

Bochner, A. P., & Eisenberg, E. (1987). Family process: Systems perspectives. In C. R. Berger & S. H. Chaffee (Eds.), *Handbook of communication science* (pp. 540–563). Newbury Park, CA: Sage.

Bryant, J. A., & Bryant, J. (2006). Implications of living in a wired family: New directions in family and media research. In L. H. Turner & R. West (Eds.), *The family communication sourcebook* (pp. 297–314). Thousand Oaks, CA: Sage.

Bulmer, M. (1979). Concepts in the analysis of qualitative data. *Sociological Review, 27*, 651–71.

Charmaz, K. (2000). Grounded theory: Objectivist and constructivist methods. In N. K. Denzin & Y. S. Lincoln (Eds.), *The handbook of qualitative research* (pp. 509–535). Thousand Oaks, CA: Sage.

Cohen, S. G., & Bailey, D. E. (1997). What makes teams work: Group effectiveness research from the shop floor to the executive suite. *Journal of Management, 23*, 239–290.

Daly, K. (1992). The fit between qualitative research and characteristics of families. In J. Gilgun, K. Daly, & G. Handel (Eds.), *Qualitative methods in family research* (pp. 3–11). Newbury Park, CA: Sage.

Davis, C. S. (2006). Sylvia's story: Narrative, storytelling, and power in a children's community mental health system of care. *Qualitative Inquiry, 12*(6), 1–24.

Davis, C. S. (2008). Competing narratives: How peer leaders use narrative to facilitate change in community mental health groups. *Small Group Research: An International Journal of Theory, Investigation, and Application, 39*(6), 706–727.

Eber, L., Nelson, C. M., & Miles, P. (1997). School-based wraparound for students with emotional and behavioral challenges. *Exceptional Children, 63*, 539–555.

Epstein, M. H., Jayanthi, M., McKelvey, J., Frankenberry, E., Hardy, R., Dennis, K., & Dennis, K. (1998). Reliability of the wraparound observation form: An instrument to measure the wraparound process. *Journal of Child and Family Studies, 7*, 161–170.

Epstein, M. H., Nordness, P., Kutash, K., Duchnowski, A., Schrepf, S., Benner, G., & Nelson, J. R. (2003). Assessing the wraparound process during family planning meetings. *Journal of Behavioral Health Services and Research, 30*, 352–362.

Faenza, M. M., & Steel, E. (1999). Mental health care coverage for children and families. In T. P. Gulotta, R. L. Hampton, G. R. Adams, B. A. Ryan, & R. P. Weissberg (Eds.), *Children's health care: Issues for the year 2000 and beyond* (pp. 117–135). Thousand Oaks, CA: Sage.

Glaser, B., & Strauss, A. (1967). *The discovery of grounded theory.* Chicago: Aldine.

Goffman, E. (1967). *Interaction ritual: Essays on face-to-face behavior.* New York: Pantheon.

Goffman, E. (1974). *Frame analysis.* New York: Harper & Row.

Gumperz, J. J. (1997). Contextualization and understanding. In A. Duranti & C. Goodwin (Eds.), *Rethinking context: Language as an interactive phenomenon* (pp. 229–252). New York: Cambridge University Press.

Guzzo, R. A., & Dickson, M. W. (1996). Teams in organizations: Recent research on performance and effectiveness. *Annual Review of Psychology, 47*, 307–338.

Halfon, N., & Newacheck, P. W. (1999). Prevalence and impact of parent-reported disabling mental health conditions among U.S. children. *Journal of the American Academy of Child and Adolescent Psychiatry, 38*, 600–608.

Hernandez, M., Gomez, A., Lipien, L., Greenbaum, P. E., Armstrong, K. H., & Gonzalez, P. (2001). Use of the System-of-Care Practice Review in the National Evaluation: Evaluating the fidelity of practice to System-of-Care principles. *Journal of Emotional and Behavioral Disorders, 9*, 43–52.

Hoagwood, K., & Olin, S. S. (2002). The NIMH blueprint for change report: Research priorities in child and adolescent mental health. *Journal of the American Academy of Child and Adolescent Psychiatry, 41*, 760–767.

Hoffman, L. (1981). *Foundations of family therapy*. New York: Basic Books.

Janis, I. (1982). *Groupthink: Psychological studies of policy decisions and fiascoes*. Boston: Houghton Mifflin.

Kayser, T. A. (1994). *Building team power: How to unleash the collaborative genius of work teams*. Carlsbad, CA: Irwin.

Laing, R. E., & Esterson, A. (1970). *Sanity, madness, and the family: Families of schizophrenics*. Middlesex, England: Penguin.

Laveman, L. (2000). The Harmonium project: A macrosystemic approach to empowering adolescents. *Journal of Mental Health Counseling, 22*(1), 17–31.

Lezak, A., & MacBeth, G. (2002). *Overcoming barriers to serving our children in the community: Making the Olmstead decision work for children with mental health needs and their families*. Washington, D C: Center for Mental Health Services, Substance Abuse and Mental Health Services Administration, U.S. Department of Health and Human Services.

Luckmann, T. (1978). *Phenomenology and sociology: Selected readings*. New York: Penguin.

Mabry, E. A. (1999). The systems metaphor in group communication. In L. R. Frey, D. S. Gouran, & M. S. Poole (Eds.), *The handbook of group communication theory and research* (pp. 71–91). Thousand Oaks, CA: Sage.

Minuchin, S. (1993). *Family healing: Strategies for hope and understanding*. New York: The Free Press.

Minuchin, S., & Fishman, H. C. (1981). *Family therapy techniques*. Cambridge, MA: Harvard University Press.

Orpen, C. (1997). The interactive effects of communication quality and job involvement on managerial job satisfaction and work motivation. *The Journal of Psychology, 131*, 519–522.

Parker, G. M. (1994). *Cross-functional teams: Working with allies, enemies, and other strangers*. San Francisco: Jossey-Bass.

Poole, M. S. (1999). Group communication theory. In L. R. Frey, D. S. Gouran, & M. S. Poole (Eds.), *The handbook of group communication theory and research* (pp. 37–70). Thousand Oaks, CA: Sage.

Sabourin, T. C. (2006). Theories and metatheories to explain family communication. In L.H. Turner & R. West (Eds.), *The family communication sourcebook* (pp. 43–60). Thousand Oaks, CA: Sage.

Schmeeckle, M., & Sprecher, S. (2004). Extended family and social networks. In A. L. Vangelisti (Ed.), *Handbook of family communication* (pp. 349–375). Mahwah, NJ: Erlbaum.

Seligman, M., & Darling, R. B. (1997). *Ordinary families, special children: A systems approach to childhood disability*. New York: Guilford.

Senge, P. M. (1990). *The fifth discipline: The art and practice of the learning organization*. New York: Doubleday.

Sieburg, E. (1985). *Family communication: An integrated systems approach*. New York: Gardner.

Stake, R. (1995). *The art of case study research*. Thousand Oaks, CA: Sage.

Strauss, A., & Corbin, J. (1990). *Basics of qualitative research: Grounded theory procedures and techniques*. Newbury Park, CA: Sage.

Stroul, B. A., & Friedman, R. M. (1994). *A system of care for children and youth with severe emotional disturbances. (Revised edition).* Washington, DC: Georgetown University Child Development Center, CASSP Technical Assistance Center.

Sykes, R. E. (1990). Imagining what we might study if we really studied small groups from a speech perspective. *Communication Studies, 41,* 200–211.

Turner, M. E., Pratkanis, A., Probasco, P., & Leve, C. (1992). Threat, cohesion, and group effectiveness: Testing a social identity maintenance perspective on groupthink. *Journal of Social Psychology, 53,* 69–79.

Watzlawick, P., Beavin, J. B., & Jackson, D. D. (1967). *Pragmatics of human communication.* New York: Norton.

Watzlawick, P., Weakland, J. H., & Fisch, R. (1974). *Change: Principles of problem formation and problem resolution.* New York: Norton.

Weick, K. E. (1995). *Sensemaking in organizations.* Thousand Oaks, CA: Sage.

Weigel, D., & Murray, C. (2000). The paradox of stability and change in relationships: What does chaos theory offer for the study of romantic relationships? *Journal of Social and Personal Relationships, 17*(3), 425–449.

Yerby, J. (1995). Family systems theory reconsidered: Integrating social construction theory and dialectical process. *Communication Theory, 5*(4), 339–365.

9 Early Intervention or Early Imposition

A Bona Fide Group Perspective Analysis of the Parent-Child–Early Intervention Relationship

Carol B. Mills and Kasey L. Walker

All families have experience interacting with groups outside the family unit, from doctors' offices and schools to music ensembles and team sports. In fact, as many parents envision having their first child, part of their ongoing fantasies involve how they and their child will interact with these outside groups and agencies: the child's first playgroup, the first day of kindergarten, soccer teams, baseball games, and dance lessons. Part of forecasting life with a child is contemplating how the parent and child become part of the larger world we know as "parenthood" and "family." One group or system that parents rarely, if ever, imagine themselves participating in is known as Early Intervention (EI). In fact, for "outsiders" EI is almost invisible, but for participants, it can have a profound impact on their lives, both short- and long-term.

In brief, Early Intervention is a collection of services designed to support the development of children with disabilities under 36 months of age and to provide support for family growth and stability as they learn more about the child's diagnosis. Ideally, providers and families work together to help maximize the child's development and identify the family's strengths, as well as provide assistance for potentially problematic areas. When effective teams exist, studies have found tremendous benefits to families involved in the EI system. Pelchat, Lefebvre, Proulx, and Reidy (2004) report that EI programs help parents find information about their child's disability, reduce parental stress associated with learning of a child's disability, and empower parents to become involved in their children's therapies and educational activities. And, both short-term and long-term academic gains for the child in EI have been documented as well (Guralnick, 1997, 2005).

Although much of the research to date highlights the benefits of EI, some sources indicate that not all parent-child-EI provider relationships are positive. Mills (2005), for example, provides instances in which parents identify the interactions with EI professionals as intrusive and counterproductive:

> There is often a love-hate relationship with doctors and therapists. Parents want their children to reach their full potential ... but evaluations and therapy sessions are also a constant reminder, even barrier, to leading a "normal life" for many families. (p. 205)

Similarly, Bridle and Mann (2000) argued that EI creates "the 'ultimatum' and the meaning of disability" (p. 7) that instantiates the idea that children with disabilities are "broken" and can be fixed by therapies if parents diligently follow the EI program created by the therapists. Bridle and Mann also assert that the EI system has been responsible for a shift from thinking about children with disabilities as helpless, even worthless, to framing them as projects to be tackled, where "level of functioning" reflects outcomes of early intervention and parental efforts. As many scholars have pointed out, this "fix them" mentality belies the notion that disability is natural, and that the real problems with disability are not from those with support needs, but from society's reactions to disability itself (e.g., see Morris, 1993; Newell, 1994).

Clearly, then, the relationships between EI providers and the families they serve are complex, complete with success stories of academic, social and physical improvements, and satisfied participants, as well as narratives of challenge, disappointment, and frustration. Given the limited focus of most prior studies, the strengths and weaknesses entailed in the parent-child-EI provider relationship has not been adequately explored. To date, studies tend to focus on perceptions and practices of EI providers (Keenan-Rich, 2002; Vanderhoff, 2004) or on the perceptions and outcomes for parents and their children (Bridle & Mann, 2000; Pelchat et al., 2004). These discussions treat the groups as two discrete systems interfacing with one another, thereby ignoring the vital interactions that help combine and/or define the systems themselves.

We propose that using the Bona Fide Group perspective (Putnam & Stohl, 1990) can help reconceptualize the multiple relationships realized in the intersection between EI providers and the family. Far from considering the parent-child- EI provider relationship as immutable, this perspective examines the family system as it relates to the EI system and the coterminous systems the family is now a part of (e.g., the disability community). This chapter will review the extant literature on Early Intervention and the parent-child relationships, and then delineate the ways in which the Bona Fide Group perspective (BFGP) changes our conceptualization of those relationships and finally propose an agenda for research based on those changes. In doing so, we will focus on the ways that the key elements of the BFGP, including (a) stable, yet permeable boundaries, (b) interdependence with context, and (c) unstable and ambiguous borders, are communicatively co-constructed.

The Early Intervention System

In the United States, Early Intervention had its beginnings in 1975 with "The Education for All Handicapped Children Act" that served as the progenitor of what we now have as Part C of The Individuals with Disabilities Education Act (IDEA). IDEA requires that states provide services for children from birth to 36 months who have, or are at risk for, developmental delays. Essentially these services, provided with assistance from government funds, are designed to help reduce developmental delays through a system of therapies, including but not limited to speech, physical, and occupational.

At the earliest EI meetings, the child's disability and its impact on the family are discussed at length. The parent-child dyad (or entire family, if desired) works with the EI provider to talk about the child's developmental trajectory possibilities, developmental priorities, family concerns, and even financial and emotional resources. Together, parents and providers develop goals for the child, and discuss how the family can help support those goals utilizing a wide variety of therapeutic tools to improve the child's skills, reduce the extent of the child's delays, and ultimately, help the family thrive, including assisting them in finding support groups and developing advocacy skills (Vanderhoff, 2004). In many cases, the child is referred to early intervention at birth or early infancy, so the child cannot speak for him or herself. Yet, it is clearly the needs of the child, and the desire of the parents to help the child reach his or her full potential, that drive the meetings. Parents, then, become the voice of the child in the earliest meetings with care providers.

As IDEA evolved, Part C, a major component of the act, mandated that services should be provided "in the child's natural environment to the maximum extent possible." Quite simply, the natural environment is the home or daycare setting where the child spends his or her days. Providing services in the child's natural environment serves multiple goals: (a) children often learn best in familiar situations, (b) families and/or daycare providers present during services learn proper therapy techniques that can be implemented into the child's daily routine, (c) the therapists can observe what is happening in the home and determine if the natural environment is constructed to help support the goals they set in conjunction with the parents, and (d) therapists can more easily identify additional support needs that the family might have when they can observe "natural" life (Peterander, 2000). In fact, while Part B of IDEA requires that services for individuals from age 3 to age 21 be "child centered," Part C is explicitly family-centered. Similarly, rather than the "Individualized Education Plan" completed for the 3- to 21-year-old group, the plan for the birth to 3 (EI) group is called the "Individualized Family Services Plan." Thus, at its foundation, EI services are not just about the child, but are designed to help support the entire family as they learn about disability and how they can improve the entire family's quality of life. The communication that occurs between the parent-child and EI providers is central to the goals of the Early Intervention system itself.

While the therapy goals and activities are best left to the therapists, the communicative exchanges that comprise the parent-child-EI provider interactions are critical to the EI program's and family's success. To date, the goals of EI and the nature of the relationship between the EI system and the family have been studied separately, rather than as a system in which interaction, goals, identity, and boundaries have concomitant influence. By applying the Bona Fide Group perspective (BFGP) to the current literature focusing on varying aspects of the EI system, we offer a new and dynamic way of looking at these services and relationships. Pragmatically, this approach can yield insights to both therapists and parents involved in EI. Theoretically, this contributes to the extant work on the BFGP and family communication.

Bona Fide Group Perspective

The Bona Fide Group perspective was originally developed in response to calls for group communication research to move away from zero-history laboratory groups to groups "embedded in natural contexts" (Putnam, 1994; Putnam & Stohl, 1990, 1996; Stohl & Putnam, 1994, 2003). The BFGP has become increasingly utilized (see for example Ellingson, 2003; Kramer, 2002; Lammers & Krikorian, 1997; Sunwolf & Leets, 2004), and the significance of its impact on small group communication research is clearly evidenced by a recent edited volume devoted to the further exploration of this perspective (Frey, 2003). The BFGP challenges researchers to think differently about groups and impacts our very conceptualization of a group and what variables are most salient for understanding group processes (Putnam & Stohl, 1990).

The BFGP can be especially useful for the study of families and their relationships with "external" groups. Studying the family as a group is not new, and families have been studied in a variety of group contexts, most frequently in therapy or social support groups. However, in communication studies, the intersection between group research and family communication is much more recent and not as well explored (see Barker et al., 2000, for an exception to this), with earlier sociological efforts abandoned in large part to small group researchers' focus on zero-history and task groups and family communication research agendas that focused more on interpersonal communication (Socha, 1999). Socha argues that small group research can benefit from the study of families, pointing to the "considerable overlap. . .between the concepts of 'family' and 'group'" (p. 476) and the importance of investigating this "first group" as critical for a full understanding of an individual's participation in small groups throughout his or her lifespan. In turn, "focusing on the group as a collective entity, of course, is a strength of group communication research, and family communication scholars can learn from this work" (Socha, p. 476).

The BFGP has great potential heuristic value for understanding family communication (Socha, 1999) and has already been employed in some authors' studies of families (see, for example, Petronio, Jones, & Morr, 2003, and see Duggan & Petronio, this volume). In particular, the BFGP can facilitate our investigation of a family's interaction with external systems, such as EI. The BFGP explicitly "posits that agencies external to a group have a much more powerful role in group life than most current theory acknowledges and it challenges researchers to consider explicitly the group's relation to 'outsiders'" (Poole, 1999, p. 59). The parent-child-EI provider relationship creates a nexus (Stohl & Putnam, 2003) of insider/outsider relationships. As such, we use the three key characteristics of the BFGP to reframe the parent-child-EI provider relationships.

Method

Our purpose in this chapter is to provide a theoretical framework through which relationships between parent-child dyads and early intervention providers can be viewed. In doing so, we hope to significantly extend work that has been done on this relationship, as well as allow us to more clearly examine the complexities of this relationship. We do not aim to test the Bona Fide Group Perspective in this chapter, but rather to provide a conceptual analysis using this framework.

The examples in this chapter are drawn from publicly available, online sources, such as training manuals for early intervention providers, and stories about parent-child and EI provider relationships on nonrestricted bulletin boards and parenting sites. The data were chosen from educational sites for EI providers and therapists, as well as from parenting boards for children with special needs. The examples presented in this were chosen because they helped demonstrate how the BFGP can be used to understand the nuances and issues involved in this relationship, not because they are representative nor inclusive of all possible concerns. We hope, however, that this first step toward a theoretical understanding of the interactions will help us explicate our emerging conceptual analysis that grounds the understanding of the parent-child, early intervention interactions as part of a group communication phenomenon.

Reframing the Parent-Child-EI Relationship

Boundaries

The first element of the BFGP is stable yet permeable boundaries. These boundaries are manifested in "overlapping group membership, relationships among group members in other contexts, and fluctuations in membership within groups" (Putnam & Stohl, 1990, p. 257). Boundaries allow groups to differentiate themselves from their context (Poole, 1999) by determining what constitutes group membership and the degree to which the group will remain "open" to their various contexts. In the parent-child-EI relationship, while the family boundary remains stable (i.e., a family's criteria determining who is and who is not a family member), the permeability of the family's boundary is more significantly affected (see Duggan & Petronio, this volume). Upon entering EI, the parent-child relationship is increasingly influenced by outside groups; as these outside influences are "let in" or "forced" to the family, and as the family's boundary becomes increasingly permeable, the parent-child relationship will change (e.g., see Duggan & Petronio, this volume, regarding privacy). One parent notes how attending the IFSP meetings to discuss her daughter's progress changes how she perceives her daughter, at least until she returns home.

> Ok, I know it doesn't really matter … it's just to let the teachers know where she's at and to present "proof" to the State that she is eligible. But it still kind of stings. It was weird coming home after the meeting when

we sat there and talked about this "abstract being" who is my daughter. It was all concepts and skill sets, but when I got home, this "skill set" was a gorgeous little girl who was happy to see us. So I just have to remember that whenever I go to these stupid but necessary meetings.

The content of EI meetings permeate this family's boundary and therefore the parent-child relationship itself. Though the toddler did not participate in the evaluation meetings, the power of the assessments to alter the relationship between her and her mother is clear. At the meetings, the child is represented by tests, scores, and milestones that were (not) achieved. The parent representing the child then has to reconnect with the child on a personal level, and to interact with her baby girl, remembering that the meetings are not the sum total of who her child is or the only tool she has for deciding how to best interact with her daughter.

Further, parents, children, and EI providers are now members of multiple relationships, with multiple identities; for example, parents are now parents, functional therapists, special needs advocates, and students of disability rights. For some parents, embracing multiple identities becomes a natural part of the redefined parenting role in which advocate and therapist are embraced as part of parenting obligations. As one mother discusses, she even thinks that becoming parent/functional therapist is critical to the success of her child:

> I think this bears repeating. We had a good experience with EI, but a portion of our 1 hour a week was spent learning about our therapy tasks for the week. That has also been my experience with private therapy—part of the appointment has been spent discussing the steps we need to take at home. If the specialists don't train the parents to be the primary therapists, there isn't much point—1 hour a week doesn't lead to much progress in anything.

In other words, this mother recognizes that the boundary of therapist is not only demarcated in space, but in time. Though an EI provider may see a child weekly, or less, the parent can apply those skills and techniques daily.

Not all parents readily embrace this boundary shift; additional roles for some parents might make the parent role, itself, seem overwhelming. Bridle and Mann (2000) discuss this tension, asserting that:

> as parents we teach our children a great deal, but this is usually a seamless part of our very multi-faceted roles as a parent. With our children with disability this role threatens to overwhelm these other roles. It may even undermine the integrity of the whole relationship. (p. 64)

In fact, the stress created by boundary overlap between the primary parenting role and the parent-as-therapist role can be seen in the comments of another mother:

I know that all of the things I am doing for Charlie are helping, but some-times I'd like to just play with him and not wonder if babytalk will hurt his speech more, of if this toy will make it harder for him to walk later. With my other kids it was just so easy to be with them and play. Now I'm doubting myself and wondering if I'm good enough.

The tensions created by these multiple identities are continually negotiated through parents' communication with their own children, the EI provid-ers, and related social agencies. And, yet, though we know that parents are stressed by seeing their children as "projects," we see that children are children first. Given the very young ages of the children involved in EI, they are often unaware of their disabilities and interact with their parents and others solely on the basis of their own experiences, uncolored by definitions of disability and intervention.

The concept of stable yet permeable boundaries also calls particular atten-tion to changing group membership. Changes in the family group (e.g., the birth of a new child or a divorce) and changes in the EI providers (e.g., new therapists) must be important considerations as well. One of the key stressors in negotiating boundaries is the potential need to alter membership in the therapy team. Though both parents and providers ultimately are supposed to act in the best interests of the child in the EI system, sometimes the relation-ships between the participants are strained, or minimally effective. And in some cases, the child does not seem to work effectively with a particular pro-vider. As one mother reminded her online friend:

> Do NOT forget u can change therapists or even the companies that pro-vide the therapy (or at least u can in VA). I would sit down & talk to the therapist & tell them what u need & see how they react. If they are resis-tant tell your EI coordinator u want to switch. Do NOT feel guilty ... what is best for your little girl is the most important thing.

Other parents discussed how changing the team has worked for them, too. One mother with a young girl with multiple disabilities recounted her experiences:

> I think I'm just tired, and I see a long road ahead in terms of breaking through whatever this barrier is with her ... maybe the barrier is "Two Years Old"?!? Anyway, we're definitely not afraid to change people out, and we have already switched her ST and love her new one. I've already told the therapists I love and the coordinator that they're not allowed to stop working with her!!!

In this situation, the mother makes it clear that the boundaries have shifted, but that this shift can be beneficial when they find the right balance for the parent-child-provider interactions.

These boundaries are often tested and shaped because of the emotional nature of the interaction: a team of professionals and participants developed to help a child with some degree of delay maximize his or her potential. Who is part of this team, and for how long, are often simple matters, and other times more complex. For example, siblings are clearly part of the parent-child relationship, but do not always have a clear role in the therapeutic relationship and parents and therapists often do not know how to include siblings, or if they should exclude them. One mother discusses her struggle with this boundary concern:

> I hate that Katie is ignored when the therapists come to the house. I wish they would realize that when they leave, Katie spends tons of time with Max. If they included her, maybe she could help throughout the week, right??? But, when I say something, they ask me to keep her busy? And, if I'm supposed to carry on this work all week with Max, who is going to keep her busy then? I'm ready to scream!

This parent's concern is not uncommon. One state's Web site for EI providers addresses this very issue and advises therapists to start:

> [P]racticing in a way that supports the competence and confidence of parents/caregiver in their ability to meet the developmental and health related needs of their child, we need to meet them where they are. If siblings are an issue for you, you can bet they're an issue for the parent/caregiver who is going to be trying to implement the strategies you're developing. The ideal thing to do would be to involve the sibling(s) in the activities you are doing. It is only natural for children to be intrigued by a home visitor. (Illinois Department of Human Services, 2007)

The BFG element of stable yet permeable boundaries calls attention to the ways in which the "outside" EI system influences the parents' interactions with their own children, from the way they perceive them to the way they play with them. The parents' and siblings' multiple identities and potential changes in the therapy team membership all demonstrate the key role that boundaries play in negotiating the relationships between parent-child and the EI system and providers.

Interdependence with Context

While stable yet permeable boundaries highlight how groups differentiate themselves from the environment, another property of the BFGP focuses specifically on how the group's interdependence with context is communicatively constructed. Interdependence with context is evidenced in "interlocked behaviors, message patterns, and interpretive frames within and between groups" (Putnam & Stohl, 1990, p. 258). Rather than conceptualizing the context as merely a set of variables or conditions affecting the group, the BFGP focuses on the ways in which the group and its external environments are co-constructed through communicative interaction (Frey & Sunwolf, 2005).

Engagement in the EI system makes the context salient for these families in a way that is not true for families of children without disabilities. A cornerstone of early intervention is that services should be conducted in the child's "natural environment," meaning settings that are natural or normal for the child's age peers who have no disabilities (U.S. Code of Federal Regulations 303.1, 1989). These services are conducted in home, neighborhood, or community settings in which children without disabilities participate. Thus, not only are children going into other environments seen as "therapeutic" such as a doctor's or therapist's space which entail a feeling of disability and intervention, but also EI can be seen as intruding upon spaces otherwise seen as "non-disabling" or places where disability is not expected to be the center of focus. One mother discussed a therapist watching her child finish lunch:

> Yes, Stella is delayed but so are a lot of kids they just don't have someone watching, evaluating and analyzing there every move. Nobody is watching to see if they suck the straw right, get to a standing position or sit the "right" way.

This mother was frustrated with the conflation of the EI and home context, which she believes results in constant critique of her daughter, and is in some way infringing upon her daughter's ability to grow as other children do. Another parent, who has a child with a non-specific diagnosis said:

> It's annoying that therapy seems to be everywhere! I feel like every toy in house has a purpose and sometimes I just want to have fun like I did with Jack and Trey. At times, I feel like I'm cheating Chrissie out of a normal childhood and maybe that is hurting her, too.

The idea that the context of therapy as overwhelming "normal" childhood was apparent in another parent's discussion about her interactions with a therapist. Her son had started scooting to move from one area to another, and the therapist strongly discouraged it, saying it was improper locomotive technique. The mother was happy her son was moving on his own and frustrated by the discouraging response:

> We felt horrible telling Garrett he was doing something wrong when he's finally able to explore his environment. I'm going to see what our Early Ed chicky says this morning (she comes at 9:30). She used to be our coordinator, but now our PT is (figures, huh?). What really bugs me is that on our sheet that the PT leaves (with what we've done, and our future plans) she wrote "Davey has also begun to scoot—plan to discourage scooting". Ugh. Thanks for listening to me vent! I'll keep you posted on the butt-battle!

Government agencies, and people who proclaim to be experts in their child's development, are now in the family's home. While other families interact with health care providers, this interaction is less frequent and generally occurs in the health care space. In the parent-child-EI system, home and public (or front-stage and back-stage areas) are conflated. However, not all parents respond negatively to the overlap between the EI and home context; rather, they see the benefits of combination. A parent who has a child with CP talks about the importance of natural environment EI:

> Mattie is only 3 and getting ready to age-out. I'm so glad we had in home PT because he needed to learn to get around his own house, how to open his refrigerator, how to get into his bed, and how to play with his own toys. We tried private PT, too, but everything was so different than at home. Our PT even went to the playground with us a few times and showed us how to get him on and off the swings and stuff there. I'm hoping to get a good person when we go to the ps [public school] system now. I'm really scared!

A mother of a young boy reminds an online group that Early Intervention is responsible for many developments in the abilities of children with special needs, and reminds parents that the services are:

> Not for convenience of the parents or how it may be hurtful to hear the extent to which their child is delayed. Therapy can be made fun, and part of your daily lives. Some is not even "therapy" but many new parents may not know this and never give tummy time when needed and use sensory stimulation when appropriate. Many have feeding issues that need to be addressed.

In her comments, she makes several critical points. First, though EI may seem intrusive, it is for the sake of the child. Thus, as we consider how the parent-child-EI relationship is affected by context, it centers on the notion that the parent's and child's needs themselves may be different. Though it is easy to consider the "parent-child dyad," it may be important to recognize that sometimes the very parent-child relationship may be strained as they interact with the system. Thus, in order to fully understand the context of EI, we need to address the complexities that arise in that relational arrangement. Second, though natural environment therapy may seem invasive, it may be a critical way of determining what the child's daily life really looks like, in order to make meaningful changes that can affect the ways in which daily tasks are done. Artificial settings may mask issues that only appear when the child feels comfortable and safe, and is engaged in his or her daily activities.

Given the complexities of the issues of context, perhaps the most interesting element of the interdependence between family and EI provider is the degree to which interpretive frames are adopted and/or resisted. For example, despite the mission statement that EI is family-centered and that families are empowered to make changes and implement plans, the very notion of "intervention" sets the stage for the agenda that EI sets, namely that the family has a responsibility to work with their child to see that he or she becomes as "high functioning" as possible. Interestingly, families may actively resist this "normalizing" of their child while at the same time working toward helping that child achieve all that he or she can (see Mills, 2005). One mother's comments illustrate this seeming contradiction:

> that's another thing- if I hear one more time, "Wow she's doing really well!" in a surprised voice ... grrr!! yes, she's doing well compared to a severely delayed child, which she could have been, but compared to a typically developing child, she aint' doing that hot people! let's get going on everything we need to do to help!

And while the EI provider may privilege disability in explaining a child's particular behavior, the family may instead point to the child's age, siblings' similar behavior, or any number of explanations other than disability:

> My friend's daughter is about where your son is and I would not put a label on it at all. That is just his pace. I think people are too quick to label our kids just because they can. There is a reason they tell you that you do not know what their potential is until they have reached it and at 19 months your DS is nowhere near his potential. Keep doing what you are doing and he will be just fine.

Thus, through the parent-child-EI provider interaction, the definition of disability and the family and society's response to a child's disability is constantly renegotiated. One parent's comments regarding "talking" specifically address this issue:

> I too find the "what is talking" definition a problem. My not-quite-three-year-old has never had any problems talking—her problem is in being understood!... Frustrating all round. What really upsets me though is the number of people who say "oh, isn't she talking yet?" As far as I'm concerned she is talking, and so is any child who is communicating effectively with their family. More to the point she considers that she is talking, and as long as we respond to her attempts she continues to try to speak more clearly.

The disability frame is continually negotiated, and perhaps most clearly in the IFSP and the written assessments of the child's progress:

> They just see him as a baby with DS, and not as the unique, talented and intelligent little boy that he is. After his last assessment, I actually made

them rewrite parts of the report. They referred to his drooling (which he doesn't do) and to his "frequent hospitalizations" (he's been in the hospital 1 time in 21 months). I thought they would just think I was "in denial" if I complained, but I went ahead & made them change it anyway.

Articulately capturing the concerns of many parents on multiple boards, Trent's mother explains her preparation for her EI meeting:

Trent has his first annual review coming up after Thanksgiving. I spoke to his PT (also his case manager) today about my desire to word his report in positive terms (i.e., what Trent CAN do) rather than a deficit model (i.e., what his delays are). She was amenable, but said that she has never done this before. I told her that I'm not deceiving myself into thinking that if she doesn't spell out the delay that it doesn't exist, just that I don't really care about a "delay," I care about where Trent is, where he has come from, and where we should be going from here.

The family is clearly interdependent with the context. And the interactions between the parent-child and the EI system is reflected in a myriad of ways, from the conflation of the therapy and home settings to the ongoing negotiation of disability and the child's progress.

Borders

Finally, to fully examine how communication co-constructs the parent-child-EI provider relationship, scholars must investigate the construction of group identity and the creation of alliances among these systems. These unstable and ambiguous borders are the third key element of the BFGP. The concept of unstable and ambiguous borders recognizes that "groups continually change, redefine, and renegotiate their borders to alter their identities and embedded context" (Stohl & Putnam, 1994, p. 291). Stohl and Putnam (2003) later clarified and extended this concept with a call to focus on the group nexus, "which centers on the points of connection or overlapping group links" (p. 410).

While boundaries are focused on differentiating groups from the context by demarcating group membership and focusing on individual group members' multiple identification, borders differentiate the group through the ongoing construction of a unified whole, the overall group identity. For example, the parent-child-EI provider intersection can lead to changes in the family's identity. Clearly, having a child with a disability may challenge many families' notions of what it means to be a "family" and the parent-child relationship itself; their "family" has become the "family of a child with a disability" and the ambiguity of their new identity is compounded by a system in which the family becomes a "family of a child with a disability in multiple therapeutic and intervention settings." Part of group identity is constructed in the ways in which a group allies itself with other groups. In the parent-child/EI coalition, family discourse clearly demarcating "us," as parents of children with special needs, from "them," parents of typically-developing children, creates an identity for the family as part of "special needs community," creating a new identity and alliance for the family.

Expressing their membership in this new alliance is critical for the family's identity as they become sojourners in a new territory. Multiple examples of the country and border metaphors (e.g., territory, passport, and new world) which dominate special needs bulletin boards for nearly all types of disabilities arguably arise from an oft-quoted poem, "Welcome to Holland" by Emily Perl Kingsley, a mother of a son with Down syndrome. In this poem, Kingsley makes use of a very literal country and border metaphor. She describes the experience of having a child with special needs as visiting an unexpected country, Holland, when all plans had been made to visit a more popular, common destination, Italy. She identifies her feelings of being in a new group:

> So you must go out and buy new guide books. And you must learn a whole new language. And you will meet a whole new group of people you would never have met ... But everyone you know is busy coming and going from Italy ... and they're all bragging about what a wonderful time they had there. And for the rest of your life, you will say, "Yes, that's where I was supposed to go. That's what I had planned." (Kingsley, 1987)

While Kingsley closes with thoughts that give hope to new parents about appreciating the beauty of the new land and all it has to offer, such as tulips and Rembrandts, it is clear that for her, and the many who quote her work, that the terrain is different, not what they expected, and must be explored and, to a certain extent, conquered. The family's territory has shifted, and its identity will change as they learn to navigate the new topography and alliances.

Even within this new land, the special needs community, the borders are not stable. For some parents, when the educational goals of the child are not met, they may perceive their role as border patrol work—with some forces in the educational land trying to keep out a child from a nontypical territory. One parent of a child with autism wrote:

> When our girl was first diagnosed we had her enrolled in our County's Special Needs Early Intervention Pre-School Program right away and from the start the School has been nothing but a problem. We've tried so hard to find someone, anyone that would HELP our girl.

Other parents quickly responded, both confirming her fears, and reassuring her that she had a place inside the group of parents of children with autism with comments such as: "Unfortunately, there is still a big part of the world that still just don't get it," "You're a great mom, and not to blame for the way the system has betrayed you and your sweet daughter," and "We are all behind you on this one! Best of luck." Another parent talks about the necessity to fight for your child's needs, to protect their identity as a child who needs services:

> Don't give up. They are in the wrong here. I don't know if you've had to fight for services for him yet. I did when Matthew was in EI and it was not pretty, but in the end, he got what he needed. Remember that you are his best (and sometimes only) advocate. If you don't see that he gets the services he needs, no one will.

These parents actively negotiate their family's borders, seeking allies to support their efforts to secure the services and help they believe their children need. In many ways, the simple existence of online support groups allows parents the ability to immerse themselves within a group of people who understand this nontypical terrain, and they can discuss the issues that are problematic in nonthreatening and supportive ways.

Even when basic communication and goals are being met, in some cases families may view their relationship with the EI provider as a competitive one; the family vies for limited resources and time with the therapist who is balancing an already heavy caseload with other families in similar situations. Thus, when a therapist can only give a child 1 hour each week and the parents seek 3 hours, the "cooperative" relationship between parents and EI-providers can become antagonistic. A parent of child with hearing loss says:

> Luke, 6 months deaf, is getting little help. Well at the doctor today I was talking to a mom who receives EI and her son is HOH and she has a deaf ed teacher come in once a week and teach them both sign.... I do a lot on my own and I don't think just because we live in a rural area that we should receive less you know.

As a result, many parents feel forced to occupy an adversarial position with the EI-providers and state agencies to act as an advocate for their child. One parent supports Luke's mother by saying:

> You are an advocate and will need to be one for the sake of your child. I cannot tell you the importance of advocating as you are the best one as you know your child best. Keep up the fight. Your child will thank you someday for doing such a good job.

Luke's mother's response clearly indicates that she has become disillusioned with the EI system and no longer classifies the relationship to the family as positive:

> It's easy to be your child's advocate, it's hard to know what to know what to advocate for, and by that I mean options, help, support, education and what not. I'm a trusting person so I believe people are here for my sons best interest, now I know better is all.

The alliance between the family and the EI system is a complex one. EI literature sets up the "team" consisting of the EI providers, the parents, and the child with a disability, siblings, and key care providers. This team, then, relies on the cooperation among all of its members. In fact, EI providers are trained and exposed to the nature of collaboration in teams with families, yet as EI provider Nancy Keenan-Rich discusses of her own experiences:

> Family beliefs, values, and priorities became the backdrop for services. Whereas I previously held an ideal concept of how family members might participate in EI, I now began, for the first time, to appreciate circumstances within the family that might influence the process—parent personalities, stress, boundaries, and the various pressures created by an extended family. (Keenan-Rich, 2002, p. 5)

The alliance, then, between a family and the EI system is often uneasy. In fact, some research (Bridle & Mann, 2000; Mills, 2005) indicates that frequently a family's "cooperation" is more like "compliance" with the EI provider prescriptions, creating a submissive or combative rather than a truly collaborative relationship. The BFGP's focus on unstable and ambiguous borders directs our attention to the family's membership in the special needs community, its alliances with the EI system and other support groups, and its shifting identity as a result of these ongoing ambiguities.

Conclusion

When examining parent-child dyads, and how they interface with external constituencies, it is important to examine how the groups interact in multiple, changing, and complex ways. As noted, one of the primary issues in this triadic relationship, parent-child-provider, is that the child involved is an infant, or at oldest a toddler. Therefore, the child in this relationship cannot speak for him or herself verbally, and the parent must try to understand the needs of the child. The parents pay attention to all of the cues the child displays, not only about developmental progress, but also in regards to emotional development, family bonding, and overall happiness. Clearly, the child is an active participant, demonstrating emotions and achieving developmental milestones, yet the parent must stand in as that child's verbal expression.

By applying the Bona Fide Group perspective, we offer a reconceptualization of relationships created through the parent-child-EI interface. This perspective extends prior calls for studying family communication from a group perspective (Socha, 1999) and the formulation of these concepts can clearly be applied to other parent-child interfaces with external groups. By highlighting the dynamic and fluid nature of boundaries, contexts, and borders, we illustrate how the parent-child dyad and EI providers are active participants in their own reality construction through communication, as well as offer pragmatic insight for EI participants (both families and therapists).

References

Barker, V. E., Abrams, J. R., Tiyaamornwong, V., Seibold, D. R., Duggan, A., Park, H. S., et al. (2000). New contexts for relational communication in groups. *Small Group Research, 31,* 470–503.

Bridle, L., & Mann, G. (2000). *Mixed feelings: A parental perspective on Early Intervention.* Paper presented at the National Conference of Early Childhood Intervention Australia, Brisbane, June 2000.

Ellingson, L. L. (2003). Interdisciplinary health care teamwork in the clinic backstage. *Journal of Applied Communication Research, 31,* 93–117.

Frey, L. R. (Ed.). (2003). *Group communication in context: Studies of bona fide groups.* Mahwah, NJ: Erlbaum.

Frey, L., & Sunwolf. (2005). The symbolic-interpretive perspective of group life. In M. S. Poole & A. B. Hollingshead (Eds.), *Theories of small groups: Interdisciplinary perspectives* (pp. 185–240). Thousand Oaks, CA: Sage.

Guralnick, M. J. (Ed.). (1997). *The effectiveness of early intervention.* Baltimore: Brookes.

Guralnick, M. J. (2005). Early intervention for children with intellectual disabilities: Current knowledge and future prospects. *Journal of Applied Research in Intellectual Disabilities, 18,* 313–324.

Illinois Department of Human Services, (2007). Retrieved July 22, 2007, from http://www.dhs.state.il.us/page.aspx?item=31744

Keenan-Rich, N. (2002, January-March). Early Intervention: Is being a good SLP enough? The ASHA Leader Online. Retrieved July 12, 2007, from http://www.asha.org/about/publications/leader-online/archives/ 2002/q1/020205_e.htm

Kingsley, E.P. (1987). Welcome to Holland. Retrieved July 12, 2007, from http://www.our-kids.org/Archives/Holland.html

Kramer, M. W. (2002). Communication in a community theater group: Managing multiple group roles. *Communication Studies, 53,* 151–170.

Lammers, J. C., & Krikorian, D. (1997). Theoretical extension and operationalization of the bona fide group construct with an application to surgical teams. *Journal of Applied Communication, 25,* 17–38.

Mills, C. B. (2005). Catching up with Down syndrome: Parents of children with Trisomy 21 learning to deal with the medical community. In E. B. Ray (Ed.), *Health communication in practice: A case study approach* (pp. 195–210). Mahwah, NJ: Erlbaum.

Morris, J. (1993). Prejudice. In J. Swain, V. Finkelstein, S. French, & M. Oliver (Eds.), *Disabling barriers-enabling environments* (pp. 101–106). London: Sage.

Newell, C. (1994). A critique of the construction of prenatal diagnosis and disability. In J. Mc Kie (Ed.), *The Proceedings of the Conference: Ethical Issues in Prenatal Diagnosis and the Termination of Pregnancy* (pp. 89–96). Melbourne, Australia: Monash University.

Pelchat, D., Lefebvre, H., Proulx, M., & Reidy, M. (2004). Parental satisfaction with an early family intervention program. *Journal of Perinatal Neonatal Nursing, 18* (2), 128–144.

Peterander, F. (2000). The best quality cooperation between parents and experts in early intervention. *Infants and Young Children, 12,* 32–45.

Petronio, S., Jones, S., & Morr, M. C. (2003). Family privacy dilemmas: Managing communication boundaries within family groups. In L. R. Frey (Ed.), *Group communication in context: Studies of bona fide groups* (pp. 23–55). Mahwah, NJ: Erlbaum.

Poole, M. S. (1999). Group communication theory. In L. R. Frey (Ed.), *The handbook of group communication theory and research* (pp. 37–70). Thousand Oaks, CA: Sage.

Putnam, L. L. (1994). Revitalizing small group communication: Lessons learned from a bona fide group perceptive. *Communication Studies, 45,* 97–102.

Putnam, L. L., & Stohl, C. (1990). Bona fide groups: A reconceptualization of groups in context. *Communication Studies, 41,* 248–265.

Putnam, L. L., & Stohl, C. (1996). Bona fide groups: An alternative perspective for communication and small group decision making. In R. Y. Hirokawa & M. S. Poole (Eds.), *Communication and group decision making* (pp. 147–178). Thousand Oaks, CA: Sage.

Socha, T. J. (1999). Communication in family units: Studying the first "group." In L. R. Frey (Ed.), *The handbook of group communication theory and research* (pp. 475–492). Thousand Oaks, CA: Sage.

Stohl, C., & Putnam, L. L. (1994). Group communication in context: Implications for the study of bona fide groups. In L. R. Frey (Ed.), *Group communication in context: Studies of natural groups* (pp. 285–292). Hillsdale, NJ: Erlbaum.

Stohl, C., & Putnam, L. L. (2003). Communication in bona fide groups: A retrospective and prospective account. In L. R. Frey (Ed.), *Group communication in context: Studies of bona fide groups* (pp. 399–414). Mahwah, NJ: Erlbaum.

Sunwolf, & Leets, L. (2004). Being left out: Rejecting outsiders and communicating group boundaries in childhood and adolescent peer groups. *Journal of Applied Communication Research, 32,* 195–223.

U.S. Code of Federal Regulations 303.1 (1989). Retrieved July 25, 2007, from the U.S. Department of Education Web site: http://idea.ed.gov/static/partCNprm

Vanderhoff, M. (2004). Maximizing your role in early intervention. *PT-Magazine of Physical Therapy, 12,* 48–53.

10 Parent-Talk and Sport Participation

Interaction Between Parents, Children, and Coaches Regarding Level of Play in Sports

Paul D. Turman, Angela Zimmerman, and Brett Dobesh

Youth sports has found itself at a crossroads as our society has shifted from a game to a sport culture, whereby the athletic activity of young athletes is controlled and maintained by a combination of parents, coaches, and administrators. For many families, sports consume a significant portion of their leisure activities, including the enactment, consumption, and performance of sports (Kassing et al., 2004). For larger families with multiple youth athletes, it is not uncommon for sport to constitute a central role in parent-child interaction (i.e., talk about practice and competitive experiences), parent-child time together (i.e., transporting to practice, coaching etc.), and family leisure time (i.e., multiple family members assuming spectator roles). As more family time and resources are devoted to sports, there is further opportunity for parents to provide feedback (both support and pressure) to encourage participation. Previous research suggests parental pressure is correlated with athlete drop-out and retention rates (Gould, 1982; Gould, Feltz, & Weiss, 1985), stress (Hellstedt, 1987, Jellineck & Durant, 2004), increased sport anxiety (Anderson, Funk, Elliott, & Smith, 2003), and reduced self-concept (Hoyle & Leff, 1997). Despite these research findings, limited research has examined issues about youth sports participation that necessitate parent-child interaction about sports in the private family setting.

Not only do parents spend time providing feedback to their children, but youth sport participation often necessitates the need for parent-coach interaction. Parents and coaches have been found to collide over the objectives for sport participation (i.e., skill development vs. fostering competitive environment), and much of this disagreement emerges as a result of miscommunication between these two entities (Yan & McCullagh, 2004). Kidman, McKenzie, and McKenzie (1999) described instances of parents being banned from sporting events for behavior such as tripping or hitting players from opposing teams or berating coaches and officials. The competing notions of "everyone should be allowed to play" and "win at all costs" provide opportunities for conflict between parents and coaches, resulting in the need for these sports organizations, and coaches especially, to establish boundaries that restrict parent access to the rationale, justification, and decisions for playing one child over another. Despite a coach's attempt to establish rigid boundaries for communicating with parents, playing status appears to be a unique factor that necessitates the need for parents to maintain direct and indirect control over their child's playing time. In her description of Communication Privacy Management (CPM), Petronio (2002) argues, "The regulation process is fundamentally communicative in nature. Consequently, CPM places communication at the core of private disclosure because it focuses on the interplay of granting or denying access to information that is defined as private" (p. 3). Taking this theoretical perspective toward parent-child and parent-coach sport boundaries, the purpose of this study was twofold: (a) to determine what topics or issues about sports participation parents discuss with their children; and (b) to identify the techniques parents use to develop relationships with coaches to facilitate their child's participation levels.

This investigation has significance on a number of levels. First, Baxter-Jones and Maffulli (2003) suggested parents with an active interest in sports are more likely to expose their children to sports at an early age and allow sports to become an important part of the family's leisure time. Family scholars (Fitzpatrick & Vangelisti, 1995) argue that the family is an important socializing agent for children and the way children view their athletic experience is dependent on the way their parents communicate to them about what occurs. As more family time and resources are devoted toward sports, there is an increased opportunity for parents to provide feedback (both support and pressure) to encourage participation and influence coaching decisions.

Second, many coaches have observed that parents serve as one of the primary obstacles in their attempt to coach young athletes. Mach (1994) noted that "Misunderstandings between the coach and the parent later leads to clashes of opinion between the parent and the child and then between the coach and the child" (p. 5). Coaching proverbs such as "The best coaching jobs are in orphanages because there are no parents there," or "If it isn't one thing it's a mother," add credence to the fact that coaches struggle with the interaction they have with parents. Recent findings report that youth sports in our society have been recently scarred by increased accounts of parental violence surrounding young athlete playing status. Stories of such events are rampant and difficult to ignore. As the frequency and severity of these parent-coach interactions increase, further research is needed to assess the nature of parent-coach communicative boundaries regarding participation.

Parent-Child Sport Interaction

Despite the perceived benefit for parents and children, sport participation can produce emotions ranging from excitement to apprehension, and research suggests these responses can be directly influenced by interaction with parents (Hoyle & Leff, 1997; Roberts, Treasure, & Hall, 1994). To encourage sport participation, parents often find themselves serving as motivators, coaches, or facilitators, yet many have different ego orientations for their child's sport participation (i.e., having fun, winning, increased physical activity). As a result, their direct and indirect messages about sport participation can either foster or deter child involvement (Kidman et al., 1999), stress (Hirschhorn & Loughead, 2000) and drop-out rates (Bergin & Haubusta, 2004). Most recently, research has begun to examine specific types of feedback provided by parents to young athletes; parental support and parental pressure. Research suggests parental support produces positive results for young athletes and is correlated with increased enjoyment and self-esteem (Hoyle & Leff, 1997) and increased sport involvement (Anderson et al., 2003). However, parental pressure has been found to relate to athletes' fear of failure, guilt, and sport anxiety (Scanlan, Stein, & Ravizza, 1991) and to be inversely related to athlete enjoyment (Anderson et al., 2003).

Parental Support

Social support is a benefit many people seek from disclosure (Derlega, Metts, Petronio & Margulis, 1993) and these benefits include: (a) *esteem support* represented by support given to help a person feel loved, valued, and accepted even though the person may be going through difficult times; (b) *informational support* in which guidance, advice, or information is given to help a person cope with a problem; (c) *instrumental support* defined by tangible support given to a person who needs assistance; and (d) *motivational support* represented by encouragement from others. Research has demonstrated relationships between various forms of parent social support and sport outcomes for young athletes. Hirschhorn and Loughead (2000) observed that supportive parents (noninterfering with a focus on effort rather than winning) utilized more open communication and encouraged children to develop at their own pace. Additionally, Hoyle and Leff (1997) observed that when feedback was presented in a positive light, parental support was associated with athlete enjoyment toward the sport as well as perceived sport importance. Athletes who reported higher levels of enjoyment also displayed higher levels of self-esteem. When assessing technique for encouraging sport participation, Roberts et al. (1994) found parents to most commonly emphasize goal-reaching, followed by pointing out child's personal improvement or growth, importance of trying your best, and reward for hard work and overcoming difficulties. These findings also indicate that children perceive two conceptually different types of parental involvement, one that represents *parental facilitation* of the children's activity participation, and one that suggests *parental control* of the child's activity participation and imposes performance standards. For some athletes this parental control could be perceived as a moderate form of parental pressure.

Parental Pressure

Despite the potential positive benefits that result from parent-child sport interaction, research has also demonstrated how parental influence can produce detrimental results (Roberts et al., 1994). When examining the negative repercussions of parental involvement, messages that continually focus on success and performance-based outcomes establish an expectation in children that winning is the only way to satisfy. Ego building involves instances where parents' natural instinct is to wish for their children's success in their respective sport. Hirschhorn and Loughead (2000) found that children can develop the fear that their standing with parents is based on their on-field performance, which can produce long-term effects that influence the parent-child relationship. Often the parents will attempt to live vicariously (i.e., living through the success/failure or another's athletic performance) through their child and will believe that the performance of the child is a direct reflection of them (Hirschhorn & Loughead, 2000). This biased approach causes the child stress and lowers satisfaction of the sport itself. Roberts et al. (1994) presented a typology of negative parental attitudes that are often passed on to children, including a need to: (a) outperform their opponents, (b) show others they were the best, (c) demonstrate their superiority, (d) accomplished something others could not, and (e) exhibit dominance over others. White, Kavussanu, Tank, and Wingate (2004) found a strong correlation between parent and child sport orientation (both task and social). Specifically, young athletes who had parents who held a task orientation were also more likely to view sports in a similar fashion (i.e., effort leads to success in sports). Those parents with a high ego orientation were also more likely to have young athletes with this orientation, producing negative assumptions about sport involvement (i.e., success is achieved through deception and external factors).

Boundaries of Privacy in Sports

As the research on parental pressure supports, parental perceptions of sports necessitate the need for parents to provide a combination of private and public disclosures. Much of the existing research highlights the harmful nature of such parental comments. For instance, Kidman et al. (1999) observed that 35% of comments made by parents at sporting events resulted in forms of correcting child performance, scolding for inappropriate play, or contradicting coach recommendations. As parents view their child's athletic competition, they are further exposed to a number of factors that may mediate the need to provide feedback (both support and pressure) in a more private setting. Privacy and disclosure within the family environment has been the focus of many research studies. Communication Privacy Management (CPM) theory (Petronio, 1994, 2000, 2002) suggests that sharing private information is not easy and relegated by two factors: boundary structures and rule management (Golish & Caughlin, 2002). Communication boundary structures identify who is and who is not allowed access to private information, while rule management represents the regulation of private information that moderate boundary linkage, boundary ownership, and boundary permeability (Petronio, 2000). Petronio further described four interrelated dimensions associated with communication boundaries, including ownership, control, permeability, and levels. *Ownership* represents an individual's right to reveal or conceal private information about themselves, whereby individuals assess the amount of risk associated with revealing private information. *Control* refers to whom private information is shared with. For instance, a connection to a child's coach may make one privy to information that is restricted to other parents. Making choices about who has access to private information influences the *permeability* of one's communication constructed boundaries. Free exchange results in permeable boundary management. Finally, *levels* represent the individuals within the subsystem who have access to information (i.e., assistant coaches, players, the team, parents).

Much of the family research examining privacy and disclosure has focused on issues related to topic avoidance (Golish, 2000; Guerrero & Afifi, 1995) and communication motives (Barbato, Graham, & Perse, 2003). For active sports families, a variety of topics may necessitate the need for parents to talk to their child about their sport participation. Yet, little is known regarding issues and topics associated with a child's sport that requires parent-child interaction. How a parent talks about the problems they perceive with their child's sport can be influential in determining a child's continued participation. Thus, to uncover and assess these topics, the following research question (RQ) was set forth:

RQ 1: What sport topics necessitate the need for parents to talk with their children regarding their sports participation, and what techniques do parents use when discussing these topics with their children?

Parent-Coach Relationships

Kirk and MacPhail (2003) found that coaches believed a significant number of parents were "antagonists" who overemphasized the skills of their child and demanded that much of the coach's time and effort be devoted to his/ her child. Coaches in their investigation "held the view that the ideal parent was a willing helper who offered support and encouragement to their child but who did not interfere with the coaches' work" (pp. 39–40). In an assessment of both athlete and parent types, Kirk and Macphail completed observations and interviews with parents and athletes and classified parental positioning in relation to their child's participation at each of these levels. The "non-attenders" were likely to drop off children at practice or games but never stayed to watch. "Spectators" were those parents that attended all practices, but took no part in helping with practice or the management of the team. "The helpers" were defined as parents who contributed time and effort to assist the coach. These parents typically began as "spectators" who transitioned into assisting after their children had been properly introduced to the sport. Their final parent classification was "The committed members" who assisted the coaches, maintained contact with other parents, and assisted with the running of the sport organization over an extended period of time. Stein, Raedeke, and Glenn (1999) suggested that the level of involvement may help to influence athlete success, stress and enjoyment; yet researchers should begin to better understand "the quality of parent involvement in terms of involvement degree" (p. 597). Preliminary research examining parent-coach interaction presents evidence of tension between parents and coaches. However, little is known about the communicative rules that encourage or restrict interaction between these two entities. Thus, to further assess these communicative barriers, the following research questions were set forth:

> RQ 2: What boundaries, if at all, do coaches create that regulate interaction with parents regarding their child's sport participation, and how do parents negotiate those boundaries by developing coach-parent relationships?

Method

Participants

The participants for this study consisted of a sample of 13 male and 17 female parents with at least one child involved in organized junior high or high school team sports in the Midwest. Parents reflected on the sport experiences of their male ($n = 17$) and female ($n = 13$) children who were currently participating across a variety of team sports including 18 basketball, three football, three soccer, and at least one athlete involved in baseball, softball, bowling, volleyball, wrestling, and track. Athletes ranged between 12 to 18 years of age and varied in their level of playing time in their respective sport including 47% who started every game, 17% who were starters for at least half of the season, and 36% who were back-up or reserve players for all games. A majority (33%) of the athletes were in schools with more than 300 students per class, followed by 12 between 99 to 20 students, and 8 between 299 to 100 students.

Data Collection Procedures

A structured procedure for data collection was used to obtain consistent types of data across parents assessed in this study. For this analysis the following steps were employed. Participants were recruited through the use of a snowball sampling technique. Parents with children involved in organized youth sports between the 7th and 12th grade were asked to take part in the interview process. To comply with the regulations of the university's Institutional Review Board, the primary researchers described three aspects of the study, including: (a) the purpose of the study, whereby parents were informed that research was being conducted to determine how they communicate with their son/daughter and his/her coach about sports; (b) the method by which data collection would occur, which required the utilization of video and audio equipment to record the interview; and (c) what the data would be utilized for after transcription occurred. After parents agreed to participate, the primary researchers acquired written consent from them. Once the interview was complete, participants were asked to identify other parents that they felt would be interested in talking about their child's sport participation.

Data Analysis

After the conclusion of each interview, the primary researchers transcribed the interview data. The interviews lasted between 12 and 40 minutes, and for each interview roughly six to seven pages of transcription was obtained to yield 210 total pages of data. To complete data analysis, the data were analyzed utilizing five steps. First, the principal researcher and two additional coders (graduate students with previous coursework in qualitative methods) read through a sample of the data before analyzing transcripts from each interview. This was done to garner a holistic understanding of the interaction parents had with their children and coaches. Second, the researcher and coders then re-read each transcript, focusing on identifying and recording theme types and topics that emerged from the initial pool of transcripts. Unitizing reliability of the coding was then assessed after this first-stage of coding, yielding a coefficient of reliability at .84 or 84%.

Those messages that received agreement from all three coders during the initial stage of coding were used during the final coding process. Using the constant comparative method (Glaser & Strauss, 1967; Strauss, 1987), data were then analyzed to identify emergent themes. The principal researcher and coders independently identified initial classifications and assigned temporary labels to each. They then met to review the outcome of the initial coding and discuss a consistent scheme for the final coding of the data. Areas of disagreement were discussed among coders and consensus was achieved by further reducing the categories to those identified in the results section. The "categorizing reliability" assessed after the second-stage of coding yielded a Scott's *pi* at .80. Finally, the transcripts were read again to ensure the accuracy and consistency of the categories, looking for any rival explanations of the findings (Miles & Huberman, 1994). After the results were written, the coders then compared them to the transcripts to ensure accuracy of the findings.

Results

Topics of Sport-Talk

Research question #1 inquired about what topics or issues, perceived by parents, necessitated a need to talk with their child about the nature of their sports participation. Throughout the transcript 131 different utterances were identified that reflected topics parents discussed with their child about their sport. These were further classified into four different themes (see Table 10.1). The most common responses (35%) were categorized *Playing Time*, with 23 of the parents indicating instances where they felt a need to talk with their child

Table 10.1 Sport Topics Requiring Parent-Child Interaction

Theme	Definition	Frequency
Playing Time	Responses to perceived lack of playing time or need to discuss coach's decision to reduce playing status.	42 (35%)
Sport Politics	Factors parents perceived to exist outside the athletes control including coach favoritism and influence from team supporters.	37 (28%)
Negative Coaching Behaviors	Inappropriate coaching behaviors directly observed by parents or learned about through interaction with child.	34 (30%)
Sport Competitiveness	Overemphasis placed on winning displayed through combination of coach and parent behaviors at sporting events.	18 (14%)

Note: Frequency and percentages are represented for each major theme emerging from the data analysis.

regarding their level of play on the team. When talking about playing time, some parents were proactive with this discussion by attempting to address their child's potential dissatisfaction before it could emerge. One parent stated:

> A little bit at the beginning of the season I wasn't so sure that he would get to play so I had a conversation about 'here is the nature of the game now and not everybody gets to play. It's not like when you were in little league and there was a rule that says everybody has to play. We keep score and everybody is trying to win now, and the job of the coach is to try and figure out how to win and help you be a better player at the same time. So not everybody will get a chance to play and if you are on the bench you need to understand that your job is to support the team, and hopefully you'll get to play. (30: 62–68; here and elsewhere the numbers refer to the transcript number and the line number of the quote)

When confronted by their child's frustration about playing time, parents worked to reinterpret the situation from the coaches' perspective. One parent whose child commented about not getting enough playing time indicated, "I just listen and sometimes what doesn't seem like a lot of playing time to him, might seem like a lot of playing time to me. I will remind him that … he really had some good plays, or point out something positive that he did" (1: 57–61). Positive encouragement worked to focus athlete attention on many of the factors the athlete controlled including working to do their best and using the time on the bench to learn from teammates. Parents who discussed athlete behavior that extended beyond the athletic ability of the child, suggests that making contributions to the team and having the right attitude, were the biggest determining factor for deciding playing time. For instance one parent stated: "For a kid, I think attitude, being prepared, using good character as far as sportsmanship and rooting on the other teammates. And having all their equipment, and coming in there with a positive attitude. 'I'm ready to learn, I'm ready to work, let's do this,' and not waste time messing around" (10: 70–72). A similar sentiment was displayed by another parent: "Sports are not only about talent, there are other aspects such as team and hard work that will take a person much further than talent. If players work hard and do their best, things will fall into place and everyone will get a chance" (15: 107–109). These factors were reflective of parents who perceived athletes should de-emphasize the desire to win and become committed to the entire team effort. If an athlete was able to embrace these characteristics (i.e., motivating others, becoming a team leader, being prepared), playing time would directly follow.

The second most common responses were categorized as *Sport Politics,* which included factors outside of the control of the child's athletic ability and rested on the subjective decision making of the coach (28%). A wide range of issues were addressed by parents, including the perception that coaches showed considerable favoritism to their own children at the expense of other players on the team. A number of parents made the observation: "You look at the team, I mean you go to a game and I can always figure out who the coach's kid is. Quite often the coaches' child will play more" (28: 138–140). Another parent reported:

… there are definitely a lot of coaches in our school with high school age children who are playing on the sporting teams … I'd like to think it's ability, you know, that's what they try to say, they are playing the kids who show the best ability. (12: 80–83)

Coaches were also perceived to favor older athletes, athletes that attended camps or extra practices, and to rely on star athletes to make decisions regarding playing time.

Parents also perceived parent interaction with the coach to contribute to the politics of playing time. One parent said: "You do see parents that are really in the coach's face all the time. 'You need to play my kid,' and 'my kid's been here,' and 'my kid needs to do this,' and 'my kid takes private training,' and all this" (10: 96–98). Parents described how they observed other parents who would call coaches on a regular basis, talk directly with them after games, or volunteer to serve as assistant coaches to help increase their son/daughter's playing status. One parent referred to these as "helicopter parents. They are always hovering around the coach, the practices, the games and try and get their hands into everything in hopes of persuading the coach to play their kid more" (5: 113–115). Parents also described the extremes other parents would employ to subtly influence a coach's decision. When asked to provide an example of such behavior one parent responded:

I have seen dads especially try to butter up the coach in a lot of ways … They will do whatever it takes if it means more playing time for their kid.

I have even seen parents draft up plans and build better dugouts, conces-
sions stands and even the announcer's box. (13: 75–80)

Many of these indirect attempts extended beyond the sporting context such
as forming informal relationships, or using existing relationships as leverage.
When such behaviors were perceived, parents reported a need to talk about
the politics of sports with their child. In these instances, parents still reminded
athletes that they must work harder to overcome these hurdles. When his
daughter was losing playing time to the coach's daughter, one father said, "We
have had to discuss this with her and remind her of small town politics. It takes
time, but she often just gets more encouraged to work hard and push the other
players on the team" (15: 55–58).

Negative Coaching Behaviors was the third most common (30%) and represented actions whereby parents questioned the coach's objectivity and ethical
practices with their child or the team. A number of parents told stories about
what they perceived to be inappropriate conduct, including one parent of a
female soccer player who stated:

I just heard my daughter telling about something they did two years ago
at practice when preparing for the world cup … if they didn't get the goal,
they had to bend over with their butt in the net and let the kids aim at
them. (11: 122–124)

Another parent reported, "I heard, from a past team that he picked out a
player and had him sit on the top row of the bleachers facing the wall, and at
the end of practice they left him there (1: 77–78). In these instances, parents
learned about the coach's behavior through their child's first-hand account
of practice and locker room behavior, requiring them to explain to their
child(ren) how the coach's behavior was inappropriate. A majority of these
parents reflected primarily on the level of support or encouragement the coach
provided. These included things such as "belittling or putting down my son or
others" (3: 122–123) or "He was a yeller and a screamer" (12: 103). When faced
with coaches who displayed behaviors that fell within this classification, parents used the private family setting as a place to interpret the coaches' behavior for the child. In a number of instances, the parent's interpretation served to
contradict the motivational techniques employed by the coach.

Sport Competitiveness was the fourth most common theme that emerged
from the data (14%) and represented instances where parents' perceived sports
had become too competitive by placing an overemphasis on winning. A majority of these utterances focused on the role of parents and sports organizations
which either pushed kids or established policies that eliminated athlete enjoyment. A number of parents stated they would "like to see more just for fun …"
and that "… too much emphasis and too much money is being spent on the
kids' sporting activities" (11: 31–35). Some parents attributed this problem to
"other parents" behavior that they have witnessed while watching their children participate. One parent noted:

... there are a lot of things I would change, but I think the most important thing would be the overbearing and mouthy parents. These people forget this game is not for them and to feel good. It is for the kids to have fun. Too many parents want blood and will stop at nothing to get a win. (13: 24–27)

These parents perceived that winning was promoted to be more important than learning the sport and that overbearing parents discouraged their own desire to have their children participate. As a result, parents indicated a need to address this topic with their child as a way to encourage continued participation by deemphasizing such inappropriate behavior.

Coach Boundaries and Coach-Parent Relationships

Research question #2 sought to determine what techniques parents used to develop relationships with their child's coach, and what necessitated the need for those relationships. A limited number of the parents ($n = 4$) indicated that coaches had established explicit guidelines for parents to follow when it came to the interaction they would have with parents. This often centered on discussions about playing time and coaching decisions. One parent recalled the initial parents meeting: "... they tell you at the parents' meeting right away, 'your kid, we will decide who's going to play. Don't call. If you have a concern, we decide, we're the coaches. It's not middle school anymore. We're going to pick the best players and play them how we want.' And they come right out and tell you that, so parents know and you sign papers that you accept this and to be a good parent in the bleachers ..." (11: 57–62). Another parent described the system his son's coach employed: "... you can call them and discuss how you think your son is progressing, but you can't ask about your son's playing time" (19: 95–98). Even if coaches did not establish explicit rules or guidelines, a significant number of parents perceived interaction about playing time would be detrimental to their child's success on the team. Many provided examples of parents yelling in plays from the sidelines or bleachers, talking with the coach after the game, or calling the coach at home. One parent recalled, "I'll tell you, the ones that do approach him do it often and it's not always a positive exchange" (3: 70–71), while another said, "I wouldn't want a parent yapping at me and complaining at me either way" (21: 108–110). Because these parents perceived this form of interaction would be viewed negatively by the coach, they make a conscious effort to contain their emotions and feelings. After her son had lost a starting spot on his basketball team a female parent stated:

And at the time, which made it even harder, was that Pat's head coach was our fourth grader's teacher. And he was a poor teacher that nobody liked, and we would have requested for the good of our fourth grader to be changed out of that class, but in a small school everybody knows everything and we didn't want to jeopardize David's playing time or any chances of it because he thought we didn't think he was a good teacher. (12: 75–80)

Another parent made a similar statement about withholding feelings: "… he probably thinks I think he is doing a good job because like I said, I never let my true feelings show, cause he might take it out on my kid and I don't want that" (13: 87–88).

When assessing the transcripts for the types of relationship parents described having with their child's coach, three major types emerged (see Table 10.2). The lowest level relationship was classified as the *Spectators* (n = 9) and included parents who maximized their distance from the coach but made conscious efforts to ensure the coach recognized their presence and level of support. One parent described the relationship: "We've thanked them, we've encouraged them, we try to follow the rules in getting the kids to practice … We thank them after the season, and then we give them gift cards and things like that" (21: 124–126). These parents attended a number of practice sessions and supported their child's athletic involvement by attending all games, volunteering to provide team meals, or providing snacks or refreshments.

The second level relationship was classified as the *Enthusiast* (n = 12) representing those parents who made a point to offer insight or encouragement to the coach but who also made a conscious effort to establish only a surface-level relationship. Their interaction focused mainly on the accomplishments or actions of the team as a whole and excluded recognition of individual child accomplishments. As one male parent put it: "The conversations are usually pretty basic and may include something along the lines of 'nice game coach' or 'that other team played some pretty tight defense.' We try to avoid conversation about our child with the coach" (14: 93–95). One key distinction between the Enthusiast and the Spectator relationship were the motives behind the interaction with the coach. Parents appeared to use these opportunities to demonstrate their level of knowledge about the particular sport as a way to establish a level of status or influence over coaching decisions. A parent of a junior high football player reported, "I would be inclined to tell him something

Table 10.2 Parent-Coach Relationship Types (n = 30)

Type	Definition	Frequency
Spectator	Superficial relationship whereby parents foster connection with coach by showing support and presence.	9 (30%)
Enthusiast	Indirect relationship whereby parent offered verbal encouragement with emphasis on team rather than individual.	12 (40%)
Fanatic	Direct relationship whereby parents made point to engage the coach about their child's performance.	9 (30%)

Note: Frequency and percentages are represented for each relationship type emerging from the data analysis.

that I've noticed watching games pretty closely. I may pick things up once and a while … and say here is something I've noticed" (30: 146–149). These parents worked to demonstrate a high level of interest and subject knowledge in the sport beyond what a spectator would attempt.

The third level relationship was characterized as the *Fanatic* (n = 9), which consisted of parents who perceived permeable boundaries between them and the coach. These parents were willing to address issues and topics directly, either face-to-face or over the phone. To better understand his son's coach, one parent stated, "I did call him on the phone; I did talk to him. I feel that it is important to know who's coaching your kid and spend some time and find out where they're coming from, what's going on and be aware" (10: 83–85). This interaction was seldom described in a negative manner by parents. For instance, one parent said, "I'm not going to question issues of technique and play so much like other dads do, but I will always want to know about the decisions my son's made and my input as a parent about things in terms of the position of play" (20: 159–162). This type of parent-coach relationship was more common in smaller towns where parents and coaches often associated away from the sport. When this occurred, parents often used external interests as a logical excuse for talking about sports. The mother of a sophomore football player described the level of interaction that occurred between her husband and their son's coach: "Because (name of town) is so small it's hard not to run into (name of coach) or the assistant coaches while you are downtown. Not much else to talk about other than football so it always comes up" (29: 117–119).

Discussion

The emphasis parents place on their children's sport participation has implications for both athletes and coaches. Overall, this investigation provides insight into two important relationships that emerge through sport interaction: parent-child and parent-coach. Initially, this study sought to uncover issues or topics about sport participation that required parent-child interaction, and then assess how parents address these topics with their children. This investigation demonstrated that parents described four primary topics associated with their child's sport participation that required intervention on their part. Primarily, parents indicated a need to discuss the topic of playing time when it came to their child's sport participation. A majority of these parents encouraged the child to work harder to help control his/her playing status on the team, or highlighting the value of being a team player and supporting coaches decisions even when playing time was not at a premium. This finding is interesting when noting that parents also spent considerable time talking about the politics of sports with their child, yet only a small percentage of the parents addressed how sport politics influenced athlete playing time. Parents often made reference to what they called "other parents" who badgered coaches or overemphasized winning in their child's sport, yet they worked to downplay these aspects of the sport during interaction with their child. Dix and Grusec (1983) found that parents who focused on positive intrinsic behaviors resulted in increased physical activity by their children. Thus, by placing an emphasis on factors under the control of the athlete (i.e., working hard, supporting teammates), parents increased the potential for intrinsic motivation and increased physical activity. This is a vital implication when noting that adolescence is an important period in which one learns about physical fitness. Anderssen and Wold (1992) stated that "evidence shows the potential for preventing cardiovascular disease and all-cause mortality in a population by increasing the physical activity and physical fitness in less active groups" (p. 341).

A second implication for these findings is represented by the fact that both mothers and fathers played important roles when discussing sport topics. When assessing turning points in parent-child relationships, Golish (2000) observed that activities together, which included sporting events, were an important context for communicating closeness. Yet, findings suggested this was not a common turning point for mother-child relationships, because activities together represented an outlet for fathers to display affection and closeness through their physical presence. For the parents in this investigation, sport topics appeared to represent joint interaction between mothers and fathers, whereby they perceived equal levels of interaction regarding these sport topics.

In addition, this study sought to identify how coaches establish boundaries with parents and the techniques parents use to develop relationships and interact with their child's coach. Findings from research question #2 demonstrate that coaches feel a need to control information regarding an athlete's playing time by establishing what Petronio (2002) referred to as "ownership lines" (p. 6). These collectively held privacy boundaries about team decisions become impregnable through coaches' explicit remarks. Coaches assumed ownership of this private information as a result of the risk they perceived. Thus, playing time was viewed as a highly risky disclosure to make to parents. However, results suggest that parents perceived the development of an informal relationship worked to chip away at those boundaries to create an indirect influence on coaching decisions. Petronio (2002) argued that although we work to control our communication boundaries, one's "boundaries may also become weakened by events outside the control of the owner" (p. 6). Thus, attempts by parents, when they engage in the simple role of spectator, may be perceived as a way to gain a level of control over coaching decisions. Some parents perceived that demonstrating "I'm active and present to support the team" worked to subconsciously influence a coach's decision. The enthusiasts attacked these coach imposed boundaries more subtly demonstrating their knowledge of a particular sport, and this level of influence gave the appearance that they are privy to the private information that was influencing coaching decisions. Fanatics perceived their relationship in a way that suggested permeable boundaries; suggesting that it was appropriate to talk and interact with coaches.

Limitations and Future Research

In light of the contributions of this study, there are several limitations and directions for future researchers. First, because of the nature of the design, the findings from this examination only provide a representation of parental perceptions of sport topics of talk and coach-parent relationships. Thus, it is difficult to estimate how athletes' view the interaction they have with their parents about sports. Future research should attempt to examine athlete and coach perceptions of this same interaction. In-depth interviews or open-ended surveys would be appropriate to ask athletes and coaches to reflect on specific topics of talk and describe how parents address these topics when they arise. It would also be interesting to assess coach perceptions of parent relationships. Furthermore, along these lines, it seems warranted for future researchers to interview the combination of athlete, parent, and coach. Doing so would provide an opportunity to determine how a combination of perspectives best reflects these aspects of the athletic experience.

Second, there are additional considerations that should be examined from the athlete's perspective. This study does little to determine the athlete outcomes associated with parent discussion of these topics. Previous research on topic avoidance found that openness between parents and children is related to relationship satisfaction and solidarity (Bochner, 1982; Crohan, 1992). The examination of additional factors that contribute to the intrinsic motivation for continued sport participation would seem valuable. How does parent-child interaction about these sport topics influence athlete satisfaction and relationship with the coach? Are there certain topics that parents should avoid talking about with their children? What topics would children identify and disclose with their parents about sports? These are some questions that could be answered by examining parent-child sport-talk from a communication perspective. Research may also benefit from a different theoretical perspective on parent-child and parent-coach relationships. For instance, the foundation of CPM is grounded in the dialectal framework (Baxter & Montgomery, 1996) arguing that individuals experience tensions that necessitate change in their relationship. One primary tension is the desire to reveal and conceal information (i.e., openness vs. closedness) whereby coaches must negotiate a parents desire to uncover playing time decisions, and need for a relationship with the coach (autonomy vs. connection).

Practical Applications

Although caution should be used when suggesting practical applications from a single study, the findings from this investigation demonstrate a number of valuable applications for both new and experienced coaches. First, a number of coaches used an initial meeting with players and parents to inform them about their guidelines for discussing issues associated with playing time. It makes sense that coaches desire to control and determine how information about playing time is managed. Thus, their desire to reveal and conceal that information, presents a rigid boundary that keeps parents out of the communication sphere they have erected for the team. Parents who serve spectator roles perceive inconsistencies when other parents worked to build enthusiast and fanatic relationships. The perceptions of these relationships seemed to further negate a coach's ability to establish rigid boundaries because the "other parent" is working both directly and indirectly to negotiate relationships. This is increasingly relevant when considering that one of the major topics parents have to discuss with their child is the politics of sports. Adding to this is the notion that parents perceive factors other than athletic ability influence playing status. It was difficult for parents in this study not to perceive a need to develop at least a surface level relationship with the coach. Thus, coaches should be encouraged to fully discuss what factors contribute to playing time, or more importantly, what factors have no impact on their decision. By explicitly stating that athlete accomplishments (or lack thereof) rather than parental interaction determine playing status, coaches may help to limit the perceived need for parents to establish unwanted relationships. More important, athletic directors would be better served if they worked to establish a consistent set of guidelines and procedures whereby coaches discussed status decisions.

Second, parents highlighted coaching behaviors as a topic of discussion between them and their child. A number of the fanatic parents indicated that they called or talked directly with the coach after an incident during practice. Things that ridiculed or embarrassed athletes emerged as a rationale or justification allowing parents to break down the boundary established by the coach. Permeability seemed to be weakened by a violation of these parental expectations, suggesting that coaches should attempt to fully describe the forms of punishment he/she uses. Additionally, coaches should work to better understand the importance of maintaining an athlete's emotional stability, since such stability may work to determine type of relationships they ultimately have with parents. Hellstedt (1987) reported, "Most coaches do not feel equipped to work with parents ... They feel their main area of responsibility is with the athlete. They often block out the parent, and if they view them as problem parents they refuse to deal with them at all" (p. 151). There are times when spectators and enthusiasts can be welcome additions to a team sport experience, yet control of parents who wish to develop a fanatic relationship can be better maintained through clearly identified expectations and strict boundaries.

This study has explored topics of sport-talk within the family context. Findings suggest that four main topics require parents to discuss dissatisfaction that their child experiences in their sport. Better understanding how parents discuss these topics can help to further understand the parental role for continued sport participation. Roberts et al. (1994) stated that "in play, games and sport, children are brought into contact with social order and the values inherent in society, and are provided a context within which desirable social behaviors are developed" (p. 631). In particular, Weinberg (1981) argued that proper motivation on the part of the parent will produce the best likelihood for athletic success and continued performance. Finally, the results from this analysis further support the complexity associated with coaching, as coaches' work to serve three different constituents (parents, athletes, and administrators). Negotiating the boundaries with parents may be one of the most difficult challenges new coaches face. As youth and high school coaching retention rates have continued to decline (Raedeke, Warren, & Granzyk, 2002), further inquiry is necessary that extend beyond just the Xs and Os associated with fostering athletes' athletic ability.

References

Anderson, J. C., Funk, J. B., Elliott, R., & Smith, P. H. (2003). Parental support and pressure and children's extracurricular activities: Relationships with amount of involvement and affective experience of participation. *Journal of Applied Developmental Psychology, 24*, 241–258.

Anderssen N., & Wold, B. (1992). Parental and peer influences on leisure-time physical activity in young adolescents. *Research Quarterly for Exercise and Sport, 53*, 341–349.

Barbato, C. A., Graham, E. E., & Perse, E. M. (2003). Communicating in the family: An examination of the relationship of family communication climate and interpersonal communication motives. *Journal of Family Communication, 3*, 123–150.

Baxter, L. A., & Montgomery, B. M. (1996). *Relating: Dialogue and dialectics.* New York: Guilford.

Baxter-Jones, A. D., & Maffulli, N. (2003). Parental influence on sport participation in elite young athletes. *Journal of Sports Medicine and Physical Fitness, 43*(2), 250–255.

Bergin, D. A., & Haubusta, S. F. (2004). Goal orientations of young male ice hockey players and their parents. *Journal of Genetic Psychology, 165*, 383–399.

Bochner, A. P. (1982). On the efficacy of openness in close relationships. In M. Burgoon (Ed.), *Communication Yearbook 6* (pp. 109–123). Beverly Hills, CA: Sage.

Crohan, S. E. (1992). Marital happiness and spousal consensus on beliefs and marital conflict: A longitudinal investigation. *Journal of Social and Personal Relationships, 9*, 89–102.

Derlega, V. J., Metts, S., Petronio, S., & Margulis, S. T. (1993). *Self-disclosure.* Newbury Park, CA: Sage.

Dix, T., & Grusec, J. E. (1983). Parental influence techniques: An attributional analysis. *Child Development, 54*, 645–652.

Fitzpatrick, M. A., & Vangelisti, A. L. (Eds.). (1995). *Explaining family interactions.* Thousand Oaks, CA: Sage.

Glaser, B. G., & Strauss, A. L. (1967). *The discovery of grounded theory: Strategies for qualitative research.* New York: Aldine de Gruyter.

Golish, T. D. (2000). Changes in closeness between adult children and their parents: A turning point analysis. *Communication Reports, 13*, 79–97.

Golish, T. D., & Caughlin, J. P. (2002). "I'd rather not talk about it": Adolescents' and young adults' use of topic avoidance in stepfamilies. *Journal of Applied Communication Research, 30*, 78–106.

Gould, D. (1982). Sport psychology in the 1980s: Status, direction, and challenge in youth sport research. *Journal of Sport Psychology, 4*, 203–218.

Gould, D., Feltz, D., & Weiss, M. P. (1985). Reasons for attribution in competitive youth swimming. *Journal of Sport Behavior, 5*, 155–165.

Guerrero, L. K., & Afifi, W. A. (1995). Some things are better left unsaid: Topic avoidance in family relationships. *Communication Quarterly, 43*, 276–296.

Hellstedt, J. C. (1987). The coach/parent/athlete relationship. *The Sport Psychologist, 1,* 151–160.

Hirschhorn, K. H., & Loughead, T. O. (2000). Parental impact on youth participation in sport: The physical educator's role. *The Journal of Physical Education, Recreation & Dance, 71*(9), 26–29.

Hoyle, R. H., & Leff, S. S. (1997). The role of parental involvement in youth sport participation and performance. *Adolescence, 32,* 233–245.

Jellineck, M., & Durant, S. (2004). Parents and sports: Too much of a good thing? *Contemporary Pediatrics, 21*(9), 17–20.

Kassing, J., Billings, A. C., Brown, R., Halone, K. K., Harrison, K., Krizek, B., et al. (2004). Enacting, (re)producing, consuming, and organizing sport: Communication in the community of sport. *Communication Yearbook, 28,* 373–409.

Kidman, L., McKenzie, A., & McKenzie, B. (1999). The nature and target of parents' comments during youth sport competition. *Journal of Sport Behavior, 22,* 54–68.

Kirk, D., & MacPhail, A. (2003). Social positioning and the construction of a youth sports club. *International Review for the Sociology of Sport, 38,* 23–45.

Mach, F. (1994). Defusing parent-coach dissidence. *Scholastic Coach, 63*(10), 5–6.

Miles, M. B., & Huberman, A. M. (1994). *Qualitative data analysis* (2nd ed.). Thousand Oaks, CA: Sage.

Petronio, S. (1994). Privacy binds in family interactions: The case of parental privacy invasion. In W. R. Cupach & B. H. Spitzberg (Eds.), *The darkside of interpersonal communication* (pp. 241–257). New York: Wiley.

Petronio, S. (2000). The boundaries of privacy: Praxis of everyday life. In S. Petronio (Ed.), *Balancing the secrets of private disclosures* (pp. 37–49). Mahwah, NJ: Erlbaum.

Petronio, S. (2002). *Boundaries of privacy: Dialectics of disclosure.* New York: State University of New York Press.

Raedeke, T. D., Warren, A. H., & Granzyk, T. L. (2002). Coaching commitment and turnover: A comparison of current and former coaches. *Research Quarterly for Exercise and Sport, 73,* 73–86.

Roberts, G. C., Treasure, D. C., & Hall, H. K. (1994). Parental goal orientations and beliefs about the competitive sports experience of their child. *Journal of Social Psychology, 24,* 631–645.

Scanlan, T. K., Stein, G. L., & Ravizza, K. (1991). An in-depth study of former elite figure skaters: III. Sources of stress. *Journal of Sport and Exercise Psychology, 13,* 103–120.

Stein, G. L., Raedeke, T. D., & Glenn, S. D. (1999). Children's perceptions of parent sports involvement: It's not how much, but to what degree that's important. *Journal of Sports Behavior, 22,* 591–601.

Strauss, A. (1987). *Qualitative analysis for social scientists.* New York: Cambridge University Press.

Weinberg, R. (1981). Why kids play or do not play organized sports. *The Physical Educator, 38,* 71–75.

White, S. A., Kavussanu. M., Tank, K. M., & Wingate, J. M. (2004). Perceived parental beliefs about the causes of success in sport: Relationship to athletes' achievement goals and personal beliefs. *Scandinavian Journal of Medicine & Science in Sports, 14,* 57–68.

Wold, B., & Anderssen, N. (1992). Health promotion aspects of family and peer influences on sport participation. *International Journal of Sport Psychology, 23,* 343–359.

Yan, J. H., & McCullagh, P. (2004). Cultural influence on youth's motivation of participation in physical activity. *Journal of Sport Behavior, 27,* 378–391.

11 Coaching Your Own Child

An Exploration of Dominance and Affiliation in Parent-Child Communication in the Public Sphere

Robert S. Littlefield and Cindy Larson-Casselton

From birth, children begin negotiating the way they communicate with their parents and establish communication boundaries. As they develop a clearer sense of their autonomy within the family unit, they often seek more privacy and begin to develop their own privacy rules that may differ from those of their parents. In an effort to negotiate this privacy boundary, and to maintain a close affiliation with their children, parents often strive to keep the lines of communication open (Noller, 1995; Noller & Bagi, 1985; Petronio, 2002). Depending upon the changing nature of their relationship, the way they communicate also changes (Mazur & Hubbard, 2004; Stein, Raedeke, & Glenn, 1999).

In an effort to retain some level of control, and find ways to affiliate with their children, parents often extend their involvement from the home to the school setting by taking on the role of the coach or director for their child's activities (Barber, Sukhi, & White, 1999; Noller, 1995).[1] Complicating the changing roles for both parent and child is the nature of the communication that is shared when they move from private to public spheres. The intersection of the private and public contexts and how the parent and child negotiate what they will and will not reveal is the focus of this chapter.

Conceptual Framework

Relational Communication

Scholars of relational communication suggest that individuals communicate nonverbally and verbally how they feel about each other, their relationship, and themselves in the relationship (Burgoon & Saine, 1978). This communication not only transmits information, but also defines the nature of the relationship (Burgoon & Hale, 1984; Watzlawick, Beavin, & Jackson, 1967). Dillard, Solomon, and Palmer (1999) built upon earlier research suggesting that despite the range of components, relational communication boils down to variations of two elements: dominance and affiliation. Dominance is defined as "the degree to which one actor attempts to regulate the behavior of the other," while affiliation reflects "the extent to which one individual regards another positively" (p. 53). Dillard et al., found that individuals generally do not attend to both concepts simultaneously, focusing on one or the other.

The element interacting with dominance and affiliation is involvement, defined as "the degree to which two interactants engage with one another or their behaviors are mutually dependent" (Dillard et al., 1999, p. 53). Operating as an intensity variable, level of involvement indicates a tendency toward more or less. As one member of the relationship changes the level of involvement, the elements of control and affiliation are affected. Greater involvement by an individual may lead to greater dominance, or it may prompt submissiveness to the other in the relationship. Greater involvement also may lead to either intense liking or intense disliking on the part of either individual, depending upon the nature of the relationship.

While the majority of the studies have focused on mating dyads, Dunbar (1988) suggested that research be expanded to include parent-child relationships. The present study explores how messages of control and affiliation are reflected in the way parents and children communicate in a coaching relationship when the level of parental involvement is increased.

Family Communication

While family research has increased our understanding of communication and families (Vangelisti, 2004), "the area of parent-child communication and relationship quality remains relatively uncharted" (Perry-Jenkins, Pierce, & Goldberg, 2004, p. 550). This gap has far-reaching implications, as Socha and Stamp (1995) suggested, because what children learn about communication in the family setting will be reflected in their future communication with individuals outside of the family. As parents and children communicate within the family, the type of interaction and the level of control exerted by family members affect the parent-child relationship. These family communication patterns may be examined through conversation and conformity orientations.

Koerner and Fitzpatrick (2004) described the differences between conversation and conformity orientations within families. Conversation orientation is, "the degree to which families create a climate where all family members are encouraged to participate in unrestrained interaction about a wide range of topics" (p. 184). Families with a conformity orientation stress "a climate of homogeneity of attitudes, values, and beliefs" (p. 184). The effects of these two dimensions on parent-child communication are interdependent and both must be considered when determining the nature of communication within a family (Koerner & Fitzpatrick, 2004). However, an investigation of the assumption that these orientations remain stable in different contexts has yet to be undertaken (Perry-Jenkins et al., 2004).

Communication Privacy Management

As parents and children negotiate levels of control and affiliation, they alter the ways they communicate with each other in private and public settings.

Communication Privacy Management (CPM) Theory (Petronio, 2002) provides a means for explaining how this negotiation functions within and outside of the family unit, as "people make choices about revealing or concealing based on criteria and conditions they perceive as salient" (p. 2). As parents and children become *co-owners* of information, rules are established that determine what should and should not be revealed. These negotiated boundary rules link the co-owners relationally. When boundary rules are broken and information permeates an established boundary, turbulence may occur until synchronized coordination can be established again. As more individuals co-own information (e.g., groups, teams, organizations), the negotiation of boundary rules becomes more complicated (Petronio, 2002).

In a coaching context, the parent/coach and child/team member may co-own information that they do not share with other family members. Similarly, when the family is together as a unit, the family members may co-own information that they do not share with individuals outside the family. Within the team, the coach and team members share information that is not disclosed to family members, the press, or general public. In contrast, there may be times when open disclosure is necessary between coach, player, press, and public. Despite the co-ownership of information, "if a person breaches the agreed-upon rules, the other members will enforce the sanctions that are generated to keep everyone on common ground" (Petronio, 2002, p. 133). This reinforces the notion that central to boundary management is the issue of power and control.

Instructional Communication

The literature of instructional communication provides insight into the nature of parent-child communication when the parent becomes the child's coach in a competitive context. Previous studies suggest that coaches, like teachers in the classroom, utilize instructional principles as they help guide their students to learn and to succeed (Hodges & Franks, 2002; Turman, 2003). Furthermore, just as teachers influence the affective learning of their students through immediacy, willingness to communicate, affinity-seeking behaviors, caring, and humor (Turman & Schrodt, 2004), coaches impact how team members come to view their activity (Roberts, 1984; and see Turman, Zimmerman, & Dobesh, this volume).

It follows that when parents become coaches, they also use instructional principles when working with their own children as members of the team. The attitude and approach of the parent/coach can affect how the child comes to view participation and interest in the activity. Despite calls by scholars to study how the parent/coach influences the child/participant (Brown, 1985; Brustad, 1992; Weiss & Chaumeton, 1992), only one study has explored the impact of parent/coaches on their children (Barber et al., 1999). These researchers found the presence of a parent-as-coach not to be perceived as detrimental by the child. However, the study did not examine how the context of the coaching situation influenced the nature of the communication between parent and child when the roles were changed to that of coach and team member.

In related research, studies have examined the presence of parents within teaching environments. For example, some have focused on teaching parents to play complementary roles to that of classroom teachers when helping their children to learn or develop particular academic skills or social abilities (Elksnin & Elksnin, 2000; Haney & Hill, 2004; Resetar, Noell, & Pellegrin, 2006). A more direct role for parents as teachers emerged from popular literature pertaining to home schooling (Luffman, 1998). However, few studies directly examined the effects of parents as teachers in the home school environment (e.g., Suizzo & Stapleton, 2007). Absent from all of these studies was an examination of how the parents and children communicate about their respective roles to each other or to those outside the family in the public and private spheres. Despite the call by Sprague (2002) to expand the educational contexts being investigated by instructional communication researchers, scholars have not extended previous studies to the parent/child coaching dynamic. This study provides insight into the way parents and children communicate in different contexts about practices used by the parents when coaching their children.

Method

Participants

Twenty parent-child dyads were identified as participants in the study using a convenience sampling method. The dyads were selected because of their willingness to discuss the nature of their coaching relationship and their communication patterns. In addition, all dyads were engaged in what appeared to have been stable coaching relationships for extended periods of time (median = 6 years). To be interviewed, the child had to be 18 years of age or older, the parent had to have coached the child in a competitive activity at some level, and both had to be present for the interview. The type of aesthetic activity did not matter.[2]

Five pairs involved a mother and daughter, 8 pairs were a mother and son, 1 pair was a father and daughter, and 6 pairs were fathers and sons.[3] All of the parent/coaches identified their occupation as having something to do with education. All 20 children had experienced some level of education following high school graduation.[4]

Instrument

To elicit open-ended responses from parents and children describing their thoughts or feelings about the nature of their communication relationship (Lindlof & Taylor, 2002), a 14-item instrument was generated by the researchers based upon their preliminary unpublished study of parents and children involved in coaching relationships where relational communication themes were identified. The instrument was pilot tested with a parent and child who had a coaching relationship, and minor modifications were made so that both

researchers could comfortably use the instrument when interviewing participating dyads.

The 14 structured questions focused on four different aspects of the coaching
dynamic: Coaching background; coaching stories; the nature of the communication between parent/coach and child/participant in different contexts; and
reflective questions about their views of the relationship.[5] The four questions
used for the present study included: "In what ways did/do you talk about your
coaching relationship between just the two of you," "In what ways did/do you
talk about this coaching relationship when you are in public," "How do you
think your coaching relationship affected your communication with other family members," and "How do you think your coaching relationship affected the
way you communicated with other team members?" The narrative responses
provided insight into how the participants viewed themselves, their relationships, and their personal experiences (Cohler, 1991; Friese & Grotevant, 2001).

Procedure

Following Institutional Review Board approval, interviews were scheduled at
the convenience of the participating dyads, usually in informal settings, such
as: coffee shops, restaurants, offices, or in the participants' surroundings. The
interviews varied in length, but took between one half and 1 hour to complete.
The conversations were tape recorded to "capture the interview more or less
exactly as it was spoken" (Lindlof & Taylor, 2002, p. 187).

Participants were given pseudonyms and all specific references to people,
places, and events were changed to protect anonymity. Two college students
unrelated to any of the participants transcribed the tapes. Four tapes and transcripts randomly were selected and reviewed by the researchers to check for
accuracy. No discrepancies were found. The transcripts were saved for data
analysis and audiotapes were erased.

Analysis of the Data

The transcripts from the interviews were analyzed utilizing an etic approach,
whereby pre-established categories reflecting the private and public settings
in which the communication occurred were used to sort the data. Within
these public and private settings, the data were inductively examined to identify examples of parent/coach dominance and parent/child "negotiated dominance," along with the impact of these dimensions on the family.

Communication of Dominance

Private Settings

In private, examples of parental dominance and child compliance centered on
how the child should perform or behave. These included: telling the child what
to do or how much the child would practice, and how to deal with problems.

Parent/Coach Dominance   One father said, "I think that I was too domineering ... I didn't let him give his own opinions on that a lot. I was trying to do the correcting part of being the teacher." One mother agreed: "Yes, I told him straightforward, 'you need to do this because it's going to work better.' 'I don't think this is going to work; it's not coming across. We need to change this....'" For one parent/coach, the private interaction with her daughter provided an opportunity for her to provide suggestions about how to deal with the conflict she was having with other students in a dramatic production:

> I remember one time coming home from rehearsal, and some kids were being terrible to her ... I was so, so sad for her. We got in the car and she just started crying. We drove home and we sat in the driveway for a long time and we did a lot of talking. I was trying to teach her self-talk, how to get strong in all situations: How to look at it, how to analyze it, and then how to respond to it. I remember role-playing with her.

Her daughter reflected later that she came to depend upon her mother for emotional support: "I think that I was just so insecure in a lot of ways. I have always felt that my mom was the only person who made me feel better."

Negotiated Dominance   The private setting also provided an opportunity for parent/coaches and their children to negotiate the boundaries about who would hold the dominant position in the coaching relationship. The child sometimes was viewed by some parent/coaches as a source of information about the team. One mother said, "I guess I sometimes tried to get information out of [my son], regarding kids or maybe I'd heard a rumor or something and asked them if they could validate it just because I was concerned about eligibility, perhaps, or ethics." She indicated that her son did not often conform to her request to share information. One father commented on the difficult position the parent/coach experienced when trying to exercise control while providing some freedom for the child: "I want to know if somebody is asking you to get into trouble, but at the same time, I don't want to get that kid in trouble because I am your dad. That's unfair."

Some children commented that they were more open to disagreeing with their parent/coaches in private than they would be in public where the negotiated boundary of conformity would be expected. One mother described the private relationship with her son this way: "When we talk about the coaching aspect and we're alone, I think we're much more open about what we both think." Her son concurred: "When it's just the two of us, it's much more like, 'this is what I think, you know, let's try to figure out ways.' Whereas, if it's me and her and other students; and she goes, 'you should try this,' then I'm going to try that." Another son, who now coaches with his father/coach, described a similar negotiated relationship:

In private, we might argue about who should start at a certain weight, or you know, those kinds of things. I have a different role now. I'm his assistant. So I have my role as an assistant.... Out in public, we're on the same team. We talk about how we're going to approach something; and ... I don't go and say, 'well, I disagreed with him on that' ... I don't do that in public.

The parent/coaches recognized the difficulty in forcing their children to conform without some level of negotiation: "I didn't feel like I had the same kind of ability to say 'this is what we are doing.' I think you negotiate that more with your child than you do with a student."

Parent/coaches also used private communication to negotiate the level of attention they could pay to their child in public. One mother/coach commented: "We talked about how I was going to have to treat [her] like I treated my other students." Another mother/coach, facing a daughter who wanted her to intervene to do something about a student who was causing problems for her, was forced to respond by saying, "It's not a problem I can fix."

Impact on the Family   The most common examples depicted how the parent and child negotiated the way they would convey information about the activity. One father/coach remarked on the difference between talking with his daughters (who were basketball players) and his wife (who was not): "I think that when I talk with my children, we talk on a more technical level than if my wife happens to be in the room."

Control of information about the child was another way communication was influenced due to the coaching relationship. In the immediate family, one mother would ask her son, not her husband, about what was going on at practice. The father/coach acknowledged: "She always asked questions—more questions about Daniel, I think than of me—because she knew she'd get the answer out of me, but she wanted to hear the answer out of Daniel." A mother/coach cautioned about sharing information about her child and coaching with the extended family: "You have to be much more cautious about talking about your coaching and your accomplishments. They think you're bragging, they think that, 'oh, you're just talking about it because you coach him,' and it's going so well, and blah, blah, blah."

The amount of time spent by the child with the parent/coach was another issue of control in the family, particularly for a divorced couple because the activity and tournaments with the mother/coach took the son away from the father's custody time on weekends. As a result, the son did not discuss the activity with his father because it was a source of tension: "Forensics was a tough subject to discuss. We would periodically talk about the [debate] resolution or something like that.... But, if we got too into it, it would become an argument about me being there on weekends...."

The role of the mother, as mediator for the son with his father/coach, was another aspect of dominance in the family dynamic. For one son, his mother kept the lines of communication open: "When I was younger, when he was kind of really tough on me, I refused to talk to him about it. I'd just walk away, and he'd get kind of mad, and then she'd have to go back and forth between us." Another son commented: "I think Mom was ... my biggest defender. There were times when it was tough, maybe I didn't play well or he was angry or I was mad at him for not playing me in a certain way. But we always had Mom to get us through some of those tough times." Her strategy for keeping peace at home was making sure there were other things in their lives, "like going to a play or a movie. She was really helpful at keeping us somewhat sane."

Public Settings

In public settings, both parent/coach and child offered examples of negotiated dominance. The parent/coach wanted the child to respond to directives regarding appropriate behavior, a more disciplined effort, and requests made in different contexts. The children sought more parental attention and less pressure to prove themselves.

Parent/Coach Dominance   One mother/coach was very explicit about what behavior she expected: "I said, 'Ernie, school starts in a week. That green goatee will either be shaved off by the time schools starts of you will dye it back to its natural color because you will not go to a tournament with a green goatee.' And within two days, it was back to its natural color." One mother/coach described how she felt when her daughter didn't behave as other team members were expected to behave: "I remember the one time you were late for the bus, and it was like I am angry because I am a parent and it is my own child coming late for the bus; therefore I am embarrassed and every kid on the bus is watching to see if I get as angry at her as if I'd gotten annoyed with them....."

Parent/coaches also sought dominance regarding their child's level of performance. Many expressed how they tried to get their child to be more focused and disciplined. One child viewed her mother's efforts this way: "We were practicing at this dome .... and she kept making me do this trick over and over. She was just being a Nazi about it." Many parent/coaches indicated their desire to treat their own child like everyone else. However, most acknowledged they probably were harder on their own children than on other team members: "There were . . . times I would dwell on it. Rob would make a mistake and he would know it, but I'd shove it in his face three or four times and that is not a situation that you like to do."

Child Dominance   Parent/coaches were not alone, as children also exerted pressure on the parent by seeking more personal attention and by not continually being forced to prove themselves. The child/participant often wanted more attention of their parent than they received, as one daughter reflected: "I have a problem sharing sometimes, but I was always like, 'Mom, come over here. Come over here, come on, I need your help.' And you know ... I was pretty demanding."

Other children wanted less pressure to continually prove themselves to their parent/coaches and others on the team. One son reflected on having to constantly prove himself in wrestle-offs: "At the time, I thought that was unfair, and I wasn't sure if that was because I'm his son and he didn't want to see favoritism ... but other than that, I mean, he treated me just as bad as everyone else."

Team Dynamic   The influence of the team had its effect on the relationship of the parent/coach and child and negotiated boundaries. Several children provided examples of how their teammates tried to use them to get through to the coach. Conversely, children often had to demonstrate to their teammates that they could be trusted not to report back to their parent/coach when they were having difficulties. Through it all, parent/coaches tried to avoid showing favoritism.

When teammates wanted one son to intervene on their behalf, he said that rather than getting in the middle, "I just sent them my mom's way or whatever." When asked about what his father was thinking, another son told his teammates: "Why don't you ask him? I don't know. I'm not going to go ask for you, you just ask him yourself. He's right there, he's the coach."

Children also had to show they weren't going to report back to their parent/coaches immediately about what their teammates were thinking or doing, or about things that were happening. One son described how having his father as coach affected his relationship with teammates: "If they weren't happy and they were venting, I wouldn't go tell him.... It's their beef. I don't need to be the team rat, and I don't want to feel like that. I just want to be one of the guys." One daughter had a difficult time with her teammates when she was captain of the basketball team and her father was the coach. She explained: "When the team got together my senior year, they didn't want to have me involved because I was his daughter. Like I was going to say things and I was going to do things. So they would have their meetings without me. I was the only one on the team not involved." Her father/coach acknowledged that "it was real uncomfortable for both of us."

At times, the children found themselves in difficult situations. Rather than seeking assistance from their parent, they kept their parent/coaches out of it. One father/coach was given this advice by his daughter: "No matter what you do, Dad, they're going to think you're doing this because I'm your daughter. Just leave it alone and I'll deal with it." One son described the pressure of his teammate's criticism and how he dealt with it himself: "Whether it was jealousy, whether it was just thinking they were better than they actually were or I was worse than I actually was, they said, 'you're here because of your Dad.' There were some really tough comments and so my whole thought process was, 'I've gotta prove. I've gotta prove.'" He did not say anything to his father/coach about the situation to avoid influencing his father/coach.

Generally, the parent/coaches were concerned about giving the appearance of favoritism to their children. Some tried to separate themselves at competitions, as one mother noted: "I'd kind of stay away and I'd let her just be with the rest of the kids, you know, and I wouldn't ask her anything personal during the speech meet, like 'what are you doing tonight?' I would try to keep it all real generic so that all the kids were feeling as special as she was."

Communication of Affiliation

Private Settings

The affiliation between parent/coach and child was very apparent in one-on-one communication. The examples fall into the two main categories of relational closeness and shared experiences.

Relational Closeness   The theme of relational closeness was evident from both parent/coaches and children. One mother/coach described their closeness: "I think it's easier when it's just the two of us.... I think we're really open to each other." One father/coach later realized and told his son how he felt about the time they spent in their coaching relationship: "It took a long time to talk to him about it. I think it was only a couple of years ago that I told him that I really appreciated what he had done ... I wanted him to know that those five years were very precious to me."

Shared Experiences   A son described how shared experiences helped him relate to his mother/coach: "In coaching track and field, for me to go and talk to somebody who doesn't know anything about track, they don't understand how time consuming it is to be a coach. And it's nice that my mom can relate to the way I feel about things and she knows that I definitely fill up my day with athletics and coaching." For one mother/coach, shared experiences become the subject for deep discussion: "There were times when we'd come home from a Friday night and talk until one, two o'clock in the morning about what happened and what was said, and those kinds of things.... I loved it."

Family Dynamic   In the family, themes of inclusion, open communication, and parental focus predominated, as reflective of the conversational orientation. One son described how the entire family was included in the discussions about the activity and what he was doing: "One thing I remember was when we'd have a Saturday tournament and then on Sunday, our whole family would go out to lunch or something and then we'd always rehash the tournament the day before over it, and ... that was kind of cool." Oftentimes, the spouse shared an interest in the activity. As one coach described: "My wife grew up with wrestling, too. And if anything, sometimes she was the one who would talk about it more than we would, you know?"

Several of the children were the youngest in their family or an only child. This made them the focus of their parents' attention and influenced the communication taking place in the family. As one daughter explained: "By the time I was even in high school, my brother and sister had left the house. And so I would like, call myself the only child to a certain extent, because for five years, if you're alone with your parents, I got them to myself."

Public Setting

When in public, children tended to positively acknowledge their affiliation with parent/coaches (Dillard et al., 1999), while functioning in the conformity orientation by subordinating their behaviors to those directed by their parent/coaches (Koerner & Fitzpatrick, 2004). However, there were parent/coaches who were not as open about acknowledging a parental relationship with their children in order to deflect criticism or to afford their child the opportunity to resolve tensions with team members. When the team dynamic was introduced, positive affiliation was attributed to the parent/coach's extended contact with kids outside of the coaching environment and the children of coaches often made friends with those who liked their parents.

Parent-Child Acknowledgment   Children were almost unanimous in their acknowledgment of identifying their parent/coach by "mom" or "dad" in almost every context, with the exception of three athletes who commonly called their fathers "coach." Several children shared stories about trying to get their parent's attention by using the unexpected; either by name (e.g., "Mrs. D" instead of "mom") or by relationship (e.g., "Dad!" instead of "coach"). One daughter even suggested that although she might have appeared as if she wanted to distance herself from her mother, "I truly didn't want to. I wanted to talk to her. I wanted to see her." The parent/coaches were less willing to openly acknowledge their parental connection in public. One mother/coach was very explicit about who she was supposed to be in public: "Now remember, while we're at the gym, I'm your coach and not your mom." Another mother/coach said: "I don't think we really claimed ourselves as coaches." Their son agreed: "Yeah, they didn't talk about themselves as coaches to outside people."

Extended Contact of Parent/Coach   When the team dynamic was considered, affiliation was based on the extended contact of the parent/coach outside of the coaching context. For example, in many instances, the team members had known the parent/coach for many years. One daughter described how her mother became everyone's mother: "They used to call her 'Mama C.' because she cared about them a lot. I probably didn't feel that much different than a lot of kids on the team felt toward her." One of the father/coaches commented on how he is still identified by members of the team as "Daniel's dad." He said, "I'm still treated that way, you know. It's fun the kids all know who I am."

Selection of Friends   While the parent must coach everyone on the team, the child often faces criticism and resentment from some team members who do not get to play as much, have a leading role, or be as successful. This often causes the child of a coach to seek out those who affiliate with the parent/

coach or who genuinely like the child. For the son on a middle school travel team, the tension was minimal: "The seven kids I played with were probably some of my closest friends, if not my best friends, so it didn't really change.... They knew my dad as my dad, not as coach." At the high school level, one son noticed how members of the team would criticize him for being the coach's son, but yell at him to be the leader when the game got rough. When they'd lose, he described his feelings this way: "I'd feel like I let the team down, and I let my dad down, and I wouldn't go crying to him about it, I'd just keep it to myself, but it kind of ate me up sometimes.... I started to be more picky about who my friends were ... because I had friends that I knew wouldn't say a word about it." At the collegiate level, the competition became rougher on relationships. One father/coach described the conflict for his son: "The guys ... who were really on his rear or on mine were the guys that thought they were good enough to start, but weren't really good enough.... And there were times when he said, 'Dad, I'm handling this.' When he said that I pretty much knew I should keep my nose out of it."

Implications

Relational Dominance in Communication Privacy Management

The narratives from the private communication between parent/coaches and their children provided examples of both parental dominance and negotiated dominance based upon the nature of the relationship. The parental dominance reflected the authority to make decisions about what the child would or would not be allowed to do, consistent with high conformity orientation. The negotiated dominance reflected the role of the coach in the instructional process of seeking information, providing instruction, solving problems, and maintaining a smooth working relationship with the child, reflective of low conformity orientation and high conversation orientation.

Just as dominance appeared in the private interactions of parent/coach and child, elements of the conformity orientation were found in the negotiated boundaries about how communication would occur in the family. Specifically, examples suggest that the coaching relationship reflected how information about the activity was to be shared, how information about the child was presented, how the non-coach parent viewed time spent with the parent/coach, and how the non-coach parent functioned as mediator between the parent/coach and child.

In the examples of dominance between the parent/coaches and children in public settings, there appeared to be less public negotiation about what each person expected and how communication was managed. The parent/coaches expected conformity to the norms of appropriate behavior, a more disciplined effort, and compliance about requests made in different contexts. When the team dynamic became a part of the communication, teammates tried to use the child to violate the privacy boundaries to get to the coach and the child often felt compelled to deal with difficult situations without the involvement of the parent. The parent/coaches reflected the hierarchical nature of conformity orientation by not appearing to be willing to publicly treat their children differently that others on the team, thereby making negotiation in public a less viable option. The children sought more parental attention, less pressure to continually prove themselves, and less pressure to report to the parent about everything that happened to them in the public arena. This move toward more independence from the family structure is reflective of low conformity orientation. Children used their resistance to parental authority to bolster their public image with their teammates in certain situations.

Affiliation and Relational Dynamics

When examining the narratives for examples of affiliation, positive relational dynamics between parent/coach and child were very apparent in one-on-one communication settings. The closeness, felt by both the parent/coach and child, created a positive bond that enabled them to interact at what one son described as a level of "communication intimacy" that is characteristic of high conversation orientation. Shared experiences provided for a more technical or complex level of communication because both understood what the other was experiencing or describing. When considering the family dynamic, the inclusion of the entire family appeared to be a natural development altering the coach-team member boundary, stemming from the involvement of most family members. The result was open communication between members in the family, and in some cases, a total focus of the parents on the welfare of the child. This also reflected a high conversation orientation.

Positive affiliation and high conversation orientation was reflected when the children wanted to talk with their parents in public contexts about what was going on in the competition or when they sought their parent's attention through the public identification of their parent/coaches by name as "Mom" or "Dad." However, some parent/coaches considered this to be boundary turbulence and were not as open about acknowledging their children, either to deflect criticism or to maintain the appearance of not showing favoritism. When the team dynamic was introduced, affiliation was attributed to the parent/coach's extended contact with team members outside of the coaching environment and the children of coaches often made friends with those who liked their parents, reflecting a conformity orientation (Koerner & Fitzpatrick, 2004).

Conclusions and Directions for Future Research

This study contributes to a better understanding of interaction of relational, family, and instructional communication theories in several ways. Koerner and Fitzpatrick (2004) suggested that families differ in their communication between conversation and conformity orientations; and Socha and Stamp (1995) argued that the communication patterns established in the home informs their communication with individuals in other contexts. If we accept these viewpoints, then established patterns of parent-child communication in the family unit should be similar in different contexts. Perry-Jenkins et al. (2004) called for studies to determine if this were the case. In the present study, this conclusion is not supported. The narratives show that in private, parent/ coaches were willing to negotiate dominance about particular instructional strategies, reflective of low conformity orientation and high conversation orientation; whereas, in public contexts, parent/coaches sought to deemphasize affiliation and stressed high conformity from their children in order to promote higher levels of performance and to avoid the appearance of showing favoritism. The differences in orientation suggest that the four family types (consensual, pluralistic, protective, and laissez-faire) described by Koerner and Fitzpatrick (2004) should be expanded to include an additional family type more reflective of the coaching dynamic influencing the communication because the coach and child have a high conversation orientation (subject and symbolic) and sometimes a negotiated conformity orientation (behavior and practices). Dillard et al. (1999) suggested that individuals in relationships do not attend to dominance and affiliation simultaneously. The findings of this study support this conclusion. In private, parent/coaches negotiate their dominance due to a desire for high affiliation with their children. This negotiation is less prevalent in public contexts where parent/coaches seek more conformity from their children about their behavior and performance on the team and downplay their relationship or affiliation, even though they may be masking their true feelings of care and concern for the child's welfare.

The use of Communication Privacy Management Theory to explain how co-owned information held by the parent/coach-child/team member in different contexts aids in understanding how changing roles causes boundary turbulence. Petronio (2002) discussed the intersection of interior and exterior family boundaries. When internal and external boundaries are congruent, there is little boundary turbulence. When there is incongruence, the boundary turbulence may be substantial. Based upon the findings from this study, the most common congruent combination is moderate interior and moderate exterior permeability. This is to say, children and their parents negotiate a set of rules that enables the child to maintain some privacy within the relationship of peers on the team, as well as a degree of openness with the parent about the nature of the team relationship. In contrast, the most common incongruent combination is moderate interior and low exterior permeability. Here, the children and parents negotiate a set of rules that allows the child to maintain some privacy within the family about what peers are saying or doing, but establishes a united front and low permeability about how the family may feel or be reacting to outside pressures.

The findings also extend the introduction of instructional communication into the family setting, providing new insight into orientations of family communication and their transference into different contexts. Millar and Rogers (1976) suggested that the communication process relies on negotiation as individuals define their relationships and themselves. In the present study, the relationship between the parent/coach and child was consistently positive. One explanation for this finding is the willingness of the child to accept the dominance of the parent in the public contexts when instructional strategies were introduced. While there was some negotiation in private settings, as long as the child accepted the direction of the parent/coach in public, the coaching relationship remained functional. One might speculate that when private negotiation about following the instructional strategies spills over into the public context, and the child becomes less willing to conform to the dominance of the parent/coach, the coaching relationship will become dysfunctional and, ultimately, end. How this decision to discontinue participation in an activity because of a dysfunctional coaching relationship affects the communication in the family is another area for future study. Initially, the child controls the boundary by selecting an activity. If the parent steps into the arena as coach only to create dysfunction, the communication in the family also may be impacted. In this study, the fact that dyads functioned and relationships were strengthened suggests that communication can be enhanced through coaching. Further study of parent-child dyads that resulted in early termination is needed to determine the effect of a negative experience on communication in the family.

This study provided a general overview of coaching across different activities. One limitation of the study may be related to the demographic characteristic of the parent/coaches indicating that all 20 were at one time in the field of education. Despite the reality that they were already *teachers in the home*, the present study is useful in presenting the subtleties of how the parent/coaches managed their communication in different contexts because of their public role in the school and community. In addition, researchers might find specializing in athletics or fine arts to produce unique findings. Focusing on the coaching of particular age groups also might be especially insightful. How dominance and affiliation interact to produce successful competitors is another possible area of study. Furthermore, the identification of specific instructional communication strategies and their effect on the relational dynamics of dominance and affiliation may assist parent/coaches in the future to be more successful in navigating the boundaries that children create as they seek greater independence.

Notes

1. A coach is defined variously, ranging from someone in charge of training a team to someone giving private instruction. Coaches regularly provide students with constructive feedback designed to improve learning and "push" performance toward higher levels of achievement. For the purpose of this study, a coach is operationally defined as an individual with expertise in a particular activity or event having the official responsibility to direct children/students in that competitive or creative activity. A coach is responsible for preparing a team or individual for practice, presentation/competition, and some form of reward or evaluation.

2. These activities were included: basketball (middle school travel team, high school, and college), football (middle school and high school), wrestling (high school and college), track (middle school and high school), soccer (high school), baton twirling (middle school and high school), speech activities (middle school and high school), and drama (high school).
3. The median age of the 13 mothers was 50, while the median age of the 7 fathers was 53. The median age of the 6 daughters was 23, and the median age of the 14 sons was 23. Of the parents, 19 were married at the time they coached their child. Eighteen of the children had siblings while their parent coached them. The researchers drew the dyads from the same region of the country. Dyads were not asked to provide their ethnicity since ethnicity was not a variable in this particular study.
4. Sixteen of the parent/coaches were current or former high school teachers; and 4 were employed at the collegiate level in some aspect of teaching or coaching. Seventeen of the children interviewed were currently engaged in education in some way, either as a high school senior or current college/university student, high school teacher, or college teacher/coach.
5. Two questions sought information about the coaching situation in which the parent and child were involved, and where and how long the parent coached the child. Five questions asked the dyads to describe their favorite stories/memories, least favorite stories/memories, humorous stories, sad stories, and any other stories they wanted to share about their coaching relationship. Four questions explored the communication dynamic of the dyad when they were alone, in the family, with team members, and in public. The dyads were asked to reflect on how often they thought about their relationship as coach and team member, as well as to provide a theme or metaphor to describe their coaching relationship. Finally, the participants were asked if they wanted to make any additional comment about their coaching relationship or about parents being involved in coaching their children in competitive activities.

References

Barber, H., Sukhi, H., & White, S. A. (1999). The influence of parent-coaches on participant motivation and competitive anxiety in youth sport participants. *Journal of Sport Behavior, 22*, 162–180.

Brown, B. A. (1985). Factors influencing the process of withdrawal by female adolescents from the role of competitive age group swimmer. *Sociology of Sport Journal, 2*, 111–129.

Brustad, R. (1992). Integrating socialization influences into the study of children's motivation in sport. *Journal of Sport and Exercise Psychology, 14*, 59–77.

Burgoon, J. K., & Hale, J. L. (1984). The fundamental topoi of relational communication. *Communication Monographs, 51*, 194–214.

Burgoon, J. K., & Saine, T. (1978). *The unspoken dialogue: An introduction to nonverbal communication.* Boston: Houghton Mifflin.

Cohler, B. J. (1991). The life story and the study of resilience and response to adversity. *Journal of Narrative and Life History, 1*, 169–200.

Dillard, J. P., Solomon, D. H., & Palmer, M. T. (1999). Structuring the concept of relational communication. *Communication Monographs, 66*, 49–65.

Dunbar, R. I. M. (1988). *Primate social systems.* Ithaca, NY: Cornell University Press.

Elksnin, L. K., & Elksnin, N. (2000). Teaching parents to teach their children to be prosocial. *Intervention in School & Clinic, 36*(1), 27–34. Retrieved May 5, 2008, from http://ebscohost.com

Friese, B. H., & Grotevant, H. D. (2001). Introduction to special issue on "Narratives in and about relationships." *Journal of Social and Personal Relationships, 18,* 579–581.

Haney, M., & Hill, J. (2004). Relationships between parent-teaching activities and emergent literacy in preschool children. *Early Child Development & Care, 174*(3), 215–228. Retrieved May 5, 2008, from http://ebscohost.com

Hodges, R. L., & Franks, I. M. (2002). Modeling coaching practice: The role of instruction and demonstration. *Journal of Sports Sciences, 20,* 793–911.

Koerner, A. F., & Fitzpatrick, M. A. (2004). Communication in intact families. In A. L. Vangelisti (Ed.), *Handbook of family communication* (pp. 177–196). Mahwah, NJ: Erlbaum.

Lindlof, T. R., & Taylor, B. C. (2002). *Qualitative communication research methods* (2nd ed.). Thousand Oaks, CA: Sage.

Luffman, J. (1998). When parents replace teachers: The home schooling option. *Canadian Social Trends, 50,* 8–11. Retrieved May 5, 2008, from http://ebscohost.com.

Mazur, M. A., & Hubbard, A. S. E. (2004). Is there something I should know?: Topic avoidant responses in parent-adolescent communication. *Communication Reports, 17,* 27–37.

Millar, F. E., & Rogers, L. E. (1976). A relational approach to interpersonal communication. In G. R. Miller (Ed.), *Explorations in interpersonal communication* (pp. 87–104). Beverly Hills, CA: Sage.

Noller, P. (1995). Parent-adolescent relationships. In M. A. Fitzpatrick & A. I. Vangelisti (Eds.), *Explaining family interaction* (pp. 77–112). Thousand Oaks, CA: Sage.

Noller, P., & Bagi, S. (1985). Parent-adolescent communication. *Journal of Adolescence, 8,* 125–144.

Perry-Jenkins, M., Pierce, C. P., & Goldberg, A. E. (2004). Discourses on diapers and dirty laundry: Family communication about child care and housework. In A. L. Vangelisti (Ed.), *Handbook of family communication* (pp. 541–61). Mahwah, NJ: Erlbaum.

Petronio, S. (2002). *Boundaries of privacy: Dialectics of disclosure.* Albany: State University of New York Press.

Resetar, J. L., Noell, G. H., & Pellegrin, A. L. (2006). Teaching parents to use research-supported systematic strategies to tutor their children in reading. *School Psychology Quarterly, 21*(3), 241–261. Retrieved May 5, 2008, from http://ebscohost.com.

Roberts, G. C. (1984). Achievement motivation in children's sport. *Advances in Motivation and Achievement, 3,* 251–281.

Socha, T. J., & Stamp, G. H. (1995). Expanding the conceptual frontier. Parents, children, and communication. In T. J. Socha & G. H. Stamp (Eds.), *Parents, children, and communication: Frontiers of theory and research* (pp. ix–xiv). Mahwah, NJ: Erlbaum.

Sprague, J. (2002). Communication education: The spiral continues. *Communication Education, 51,* 337–354.

Stein, G. L., Raedeke, T. D., & Glenn, S. D. (1999). Children's perceptions of parent involvement: It's not how much, but to what degree that's important. *Journal of Sport and Behaviour, 22,* 581–600.

Suizzo, M., & Stapleton, L. M. (2007). Home-based parental involvement in young children's education: Examining the effects of maternal education across U. S. ethnic groups. *Educational Psychology, 27*(4), 533–556. Retrieved May 5, 2008, from http://ebscohost.com

Turman, P. D. (2003). Athletic coaching from an instructional communication perspective: The influence of coach experience on high school wrestlers' preferences and perceptions of coaching behaviors across a season. *Communication Education,* *52,* 73–86.

Turman, P. D., & Schrodt, P. (2004). New avenues for instructional communication research: Relationships among coaches' leadership behaviors and athletes' affective learning. *Communication Research Reports, 21,* 130–143.

Vangelisti, A. L. (Ed.). (2004). *Handbook of family communication.* Mahwah, NJ: Erlbaum.

Watzlawick, P., Beavin, J., & Jackson, D. D. (1967). *Pragmatics of human communication.* New York: W. W. Norton.

Weiss, M. R., & Chaumeton, N. (1992). Motivational orientations in sport. In T. S. Horn (Ed.), *Advances in sport psychology* (pp. 61–99). Champaign, IL: Human Kinetics.

12 Commentary

Communication and Family Health and Wellness Relationships

Gary Kreps

The family is a primary site for health education, information, and support that has a powerful influence on promoting health and wellness (Baxter, Bylund, Imes, & Scheive, 2005; Bylund, Imes, & Baxter, 2005; Kreps, 1990; Kreps & Sivaram, 2008; Zhang & Siminoff, 2003). Family communication performs a crucial role in socializing family members' development of powerful culturally engrained beliefs about health and illness that influence health behaviors (Botelho, Bee-Horng, & Fiscella,1996; Kreps & Kunimoto, 1994). Family members are significant sources for providing needed health information to other family members that strongly influence their adoption of health promotion, disease prevention, and health care activities (Arrington, 2005; Pecchioni, Thompson, & Anderson, 2006). Furthermore, family members (especially wives, mothers, grandmothers, sisters, and daughters) often provide needed home care to spouses, parents, and children and face tremendous stress as informal caregivers (Ballard-Reisch, 1996; Kreps, 1990). Parents also serve as health role models and have powerful influences on the development of their children's orientations toward primary health issues such as nutritional patterns, exercise behaviors, leisure activities, and personal relationships (Weihs, Fisher, & Baird,, 2002). Family members provide important support and advocacy for one another within the complex health care system (Beach & Good, 2004; Petronio, Sargent, Andea, Reganis, & Cichocki, 2004; Rabow, Hauser, & Adams, 2004). Despite the central role that family communication performs in health, health care, and health promotion, there has been relatively little attention paid to studying the influences of family communication on health within the scholarly literature (Jones, Beach, & Jackson, 2004; Pecchioni & Sparks, 2006). The vast majority of health communication research has focused on formal health care delivery systems, such as doctor's offices, hospitals, clinics, and public health settings, and not on the far more pervasive and ubiquitous delivery of informal care and health promotion within the family (Kreps & Bonaguro, 2009). I am hopeful that the chapters on family communication and health/wellness in this section of this book will encourage more careful study of the health-related influences of family communication. In this commentary, I will examine the contributions of the individual chapters in this section and provide guidance for future research on family communication, health, and wellness.

Communication Between Parents and Physicians

In chapter 7, Ashley Duggan and Sandra Petronio provide vivid illustrations of the ways strategic and sensitive health communication between parents and physicians can help address significant concerns parents typically have about their children's well-being in times of serious health threats, as well as the significant psychosocial, emotional, and support needs of these parents. They frame their insightful analysis of conversations between physicians and parents of children admitted to neonatal intensive care in Communication Boundary Management theory and a relational approach to consumer-provider communication. Their analysis describes how sensitive issues, barriers, and boundaries concerning children's health care can be negotiated through the skillful disclosure of relevant information and the use of supportive nonverbal cues. Both parents and physicians have access to specialized information that can be shared though strategic disclosure to promote collaboration, adaptation, and coordinated care. I particularly appreciate the specific recommendations suggested by the authors for parents and health care providers to use to increase the sensitivity and effectiveness of care for children. Communication scholarship can provide significant insights into the best strategies for parents to use to promote the best care for their children.

Family Communication in Mental Health Care

In chapter 8, Christine Davis, Norin Dollard, and Keren Vergon provide an in-depth examination of the ways that child, parent, and provider interactions influence care for children with severe emotional disturbances. They establish a strong theoretical underpinning for their investigation in the application of open systems theory to focus their analysis on the powerful interdependent communication relationships between the many different key participants in the health care system at multiple levels of social organization. This is a particularly valuable theoretical framework for illustrating the importance of a team-based comprehensive, coordinated, community approach to helping children and families. They report a longitudinal analysis of communication over 3 years in children's mental health system of care team meetings to explore child-family-provider interactions. They use a multiple case study approach to evaluate system of care practices in their naturally occurring contexts. The study identifies five communication processes through which child-family-provider team meeting interactions influence the ability of families to participate fully in the planning and delivery of services: the use of a systems orientation, the use of framing and sense-making, the development of meeting structure and communication networks, the empowerment of team members, and the management of role ambiguity. This chapter illustrates the power of formal group communication processes within the health care system for influencing family participation in treatment decision making and the delivery of care.

The Parent/Child Early Intervention Relationship

In chapter 9, Carol Mills and Kasey Walker provide an interesting conceptual analysis of the applications of the Bona Fide Group Perspective (BFGP) to understanding the communication processes that influence early intervention services for supporting development of children with disabilities under 36 months of age and supporting family growth and stability. The chapter illustrates how communication in Early Intervention (EI) meetings between health care providers and family members help increase awareness and understanding about the child's disability, the impact of the disability on the family, the child's developmental potential and priorities, as well as about family concerns, constraints, and opportunities for supporting the child's development. In these meetings, parents and providers work together to develop goals for the child, examine how the family can help promote those goals, improve the child's skills, reduce the child's delays, and help the family adapt, adjust, and grow. The authors show how the communicative exchanges that comprise the parent-child-provider interactions are critical to the success of the EI program and to the family. The BFGP approach suggests that critical issues such as the development of stable, yet permeable boundaries, group interdependence with context, and unstable and ambiguous borders influence communication processes and health outcomes for EI groups. The chapter illustrates how communication interactions between parents, child, and EI providers can promote adaptation, growth, and support for the disabled child and the family.

Interaction Between Parents, Children, and Coaches in Sports

In chapter 10, Paul Turman, Angela Zimmerman, and Brett Dobesh move this section of this book in a different direction by examining the family communication dynamics of participation in youth sports. Youth sports activities occupy an increasingly large portion of family time and often involve emotionally intense communication interactions within the family and between family members, coaches, and other youth sports participants. There are some interesting parallels between youth sports and health care for children. Both systems are designed to promote the growth, development, and wellness of children. Both systems are also complex social settings that challenge family dynamics and demand effective family communication. The authors employ Communication Privacy Management Theory as a conceptual grounding to study parent-child and parent-coach sport boundaries. They report an interesting study that examines the topics concerning sports participation that parents discuss with their children; and also identifies the communication strategies that parents use to develop relationships with coaches to influence their childrens' levels of participation in sports activities. They found that in sports-related parent child communication there were four (rather negative) primary topics that were discussed: the lack of playing time for the child, the politics of sports (such as a coach's favoritism towards certain players), inappropriate coaching behaviors, and over-emphasis that is often placed on winning (sometimes at any cost). They found three primary communication relationship styles parents use with coaches that vary in level of involvement and intensity: the relatively mild style of the parent as a sports spectator, the more direct communication style of the parent as a sports fan/enthusiast, and the most intense (and often over-the-top) communication style of the parent as sports fanatic. The study illustrates the complex communication strategies used in sports to negotiate boundaries between parents, children, and coaches, as well as the serious problems these strategies can pose for family communication and well-being.

Coaching Your Own Child

In chapter 11, Robert S. Littlefield and Cindy Larson-Casselton build upon the previous chapter by examining the unique relational communication dynamics that develop between parents and children when the parent serves as a coach for his/her child. They examine this unique parent-child dynamic through the lens of relational communication research to illustrate interdependent issues of relational dominance, affiliation, and involvement. They use Communication Privacy Management Theory as a lens to illustrate the ways communication between parents and children is used to negotiate boundaries between public and private domains concerning decisions about the kind of information that can be shared and the kind of information that should remain private. They also use the literature of instructional communication to illustrate the pedagogical teaching aspects of the coaching relationship with children. To illustrate these communication processes they report an evocative study where they interviewed 20 parent-child dyads to generate narratives about the ways these dyads communicated about their coaching relationship in public and in private and how that talk affected their family and team communication. The narratives collected showed that in private family contexts the parents/ coaches negotiated dominance about particular instructional strategies with their children, but in public sports contexts the parents/coaches deemphasized affiliation and stressed high conformity from their children to promote high performance and to avoid showing favoritism. The study found that children and their parents negotiated rules to enable the child to maintain privacy within the relationship of peers on the team, as well as a degree of openness with the parent about the nature of the team relationship. The study also found that children were willing to accept the dominance of the parent/coach in the public team context when instructional strategies were introduced. The study provides interesting insights into the ways parents and children negotiate their relationships in public when they are participating in coaching relationships, as well as in private within their normal family relationships.

Future Directions for Scholarship on Communication, Family Health, and Wellness

The chapters in this section of this book provide unique insights into the ways family communication is used, both effectively and ineffectively, to enable parents and children to negotiate their family and external relationships to achieve personal and family goals for promoting health, wellness, growth, and personal development. It is clear that the family is a major social context for promoting health and wellness, yet achieving these desired outcomes depends mightily on the effectiveness of strategic family communication. The authors use a variety of unique theoretical and methodological frameworks for their investigations to illustrate interesting nuances and dilemmas to effective family communication. It appears that these studies are all breaking new ground and there is much left to be learned about the dynamics of family communication for promoting health and wellness. I was struck by the complex relational choices and conflicts that abound in health and recreational contexts for both parents and children. It was frustrating to note the difficulties families often have in negotiating the best care for their members and the negative tone of much of the family communication concerning sports participation. These are areas of investigation that will clearly benefit from future research, theorizing, and application, especially if future work can be translated into the development of powerful communication interventions to improve the quality and outcomes of family communication that will ultimately promote health and well-being.

References

Arrington, M. I. (2005). "She's right behind me all the way": An analysis of prostate cancer narratives and changes in family relationships. *The Journal of Family Communication, 5*, 141–162.

Ballard-Reisch, D. (1996). Coping with alienation, fear, and isolation: The disenfranchisement of adolescents with cancer and their families. In E. Berlin Ray (Ed.), *Communication and disenfranchisement: Social health issues and implications* (pp. 185–208). Mahwah, NJ: Erlbaum.

Baxter, L. A., Bylund, C., Imes, R., & Scheive, D. (2005). Family communication environments and rule-based social control of adolescents' healthy lifestyle choices. *Journal of Family Communication, 5*, 209–228.

Beach, W. A., & Good, J. S. (2004). Uncertain family trajectories: Interactional consequences of cancer diagnosis, treatment, and prognosis. *Journal of Social and Personal Relationships, 21*, 8–32.

Botelho, R. J., Bee-Horng, L., & Fiscella, K. (1996). Family involvement in routine health care: A survey of patients' behaviors and preferences. *Journal of Family Practice, 42*, 572–576.

Bylund, C., Imes, R. S., & Baxter, L. A. (2005). Parents' perceptual accuracy of their college student children's health and health risk behaviors. *Journal of American College Health, 54*, 31–37.

Jones, D. J., Beach, S. R. H., & Jackson, H. (2004). Family influences on health: A framework to organize research and guide intervention. In A. L. Vangelisti (Ed.), *Handbook of family communication* (pp. 647–672). Mahwah, NJ: Erlbaum.

Kreps, G. L. (1990). Communication and health education. In E. B. Ray & L. Donohew (Eds.), *Communication and health: Systems and applications* (pp. 187–203). Hillsdale, NJ: Erlbaum.

Kreps, G. L., & Bonaguro, E. (2009). Health communication as applied communication inquiry. In L. Frey & K. Cissna (Eds.) *The handbook of applied communication research* (pp. 970–993). Hillsdale, NJ: Erlbaum.

Kreps, G. L., & Kunimoto, E. (1994). *Effective communication in multicultural health care settings.* Newbury Park, CA: Sage.

Kreps, G. L., & Sivaram, R. (2008). The central role of strategic health communication in enhancing breast cancer outcomes across the continuum of care in limited-resource countries. *Cancer, 113*(S8), 2331–2337.

Pecchioni, L. L., & Sparks, L. (2006). Health information sources of individuals with cancer and their family members. *Health Communication, 21*(2), 1–9.

Pecchioni, L. L., Thompson, T. L., & Anderson, D. J. (2006). Interrelations between family communication and health communication. In L. H. Turner & R. West (Eds.), *The family communication sourcebook* (pp. 447–468). Thousand Oaks, CA: Sage.

Petronio, S., Sargent, J., Andea, L., Reganis, P., & Cichocki, D. (2004). Family and friends as healthcare advocates: Dilemmas of confidentiality and privacy. *Journal of Social and Personal Relationships, 21,* 33–52.

Rabow, M. W., Hauser, J. M., & Adams, J. (2004). Supporting family caregivers at the end of life: "They don't know what they don't know." *Journal of the American Medical Association, 291,* 483–491.

Weihs, K., Fisher, L., & Baird, M. (2002). Families, health, and behavior. *Families, Systems and Health, 20,* 7–46.

Zhang, A.Y., & Siminoff, L.A, (2003). The role of the family in treatment decision making by patients with cancer. *Oncology Nursing Forum, 30*(6), 1022–1028.

Section III

Parent-Child-Society
Relationships & Media

13 Powerful Media Tools

Arming Parents with Strategies to Affect Children's Interactions with Commercial Interests

Erica Weintraub Austin, Stacey J. T. Hust, and Michelle E. Kistler

No loving parent would let a toddler play unattended in a garage that provided easy-access to plugged-in power tools. At the very least, most parents would tell their children the tools are off limits, not because the tools are harmful machines, but because most parents understand the proper use of power tools requires appropriate skills and safety precautions beyond the understanding of most children. It is interesting, however, that many parents actively send their children into their entertainment rooms and bedrooms with plugged-in media tools readily available. In fact, these powerful tools often are used to help children keep busy while their parents do household chores.

Although most people consider media, such as televisions and radios, as toys, they actually perform useful tasks like most other power tools. In fact, some people assert media messages make people quit smoking, buckle their seat belts, cast a vote, and donate millions to help others recover from disaster. Yet media often seem like toys. They are easy to access and lots of fun. So fun, in fact, that it is easy to forget they serve a purpose.

The difference between a tool and a toy is that a tool performs useful tasks but requires precautions and skill for safe operation. A toy, on the other hand, is supposed to be safe to use, and usually does not perform any useful function. What makes a tool dangerous or helpful is *how it gets used*. Most adults wouldn't attempt to use a power saw without the proper safety mechanisms in place or without reading the safety messages, yet people often neglect to consider precautionary messages for the media.

Electronic media are powerful tools that advertisers and broadcast media use to gain influence and profit. In fact, much of the profits reaped by broadcast media come simply from getting people to use them. A 30-second ad on the 2006 Super Bowl was worth $2.5 million because it reached more than 45 million households, and many of those households had multiple pairs of eyes glued to the TV (Horovitz, 2006). Admittedly Super Bowl ads are a high extreme, but television advertising, even during regular viewing times, is a lucrative business. The average prime-time TV show in 2005–2006 charged about $17,000 per million households, which meant that it raked in more than $3 million per hour.

Using media tools to gain profit and influence seems straightforward. An advertiser that wants to sell its product can purchase high-volume advertising space so that a higher number of viewers would see the advertisement. A greater number of views should translate into a higher number of product purchases. Yet, the result of any given advertisement depends on the audiences' use of it as well.

Given this, children are a key audience for marketers and advertisers because they tend not to be perceptive consumers, they attend to a lot of media and they have significant buying power. In this chapter, we discuss how youths' buying power and their heavy media use makes them among marketers' favorite consumer groups. We discuss marketing practices related to children and then, within the context of what we know about media effects, we point out why children may not be the most savvy media consumers. Finally, we discuss how parents can use mediation strategies to serve as intermediaries between their children and television advertisers.

Youths' Media Use and Buying Power: An Attractive Target for Advertisers

One quarter of the United States population is under the age of 18 (U.S. Census, 2006), and experts estimate that their buying power rivals that of any other age group, including the baby boomers (McNeal, 1999). James McNeal, an influential youth-marketing expert, told the *New York Times* that the youth market is the largest consumer market there is (Leimbach, 2000). This large consumer market is attractive to advertisers because youth have significant buying power, frequently attend to the media, and are susceptible to advertisers' techniques and tactics.

Youth's Buying Power

Youth's spending has doubled each of the past three decades (McNeal, 1999). By 2002, the direct buying power of children 4 to 12 years old was more than $30 billion (McNeal, 1999). With an even greater buying power, 12- to 19-year-olds accounted for $170 billion of personal spending this same year, which equates to a weekly average of $101 per week (Schor, 2004). This equates roughly to a $1,500 yearly discretionary income for a "tween," someone between the age of 9 to 12, that increases to $4,500 by the time she reaches 16 years old (Magazine Publishers of America, 2003). Youth spend at least one third of their income on their highest spending category of sweets, snacks, and beverages, and they spend a large portion of their income on toys and clothes (Schor, 2004).

Yet, teens' buying power extends past their weekly allowances or their summer jobs. According to James McNeal, an influential youth-marketing expert, children ages 4 to 12 influenced $600 billion worth of family purchases as of 2003, more than 100 times more than they had influenced in the 1960s (McNeal, 1999). Overall, parents would not make many of their purchases if their children did not make the request (McNeal, 1999).

McNeal (1999) found that children had a 40% "influence factor" on hobby items, peanut butter, bicycles and packaged cookies, and an even greater influence on toaster products (45%), children's shoes (50%), toys (70%), hot cereal (50%), fruit snacks (80%), video games (60%), and children's beauty aids (70%). Their influence on candy, cold cereals, and salty snacks was surprisingly less weighty although their 35% control of fast food purchases, for example, still translated into $22.75 billion to the industry. Their 30% influence on soda pop purchases garnered $13.98 billion. Children's role in big-ticket purchases might not have been large, but it had huge ramifications for their potential profits. For automobiles, for example, children's 4% of influence translated into $8.87 billion in industry sales.

Marketers call children's ability to influence their parents' spending the "nag factor" or "pester power." One study of adolescents found them willing to readily and repeatedly ask their parents to buy something they know their parents will disapprove of. They'll keep asking up to an average of nine times to get their parents to give in. In fact, more than 10% of the tweens claimed that they would continue to ask more than 50 times if necessary. Children also perceive that their nagging and pestering strategies work as more than half of those surveyed said their parents usually give in and purchase the product.

In addition to the "nag factor," increased demands on parent's time and attention have influenced their willingness not only to let children influence consumer purchases but to purchase products for their children (Schor, 2004). Parents who spend less time with their children tend to spend more money on them, which these parents often refer to as "guilt money," (Schor, 2004, p. 25). According to Schor, parents pressed for time may also rely more on their children's personal tastes so that they do not have to argue about consumption. For example, a parent may allow their child to choose their favorite brand of hot breakfast cereal instead of risking an argument about eating breakfast in the hurried moments of the morning.

Some companies depend on this nag factor and guilt money to make profits. A study by Western Initiative Media found that 41% of the parents who took their children to a kid-oriented entertainment facility did it at the behest of their children. The executive vice president of Chuck E. Cheese's Pizza told the *Selling to Kids* newsletter (MarketResearch, 1999), "Kids are critical to the whole purchasing process." As a result, they target the majority of their advertising to children. In fact, the research team that identified the nag factor advised marketers to provide children with useful ammunition in their own sales pitches.

Youths' buying power exceeds the actual dollar figure they are able to spend directly or indirectly as they also help set the trends for what is "hot" and what is not among their peers and younger children. One profile of the teen market suggested that marketers should focus on teens because they "establish and affect fashion, lifestyle, and overall trends" (Magazine Publishers of America, 2003, p. 3). Yet, most marketers begin to target "teens" much earlier, when they have a greater likelihood to make an impact.

Research indicates that even toddlers and young children can recognize brands (e.g., Buijzen & Valkenburg, 2005; Schor, 2004). In Buijzen and Valkenburg's study (2005), 2- to 3-year-olds recognized two thirds of the 12 brand logos researchers showed them, and 8-year-olds recognized 100% of the brand logos. Other research indicates that by the age of 12, young people use their perceptions of brands to make consumer judgments (Achenreiner & John, 2003). In fact, such judgments may be key to their social success. Alissa Quart (2003) articulates in her insightful text *Branded* that teens must be brand conscious if they want to navigate the complexities of the teenage world and high school cliques.

Youths' Media Use

Almost half of all children under 2 years old watch television every day, and about one third of them started tuning in before they turned 1 year old. In fact, very young children, those under 6 years, spend an average of 2 hours each day with electronic screen media, such as television, videos, and computers (Roberts, Foehr, & Rideout, 2005). Their television use continues to increase until it peaks at age 10. Between the ages of 8 to 18, children spend about 4 hours each day with television (Roberts et al., 2005). Television use does not return to pre-adolescent rates, as Figure 13.1 shows, until individuals enter young adulthood (around age 20).

In addition to television, children spend a significant amount of time with other media. On average, children between the ages of 8 and 18 spend about 6½ hours with the media each day (Roberts et al., 2005). This means that many young people spend more time with television and other media than they spend doing anything else. Given that preschoolers need 11–12 hours of sleep, they are spending about one third of their waking time with media. Many sleep-deprived teenagers spend more time with media than they spend sleeping.

The media may even make up an even bigger part of some youngsters' days. More than two of every three preschoolers live in a household in which the TV stays on at least half of the day, even if nobody is watching it. About one of every three youngsters grows up in a "constant television" household, in which the television stays on most of the day.

Not only do some children live in homes where the television is constantly on, many of them have media tools in their own bedrooms. In fact, they live in media-centered worlds (Kunkel et al., 2003). One quarter of infants and toddlers (children under age 2) have their own television in their bedrooms. By the time they reach school age, almost half of American youth have a personal TV in their bedroom.

These days a typical child's bedroom houses a CD/tape/MP3 player, a radio, a television, and a VCR or DVD player. Almost half of 8- to 18-year-olds have their own video game console. More than one third have their own bedroom connection to cable or satellite TV. Almost one third have their own computer although less than 25% have their own internet access. Almost half have their own cell phone. Their individual, independent media environment gets more extensive as they get older.

It matters that children saturate their lives with mediated experiences because children—and adults, too—learn from every experience they have. As social learning theory posits, most of this learning happens through observation as children watch what other people do and listen to what other people say. In fact, one of the skills that make human beings so different from other animals is our ability to learn from observation, through "vicarious experience." Because individuals can create and interpret symbols, such as words, we can learn about faraway places and times where we never physically can go.

It also is important to keep in mind that young children are especially wired to soak up information. The preschool years are a period for fantastic brain growth and the development of language skills. In fact, most language development happens by age two. If it's true that children learn from every experience they have, then given the amount of time they spend with the media, one third of what the average youngster learns is coming from the media. As one writer put it, the media make it possible for children to travel the world well before they can even cross the street by themselves.

The upshot is that children want to, and do, learn from every source they can, to the extent their abilities allow. They discover what information sources are available to them. They learn what happens when they imitate what they see and hear, and they watch what happens when people around them do the same thing. They notice which messages others react to with approval, laughter, disapproval, tears or even indifference. They begin to make choices about which messages deserve their attention. They use media *as tools*.

Marketing Techniques: Leveraging the Buying Power of Youth

Given that marketers favor younger audiences due to their significant potential to influence purchases both indirectly and directly, it's not surprising that youth see more than 40,000 ads per year. That's double the number their parents saw in the 1970s (Robinson, Saphir, Kraemer, Varady, & Haydel, 2001). Even if television and the Internet are banned at home—a rarity—young people are bound to encounter advertising, news, and other media messages on billboards, in stores and doctor's offices, in airports, and even in school. Currently, more than 200 companies market their products in schools with educational videos, books, posters and prizes. For example, kids can earn Pizza Hut® coupons by reading Crayola® counting books and the memoirs of teen pop stars. They can keep up with the news by reading about forthcoming movies in *TIME for Kids* or by watching the 10-minute television news show, *Channel One*, produced with two minutes of commercials for secondary schools and viewed by a larger teen audience than sees MTV.

According to the Food Institute, food and beverage industries alone now spend about $13 billion annually marketing their products to kids, and it pays off handsomely. Even companies that sell products of little use to children, such as automobiles, frequently target children because of the significant indirect influence on the market. In 2005, 12- to 19-year-olds spent about $159 billion of their money (Teen Research, Inc.) and convinced their parents to buy hundreds of billions more, which translated into about $22 for every dollar marketers had spent on them, or $3 for every dollar marketers spent on *all consumers combined*. That's an amazing payoff for any investment. Marketers can do this well because the playing field is not level. They devote a lot of resources to make sure they know how to use the media better than their targeted audiences do.

Most of the research done on marketing to young people is proprietary and not easily available, but check out just what is easily available over the internet. For $249 an individual can subscribe to the *Kidtrends* newsletter that provides "timely information … to tap into this burgeoning market segment." The *Targeting Teens* newsletter, meanwhile, promises to help marketers succeed with this "elusive but economically powerful market segment." More detailed reports are available for $1,295 each. Then, for $5,695 a company called Mind-Branch, Inc. will analyze trends and provide "action points" for selling just to 3- to 9-year-olds.

Marketers realize they take unfair advantage. A survey of youth marketers by Harris Interactive found that only 30% believed that children are well equipped to deal with the messages thrown at them. Although two thirds of them considered their own organization more ethical than other youth marketers, only 24% thought the industry did enough to police itself.

Even worse, the youth marketers on average indicated that it is appropriate to begin marketing to young people by age 7, even though they believed that most young people can begin to view advertising critically only at age 9, can separate fantasy from reality at age 9, and cannot make intelligent choices as consumers until nearly age 12. Over 90% acknowledged that young people are sold things "in ways they don't even notice." Almost two thirds agreed that too much marketing and advertising is directed towards children.

Meanwhile, people should expect more of it rather than less. At the Youth Marketing Mega-Event 2006, 70 sessions and 80 speakers were scheduled to help youth marketers do an even more effective job. Sessions included "Launching the next big 'gotta have it' for tweens," "R U ready 2 Talk Teen?" and separate live panels with kids, tweens, teens and college students. The campus media group even arranged for a keg party at the beginning of the conference to get the adult participants in the right frame of mind for networking.

Young people participate in their own manipulation by helping marketers target them more effectively. They answer surveys online, by telephone, by mail and in shopping malls. Visits to the Web site teenfreeway.com, for example, will score freebies as long as guests pretend to be 13 or older. Young people participate in discussion groups and even permit market researchers to peruse their closets. Researchers, called "consumption sociologists" tag along with teens identified as opinion leaders or trend setters while they shop. They pay visits to do in-home interviews and observe teens' family dynamics and friendships. They recruit teens to report back to them about other teens. They even arrange for schools and community groups to test out products and provide feedback.

After collecting all this information about teens, marketers are keen to put it to good use. Although they primarily market toys and foods high in sugar and fat content that may be especially appealing to young children, they also employ a number of techniques intended to capture young children's attention (Calvert, 2008). For example, advertisers place their names on toys, use cartoon characters in ads, and employ humor that is appealing to young people (e.g., Calvert, 2008). Marketers make sure their products are associated with fun, relaxation, and being "cool" (e.g., Austin & Hust, 2005, Folta, Goldberg, Economos, Bell, & Melter, 2006). They also embed products in media content such as popular video games and television programs so that young children cannot discern that they are being sold a product.

The Effects of Being a Sought after Audience

It is important to acknowledge that young people can learn positive lessons from the media just as tools used properly can build useful things. The majority of health practitioners and scholars, however, are concerned with the potential negative effects that may result from overexposure to advertising that emphasizes messages that do not make the welfare of young people a priority. This has become such a serious issue that the American Academy of Pediatrics issued a policy statement in 2006 warning against advertising's effects on children and adolescents.

In part, youths' exposure to advertising is disconcerting because they tend to agree that they do not have the cognitive ability to understand that advertisers are selling a product and oftentimes cannot differentiate between factual information and marketing techniques. In fact, the Academy of Pediatrics argued that young people, especially those under 8 years old, are both cognitively and psychologically unable to defend themselves against the barrage of marketers' targeted advertisements. The Academy identified that tobacco, alcohol, and food advertising have the greatest negative impact on young audiences. In fact, the majority of research on the effects of advertising on children has been concentrated in these areas. Overwhelmingly, this research indicates that children's exposure to such advertising is positively linked to their intent to consume alcohol, tobacco, and fast foods or foods low in nutrition.

Research on advertising's effects on youth also has identified that it is associated with materialistic attitudes, family conflict, and request for products (Buijzen & Valkenburg, 2005).

Parents are picking up on these effects, as well. One common concern among parents is the sheer ubiquity of the media in comparison to their own influence as a parent; in essence, the ability to take effective action in the face of competing media messages (Padilla-Walker, 2006). In a 2003 Common Sense Media Poll of American Parents (Penn et al., 2003), parents reported media negatively affect children because it encourages them to become too materialistic, experience a loss of innocence too early, and behave in antisocial or violent ways.

Despite their concerns, it seems that many parents have given up trying to control their children's media environment. Only about one quarter of 7th–12th graders have parental controls or filters on their computers, and very few have parents who check the advisory labels on music or video games. Hardly any parents use the V-chip that controls television program access. Indeed, parents seem to encourage media independence from toddlerhood, when most preschoolers master the use of a computer mouse. Almost half of 0- to 6-year-olds can load a CD-ROM by themselves and more than one third can turn on a computer by themselves. In the process of using these technologies, children and adolescents encounter a tremendous number of media messages.

Even though parents have identified that the media may negatively affect their children, they rarely consider doing without it (Wilson, Duffett, Johnson, & Farkas, 2002). Rather than eliminate the potential nuisances presented by television, parents may try to monitor, regulate or eliminate their children's access to it. Previous research has found that negative attitudes about television, conceptualized as how negative of an influence it had on children, were significantly related to greater parental regulation of children's television viewing (Christopher, Fabes, & Wilson, 1989).

Parents Can Be Strategic Too

Successful parenting in our media-saturated, capitalistic society requires caregivers to act as strategically as marketers already do. Savvy parents will move beyond reliance on blocking tools such as the V-chip and Internet filters to a focus on direct interpersonal communication with their children. As children's first and primary sources of information, parents play a primary role in shaping children's values along with their strategies for seeking and interpreting information. As a result, parents serve as a powerful buffer between advertising messages and children. It also, however, is important for parents to realize that children also influence their parents.

Children do not take a passive role in their own socialization process. As a result, this section first focuses on socialization in its broader context and discusses implications for the acquisition of family and media values. Next, we turn to how parenting styles and parent-child communication patterns affect and are reflected in children's development, followed by a description of commonly adopted parent-child mediation strategies. Then we address the relative effectiveness or ineffectiveness of these strategies.

Bidirectional Socialization in its Broader Context

The media present certain values to children—such as consumerism—as do parents. Indeed, the main concern with children's exposure to media in general, and to advertising in particular, is its ability to persuade children of various ages into wanting products or into adopting particular belief systems that parents finds objectionable. Parents often feel they are up against a media Goliath (Padilla-Walker, 2006). As a result, although much of the media effects literature focuses on the effects of frequent exposure and to content in various genres, it may be most useful for parents to focus on the media's role in values acquisition. Values are not transmitted but instead are constructed, and parents can play a major role in the child's construction process through discussion that acknowledges media as an important part of the child's environment (Bronfenbrenner, 1986; Kuczynski, Marshall, & Schell, 1997; Smetana 1997). Parents and children each possess beliefs, values, skills, attitudes, and motives which are influenced by their interactions with each other and by external social systems such as siblings, peers, school, and media. The more parents understand and discuss the other influencers, the greater their own influence will be.

Parenting Goals

This approach corresponds to the view of Baumrind (1996), who has maintained that two primary goals of effective parenting are the development of the child's (a) character and (b) competence. *Character* is defined by a sense of accountability, cultural and social responsibility, and self-discipline, while *competence* connotes self efficacy in navigating and interpreting the world. At the same time, parents' goals often emphasize *compliance* by the child more than character or competence (Grusec, 2002; Grusec, Goodnow, & Kuczynski, 2000). Family development researchers have distinguished these as *child-centered* vs. *parent-centered* goals (Grusec, 2002; Sigel & McGillicuddy-De Lisi, 2002).

Most families incorporate each orientation at some point or another depending on the context and the child's behavior. Parent-centered goals typically rely on punitive measures and aim for short-term compliance (a child misbehaving at the grocery store, for example). Child-centered goals are more concerned with the (longer-term) social and cognitive development of the child (Grusec, 2002). In terms of affecting the internalization of values by the child, evidence supports the child-centered approach as most effective, because it incorporates more reasoning on the part of the parent, negotiation between parent and child, and an overall relationship-oriented approach.

Parents who continually take a parent-centered perspective may achieve compliance by the child out of acquiescence or fear, but they may fail to achieve long-term internalization on the part of the child (Grusec, 2002; Smetana, 1997). Children whose parents take a firm yet not overly coercive approach, sharing clear and consistent expectations and guidelines, and expressing emotional warmth and responsiveness, tend to internalize family values more than children whose parents take a strongly authoritarian approach, act emotionally neglectful, or too permissive (Baumrind, 1978; 1996; Grusec, 2002). The most effective parenting approach is known as an *authoritative* approach and has been linked with stronger internal locus of control (i.e., self-efficacy), more positive feelings of self-worth, more mature problem-solving abilities, and better long-term social adjustment in children compared to other parenting styles (Lamborn, Mounts, Steinberg, & Dornbusch, 1991; McClun & Merrell, 1998; Pettit, Bates, & Dodge, 2000; Steinberg, Blatt-Eisengart, & Cauffman, 2006).

Impact of Child Variables

Even while parenting styles affect the character and competence of children, children also affect parenting. Variables such as the gender of the child, age, birth order, child temperament, and the child's attachment status to the parent all play a role in how a parent reacts to the child. For example, parents may take a more or less punitive approach to childhood aggression depending on whether the child is a girl or a boy. Older children are granted more autonomy and input than younger children. Children further down in birth order are often granted more freedoms at a younger age compared to first-borns, and siblings often have very different perceptions of the workings and health of the family system even though they were raised by the same parents in the same immediate environment. Psychological characteristics of the child also have an impact as parents adjust their parenting styles to accommodate each child's needs (Grusec, 2002). In addition, the attachment security of children also affects their internalization of values and may require some adjustments in communication style (Bowlby, 1979; Bretherton, Golby, & Cho, 1997; Grusec, 2002).

The Transition to Adolescence

During adolescence, the peer group, including perceived super peers in the media (Strasburger, 2007), takes a pronounced role as socialization agent, much to the chagrin of many parents. In general, teenagers exert more autonomy, with parents having less direct control over their children's activities, including their media consumption. This can magnify the media's potential for influence but does not neutralize the influence of parents. For example, in certain domains such as health behavior, adolescents typically accept a fair degree of parental monitoring and input (Smetana, 1997). Parents also continue to play a role to the extent they maintain a level of discussion about issues and other influencers. This role presents challenges, particularly because parents are now "immigrants" in their children's native social and media milieu (Rushkoff, 2006). The adolescent media world now presents a continuum of media *creation* opportunities that never existed for their parents, ranging from self-directed media consumption [or selective exposure; also see Arnett (1995)] through creation of media content (such as video postings on YouTube®). This makes the child-centered approach even more essential than before, requiring parents to listen to their teens, learn from their teens, and try to experience the world through their teens' eyes in order to communicate effectively about their media-saturated—and product placement-filled—worlds. Without parental guidance, the media become increasingly important and authoritative sources of information for children (Brown, Halpern, & L'Engle, 2005; Strasburger, 2004, 2007).

Parental Mediation as Values Acquisition

Parent-Centered vs. Child-Centered Goals Revisited

Because parental guidance plays a crucial role both as buffer between media and children and as a facilitator of children's competence to consider media messages for themselves independently, it is important to evaluate parental communication and mediation strategies in terms of their effectiveness. A child-centered approach focuses on the child's eventual need to operate effectively as an independent consumer. This approach will acknowledge the child as an active agent in her or his own socialization and development, and it will engage the child to think critically about the pros and cons of engaging in media-depicted models of behavior. The ideal approach to parental mediation will be *strategic* and *involved*.

Strategic means goal oriented. Parents can approach discussions and interactions with their children regarding advertising content with the goal of independent competence in mind, with or without involving themselves in their children's activities or media use (Warren, 2003). One strategy for countering advertising's effects is through the application of general family communication styles that influence children's information seeking patterns in beneficial ways. Additionally, parents can choose specific intervention strategies. These strategies fall into two general categories—*avoidance strategies* and *involvement strategies*. Avoidance strategies include rulemaking, passive coviewing and deference, and involvement strategies include parental mediation and active coviewing. Some strategies generally have more effectiveness than others, and the relative effectiveness of each also will depend on the child's environment and social-cognitive development.

General Family Communication Patterns

Different parents approach discussions about advertising and its effects in different ways, in large part because of different within-family norms guiding their family communication patterns. Some parents, for example, foster an exchange of ideas with their children and invite them to participate in rigorous discussions and debates. In contrast, others impose strict rules and avoid the discussion of controversial ideas, which then tends to limit communication overall.

Socio-Oriented vs. Concept-Oriented Family Communication

The Family Communication Patterns (FCP) model identifies two key dimensions of communication norms that have been used to study the association between family communication styles and media effects (McLeod & Chaffee, 1972). The FCP differentiates between families who emphasize conformity while avoiding disagreement (socio-orientation) with those who emphasize individualization while encouraging debate (concept-orientation). Much of the research on FCP focused on parents' reports of their behaviors, but subsequent research from the child's perspective has helped to clarify how children perceive different styles of communication patterns and how these perceptions relate to media effects (Austin, 1993; Fitzpatrick, Marshall, Leutwiler, & Krcmar, 1996; Fujioka & Austin, 2003). Overall, researchers have found that pluralistic families emphasize give-and-take conversation and de-emphasize conformity to address issues with their children, consensual families emphasize conversation but also emphasize conformity, protective families engage in low amounts of conversation but expect high conformity, and laissez-faire families appear to be relatively uninvolved overall, emphasizing neither conversation nor conformity to address issues. Although some gender differences exist, with girls being more resilient than boys, research has shown that even though socio-orientation families prioritize conformity, children from concept-oriented families are far more likely to internalize family norms and achieve healthier social and behavioral outcomes (Fitzpatrick et al., 1996; Fujioka & Austin, 2003; Ritchie, 1991; Ritchie & Fitzpatrick, 1990).

Important differences exist between the two communication styles as well. Socio-orientated families tend to watch greater amounts of television (Chaffee, McLeod, & Atkin, 1971; McLeod & Chaffee, 1972), while concept-oriented families tend to have more discussion of television content (Fujioka & Austin, 2002). Concept-orientation is also associated with critical discussions and negations of television messages (Austin & Chen, 2003). Research applying the FCP model to the context of persuasive messages has shown that concept-orientation tends to provide a more effective protective factor against commercial messages. On the other hand, children from socio-oriented families are more easily persuaded by media messages, presumably because they have less practice with counter-arguing and comparing arguments against evidence (Austin, 1993; McLeod & Chaffee, 1972; Messaris & Kerr, 1983). Finally, a concept-oriented approach is more likely to encourage discussion of difficult issues (Austin, 1995) and child-to-parent socialization such as in the context of politics or civic issues (Saphir & Chaffee, 2002).

Developmentally-Appropriate Parental Interventions

The complexity and appropriateness of parent intervention strategies coincide generally, but not uniformly, with the child's age, mostly because of limitations or advances in the child's cognitive processing abilities, language acquisition, and need for autonomy. This is particularly true for avoidance strategies, which are better suited for young children not yet ready to sort through the complexities of media messages. Involvement strategies are beneficial for children and adolescents of all ages, but the type of communication elicited by the parents and the child will differ depending on the child's developmental level (Fortman, Clarke, & Austin, 1998; Meadowcroft, 1986). Most parents attempt to use all of the avoidance strategies of *rulemaking, passive coviewing,* and *deference,* and the involvement strategies of *active coviewing* and *parental mediation* at some time or another, yet the degree and effectiveness of each strategy will vary with child- and parent-specific traits, with the manner in which parents convey the information, and with the degree of parent-child accuracy and congruency in developing a shared meaning of the intervention (Ritchie, 1991).

Avoidance Strategies

Avoidance strategies take three basic forms: rulemaking, passive coviewing, and deference.

Rulemaking   Rulemaking, or "cocooning" according to some researchers (Goodnow, 1997), refers to restrictions placed on children's length of time with television and other media, and/or prohibitions on watching certain programs.

Rulemaking approaches can be either *reasoned* or *controlled.* A reasoned approach includes explanation by the parent as to why certain television programming is off limits to the child, whereas a controlled approach includes no explanation for the imposed rules (Goodnow, 1997). Some research evidence shows that the degree of imposed rulemaking is related to parents' perceptions of the media threat. That is, the more parents perceive that media exposure is dangerous for their children or poses a threat to family values, the more likely they are to adopt a rulemaking approach (Padilla-Walker, 2006; Padilla-Walker & Thompson, 2005). Other researchers have called rulemaking or cocooning "restrictive mediation" (e.g., Nathanson, 2002a), yet we choose to reserve the term "mediation" to connote an active and bidirectional approach rather than an avoidant and unidirectional stance that parents take with their children with regard to media uses and effects. Research suggests that unreasoned or controlled rulemaking is appropriate primarily for infants and toddlers (ages 0– years). After the age of 2, however, parents should begin to explain their reasons for television restriction to their children using developmentally-appropriate language.

Scholars have found that the benefits of rulemaking appear to lie less in the actual rules than in the broader communication patterns that take place when the rules are developed (Alexander, 1990; Andreason, 1990). Concept-oriented families, for example, may discuss whether a particular program or channel has more advertising than others, which add to a youth's understanding of advertisers' techniques. In contrast, socio-oriented parents tend to decide the channels themselves, without indicating to their children why a channel is more appropriate than others (Krcmar, 1996).

Passive Coviewing   Coviewing simply involves using media such as television with one's children (Austin, 2007). It is important to distinguish between *passive coviewing*, which entails watching television with one's children without discussion of the media content, and *active coviewing*, which includes parent-child discussion of media content during the act of coviewing (discussed later as an involvement strategy). In passive coviewing of the media, parents attend to media with their children but do not engage in conversation about the media's content. Parents and children often use media together to share enjoyable time together and, as a result, may not invest energy in critiquing messages. As such, some researchers have used the term "nonmediation" to denote passive coviewing, since passive coviewing is simply that—no conscious action on the part of the parents to influence media's impact on their children (Austin, Bolls, Fujioka, & Engelbertson, 1999).

Although passive coviewing involves no *conscious* action on the part of parents, passive coviewing nevertheless can influence children's attitudes about advertising messages and other media content. In fact, children may assume that their parents endorse the advertising material because they do not hear their parents mentioning negative aspects of the content (Bandura, 1969, 2002). When these parents *do* discuss the media, they tend to mention content they like (Austin et al., 1999). This can further lead to reinforcement of messages that parents may not intend to reinforce, such as alcohol advertising (Austin & Chen, 2003; Austin, Chen, & Grube, 2006). As a result, passive coviewing strategies are not recommended at *any* stage of a child's development.

Deference   A final type of avoidance strategy is deference, whereby parents relent to the children and let them make their own decisions, even if contrary to family values (Padilla-Walker & Thompson, 2005). This approach may be attractive to families who wish to avoid conflict, or for parents who adopt a permissive parenting style (Baumrind, 1978). It also can reflect low involvement, making it consistent with the laissez-faire type of Family Communication Patterns generally. Such a parenting style is typically not associated with positive social outcomes in the long-term, however, because these children lack negotiation skills and tend to be overly aggressive with other children in an effort to get their way (Grusec, 1997), This may reflect the tendency of permissive parents to overly personalize situations to the child without making sweeping moral judgments toward behavior (Smetana, 1997). Deference strategies rarely are appropriate, except with older adolescents *whose parents typically have adopted involvement strategies throughout the child's life*. In this case, involved, reflexive parenting (Grusec, 2002) may include the incorporation of a deference strategy as these children become more autonomous, presumably having demonstrated the ability to think critically about media messages on their own.

Avoidance Strategies and Socio-Orientation   With some exceptions (such as with "reasoned rulemaking" and the "deference-as-reflexive-parenting" examples described above), a socio-oriented family communication style generally correlates with the adoption of avoidance strategies toward advertising influences (Fujioka & Austin, 2002). Parents of socio-oriented families in particular may choose to avoid talking directly about advertisings' potential effects. These parents avoid discussion either through establishing rules that keep their children away from the advertisements or by watching the advertisements passively with their children (passive coviewing). Neither of these strategies has been found to be effective at mediating media content and, instead, can strengthen children's receptivity to persuasive messages (e.g., Austin & Chen, 2003; McLeod & Chaffee, 1972).

By the time children reach adolescence, the effects of a continued rulemaking approach, in combination with the absence of involvement strategies, can have detrimental results, with adolescents developing less positive attitudes toward their parents, more positive views of the undesirable content, and a greater likelihood of "rebellion" simply by watching the undesirable content with friends (Nathanson, 2002b). This illustrates the disadvantages of adopting a communication style centered more on parent goals rather than child-oriented goals. A parent-centered approach tends to focus more on behavioral control of children and avoidance of content the parents do not like, regardless of what the children or adolescents think of the content. Involvement strategies, which are more child-centered in nature, tend to result in more beneficial outcomes.

Involvement Strategies

In contrast to parents who rely on avoidance strategies, some parents, typically concept-oriented families (Fujioka & Austin, 2002), use strategies that require active conversation or involvement. Key to an involvement strategy is *active coviewing*, which requires *parental mediation* during the viewing event. Importantly, parental mediation can also take place in the absence of coviewing. That is, parental mediation can take place outside of the viewing event, but *active* coviewing cannot occur in the absence of parental mediation. This is an important distinction when discussing involvement strategies, as the two constructs are conceptually intertwined, but they are not the same.

Parents who use involvement strategies actively engage their children in conversations and debates about advertising content. Unlike avoidance strategies, these strategies tend to foster children's critical thinking toward advertising content and media-presented values because they take a more child-centered approach, which emphasizes the development of socio-cultural competencies in the child. A child-centered approach tends to lead to the child's internalization of family values (such as the importance of critical thinking toward media) and achieve mutual understanding of parent and child goals (Grusec, 2002; Grusec, Goodnow, & Kuczynski, 2000; Sigel & McGillicuddy-De Lisi, 2002; Smetana, 1997). Much of the evidence supporting this type of approach has measured effectiveness of the strategy in terms of decreased purchase requests by children, lower parent-child conflict, and lower materialism among children (Buijzen & Valkenburg, 2005; Robertson, 1979). While findings such as these contribute worthwhile information to the field, outcomes such as fewer purchase requests and lower parent-child conflict, which are parent-centered goals, should not be confused with fostering critical thinking (a child-centered goal). Other research has shown that child-centered outcomes such as communication competence, resistance to persuasive messages about alcohol, and increased civic engagement also result from the use of these strategies (Austin, 1993; Austin et al., 2006; Austin, Pinkleton, & Fujioka, 2000).

Active Coviewing   Although little existing research differentiates between active and passive coviewing, it is clear that not all coviewing practices are similar. Unlike passive coviewing, parents who actively coview not only watch television or other media with their children, but also discuss positive and negative aspects of the media with their children. That is, they engage in parental mediation while watching. In doing so, parents assist their children in critically evaluating media messages and directly point out areas of concern, such as the persuasive intent of advertising, and depictions of substance use, sexual activity, and violence. During active coviewing, the act of attending to the media is not only about entertainment but also is about seizing potential teaching opportunities within media content.

What parents choose to point out to children during active coviewing also is of significance. Nathanson and colleagues (Nathanson, 2004; Nathanson, Wilson, McGee, & Sebastian, 2002) make this distinction using the terms *factual* vs. *evaluative* approaches to active coviewing in her studies of children's interpretations of media violence and sexual stereotypes. A factual approach focuses on telling children that what they are seeing on television is not "real," or that what they are seeing is the result of special "camera tricks." An evaluative approach focuses on the characters' behaviors, whereby the coviewing adult expresses verbal disapproval of unacceptable behaviors during the viewing episode. For example, "That is not the way we should treat people" or "This advertisement is not telling the truth" are examples of evaluative statements utilizing negative mediation during a viewing event. (Positive and negative parental mediation are discussed in more detail later.) Young children generally do not understand factual information regarding television production, and a factual approach with older children may in fact increase their interest in the programming. Therefore, an evaluative approach focusing on depicted media norms and values in relation to family norms and values, which are often in opposition to each other, has been related to more positive child outcomes in terms of values acquisition (Nathanson, 2004). While more research in this area is needed, preliminary results reveal the superiority of an evaluative approach over a factual approach for children of various ages. That is, an evaluative approach (i.e., active coviewing, or, mediation during a viewing event) has resulted in desirable norms and values outcomes such as less positive attitudes toward violent characters and gender stereotyped media content, less perceived justification for media violence, less involvement with violent perpetrators and more empathy for victims, and less acceptance of gender stereotyped attitudes (Nathanson, 2004; Nathanson & Cantor, 2000; Nathanson, et al., 2002).

Parental Mediation As mentioned above, it is difficult to distinguish between active coviewing and parental mediation. For clarity, Figure 13.1 depicts the process by which categorization takes place. Active coviewing, by definition, necessitates that parental mediation take place during the viewing event. Parental mediation, on the other hand, does not by definition need to occur in conjunction with viewing media content. In fact, some of the most in-depth media discussions between parents and children can take place away from the television set, such as while driving in the car. Scenarios such as these may even be preferable when the parent and child wish to hold each others' attention for extended periods of time without distraction.

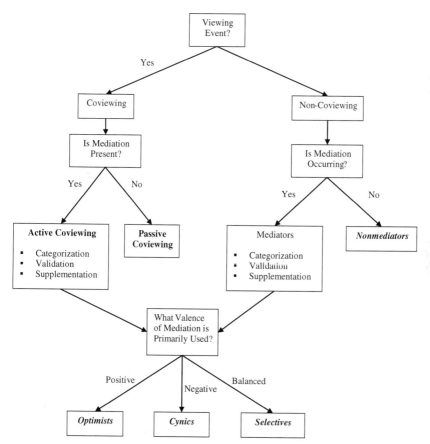

Figure 13.1 Model for ascertaining parental mediation and coviewing styles (adapted from Austin, 1993; Austin, Bolls, Fujioka, & Engelbertson, 1999).

Parents mediate by refuting or reinforcing television content in three key ways: categorization, validation, and supplementation (Austin, 1993; Messaris, 1982). Parents may *categorize* advertising content by pointing out whether and how an advertisement reflects daily life and purchases. They may *validate* an advertisement by either endorsing or condemning a new technique or advertising message. Finally, they may *supplement* advertising content with additional information that helps young people understand the ad in relation to everyday living. It is important to note that although we use advertising as the example here, the same could be said for any form of media.

Positive and Negative Parental Mediation

The goal of mediation is for parents to assist their children in understanding advertising and other media messages and their persuasive intent. Although most research on parental mediation has focused on television in general instead of advertising specifically, results indicate this strategy is related to increased knowledge and attitude change (Austin, 1993; Austin, Roberts, & Nass, 1990; Fujioka & Austin, 2003). As with the other strategies, however, mediation differs by family communication patterns, and research has just recently begun to investigate the differences in what has been called "positive mediation" and "negative mediation," with the desired outcomes described above associated with negative parental mediation rather than positive parental mediation.

Positive Parental Mediation In positive mediation, a parent typically reinforces media content rather than explaining or critiquing the content. We mentioned earlier that involvement strategies are typically associated with concept-oriented family communication. One exception to this generality is the case of positive mediation. Positive mediators (labeled "optimists" in other parental mediation studies such as Austin et al., 1999) are likely parents from socio-oriented families who also passively coview a lot of television with their children. It is possible that positive mediation is necessary in socio-oriented families so that family harmony and conformity is maintained.

When children perceive that their parents (intentionally or unintentionally) reinforce media messages, undesirable outcomes usually result. For example, children who perceive that their parents endorse alcohol consumption are less likely to be skeptical of alcohol advertisements (Fujioka & Austin, 2003). The undesirable carry-over from perceived positive mediation can be long-lasting. For example, college students who perceived that their parents positively mediated alcohol consumption when they were younger had higher positive expectancies for alcohol in college and were likely to initiate drinking sooner than college students whose parents negatively mediated alcohol consumption (Austin & Chen, 2003). Findings such as these also highlight the importance of a child-centered approach and of achieving mutual understanding during the mediation process through give-and-take discussion. It is unlikely that the parents of the students surveyed by Austin and Chen wanted their children to find alcohol consumption desirable or wanted their children to initiate alcohol consumption at younger ages than other youth. As Fujioka and Austin (2003) found in another study comparing parent reports and child reports of parent-child interactions, "No parent variables predicted anything" (p. 431). Therefore, the importance of the parent's and child's vantage points cannot be overstated here. Because of the potential for misunderstanding and its long-lasting implications, parents must be flexible and able to confirm with their children to be sure that the message they intend to convey is the message the child has received.

Negative Parental Mediation In contrast, parents employing negative mediation emphasize critical and skeptical perspectives of media content. Negative mediation occurs more frequently in concept-oriented families who encourage critical debates about media content (Fujioka & Austin, 2002). Parents who employ both positive and negative mediation in their discussions with their children have been called "selectives" (Austin et al., 1999) as opposed to "cynics," who report the most skepticism toward media content. Some research has suggested that a combination of positive and negative mediation is complementary and can encourage beneficial outcomes such as political engagement (Austin & Pinkleton, 2001).

Negative parental mediation is an especially important form of parental influence, particularly when media is viewed as a bridge from the home to the larger society. Effective parental mediation includes not only discussion of media content, but also affects children's perceptions of media values. For example, advertising directed at children has been shown to affect parent-child interactions, children's consumer behavior, and degree of materialism (Buijzen & Valkenburg, 2003; Valkenburg, 2000; Valkenburg & Cantor, 2001). Other research in this area has examined why and how children attend to certain forms of media at different ages (Valkenburg, 2004). Therefore, rather than adopt an avoidance approach, effective parental mediation focusing on advertising involves drawing children's attention to the persuasive intent of advertising and focuses on family values in comparison to those presented in advertisements. Simple statements such as, "Advertisements just try to get you to buy things, but we do not need those things to be happy" can be effective even for very young children.

Negative Parental Mediation and Developmental Appropriateness It is a common assertion among those adhering to classical theorists such as Piaget that very young children cannot grasp abstract notions such as the "intents of others" (Piaget, 1929, 1965/1932). Experimental research using more developmentally-appropriate approaches, however, has shown that this is not accurate (Donaldson, 1978). Even children as young as 18 months old are able to understand the intended acts of an adult by completing a simple task that the adult "pretends" to fail at (Meltzoff, 2000). Furthermore, these children can differentiate between a human and a mechanical pincer device that "fails" at the same tasks—that is, the children can understand that the adult confederate has intrinsically human intentions, whereas they do not attribute intentions to the mechanical device. Additionally, children as young as preschool age have shown a rudimentary ability to differentiate between lying and truthfulness, but it also has shown that they need some help—some mediation. For example, experimental evidence indicates that although preschoolers generally perceive lying as wrong, perceived severity of the transgression depends on the presence or absence of an adult reprimand for the lie. Children who see a child actor reprimanded for a lie judge the lie to be worse than the children who see the child actor's lie go unpunished (Bussey, 2000). For older children, the severity of the lie is judged equally as harshly regardless of the presence of adult reprimand, presumably because they already possess the critical thinking abilities to draw conclusions independently.

This evidence has important implications for negative parental mediation. With an age-appropriate approach, negative parental mediation is possible beginning in toddlerhood. For example, framing advertisements as a "lie" about which the parents disapprove is a developmentally-appropriate approach for young children that incorporates the importance of family values and norms (lying is wrong). If inappropriate interpersonal behaviors such as hitting, or undesirable health behaviors such as smoking are depicted, the parent can engage in negative mediation with simple statements such as, "Hitting hurts others. We don't act like that." Or, "Ew, smoking is yucky! We don't smoke!" Young children often will engage in conversation about concrete topics they can relate to their own experiences. As children grow older, parental mediation strategies can become more complex. The approach with older children will require a more reflexive, authoritative parenting approach as opposed to a control-oriented authoritarian approach, an indulgent permissive approach, or a neglectful approach (Baumrind, 1978; 1996; Lamborn, Mounts, Steinberg, & Dornbusch, 1991; McClun & Merrell, 1998; Steinberg, Blatt-Eisengart, & Cauffman, 2006).

Although longitudinal studies are rare, one study that incorporated lab and in-home observations (Bersamin et al., 2008) demonstrated that parental media intervention strategies and parent communication styles are distinct yet related constructs, and that parent communication styles in combination with various avoidance or involvement strategies resulted in differential sexual outcomes among adolescents. Specifically, teens (ages 12–16) whose parents engaged in coviewing in conjunction with discussion about sex outside of the viewing episode at Time 1 were less likely to have initiated vaginal intercourse at Time 2 than were teens whose parents coviewed with their children but did not engage in discussion (mediation), and also for teens whose parents engaged in discussion outside the viewing event but did not coview. Furthermore, teens who had engaged in oral sex perceived lower quality of parent-child communication, greater parental support for sex, and had parents who were less likely to be involved in their child's television viewing. One key component missing from this study, however, is that the authors did not investigate or distinguish between active versus passive coviewing, or between positive versus negative parental mediation—a distinction for future research which may help explain the mixed results. Nonetheless, these findings not only highlight the importance of involvement strategies, but also the importance of reciprocity and mutual understanding during the parent-child communication processes.

Conclusion

Producers and advertisers think of commercial media as tools for attracting young people's ears and eyeballs. When producers get an audience, they can get advertiser dollars, and advertisers can get the audience's dollars. They appreciate that the media are tools for persuasion and profit, and are especially interested in youth because of the high indirect and direct influence youth have on family purchases. Advertisers and marketers count on the "nag factor" and the "guilt money" as the means through which youth exert this influence.

Neither parents nor children are defenseless in this situation. Armed with developmentally-appropriate active parenting strategies with child-centered goals in mind, such as active coviewing and parental mediation, parents can socialize their children to become critical thinkers toward media content. With media literacy as a family value, parents and children alike can learn to think reflectively about media content and to operate the powerful media tools in a way that benefit them as much as or more than the professionals targeting children for their own benefit.

References

Achenreiner, G. B., & John, D. R. (2003). The meaning of brand names to children: a developmental investigation. *Journal of Consumer Psychology, 13*(3), 205–219.

Alexander, A. (1990). Television and family interaction. In J. Bryant (Ed.), *Television and the American family* (pp. 211–226). Hillsdale, NJ: Erlbaum.

Andreason, M. S. (1990). Evolution in the family's use of television: Normative data from industry and academe. In J. Bryant (Ed.), *Television and the American family* (pp. 3–55). Hillsdale, NJ: Erlbaum.

Arnett, J. J. (1995). Adolescents' uses of media for self-socialization. *Journal of Youth and Adolescence, 24*(5), 519–533.

Austin, E. W. (1993). Exploring the effects of active parental mediation of television content. *Journal of Broadcasting & Electronic Media, 37,* 147–158.

Austin, E. W. (1995). Direct and indirect influences of parent-child communication norms on adolescent's tendencies to take preventive measures for AIDS and drug abuse. In G. Kreps & D. O'Hair (Eds.), *Relational communication and health outcomes* (pp. 163–183). SCA Applied Communication Series.

Austin, E. W. (2007). Coviewing. In J. J. Arnett (Ed.) *Encyclopedia of children, adolescents, and the media, Vol. 1* (pp. 223–224). Thousand Oaks, CA: Sage.

Austin, E. W., Bolls, P., Fujioka, Y., & Engelbertson, J. (1999). How and why parents take on the tube. *Journal of Broadcasting & Electronic Media, 43*(2), 175–192.

Austin, E. W., & Chen, Y. (2003). The relationship of parental reinforcement of media messages to college students' alcohol-related behaviors. *Journal of Health Communication, 8*, 157–169.

Austin, E. W., Chen, M., & Grube, J. W. (2006). How does alcohol advertising influence underage drinking? The role of desirability, identification and skepticism. *Journal of Adolescent Health, 38*, 376–384.

Austin, E. W., & Hust, S. J. T. (2005). Targeting adolescents? The content and frequency of alcoholic and nonalcoholic beverage ads in magazine and video formats November 1999–April 2000. *Journal of Health Communication, 10*, 1–18.

Austin, E. W., & Pinkleton, B. E. (2001). The role of parental mediation in the political socialization process. *Journal of Broadcasting & Electronic Media, 45*(2), 221–240.

Austin, E. W., Pinkleton, B. E., & Fujioka, Y. (2000). The role of interpretation processes and parental discussion in the media's effects on adolescents' use of alcohol. *Pediatrics, 105*, 343–349.

Austin, E. W., Roberts, D. F., & Nass, C. I. (1990). Influences of family communication on children's television-interpretation processes. *Communication Research, 17*(4), 545–564.

Bandura, A. (1969). Social-learning theory of identificatory processes. In D. A. Goslin (Ed.), *Handbook of socialization theory and research* (pp. 213–262). Chicago: Rand McNally.

Bandura, A. (2002). Social cognitive theory of mass communication. In J. Bryant & D. Zillmann (Eds.) *Media effects: Advances in theory and research* (2nd ed., pp. 121–153). Mahwah, NJ: Erlbaum.

Baumrind, D. (1978). Parental disciplinary patterns and social competence in children. *Youth & Society, 9*(3), 239–276.

Baumrind, D. (1996). The discipline controversy revisited. *Family Relations, 45*(4), 405–414.

Bersamin, M., Todd, M., Fisher, D. A., Hill, D. L., Grube, J. W., & Walker, S. (2008). Parenting practices and adolescent sexual behavior: A longitudinal study. *Journal of Marriage and Family, 70*, 97–112.

Bowlby, J. (1979). *The making and breaking of affectional bonds.* London: Tavistock.

Bretherton, I., Golby, B., & Cho, E. (1997). Attachment and the transmission of values. In J. E. Grusec & L. Kuczynski (Eds.), *Parenting and children's internalization of values: A handbook of contemporary theory* (pp. 103–134). New York: Wiley.

Bronfenbrenner, U. (1986). Ecology of the family as a context for human development: Research perspectives. *Developmental Psychology, 22*(6), 723–742.

Brown, J. D., Halpern, C. T., & L'Engle, K. L. (2005). Mass media as a sexual super peer for early maturing girls. *Journal of Adolescent Health, 26*, 420–427.

Buijzen, M., & Valkenburg, P. M. (2003). The unintended effects of television advertising—A parent-child survey. *Communication Research, 30*(5), 483–503.

Buijzen, M., & Valkenburg, P.M. (2005). Parental mediation of undesired advertising effects. *Journal of Broadcasting & Electronic Media, 49*, 153–165.

Bussey, K. (2000). Lying and truthfulness: Children's definitions, standards, and evaluative reactions. In K. Lee (Ed.), *Childhood cognitive development: The essential readings. Essential readings in developmental psychology* (pp. 309–322). Malden, MA: Blackwell.

Calvert, S. L. (2008). Children as consumers: Advertising and Marketing. *Future of Children, 18*, 205–234.

Chaffee, S. H., McLeod, J. M., & Atkin, C. K. (1971). Parental influence on adolescent media use. *The American Behavioral Scientist, 14*(3), 323–340.

Christopher, F .S., Fabes, R. A., & Wilson, P. (1989). Family television viewing: Implications for family life education. *Family Relations, 38,* 210–215.

Donaldson, M. (1978). *Children's minds.* New York: W. W. Norton.

Fitzpatrick, M. A., Marshall, L., Leutwiler, T., & Krcmar, M. (1996). The effects of family communication on children's social behavior during middle childhood. *Communication Research, 23*(4), 379–406.

Fortman, K. K. J., Clarke, T. L., & Austin, E. W. (1998). Let's talk about what we're watching: Parental mediation of children's television viewing. *Communication Research Reports, 15*(4), 413–425.

Folta, S. C., Goldberg, J. P., Economos, C., Bell, R., & Melter, R. (2006). Food advertising targeted at school-age children: A content analysis. *Journal of Nutrition Education & Behavior, 38,* 244–248.

Fujioka, Y., Austin, E. W. (2002). The relationship of family communication patterns to parental mediation styles. *Communication Research, 29*(6), 642–665.

Fujioka, Y., & Austin, E. W. (2003). The implications of vantage point in parental mediation of television and child's attitudes toward drinking alcohol. *Journal of Broadcasting & Electronic Media, 47*(3), 418–434.

Goodnow, J. J. (1997). Parenting and the transmission and internalization of values: From social-cultural perspectives to within-family analyses. In J. E. Grusec & L. Kuczynski (Eds.), *Handbook of parenting and the transmission of values* (pp. 333–361). New York: Wiley.

Grusec, J. E. (1997). A history of research on parenting strategies and children's internalization of values. In J. E. Grusec & L. Kuczynski (Eds.), *Parenting and children's internalization of values: A handbook of contemporary theory* (pp. 3–22). New York: Wiley.

Grusec, J. E. (2002). Parental socialization and children's acquisition of values. In M. Bornstein (Ed.), *Handbook of parenting: Vol 5. Practical issues in parenting* (2nd ed., pp.143–168). Mahwah, NJ: Erlbaum.

Grusec, J. E., Goodnow, J. J., & Kuczynski, L. (2000). New directions in analyses of parenting contributions to children's acquisition of values. *Child Development, 71*(1), 205–211.

Horovitz, B. (2006). Ten rules to make ads magical. Data retrieved July 25, 2008 from http://www.usatoday.com/money/advertising/2006-02-03-super-ads-usat_x.htm

Kidtrends newsletter. (n.d.). Children's Market Research. Retrieved March 2, 2009, http://www.kidtrends.com/newsletters.html

Krcmar, M. (1996). Family communication and child compliance in television viewing. *Human Communication Research, 23*(2), 251–277.

Kuczynski, L., Marshall, S., & Schell, K. (1997). Value socialization in a bidirectional context. In J. E. Grusec & L. Kuczynski (Eds.), *Handbook of parenting and the transmission of values* (pp. 23–50). New York: Wiley.

Kunkel, D., Biely, E., Eyal, K., Cope-Farrar, K., Donnerstein, E., & Fandrich, R. (2003). *Sex on TV 3: A Biennial Report of the Kaiser Family Foundation.* Menlo Park, CA: Henry J. Kaiser Family Foundation.

Lamborn, S., Mounts, N., Steinberg, L., & Dornbusch, S. (1991). Patterns of competence and adjustment among adolescents from authoritative, authoritarian, indulgent, and neglectful families. *Child Development, 62,* 1049–1065.

Leimbach, D. (2000). Marketing; where ads aimed at kids come to life. Data retrieved July 25, 2008, from http://query.nytimes.com/gst/fullpage.html?res=9500E1DD103D F930A25751C1A9669C8B63&sec=&spon=&pagewanted=all

Magazine Publishers of America. (2003). Teen. Retrieved July 25, 2008, from http://www.magazine.org/content/files/teenprofile04.pdf

MarketResearch. (May 12, 1999). C'mon, Mom! Kids Nag Parents to Chuck E. Cheese's, Retrieved March 1, 2009, http://findarticles.com/p/articles/mi_m0FVE/is_9_4/ai_54631243

McClun, L. A., & Merrell, K. W. (1998). Relationship of perceived parenting styles, locus of control orientation, and self-concept among junior high age students. *Psychology in the Schools, 35*(4), 381–390.

McLeod, J. M., & Chaffee, S. H. (1972). The construction of social reality. In J. Tedeschi, (Ed.), *The social influence process* (pp. 50–59). Chicago: Aldine Atherton.

McNeal, J. (1999). *The kids' market: myths and realities*. Ithaca, NY: Paramount Market.

Meadowcroft, J. M. (1986). Family communication patterns and political development. *Communication Research, 13*(4), 603–624.

Meltzoff, A. N. (2000). Understanding the intentions of others: Re-enactment of intended acts by 18-month-old children. In K. Lee (Ed.), *Childhood cognitive development: The essential readings. Essential readings in developmental psychology* (pp. 151–174). Malden, MA: Blackwell.

Messaris, P. (1982). Parents, children, and television. In G. Gumpert & R. Cathcart (Eds.), *Inter/Media* (2nd ed., pp. 580–598). New York: Oxford University Press.

Messaris, P., & Kerr, D. (1983). Mothers' comments about TV: Relation to family communication patterns. *Communication Research, 10,* 175–194.

Nathanson, A. I. (2002a). Parental mediation of media effects. In J. R. Schement (Ed.), *Encyclopedia of communication and information* (Vol. 2, pp. 701–704). New York: Macmillan Reference.

Nathanson, A. I. (2002b). The unintended effects of parental mediation of television on adolescents. *Media Psychology, 4,* 207–230.

Nathanson, A. I. (2004). Factual and evaluative approaches to modifying children's responses to violent television. *Journal of Communication, 54*(2), 321–336.

Nathanson, A. I., & Cantor, J. (2000). Reducing the aggression-promoting effect of violent cartoons by increasing children's fictional involvement with the victim: A study of active mediation. *Journal of Broadcasting & Electronic Media, 44,* 125–142.

Nathanson, A., Wilson, B. J., McGee, J., & Sebastian, M. (2002). Counteracting the effects of female stereotypes on television via active mediation. *Journal of Communication, 52*(4), 922–937.

Padilla-Walker, L. M. (2006). "Peers I can monitor, it's media that really worries me!" Parental cognitions as predictors of proactive parental strategy choice. *Journal of Adolescent Research, 21,* 56–82.

Padilla-Walker, L. M., & Thompson, R. A. (2005). Combating conflicting messages of values: A closer look at parental strategies. *Social Development, 14*(2), 305–323.

Penn, Schoen & Berland Associates and American Viewpoint. (2003). *The 2003 Common Sense Media Poll of American Parents.* Available at: http://www.commonsensemedia.org/about/press/ ParentspollMay212003.ppt

Pettit, G. S., Bates, J. E., & Dodge, K. A. (2000). Supportive parenting, ecological context, and children's adjustment: A seven-year longitudinal study. In W. Craig (Ed.), *Childhood social development: The essential readings. Essential readings in developmentalpsychology* (pp. 26–57). Malden, MA: Blackwell.

Piaget, J. (1929). *The child's conception of the world.* New York: Harcourt, Brace.

Piaget, J. (1965). *The moral judgment of the child.* London: Penguin Books. (Original work published 1932)

Quart, A. (2003). *Branded: The buying and selling of teenagers.* New York: Basic Books.

Ritchie, L. D. (1991). Family communication patterns: An epistemic analysis and conceptual reinterpretation. *Communication Research, 18*(4), 548–565.

Ritchie, L. D., & Fitzpatrick, M. A. (1990). Family communication patterns: Measuring intrapersonal perceptions of the interpersonal relationships. *Communication Research, 17*(4), 523–544.

Roberts, D.F., Foehr, U., & Rideout, V. (2005). *Generation M: Media in the lives of 8–18 year-olds.* Menlo Park, CA: Kaiser Family Foundation.

Robertson, T. S. (1979). Parental mediation of television advertising effects. *Journal of Communication, 29*(1), 12–25.

Robinson, T. N., Saphir, M. N., Kraemer H. C., Varady, A., & Haydel, K. F. (2001). Effects of reducing television viewing on children's requests for toys: A randomized controlled trial. *Journal of Developmental and Behavioral Pediatrics, 22,* 179–184.

Rushkoff, D. (2006) *Screenagers: Lessons in chaos from digital kids.* Cresskill, NJ: Hampton Press.

Saphir, M. N., & Chaffee, S. H. (2002). Adolescents' contributions to family communication patterns. *Human Communication Research, 28,* 86–108.

Schor, J. (2004). *Born to buy: the commercialized child and the new consumer culture.* New York: Scribner.

Sigel, I. E., & McGillicuddy-De Lisi, A. V. (2002). Parent beliefs are cognitions: The dynamic belief systems model. In M. H. Bornstein (Ed.), *Handbook of parenting: Vol. 3. Status and social conditions of parenting* (2nd ed., pp. 485–508). Mahwah, NJ: Erlbaum.

Smetana, J. G. (1997). Parenting and the development of social knowledge reconceptualized: A social domain analysis. In J. E. Grusec & L. Kuczynski (Eds.), *Parenting and children's internalization of values: A handbook of contemporary theory* (pp. 162–191). New York: Wiley.

Strasburger, V. C. (2004). Children, adolescents, and the media. *Current Problems in Pediatric and Adolescent Health Care, 34*(2), 51–113.

Strasburger, V. C. (2007). Super-peer theory. In J. J. Arnett (Ed.) *Encyclopedia of children, Adolescents, and the media* (pp. 789–790), Thousand Oaks, CA: Sage.

Steinberg, L., Blatt-Eisengart, I., & Cauffman, E. (2006). Patterns of competence and adjustment among adolescents from authoritative, authoritarian, indulgent, and neglectful homes: A replication in a sample of serious juvenile offenders. *Journal of Research on Adolescence, 16*(1), 47–58.

Targeting Teens newsletter. (n.d.). Children's Market Research. Retrieved March 2, 2009, http://www.kidtrends.com/newsletters.html

Teen Research, Inc. (2005). TRU projects teens will spend $159 billon in 2005. Data retrieved July 25, 2008, from http://www.teenresearch.com/PRview.cfm?edit_id=378

U.S. Census Bureau. (2007). *State and County QuickFacts.* Retrieved March 1, 2009, from http://quickfacts.census.gov/qfd/states/00000.html

Valkenburg, P. M. (2000). Media and youth consumerism. *Journal of Adolescent Health, 27*(2 suppl), 52–56.

Valkenburg, P. M. (2004). *Children's responses to the screen: A media psychological approach.* Mahwah, NJ: Erlbaum.

Valkenburg, P., & Cantor, J. (2001). The development of a child into a consumer. *Applied Developmental Psychology, 22,* 61–72.

Wilson, L., Duffett, A., Johnson, J., & Farkas, S. (2002). *A lot easier said than done: Parents talk about raising children in today's America.* Retrieved March 1, 2009, from

https://www.policyarchive.org/bitstream/handle/10207/5648/easier_said_than_
done.pdf?sequence=1

Warren, R. (2003) Parental mediation of preschool children's television viewing *Journal of Broadcasting & Electronic Media, 47*,(3), 394–417.

14 Finding Adolescents through Cyberspace

Youth Workers, Teenagers, and Instant Messaging

Peggy Kendall

As the bus drops off the 15-year old girl, she runs into the house, dropping her bag at the door. With a perfunctory "hi mom" she races to the computer. Soon a sweet "blingg" is sounded. This is the time she has looked forward to all day; it is her time to "hang out" with friends. Just like generations before her, "hang-out time" is essential to adolescent social, emotional, and spiritual development. Unlike previous generations, however, hang-out time has increasingly included new technological companions that take the form of computers, cell phones, video games, or some yet-to-be-invented device. However exciting and new the technology may be, there is no doubt it fundamentally changes how adolescents and family members communicate with one another by the way it substitutes text for speech, smiley faces for smiling friends, and computer-mediated presence for real-live togetherness.

It is important to understand the implications of these changes on the social development of young people, both in terms of how they relate to their friends and how they relate to their parents. What is particularly significant is how adolescents use their technology to continue communicating with adults at the same time they are taking steps to socially and publicly separate themselves from their parents. Adults who are committed to mentor and care for young people through church, school, and community programs play an important role in the life of adolescents who might feel too old to hang out with their parents, but who are not yet old enough to operate without adult support. These mentoring adults are uniquely positioned to care for adolescents in a way that both compliments and enhances the work of parents. How these mentoring adults do that work, however, is being impacted by technology. It is no surprise that as adolescents change the way they communicate with one another, the way adults connect with those adolescents must also change. This study was developed to better understand how adults, specifically youth pastors, are integrating technology in the work they do with young people. It focuses on the opportunities and challenges of using Instant Messenger in the process of friendship formation and adolescent support. It also examines adolescent perspectives on the efficacy of adults using a tool that is primarily considered an adolescent property.

The Technology

There is no doubt that the way adolescents form and manage friendships has changed over the past decade. One of the primary changes has occurred as a result of the popularization of a fairly simple technology known as Instant Messenger (IM). It is a synchronous form of e-mail that has existed for a number of years in organizational settings. It allows users to communicate in real-time, and lets everyone on a buddy list know when a buddy is "online and available" for conversation. American adolescents have adopted this technology on a surprisingly significant scale. In 2005, the Pew Internet and American Life project found that 75% of "online" adolescents—or about two thirds of *all* adolescents—reported using IM. Forty-two percent of those adolescents reported using IM at least once a day, often for periods of more than half an hour at a time (Lenhart, Madden, & Hitlin, 2005).

While IM doesn't usually garner the media attention of technology like MySpace or the scholarly attention of technology like Facebook, there is every indication that teens have adopted IM as a socially accepted and expected form of "hanging out." According to the Pew study, IM is a place where friendships are regularly made and broken, dates are planned, gossip is spread, homework is completed, secrets are shared, and a community is created (Lenhart, Madden, & Hitlin, 2005). Unfortunately, there has been limited scholarly research that focuses on this pervasive technology. An examination of some of the foundational computer-mediated-communication (CMC) studies will serve to highlight characteristics of IM that are relevant to this study. Recent IM studies that underscore specific elements of the technology that affect adolescent-adult communication will also be examined.

Computer-Mediated Communication

The study of CMC has evolved over the past three decades, beginning with the idea that CMC was an inherently *im*personal form of communication (Walther, 1996). It was originally hypothesized that, based on theories such as uncertainty reduction (Berger & Calabrese, 1975) and media richness (Daft, Lengel, & Trevino, 1984), online communication simply lacked the physical presence and social interaction cues necessary to build deep and meaningful relationships (Hu, Wood, Smith, & Westbrook, 2004).

A contrary view of CMC developed, however, as Walther (1992) hypothesized that individuals are able to adapt to the limitations of online technology. In other words, humans "use cues available to them to manage relational development in normal (or perhaps supernormal) fashion" (Walther, 1996, p. 13). This perspective defined CMC as a type of communication that actually speeds up relationship development, liberating individuals from imposed social identities and constructs. Subsequent research has found that CMC does, indeed, tend to foster greater intimacy (Hian, Chuan, Trevor, & Detenber, 2004; Hu et al., 2004; Joinson, 2004), greater identity flexibility (Turkle, 1997), and more permeable social boundaries (Wellman et al., 2003).

One important characteristic of CMC is its tendency to produce *greater* intimacy than that found in face-to-face interactions. According to Walther (1992, 1996), CMC tends to be either "impersonal" or "hyperpersonal." Impersonal communication might take the form of shallow, silly chit-chat that takes place in teenage IM conversations every day. Hyperpersonal communication, on the other hand, has been defined as "CMC that is more socially desirable than we tend to experience in parallel FtF interaction" (Walther, 1996, p. 17). This type of communication involves intense personal disclosures and occurs much sooner in a relationship than what might be found in a parallel face-to-face relationship. It is hypothesized that the technology encourages hyperpersonal communication because it allows users to manage the risks involved in self-disclosure and intimacy-building. Users can plan risky messages and are better able to manage their identity, making intentional choices about what aspects of their identity they should reveal. A lack of nonverbal cues also reduces the perceived negative risks associated with self-disclosure; it is much easier to create imagined responses that fit within user expectations and ideals than to risk real nonverbal responses that may not provide the necessary ego confirmation (Joinson, 2004). CMC also allows the receiver to idealize or "inflate" the perceptions they form about their partners (Walther, 1996, p. 17). In sum, "the idealization of one's partner and the ability to edit one's self presentation make CMC more conducive to development of relational intimacy" (Hian et al., 2004, p. 54).

CMC has also provided a new way to become connected to a community. These communities have changed from traditional neighborhood, place-based entities to "networked societies where boundaries are more permeable, interactions are with diverse others, linkages switch between multiple networks, and hierarchies are flatter and more recursive" (Wellman et al., 2003, p. 18). Online communities provide individuals with more of a participatory voice than may be garnered from other technologies, such as the television (O'Leary & Brasher, 1996). Online communities are also more personal in nature and help meet the individual's need for support, sociability, information, social identity creation, and a sense of belonging. However, because individuals are often members of many unrelated online communities, it tends to be difficult for any one community to acquire the entire attention or passion of an individual. Additionally, users often change identities from community to community since there exist few physical signs of enduring social status or identity. According to Wellman et al. (2003), the result of this "networked individualism" is a fragmented citizenry. While CMC is, therefore, an important means of providing individuals with a valuable sense of community, it also serves to disconnect them from a unified sense of self and neighborhood.

Instant Messaging

Instant Messaging clearly creates a unique form of communication mediated by technology. It is used to form both interpersonal relationships and support communities. There are, however, certain characteristics of IM that make it different from technology that has historically been used in CMC research. Unlike chat rooms and traditional online communities where members rarely know each other and identities are easily falsified, IM is most often used to enhance existing face-to-face friendships. The communities that are served through IM are ones which already exist in face-to-face contexts (Valkenburg & Peter, 2007). Second, unlike traditional Internet bulletin boards and e-mail, IM is a unique tool that gives users "the ability to know who is connected to the shared space between or among friends, and the ability to conduct a text-based conversation in real-time" (Hu et al., 2004, p. 1). These characteristics have the potential to change the dynamic of the communication that takes place, making it more of an integrated and natural part of an individual's face-to-face social network and daily schedule. Finally, unlike most Internet-based communication technology, IM provides an opportunity for young people to communicate using language unique to the community. While IM language is often created to make things easier to type, it is also used to share secrets and jokes between friends. It identifies the conversation as uniquely adolescent and can enhance feelings of community and separateness. According to Alvestrand (2002), "this phenomenon fosters a sense of online community that perhaps no other application has done" (p. 1).

Studies focusing specifically on IM have highlighted a number of findings that are consistent with traditional CMC theories. One finding particularly relevant to the study of adolescents and how they use technology to interact with parents and other adults suggests that IM produces greater intimacy in relationships than face-to-face interactions, resulting in an increased desire to meet face-to-face (Hu et al., 2004). IM is especially conducive to "hyperpersonal" communication because of the notion of the private atmosphere that accompanies much of the IM interaction. Hu et al. found that many people use IM at home, late at night, by themselves, "where they are vulnerable and lonely" (p. 36). Perhaps as a result of this ability to create a sense of intimacy, Valkenburg and Peter (2007) found that IM tends to improve the quality of face-to-face relationships. Their results suggest that increased time spent together, both through IM and face-to-face, resulted in higher quality relationships and, in turn, resulted in a greater sense of well being. Clearly, Instant Messenger is a tool that adolescents use to manage relationships within their face-to-face communities. It tends to enhance relationships, providing an easy way for teens to connect with one another in ways that are fun, comfortable, and valued.

Relationships

As technology like IM changes the way adolescents communicate with one another, it is important to ask how those changes might impact how teens communicate with parents and other adults. The question is an especially important one for adults who seek to mentor and care for young people. There is no question that mentoring adults can play an important part in the life of an adolescent. As teenagers learn how to function independent of their parents, they still need the support, encouragement, and training only an adult can provide. Whether a church youth minister, a high school teacher, or any adult willing to spend time developing relationships with adolescents, adults can have a tremendous effect on how adolescents see themselves, how they are able to cope with everyday struggles, and how they conduct the tasks of relationship-building. This adult-adolescent relationship, however, becomes much more complex as young people gravitate toward communication technologies most adults neither understand nor embrace. As youth workers struggle to best meet the needs of the adolescents they work with, it is important to take into account the role of technology.

To better understand how technology can help meet the goals of youth workers, it is important to identify what those goals might be. Successful youth leaders have suggested a number of important goals of youth ministry, two of which are particularly relevant to this study. First is that of helping adolescents build their relationship skills. According to McDowell (2000), young people are often ill-equipped to develop and maintain committed, positive relationships. Cross-gender relationships are particularly challenging for many adolescents. "Our culture does not prepare young people for anything but romanticism. Therefore, one of your tasks as a youth leader is to teach young people how to love" (Campolo, 2000, p. 7). While helping young people determine how to effectively develop and nurture romantic relationships is certainly important to adolescents, other relationship skills such as the ability to resolve conflicts, forgive, self-disclose appropriately, and be committed in ongoing relationships are just as significant.

Role modeling positive ways to relate to one another is one of the most effective ways for youth workers to train young people how to be a good friend and how to be a valued part of a committed community. This type of role modeling is often accomplished when youth leaders share their lives with adolescents, being transparent in their struggles, disappointments, and coping strategies (Barna, 1995; McDowell, 2000). While role modeling and transparency is helpful, adolescents also need help addressing the real life issues they may be experiencing. As personal challenges arise for young people, it is important someone be there in "real-time" to help them sort out responses to specific situations and challenges, applying the same relationship skills they have seen modeled in their youth leader (Barna, 1995). This real-time help clearly allows developing adolescents to better understand what it takes to create and maintain healthy relationships.

A second important goal for youth workers is to show adolescents that they are cared for. Burns (2000) notes that "long-term positive influence on the lives of students comes from genuine connections with people" (p. 35). By being committed to the adolescents they work with, youth workers can help these young people develop the confidence and support that is needed to build healthy relationships. Developing real, caring relationships with adolescents, however, takes time, energy, and a willingness to be accessible. "Teens do not want to be managed as much as they need to feel cared for. Availability is one of the clues they examine to ascertain if they are simply being 'handled' or if they are being nurtured" (Barna, 1995, p. 119). When a youth worker demonstrates interpersonal commitment by consistently checking in on adolescents, verbalizing support and encouragement, and being available to talk and play with adolescents, that youth worker clearly communicates something very special to the adolescents he or she may work with.

Training and caring are two essential elements in any program geared toward helping teens make it through adolescence. These programs fill a unique space that, in some respects, allows parents to relegate certain training and support responsibilities to other caring adults. This transition becomes especially important as adolescents undertake the process of becoming independent, individuated adults. Because these youth workers are often seen by adolescents as "friends," they are able to communicate with adolescents in a way that is very different from the way adolescents communicate with their parents. On the other hand, these youth workers are still adults and are still bound by many of the *same* constraints as those placed on most parents. As a result, youth workers and adult mentors often walk a fine line between quasi-parent and almost-friend. The way this unique relationship is impacted by technology is of particular interest since many adolescents view their technology, especially IM, as defining a uniquely "teenage space" (Kendall, 2007). It is, therefore, important to examine how Instant Messenger is being used by youth workers in a way that respects the role of both adult and friend.

The following research questions (RQs) were proposed:

RQ #1: How are youth pastors currently using IM in their work with adolescents?

RQ #2: What do youth pastors perceive as the strengths and weakness of IM in their work with adolescents?

RQ #3: How do adolescent IM'ers perceive the use of IM by youth pastors?

Methods

Study 1

Participants   In the first study, an online survey was sent to youth pastors who served as part of the Baptist General Conference (BGC), a denominational group representing over 875 evangelical churches. A request for participation was distributed to 204 youth pastors through e-mail. Seventy-two online surveys were completed, resulting in a 35% response rate. Of youth pastors who participated in the survey, 87% were male and 13% were female. Only 3 participants were non-White. The mean age was 32 years with the average youth pastor having spent 9 years in ministry. While the average size of the respondents' youth group was 65 adolescents, the number ranged from a low of 8 adolescents to a high of over 160 adolescents.

Procedures   The initial step in the survey design included in-depth interviews with ten youth pastors who used IM in their youth ministry. The results of these interviews were analyzed by the research team made up of the primary researcher and two undergraduate assistants. A survey instrument was then designed making use of the issues identified by the youth pastors. A pilot survey was developed and administered with follow-up interviews conducted to assess the clarity of the protocol. Changes were made to address concerns about unclear questions and an overly complex response format. An online survey was then developed using multiple choice questions and five-point Likert-type statements to assess youth pastors' usage patterns of IM, purposes for using IM, and their attitudes toward using IM in ministry. Open-ended questions were also asked to assess the strengths and weaknesses of IM. The online survey was posted using Silhouette research software.

Once the surveys were completed, the responses to open-ended questions were analyzed by the research team. The data was "conceptualized and reduced," resulting in categories that seemed to best articulate common themes (Strauss & Corbin, 1998). The researcher and each assistant then used the resulting categories to go back through the data and organize and quantify the responses. Any discrepancies were discussed by the three coders.

Study 2

The second study included an online survey taken by 143 college-age students who identified themselves as having used IM in high school. Requests for participation were sent using campus e-mail lists of students attending a private Midwest university. Students were also asked to forward the survey link to their friends, resulting in a limited snowball sample. The student survey was part of a separate project and asked questions concerning student attitudes toward IM. A series of questions in the survey asked students about their high school experiences with IM'ing youth pastors. The first questions asked if they participated in a church youth group and how often their youth pastor used IM. The next question asked students if it was a good idea for youth pastors to use IM as part of their ministry. It was followed by an open-ended question asking them to explain their answer. The open-ended answers were analyzed in a method similar to study one.

Results

Youth Pastor Perspectives, Study 1

Uses of IM   Seventy percent of IM'ing youth pastors IM'ed between 1 and 5 adolescents on a regular basis. Fifty-four percent spent less than 1 hour per week on IM while 40% spent 1–3 hours per week. None of the respondents reported using IM more than 7 hours per week. When asked *when* youth pastors used IM, 42% reported chatting with adolescents in the evening. One youth pastor reported connecting with adolescents right before bed, "just chatting to see how their day went." Eighteen percent of youth pastors reported talking with adolescents during the after school hours, "especially those kids who were home by themselves," and 20% said they talked with adolescents during the day.

The most commonly reported use of IM for youth pastors tended to be "connecting and getting caught up with students (i.e., "how was your day today?" or "how did your date go?")." The second most common purpose was to "engage in small talk or just hang around." Only 33% said they often or primarily used IM for "light counseling" and very few respondents reported using IM primarily for "counseling about serious issues." Thirty-three percent of youth pastors reported that they talked with adolescents concerning issues of faith frequently or all the time while on IM.

Attitudes Concerning IM   Ninety-two percent, nearly all of the surveyed youth pastors, agreed or strongly agreed that IM helped them stay connected with adolescents. Most respondents felt that IM helped adolescents open up more, was a safe place for pastors to encourage adolescents, and helped them feel closer to those adolescents they IM'ed. Most disagreed with statements such as "I feel I compromise my personal boundaries," "IM takes too much time," and "IM promotes shallow relationships and is therefore not a good ministry tool." Overall, 61% of the youth pastors surveyed would recommend other youth pastors incorporate IM into their youth ministries (36% had no opinion).

Weaknesses of IM

When asked to identify weaknesses in IM as a ministry tool, youth pastors identified three major areas of concern including the lack of nonverbal cues, the potential for misuse, and the required time commitment (the number following each quote refers to the number of the participant).

Lack of Nonverbal Cues   Forty-two percent of respondents reported that many of the problems they experienced with IM had to do with the limited amount of nonverbal cues, often referring to problems with interpreting sarcasm or taking jokes the wrong way. Counseling also became difficult with IM because the lack of nonverbal cues resulted in an inability to gauge emotions over IM. "It's difficult to determine how depressed/upset/excited a student really is because all you see is words" (20). Along with a lack of nonverbal cues was the absence of a physical presence. "There is something about breathing the same air as the person you are interacting with that gets lost … it limits the ability of two people to really understand each other.…" (22). As a result, some respondents felt adolescents were not genuinely connecting. "Students use it as a means of bearing their souls and they do this so they don't have to actually deal with issues or talk to people.…" (13).

Potential for Misuse   A second weakness identified by 16% of the youth pastors had to do with the misuse of the technology. Many pointed to lying, gossiping, and flaming that occurred on IM. "I have had students try to tell me something, but it is just gossip and can lead to other problems" (14). One pastor described an experience where he or she was fooled when an adolescent was using someone else's screen name. Another described how a number of adolescents circulated inappropriate pictures of a young woman in the youth group. According to these respondents, since bad behavior is often a natural part of adolescence, IM becomes a high-tech showcase for inappropriate activities.

Extensive Time Requirements   A third area of weakness mentioned by 16% of respondents dealt with the issue of time. Many commented that IM could easily take up too much of their limited ministry time. "Often students will pop up and want to talk at times that I am very busy" (22), tending to interrupt other types of ministry work. Others mentioned that it was too hard to maintain a regular connection with a lot of adolescents and the task became overwhelming. Some youth pastors believed that teens were already on their computers too much and using IM simply "condoned" this type of unhealthy behavior.

There were other less mentioned weaknesses that help to highlight important areas of concern. A few youth pastors were concerned that IM only worked for a certain type of adolescent. For example, adolescents who felt uncomfortable in large group settings often felt more confident when communicating on IM. Other adolescents were naturally drawn to technological ways of communicating and often preferred IM over other channels of communication like phone calls. While IM could be very effective for these types or groups of adolescents, respondents felt it was important to balance it with other tools that may more effectively reach a broader range of adolescent.

Other youth workers suggested that sometimes parents became concerned with online conversations their child was having with an adult. In some instances, the IM context appeared too private for certain types of conversations. When parents did not feel comfortable with the technology to begin with, the idea of an older adult having unsupervised online conversations with their children seemed inappropriate. If the youth pastor had already established a trusting relationship with parents, however, these types of concerns seemed to be more manageable. Youth pastors also felt that when they talked with parents about the value of the technology and how they hoped to use it as part of their ministries, parents were much more positive about online conversations. Overall, establishing good communication with parents and providing parent training about the technology their children were using helped to overcome this apparent weakness with IM.

Strengths of IM

Participants also provided a number of positive reasons why those who work with young people should consider using IM. Some of the strengths of the tool included the ability to do counseling, the ability of the youth pastor to stay connected with adolescents, the willingness of adolescents to open up online, the ability of leaders to talk to adolescents concerning issues of faith and spirituality, and the function of IM as a "gateway" tool.

Connection   The clearest response youth pastors reported as the strength of IM was the ability to use it to stay connected to adolescents. Twenty-nine percent discussed how they were able to "be a part of the everyday life of the student and to connect even when we cannot meet face to face" (43). While this connection allowed the youth pastors to informally "hang out" with adolescents, it also allowed adolescents to see the youth pastor as "real." "It lets students know I'm human … that I do stuff that everyone else does" (13). Being online—even just having a screen name appear on adolescents' computer screens—also served as an accountability reminder, almost like having a youth pastor in the room (30). By becoming connected to their adolescents, youth leaders were able to model positive IM behavior for young IM'ers who were often faced with conversations that were "shockingly devoid of common courtesy" (27). At the same time, leaders were able to use their connections to build caring communities through IM. According to one youth pastor, "those who do use it have grown a special bond, which is a huge part of youth ministry's goal—these relationships can develop into a faith-based community" (27).

Another advantage to staying in touch is that youth pastors were able to stay connected over long distances, such as when adolescents were on vacation or gone away to college. Five percent of the respondents also noted that adolescents saw IM as "cool" and were very comfortable using it. One youth leader felt that many adolescents actually "communicate better online than in person" (49). And because they are comfortable using it, youth pastors found that IM was one of the few places where adolescents would actually take the initiative to make the connection. "It's instant and youth love it … and they think that I'm a 'kewl old guy' for talking to them online" (20).

Openness   A second, related theme dealt with the willingness of adolescents to open up through IM. Over 16% described situations by saying things like "for some reason IM isn't as intimidating to students as face-to-face conversations" (20) or "They will open up more fully when they don't have to look you in the eye" (50). In addition, some types of adolescents thrive on IM: "Our most shy students who really tend to avoid interactions except with close friends, will talk with me for an hour about life on IM" (9). This openness also included talking about issues of faith. Nineteen percent of the respondents mentioned adolescents' willingness to "ask questions about matters of faith". "By being loving and encouraging to these kids over IM, it's very easy to start spiritual conversations, or simply be a blessing" (27).

Counseling   Nineteen percent of respondents pointed to the opportunity to counsel adolescents as a strength of IM. While it should be noted that a number of youth leaders strongly warned *against* counseling because of the lack of nonverbal cues, a reduced sense of interpersonal presence, and decreased nonverbal immediacy, many gave accounts of times when IM gave them access to adolescents who needed their help. For instance, three respondents said that they had counseled young people who were suicidal and, because they happened to be online late at night, were able to intervene. Each of these individuals also reported alerting the parents and immediately setting up a time and place to meet the adolescent face-to-face. It was in those face-to-face meetings that the youth pastors reported being able to deal with significant issues in a way that helped bring understanding and healing to both parents and adolescents.

Aside from crisis counseling, however, 12% of respondents described times they simply helped adolescents get through difficult issues. An issue common to adolescents was that of how to deal with parents. By being available to "listen," youth pastors were able to reframe conflicts, helping adolescents see things from multiple perspectives and providing ideas of how to best work through conflicts in their family relationships. By being available through the technology, youth pastors were able to provide an accessible bridge between parent and child. Parental conflicts were only some of the issues mentioned by youth pastors. Whether it was talking "with a girl about her dad going to Iraq" (8), working through how a girl could make-up with her friend, or counseling a girl who didn't want to go all the way with her boyfriend, IM allowed youth pastors to be available to adolescents at the point in time those adolescents were hurting and looking for someone to talk with.

One area of disagreement among respondents involved concern with how safe it was to counsel someone of the opposite sex. Some male youth pastors said that while they would never meet with a young woman alone in a face-to-face context, "IM alleviates these concerns ... and I can save my IM conversations on my hard drive to ensure there is no concern about compromise/integrity in the relationship" (20). On the other hand, some warned about the dangers inherent in developing close relationships with someone of the opposite sex over the Internet.

Gateway Opportunities   A final strength of IM noted by youth pastors was its ability to act as a "gateway" tool. Seventeen percent of the respondents described how adolescents used IM to link non-church attending friends with their youth pastor. According to one youth pastor, "I find it a safe way for students to introduce me to their friends" (18). IM also acted as a gateway tool in that it often led to further, face-to-face conversations. One youth pastor reported IM "allows me to have a real and personal relationship with them when I see them in person" (38). While some IM conversations simply served to "grease the wheels" for face-to-face conversations, other youth pastors reported intentionally beginning deep or potentially awkward conversations online, then meeting face-to-face with students to finish the conversation.

Technical Advantages   Finally, 5% of the youth pastors saw the ability to record or archive the conversation as an advantage of the technology. One even said that because an adolescent reported living in an abusive family relationship, he was forced to report the information to the authorities. It was helpful to have a transcript of the conversation as documentation. Overall, having recorded conversations seemed to help both adolescents and youth pastors feel accountable in maintaining a positive and healthy online relationship.

Advice for Youth Workers

The final question addressed by survey respondents was to give advice for youth leaders contemplating using IM in their work with young people. Some youth pastors provided warnings. Some mentioned the potentially public nature of IM. For instance, "one has to be very careful using a tool with your name on it because students can lie and forward what you thought were private comments to a large group of students" (14). In a related comment, a youth pastor cautioned youth pastors to "assume that anything you type will be read by anyone and everyone" (24). Another individual cautioned that youth pastors make sure they are being true to their character and personality, making "sure that the person you are online is consistent with who you are offline" (22). Others advised leaders to keep control of the time online. "Budget/schedule a limited amount of minutes per day for e-mail/IM" (49). A number of individuals also talked about how important it was to "go to the student" on their level. According to one youth pastor, "though IM is not ideal and certainly not something we grew up with, it is part of the youth culture today. We can fight it and put it down, which ultimately will not change their use of it. Or we can utilize this new tool and equip our youth with the ethical and moral principles that will make their IM safe as well as allow us to connect with youth on their level not ours" (42). Probably the clearest line of advice reported by youth pastors was to view IM as a tool. By understanding its strengths and weaknesses, youth leaders can use the technology to meet the needs of adolescents in ways that make sense for each individual.

Adolescent Perspectives, Study 2

While youth pastors were very positive about the impact of using IM in their work with adolescents, adolescents were not so sure. Forty-two percent (*n* = 63) of those responding (*n* = 149) said it was a "bad idea" for youth pastors to use IM. A follow-up question found that adolescents were concerned about the depth of communication, boundary issues and miscommunication that occurred as a result of IM. For instance, a number of adolescents felt that IM is a "silly" or "cheap form of communication." According to one adolescent

"I held my youth pastor in really high regard and the conversations we had almost always had meaning. I think IM would have brought our conversations down to a much more surface level."

A second factor identified by adolescents was the inevitable miscommunication that occurred online. A problem between friends was one thing, but when it happened with a youth pastor, it could have a much wider impact.

Finally, the most common adolescent concern had to do with boundaries. Many adolescents felt that it just didn't seem right to have an adult in an IM environment. One adolescent likened it to "a youth sponsor who was frequently sitting in the student section during basketball games—it was uncomfortable. They don't belong there". A number of adolescents used the term "weird" with one stating it was "awkward if an adult hops on and tries to be 16 again. They can use a phone." Related concerns were also raised about the potential ethical problems that may arise when intimate conversations are had in such a private setting. A number of adolescents encouraged youth pastors to keep relationships more open.

While adolescents shared concerns with IM use by youth pastors, closer examination demonstrated that 91% had never IM'd their youth pastor, and those who did tended to be more positive about the potential of IM in youth ministry. An independent samples t-test was run to determine if there was a statistical difference between those who had youth pastors who IM'd and those who did not in regards to how good of an idea they thought it was for youth pastors to IM. The difference was significant (t (136) = -2.80, p = .006). It would appear, therefore, that adolescents are apprehensive about youth pastors hopping online but those who have actually experienced it found the interactions to be less "weird" than they had originally thought. In fact, a number of adolescents were quite positive at how IM conversations with their youth pastors had been encouraging, less threatening and "a great way to open up communication."

In summary, youth pastors saw IM as an important tool in their work with adolescents while adolescents were less enthusiastic. Concerns involving miscommunication, misuse of the technology, and a trivializing of the relationship were highlighted. At the same time, however, both youth pastors and adolescents saw the potential of IM as being significant. This study demonstrated that IM can provide youth pastors a way to find adolescents and talk with them at a place where they are comfortable and at ease. It can provide a safe environment for adolescents to share concerns and ask questions. It can also provide a place for youth pastors to build a friendship foundation that can be built on in face-to-face interactions. As youth workers begin using new ways of connecting with adolescents, however, this study also highlights the need for caution. IM can be a powerful tool. Because it is such an important part of adolescents' social identity and because it can become a place where adolescents communicate very personal aspects of themselves, youth workers need to be sensitive to crossing social and ethical boundaries.

General Discussion

According to experts who work with today's youth, adolescents have a desire to feel connected. They not only need someone to show them that they genuinely care, but adolescents also need someone to role model and train them in how they can create and value healthy relationships (e.g., Barna, 1995; Burns, 2000; McDowell, 2000). This requires accessibility, availability, and relationship-building on the part of the youth pastor.

One of the primary findings of this study demonstrated that IM helps youth pastors be available and accessible. While the tool can clearly become overwhelming, this accessibility allows adolescents to come to youth pastors when the needs arise, not wait to talk with them when church is in session. Because IM provides a comfortable environment for adolescents, they often take the initiative to seek out the youth pastor when they need advice or counsel. According to the youth pastor respondents, IM also allows the youth pastor to be "real" with students, sharing in jokes and everyday small talk, all the while modeling positive relationship behavior. This "hanging out" characteristic of IM helps adolescents build trust with the youth leader, which is an essential step for adolescents desiring to build and develop meaningful relationships (Barna, 1995). These data also support the "gateway" characteristic of IM, whereby young people get to know the youth leader and, in turn, have an increased desire to meet face-to-face (Hu et al., 2004), becoming an important tool for youth pastors interested in building deeper relationships.

A second key finding of this study relates to the willingness of adolescents to be open on IM, supporting the findings of Hu et al. (2004) who demonstrated that IM enhances self-disclosure. This characteristic of IM can also be an important tool for youth pastors as they to talk with adolescents about deeper issues such as faith and spirituality.

Finally, while the idea of community building was only touched on in this study, it certainly remains an important goal for youth pastors as they attempt to empower their adolescents to become committed to one another as part of a faith-based community. The finding that IM is used to connect adolescents outside of the group with the youth pastor is consistent with Wellman et al. (2003), who demonstrated that online networks and communities have significant overlap and permeable boundaries, allowing individuals to move from one community to the next, searching for the one that feels most comfortable. It is possible that, by creating an atmosphere where adolescents and youth pastors can keep each other accountable in easy and comfortable ways, communities can be built in a new and positive fashion using tools such as IM.

IM is a tool like any other communication tool that has its strengths and weaknesses. It would seem that mentoring adults undertake a balancing act as they integrate this type of technology into their work with adolescents. While the lack of nonverbal cues can allow adolescents freedom to self-disclose, it can also lead to misunderstanding and unhealthy boundaries. While the permanent nature of the written text can help protect youth pastors from false accusation, it can also serve as a public record of conversations assumed to be private. While the IM environment is an accessible place where youth pastors can go to meet their adolescents "where they are at," it is also a distinctly teenage hangout that may be unsuitable for adult intrusion (Kendall, 2007). Overall, Instant Messenger seems to provide youth workers with a unique tool whereby they can fulfill the role that lies somewhere between parent and friend.

Limitations and Future Study

It should be kept in mind that there are certain limitations inherent in this study. First and most obviously, the population was restricted to one particular denomination based in the United States. The sample did not do a good job of incorporating the perspectives of women or youth workers from non-White backgrounds. Further study should include an expanded population and greater sample size. The sample was also problematic in that it was clearly a convenience sample. Those who did not use IM, did not tend to take the survey. Additionally, because it was an online survey, those who were not comfortable in an online environment probably did not respond to the survey. However, this sample did provide insight from the individuals who were using IM in their youth ministries, thus providing the necessary information from which future research can be built.

One interesting aspect of these studies had to do with the disconnect that seemed to exist between how youth pastors see their IM use in ministry and how adolescents view youth pastors using IM. Future studies should further examine the hesitations felt by adolescents; especially those who have IM'd their youth pastor. Future studies could also examine how IM is used in the parent-child relationship. Just as youth workers find IM provides accessibility and a safe place for adolescents to self-disclose, it would be interesting to see if the same characteristics apply to parent-child IM conversations. Finally, because IM is slowly being replaced with the text-messaging function of cell phones, it would be important to examine how this mobile technology might change some of the characteristics of text-based adolescent-adult communication.

In summary, it is important for adolescents to have caring adults as part of their lives. As technology changes the lives of adolescents, it is also important that these significant adult-adolescent relationships change in an intentional and wise manner. After all, it could be a very good thing if the sweet after school "blingg" of an adolescent's computer was a caring adult just signing in to say "hi."

References

Alvestrand, H. (2002). Instant messenger and presence on the internet. *Internet Society* (ISOC). Retrieved October 9, 2007, from http://www.isoc.org/briefings/009/
Barna, G. (1995). *Generation next*. Ventura, CA: Regal Books.
Berger, C., & Calabrese, R. (1975). Some explorations in initial interaction and beyond:

Toward a developmental theory of interpersonal communication. *Human Communication Research, 1*(2), 99–112.

Burns, J. (2000). Relational youth ministry. In S. McDowell & R. Willey (Eds.), *Josh McDowell's youth ministry handbook: Making the connection* (pp. 35–38). Nashville, TN: Word Publishing.

Campolo, T. (2000). Having a heart for the disconnected world: Loving like Jesus. In S. McDowell & R. Willey (Eds.), *Josh McDowell's youth ministry handbook: Making the connection* (pp. 7–10). Nashville, TN: Word Publishing.

Daft, R. L., Lengel, R. H., & Trevino, L. K. (1987). Message equivocality, media selection, and manager performance: Implications for information systems. *MIS Quarterly, 11*(3), 354–366.

Hian, L., Chuan, S., Trevor, T., & Detenber, B. (2004, April). Getting to know you: Exploring the development of relational intimacy in computer-mediated communication. *Journal of Computer Mediated Communication, 9*(3). Retrieved October 9, 2007, from http://jcmc.indiana.edu/vol9/issue3/detenber.html

Hu, Y., Wood, J., Smith, V., & Westbrook, N. (2004, November) Friendships through IM: Examining the relationship between instant messaging and intimacy. *Journal of Computer Mediated Communication, 10*(1). Retrieved October 9, 2007, from http://jcmc.indiana.edu/vol10/issue1/hu.html

Joinson, A. (2004). Self-esteem, interpersonal risk, and preference for e-mail to face-to-face communication. *Cyberpsychology & Behavior, 7*(4), 472–478.

Kendall, P. (2007). *Rewired: Youth ministry in an age of IM and Myspace.* Valley Forge, PA: Judson Press.

Lenhart, A., Madden, M., & Hitlin, P. (2005). Teens and technology: Youth are leading the transition to a fully wired and mobile nation. *Pew Internet & American Life Project.* Retrieved October 9, 2007, from http://www.pewinternet.org/PPF/r/162/report_display.asp

McDowell, J. (2000). The disconnected generation. In S. McDowell & R. Willey (Eds.), *Josh McDowell's youth ministry handbook: Making the connection* (pp. xi–xv). Nashville, TN: Word Publishing.

O'Leary, S., & Brasher, B. (1996). The unknown god of the internet. In C. Ess (Ed.), *Philosophical perspectives on computer-mediated communication* (pp. 233–270). Albany: State University of New York Press.

Strauss, A., & Corbin, J. (1998). *Basics of qualitative research: Techniques and procedures for developing grounded theory* (2nd ed.). Thousand Oaks, CA: Sage.

Turkle, S. (1997). *Life on the screen: Identity in the age of the internet.* New York: Touchstone.

Valkenburg, P. M., & Peter, J. (2007). Online communication and adolescent well-being: Testing the stimulation versus the displacement hypothesis. *Journal of Computer-Mediated Communication, 12*(4), article 2. Retrieved October 9, 2007, from http://jcmc.indiana.edu/vol12/issue4/valkenburg.html

Walther, J. B. (1992). Interpersonal effects in computer-mediated interaction: A relational perspective. *Communication Research, 19*(1), 52–90.

Walther, J. B. (1996). Computer-mediated communication: Impersonal, interpersonal, and hyperpersonal interaction. *Communication Research, 23*(1), 3–43.

Wellman, B., Quan-Hasse, A., Boase, J., Wenhong, C., Hampton, K., Isla de Diaz, I., et al. (2003, April). The social affordances of the internet for networked individualism. *Journal of Computer Mediated Communication, 8*(3). Retrieved October 9, 2007, from http://jcmc.indiana.edu/vol8/issue3/wellman.html

15 Response to Family Crisis

Mood Disorders, Supportive Listening, and the Telephone Helpline Volunteer— Analysis and Applications

Barbara A. Penington and Raymond D. Baus

Few problems are more challenging to a family's sense of well-being and stability than those that deal with mental health issues. Unfortunately, "because mental health problems are often invisible, their pervasiveness is not well appreciated, and because they are associated with a stigma, they often go untreated" (Segrin & Flora, 2005, p. 301). Depression, for example, is "amazingly underdiagnosed" (O'Connor, 1997, p. 19) and often not taken seriously. Untreated depression costs the United States between $30 and 44 billion per year in medical expenses, work absenteeism, and lost productivity (Hurst, 2005). Depression is second only to cancer in terms of economic impact, and the number of deaths from suicide annually equals the number of deaths each year from AIDS (O'Connor, 1997). Although depression and related mental illnesses (e.g., adjustment disorder, bipolar disorder, and dysthymic disorder) touch many of today's families, family members often feel ill-equipped to handle the stressful situations that arise and seek advice and support from sources external to the family.

Although several approaches to treating depression have yielded promising results (Zarit & Zarit, 2007), a *better* treatment for those suffering depression is one of the major unmet health care priorities in the United States (Golant & Golant, 1996). While there is much that remains to be understood, the one common theme in most literatures that focus on the mentally ill is the importance of active listening. Whether active listening occurs between family members or connects family members with outside support systems, it is a valuable tool that unfortunately, many have not learned how to use effectively. Those individuals who can demonstrate supportive listening skills when called upon to assist families experiencing stress are a valuable resource.

The purpose of this chapter is to better understand how active listening impacts families under stress due to mental health issues. The chapter will provide (a) an examination of the active listening skills most helpful in these stressful family situations, (b) a critique of a volunteer's listening behavior as evidenced by interaction on a telephone helpline, (c) suggestions on the use of active listening for support individuals/agencies and family members, and (d) recommendations for future study.

Active Listening Skills

Learning to Listen Effectively

Many individuals lack the listening skills to help them interact more effectively with family members who have some degree of mental illness. Wolvin and Coakley (1996), for example, assert that schools today do a poor job of providing students with even the basics of listening. The post-secondary communication classroom is one place where persons can learn active listening skills. Yet, although basic communication course texts (Devito, 2005; Gamble & Gamble, 2005; Seiler & Beall, 2005) and interpersonal communication texts (Beebe, Beebe, & Redmond, 2005; Canary, Cody, & Manusov, 2003) consistently offer sections on listening effectively, these texts are required to cover a large amount of introductory material. Thus, most texts are unable to go into depth on supportive listening, focusing instead on general strategies to improve listening in relational, classroom, and work contexts.

Where, then, does one learn the skills needed to listen effectively to troubled individuals within or outside of one's family? Several scholars studying listening, a sub discipline of communication, provide helpful suggestions. Wolvin and Coakley (1996), for example, identify five skills of merit which may be appropriate for use with persons experiencing symptoms of mental illness. These skills will be presented and supported with information from other listening texts and from literature outside the communication discipline.

Wolvin and Coakley's Therapeutic Listening Skills

The first therapeutic listening skill identified by Wolvin and Coakley (1996) is focusing attention on the troubled sender, where the listener attempts to minimize both external and internal distractions. Psychologists, such as Amador (2000), support the idea that one's attention must be on the person with the mental illness so that the listener can better understand his or her "beliefs about the self and the illness" (p. 66). Although Amador is speaking more specifically about physician interactions with patients, his comments are useful to anyone attempting to support a student, friend or loved one.

Second, good therapeutic listeners demonstrate effective nonverbal attending behaviors. Wolvin and Coakley note that a therapeutic listener is comfortable with silence which allows the troubled sender more opportunity to verbalize his or her thoughts and feelings and feel as if they are being heard. Golant and Golant (1996) echo this notion and advocate that the supportive listener practice the "wisdom of silence" and not react automatically to what the depressed individual is saying no matter how frustrating or strange. Amador (2000) reminds us that one can accept what the mentally ill individual is saying without necessarily agreeing with the person. Arnold (1997) recognizes that the supportive listener needs to help reduce the troubled sender's anxiety and tension by keeping a calm, comforting demeanor.

The third skill identified for therapeutic listeners is the need to develop a supportive rather than defensive atmosphere (Wolvin & Coakley, 1996). The troubled sender needs to feel safe and comfortable sharing personal and potentially stigmatizing information. If the therapeutic listener can provide descriptive rather than evaluative feedback, this is helpful. Additionally, if one can refrain from telling the person what to do, but instead guide them through the problem solving process, this can add to the supportive environment. Lynn Mucha, a counselor on a midwestern university campus, found that the supportive listener must be nonjudgmental; she suggests, "Don't try to fix the problem for them" (personal communication, November 3, 2005). In keeping with developing a supportive atmosphere, Arnold (1997) recommends focusing on the present and future rather than on behaviors from the past that might be painful for the depressed sender.

Wolvin and Coakley (1996) identify empathy as the fourth skill needed for therapeutic listeners. The authors suggest that empathy involves identifying with the troubled sender's problem and trying to feel and think "with" them. Brownell (2005) discusses empathy as having cognitive, perceptive and behavioral definitions. Cognitive empathy, for example, is taking the role of the troubled sender and trying to view life from their perspective. Perceptive empathy involves sensitivity to indirect nonverbal behavior as well as the situation, so that the listener may interpret the sender's feelings. Finally, behavioral empathy is the listener's ability to convey that they are actively listening and care about the sender.

Brownell (2005) makes some important observations that can be applied in the mental health context. First, she suggests that one's personality, maturity level, attitude and motivation play a key role in one's ability to be a supportive listener. Not everyone can be an effective telephone helpline volunteer. Brownell also asserts that true empathy is difficult to "force or fake" (p. 187). The message here, especially when interacting with someone exhibiting signs of mental illness, is that one must know him or herself well. When you feel that you cannot interact with a troubled son, daughter, or spouse because you are too emotional about a topic or haven't had enough sleep making it problematic to focus your attention, it is probably not wise to put yourself in a supportive listening situation. Parents who consistently lose their tempers with family members or demonstrate behaviors indicating that they just don't care (when attempting to listen) may do more harm than good. In these cases, a person may want to seek help from other family members or outside agencies.

Brownell (2005) also reminds us that the relational nature of communication generally calls for some level of reciprocity. Because of that, the listener's ability to empathize with someone experiencing mental health symptoms is sometimes compromised. "If the other person is deliberately deceptive, silent, or judgmental you may find it very difficult to understand their perspective" (p. 188). Communication texts probably do not stress enough that developing empathy for another's situation requires the cooperation of both sender and receiver. Parents or spouses may become frustrated or angry in situations where reciprocal empathy from the depressed sender is not forthcoming.

Finally, Wolvin and Coakley (1996) highlight the need to respond appropriately when listening to the troubled sender. One type of appropriate response includes asking questions. Golant and Golant (1996) advise listeners to ask questions in a nonthreatening manner. They caution against asking questions in anger and advise listeners to use questions that are open-ended. If the supportive listener does not get an answer to their question, they are encouraged to ask in a different, but not too aggressive, way.

Another appropriate response for a supportive listener is paraphrasing the sender's words to signify understanding. Golant and Golant (1996) contend that showing care and concern is accomplished through "mirroring" which is another term for paraphrasing. The mirroring technique, however, focuses primarily on paraphrasing for emotion rather than content. For example, the authors suggest that if a teenager says, "I feel exhausted," a mirroring response would be, "I know it must be tough." Responding with advice like "Maybe you should take a nap" is not recommended because the depressed teenager wants to be heard, not told what to do.

Despite the negative stereotypes associated with competencies of the mentally ill, our assumption is that persons with mental illness can also learn to use active listening skills. In *The Bipolar Disorder Survival Guide*, Miklowitz (2002) offers the following advice to persons with bipolar disorder:

> If your parents, spouse or kids are responding to you negatively or with criticism, consider helping them modulate their anger by listening and expressing an understanding of their position, even if you do not agree with it. This is a technique called active listening, and attempts to use it will almost certainly change the outcome of what would otherwise be unproductive interchanges. (p. 264)

Miklowitz (2002) identifies maintaining eye contact, offering nonverbal acknowledgments, perception checking what was heard, and asking clarification questions about the other's point of view as important components of active listening. Professionals who work with family members who have mood disorders or other forms of mental illness should probably work with clients to help them develop stronger listening and responding skills. These children, parents, or spouses should then be encouraged to practice these skills within their families. Miklowitz observes that while active listening looks easy on its surface, it can be difficult to apply and requires regular practice. Furthermore, he advises the reader that familiarizing oneself with active listening when one is well makes the skill easier to apply when one is ill.

Clearly, when family members use therapeutic listening skills, chances are greater that the challenges engendered by mood disorders may be more effectively managed. Yet, support from outside the family rests equally on the quality of listening as well. The next section of this chapter examines the teaching and practice of active listening in a telephone helpline setting.

Active Listening in Applied Settings: Training Volunteer Call Takers to Respond to Parents' Stress

Telephone helplines play a crucial role in community outreach and offer an applied context for studying parent/child interactions with outside agencies. These helplines have been used to assess and manage children and adolescents who present with suicidal behavior and/or other manifestations of mental illness (American Academy of Child & Adolescent Psychiatry, 2001). As such, telephone helplines represent a form of telemedicine, which refers to a "process of communicating across distances for health-related purposes" (du Pre, 2005, p. 76). While parents do not necessarily feel that telephone helplines are the most appropriate medium for acquiring information about their children's mental health (Akister & Johnson, 2002), Simon (2004) notes a movement that advocates telephone outreach in the treatment of depression. In fact, calls to telephone hotlines by persons with some form of mental illness are an increasing phenomenon (Gilliard, Keady, Evers, & Milton, 1998).

Based in part on knowledge of a literature base that notes potential difficulties in telephone helpline interactions (e.g., Tracy, 2002; Tracy & Tracy, 1998), an effort was made to examine these interactions from an insider's perspective. It was believed that participant observation of interactions outside of the 911 context would afford a basis for critique of the active listening model considered thus far. Therefore, a decision was made by the second author to serve as a volunteer call-taker for the Family Management Association's (a pseudonym) parent stress line.

The Family Management Association (FMA) is a nonprofit alliance among four agencies that advances the welfare of children and families in a mid-American urban environment of approximately 200,000 persons. According to its Annual Report, the FMA has 22 paid staff and 150 volunteers. In 2004, the FMA answered approximately 10,500 calls for help, information and/or referral. Among the services provided by the FMA is an around the clock crisis helpline. Approximately 7,000 hours of volunteer time are used to staff this helpline. Volunteer call-takers include 34 females and 4 males, with age ranging from 22 to 60. Volunteers handle approximately 60% of the calls to the helpline, the vast majority of which are made by females.

Becoming part of the stress line staff required initial screening interviews first with a social work professor affiliated with the FMA, and then with the FMA's coordinator of the parent stress line. These representatives appeared to focus outwardly on the participant's motivations for volunteering, and with whether the participant had any academic or work experience related to helping behavior. Following disclosure about his motivations and profession, the second author was invited to attend training sessions. Information in the following section comes from the training manual, training sessions, and second author's personal experience as a volunteer call-taker for the FMA.

FMA Training Manual: "Content" and "Process" Emphases

According to its training manual, the mission of the FMA includes strengthening families, preventing child abuse and neglect, and promoting healing of persons affected by abuse. The manual indicates that 77% of child abuse perpetrators were parents. Recent data show that over 75% of child abuse fatalities happen to children under the age of three (National Clearinghouse on Child Abuse and Neglect, 2004).

The FMA training manual emphasizes abuse *prevention*, asserting that the solution of removing a child from parents' custody is "grossly unfair" when the crisis could have been dealt with earlier through accessible counseling services. Signs of child abuse, like bruises, skin abrasions, poor hygiene, developmental delays and delays in medical care are noted. Call-takers are urged to "remember with compassion" that parents who abuse tend to have been abused, have low esteem, little emotional support and little understanding of child development. This highlights FMA's philosophy that every person has worth, and that the cycle of abuse can be broken.

A second emphasis concerns call-takers' active listening orientation to helpline callers. The helpline's training manual specifies that having someone to listen in a nonjudgmental and understanding way can be crucial in helping parents deal with their children. An active listening emphasis is reflected in basic helpline guidelines like "be nonjudgmental," "be empathetic," "paraphrase and clarify," and "avoid giving personal advice." The manual states that caring attitudes don't by default lead to great listening. Call-takers are urged to practice "no response listening" (i.e., silence), "nudges" (or minimal response cues), reflecting feelings, and restatement of content. These suggestions bear some correspondence to descriptions of therapeutic listening (Wolvin & Coakley, 1996), and to guidelines for being a supportive listener (Burleson, 1994).

A third emphasis in FMA's training manual involves a view of the call-taker as a precious resource. Given the emphasis on burnout in the helping professions (e.g., Maslach, 1982; Miller, Stiff & Ellis, 1988), this orientation is instrumental to preservation of the FMA. The manual specifies that one responsibility of volunteer call-takers is to be sensitive to one's own emotional needs. Call-takers are urged to call the helpline coordinator to "debrief" on distressing calls. Furthermore, the manual notes the importance of developing a support system with other volunteers in order to provide an outlet for sharing feelings. In exchange for the volunteer's time, the FMA acknowledges responsibilities that it has to the volunteer. One such responsibility involves honoring the time that volunteers donate. This is, in part, accomplished through provision of letters of recommendation for employment and/or education. By supporting the volunteer, a nod is given to reciprocity, which is highlighted in the social support literature (e.g., Albrecht & Adelman, 1987; Vaux, 1985).

Helpline staffers receive 16 hours of training before answering their first live call. Call-takers are trained to recognize, among other things, that listening is therapeutic. This provides a reflection of the "larger discourses" (Tracy, 2005) that attend wellness environments in general, and the FMA in particular. Training session activities are consistent with the focus on therapeutic listening. For example, role-play asks the trainee to imagine that:

> … you are a mom of a 4-year old daughter who you are raising alone. You are yelling at her all of the time, have slapped her several times and you are afraid it's going to get worse. You need to get away. You're thinking of leaving your child at a day care center and leaving town. You think you can get the money together to do this. At the same time, you love your daughter very much. But maybe she'd be better off if you weren't taking care of her.

Trainees pair off and role-play this situation. This activity provides them with insight about the feelings that accompany such a predicament. With the guidance of trained staff, they are instructed in effective ways of responding to such calls.

One assumption in the training is that "no response" listening can be an effective strategy for call-takers to implement. In this exercise, call-takers were instructed not to say anything (with the exception perhaps, of an intermittent backchannel cue). It was believed that nonresponses essentially "forced" callers to disclose about their problem to the point of "exhaustion." There are merits to such an approach. Tracy (2002) warns about the dangers accompanying 911 call-takers' overuse of epistemic (i.e., who, what, where, etc.) and "expressive" questions (i.e., implying the questioner's negative attitude toward the speaker). Furthermore, Tracy reported that call-takers tended to ask too many questions which worked to delay the emergency response.

Another training assumption is that call-takers should recognize they are dealing with serious situations. This was conveyed through trainees' exposure to a disturbing video called *A Time To Speak*. In this video, a phone call to a 911 helpline was replayed. The caller's voice suggests that of a child around the age of 5 years. The child indicates that her mom's old boyfriend has broken into the house and is hurting her mother. Noise is heard in the background while the call-taker tries to get information and keep the child on the line. The phone call ends with the child saying that her mother is dead. Tracy and Tracy (1998) reported that such calls involved a mixture of complex emotions, not the least of which includes call-takers' feelings of powerlessness.

The importance of taking calls seriously is also reflected in role-plays involving suicide:

> You are a 29 year old woman. You have four children (ages 1, 3, 4, and 5). Your husband walked out on you about three months ago, and you have not heard from him since. You are broke and cannot find a decent job. You have no help with your children who are very upset because their daddy is gone. You have decided that the only way out of this mess is to kill yourself, but you need someone to take your kids.

Trainees are taught to assess the level of emotional distress reflected in the caller's suicidal ideations, and to distinguish between callers having high, moderate and low probabilities of acting on their thoughts. High emotional distress might be indicated by the caller's previous suicide attempts, no attempt to control suicidal thoughts or offer reasons for living, and reporting a plan to act on their thoughts within the next 48 hours. When probability is judged to be high, call-takers are urged to try to get the caller's name, address, phone number and location so that help can be sent as soon as possible. During such emergencies, it is up to the call-taker to make a quick assessment regarding which of the manual's "top referral sources" (e.g., National Alliance for the Mentally Ill; Domestic Abuse Intervention Services; Parents, Families and Friends of Lesbians and Gays) is in the best position to help.

Tracy (2002) suggests that attention be drawn to the training received by call-takers, especially in terms of call-takers' explanations for mismanaged interactions. In the following section, a narrative is provided of a phone call involving a parent, her child, and the volunteer call-taker. The conversation was selected for description and analysis because it seemed to fit under the category of "mismanagement," and because its features represented a memorable contrast from approximately fifty other calls that the call-taker handled during six months as a helpline volunteer. The narrative is based on the call-taker's own participation in the call, his call log and subsequent reflections on the conversation, and discussions about it with the training coordinator.

The mother who initiated the call can be classified as a "repeat caller." In fact, there were times when she called every volunteer taking a shift in a given day. While it was eventually learned that the mother was mentally ill, the situation was initially configured by the call-taker as a caregiving mom attempting to deal with the demands posed by her mentally disturbed daughter.

In applying communication texts' prescriptions for dealing with troubled senders, we plan to show first, how this call was mishandled. Then, by turning the circumstances of this listening situation on communication texts' listening prescriptions, we intend to show the limitations of such prescriptions.

A Report of the Mishandled Conversation

My first interaction with the caller was framed around her description of attempts to keep her daughter from physically attacking the daughter's younger sibling. The mother noted that her daughter was prone to violence—demonstrated by the child's "flipping" a glass coffee table at one mental health center—and that police had come to the family's home more than once to quell such chaos. Credence for the description of the daughter as "out of control" came from overhearing the daughter's behavior during the call. I could hear her screaming, calling her mother stupid, and telling her to shut up. I had initially conceived of "child abuse" being perpetrated by adults against their children, so I was quite taken aback when I sensed the mother restraining herself from retaliating against her child's aggression. To date, this was my closest encounter with family violence, and it gave me a different understanding of "how abuse happens" than ever before.

Subsequent calls with the mother frequently involved my not saying much, but rather, "bearing witness" as the mother tried to get her daughter to take prescribed medication, keep her from crying, hitting her mother or her sibling, or wreaking some other form of havoc (e.g., kicking a hole in one of the walls). Variation in this pattern was introduced during one call where the daughter was inconsolable (apparently due to the death of her pet cockatiel). Without warning, the mother handed the phone to her daughter.

I took the position of attempting to stop the child's tears. Remembering that she had participated in her school's band concert the previous week, I told her that her mom was proud of how well she played. The child seemed surprised that I knew this about her, and, in fact, her tears abated. Sensing that I had made progress, I continued talking. I mentioned how things would be better when the weather warmed up, because the children would have a chance to play outside and "the birds would be singing." To this, the child responded, "Not my bird. My bird's dead." Her crying resumed, vigorous as ever.

Critique of the Mishandled Conversation

A review of the reference to "birds singing" may prompt the reader to recall that time when you knew immediately after saying it, that you said the one thing you should not have said. As communication texts tell us, a basic axiom is that communication is irreversible.

Even on its surface, there are clues regarding why the call was mishandled. First, the call log acknowledges the call-taker's stereotypes about how abuse happens. Apparently, he was unaware of, or had forgotten about, the reciprocal and relational nature of violence (Cupach & Canary, 1997). In addition, the call log indicates deviation from the pattern of previous conversations. The call-taker suggests that he was taken off guard when the mother handed the telephone to her daughter. In fact, three person interactions were never discussed during the FMA's training sessions. One can imagine how such a situation becomes rather complex when the notion of "double-faced emotion" comes into play. Tracy and Tracy (1998) explained how emergency call takers were confronted with having to manage their own emotions as well as those of the caller. When three persons' emotions come into play, coping skills may be taxed beyond their capacity.

A description of this call as having been "mishandled" by the call-taker is justified in light of Wolvin and Coakley's (1996) guidelines for active listening. If the call-taker had been comfortable with silence he would not have continued speaking after the child's tears had subsided. At that point, "no response listening" would have been preferable. Furthermore, the call taker might have been instructed that one does not demonstrate empathy by attempting to structure how a person should feel, or when things will be better.

Inspection of several criteria posed by Bippus (2001) for evaluating the skill-fulness of comforting communication provides further insight about the call-taker's response.

First, listeners should demonstrate an "other orientation." This is accomplished through demonstrations of involvement, caring, and acceptance. In fact, the call-taker does demonstrate involvement because he remembers something about the child's life that her mother told him in a previous conversation. He shows caring about the child's feelings, and wants the child to know that her mother is proud of her musical accomplishments. However, the call-taker does not demonstrate acceptance of the child's emotions. Rather, he is unnerved by her screams of distress.

Second, Bippus (2001) points out that listeners might relate to the troubled sender through comforting disclosures or by diverting focus from the problem. While the call-taker attempted to divert focus from the child's deceased pet, the culmination of the conversation indicates that he was not successful. Instead, the "relating" objective might have been accomplished through disclosures about the call-taker's own loss of loved pets and the child's subsequent response to such disclosures.

Third, Bippus notes that comforting listeners refrain from general negativity. While the call-taker attempted to generate a positive climate by noting the girl's accomplishments, he inadvertently provided a prompt for the child to recall the sad event in her life. In fact, the call-taker's response represents a good example of the aphorism that "less is more." Active listeners should not be enticed by feelings of previous success to continue and say more than one should.

Fourth, application of the Bippus study leads to the conclusion that the outcome of the "comforting" message did not generate a positive mood, stop rumination about the upsetting event, or promote the child's empowerment to cope with the situation. In fact, while the volunteer was well-meaning, the conversational episode ends in a space that may situate the family in worse position than before the call was made. Gavois, Paulsson, and Fridlund (2006) reported that families tend to turn away from mental health professionals when they sense that progress with their problems is not being made.

Discussion

Use of active listening when working through family situations involving all forms of mental illness is essential. Yet, even the most well-meaning family member or family helper may misjudge and/or mismanage stressful events. The final section of this chapter discusses implications for helpers/outside agencies working with families, as well as family members themselves who cope with challenges related to mental illness. Finally, recommendations for future study are included.

Implications for Family Helpers/Outside Agencies

Our critique of the helpline volunteer's interaction with troubled callers raises concerns about both the active listening model of therapeutic discourse and the efficacy of call-taker training in responding to persons who seem to manifest mood disorders. The previous section describes a call-taker who veered from the path of active listening prescriptions. While call-takers' failure to meet minimum standards of helper behavior has been described in terms of a lack of empathy, respect, and responsiveness (Mishara et al., 2007a), the interaction described herein was beset by different circumstances. Gilgun (1992) has noted how the "busyness" (p. 239) problem complicates therapeutic listening contexts. When more than one person speaks simultaneously, call-takers are less likely to actively listen. Family members who seek helpline support do well to manage turn taking in ways that minimize the likelihood of call-taker overload. While the therapeutic discourse model tends to assume that active listening promotes effective family functioning, it should be acknowledged that effective family functioning increases likelihood of active listening.

Reasons for challenging usefulness of the active listening model also relate to the caller's "repeat" status. While an active listening emphasis may ensure an outlet for persons to vent their stress, Mishara and colleagues' (2007b) comparison of active listening and collaborative problem solving models found that repeat callers tended to benefit more from directive problem solving. In fact, these two models are not mutually exclusive and are probably best used in combination. Nevertheless, it is important to consider the caller's previous calling status when deciding how to respond.

Training volunteer call-takers in active listening should incorporate some of the factors suggested in this analysis. Uchino (2004) notes that there are occasions where potential support persons understand what behaviors are supportive to distressed persons, but their interactional anxiety prevents them from summoning the appropriate skills. Future training sessions should implement strategies for managing anxiety in the process of coping with self and other emotions. Furthermore, in addition to an ability to assess callers' risk levels, training sessions should provide more information about depression and the diseases and disorders that are associated with it. Dealing with callers who seem to demonstrate some type of mood disorder may be the very time when communication skills are in greatest demand but in shortest supply.

Implications for Family Members

There are few who would argue that being a parent is a challenging and often stress-inducing role that is exacerbated when mental health issues are involved. "There is an undeniable pattern between abnormal and problematic family interaction patterns and family members' mental health" (Segrin & Flora, 2005, p. 323). The opportunity for a parent or child to talk through a problem with a supportive listener is often helpful. Yet, while calls are usually made within the privacy of their own home, parents should not forget that calls to a telephone helpline involve contact with external agencies. These agencies have the potential to both affect, and be affected by, the family system in ways that are not always anticipated (Bronfenbrenner, 1986).

Family members who feel the need for outside support will find a wide range of telephone helplines available. The website Partners-in-Parenting (2006), for example, lists almost 100 lines available for families dealing with alcohol abuse, family violence, and other problematic issues. When using this form of support, however, caution should be exercised. Speaking as clearly and concisely as possible, although difficult in emotionally-charged conditions, is extremely helpful to the call-taker who is trying to assess the situation to offer the best help possible. Also, both parents and children must realize that the call-taker is there to listen, but not necessarily solve the problem for callers. Often, callers are told not to give advice. Callers never know the entire context of the problem nor the personality characteristics of those calling, so they refrain from giving advice that may not be applicable to the situation being described. Finally, callers must understand that volunteers, such as the individual in the case study we critiqued, are human beings who experience confusion and anxiety in responding to challenging, even crisis situations. Volunteers may mismanage an interaction. Call-in responders will not often give callers the perfect solution to their dilemma, and parents and children using helplines must be prepared to put effort into solving their own problems.

All family members who cope with issues of mood disorders and other mental illnesses, including those who use helplines, would be well-served to learn basic skills inherent in active listening for use in their own homes. Brownell (2006) asserts that it is with members of our families that "our most intense emotions are expressed" (p. 316). Use of listening with those closest to you "demonstrates both caring and a commitment to problem solving" (p. 317). Although it may be incumbent upon parents to seek out this important information, agencies outside the family can be helpful. Schools, health facilities, neighborhood organizations and the like, can work to provide parents and their children with a heightened awareness of the *importance* of listening when working though problems in family relationships as well as opportunities to learn and practice active listening skills. Listening is often taken for granted (Brownell, 2006; Wolvin & Coakley, 1996); yet when dealing with difficult family issues, it is certainly an essential tool to cope with uncertainty and arrive at a better understanding of others' perceptions and needs.

Recommendations for Future Study

As evidenced by our critique of the volunteer call-taker, agencies such as FMA may want to do more to assess the quality of their training programs and volunteers' interactions with callers so as to provide the best possible help to parents and children who need assistance. As Mishara and colleagues (2007a) point out, thousands of individuals contact helplines on a daily basis, but "there has been relatively little development of theoretical models of telephone crisis intervention and little hard data to describe how helpers actually react to callers in crisis situations" (p. 291). When conducting research to develop more effective models, input from the callers themselves must also be obtained. Callers' perceptions of the call-takers' listening behaviors or outcomes resulting from their calls, for example, would seem an essential component to uncovering more effective ways of working with families under stress. A combination of input from those managing agencies, the volunteers who take calls, and the callers themselves, would provide a more comprehensive picture of what actually occurs and what should ideally occur in the call-taking process.

In a broader sense, active listening as a potential diffuser of challenging family situations related to mental health issues, has been only generally discussed in literature relating to counseling or the giving of social support. Yet, these discussions would be enhanced if approached from a more scholarly perspective. We all know that active listening is helpful, but what specifically, in terms of strategies, is *most* effective? The "mishandled" call excerpt demonstrated that active listening skills are not always easy to use. Mishara and colleagues (2007b) suggested that frequent callers may benefit from a more directive problem solving approach instead of the call-taker using active listening only. Situations, especially in the helpline context, pose challenges for traditional, prescriptive measures for active listening use. Therefore, scholars would do well to more thoroughly investigate how active listening is used in very stressful, even crisis situations.

Research into active listening for agencies and helpers working with troubled families is important, but future studies should also focus on how best to incorporate active listening skills into the family itself. Parenting workshops or self-help books, such as *How to Talk so Kids Will Listen and How to Listen so Kids will Talk* (Faber & Mazlish, 2002) are helpful, but probably do not reach the majority of families. The role of schools in educating children on the importance of supportive listening in relationships would then seem in order. Most schools articulate "listening" as a basic language arts competency (Wolvin & Coakley, 1996), but if systematic listening instruction is provided, it is generally associated with comprehensive listening in the classroom. A more therapeutic listening paradigm is needed if we expect children to bring active listening into their family of origin and future family relationships.

Conclusion

This discussion would not be complete without acknowledging economic and sociological factors that give rise to the need for the Family Management Association's and other such call-in lines. In analyzing a father's search through America's "mental health madness," Earley (2006) describes how closing of mental health hospitals between 1960 and 1980 resulted in a fourfold decrease of patients in those hospitals and a savings of millions in tax dollars.

"Deinstitutionalization" was presented as liberating because it freed mentally ill persons to live in their communities. Their functioning would be facilitated in part, through pharmaceutical "wonder drugs" (e.g., Thorazine) that represented advances in treatment of mental illness, and through John F. Kennedy's commitment to construct a national network of community mental health centers. That commitment was not realized and, since that time, our government has not given priority to the issue of mental health. Given this unacceptable state of affairs, we should not be surprised about the increase in the number of families experiencing ramifications of mental illness or that call-in lines stay busy.

Those who study family communication are in a unique position to both support families in trouble and to train others to do so. With additional research regarding how to best use active listening and other skills associated with providing support, society will be bolstered by more effectively functioning families who set a positive pattern for families of the future.

References

Akister, J., & Johnson, K. (2002). Parenting issues that may be addressed through a confidential helpline. *Health and Social Care in the Community, 10,* 106–111.

Albrecht, T., & Adelman, M. (1987). Communicating social support: A theoretical perspective. In T. Albrecht & M. Adelman (Eds.), *Communicating social support* (pp. 18–39). Newbury Park, CA: Sage.

Amador, X. (2000). *I am not sick, I don't need help!* New York: Vida Press.

American Academy of Child and Adolescent Psychiatry. (2001). Practice parameter for the assessment and treatment of children and adolescents with suicidal behavior. *Journal of the Academy of Child and Adolescent Psychiatry, 40,* 24S–51S.

Arnold, W. E. (1997). Listening and the helping professions. In M. Purdy & D. Borisoff (Eds.), *Listening in everyday life* (pp. 267–284). Lanham, MD: University Press of America.

Beebe, S. A., Beebe, S. J., & Redmond, M. V. (2005). *Interpersonal communication: Relating to others.* Boston: Pearson Education.

Bippus, A. (2001). Recipients' criteria for evaluating the skillfulness of comforting communication and the outcomes of comforting interactions. *Communication Monographs, 68,* 301–313.

Bronfenbrenner, U. (1986). Ecology of the family as a context for human development: Research perspectives. *Developmental Psychology, 22,* 723–742.

Brownell, J. (2006). *Listening: Attitudes, principles, and skills.* Boston: Pearson.

Burleson, B. (1994). Comforting messages: Significance, approaches, and effects. In B. Burleson, T. Albrecht, & I. Sarason (Eds.), *Communication of social support: Messages, interactions, relationships, and community.* Thousand Oaks, CA: Sage.

Canary, D. J., Cody, M. J., & Manusov, V. L. (2003). *Interpersonal communication: A goals-based approach.* Boston: Bedford's/St.Martins.

Cupach, W. R., & Canary, D. J. (1997). *Competence in interpersonal conflict.* Prospect Heights, IL: Waveland.

Devito, J. (2005). *Human communication: The basic course.* Boston: Pearson Education.

du Pre, A. (2005). *Communicating about health: Current issues and perspectives.* New York: McGraw-Hill.

Earley, P. (2006). *Crazy: A father's search through America's mental health madness.* New York: Berkley Books.

Faber, A., & Mazlish, E. (2002). *How to talk so kids will listen & how to listen so kids will talk.* New York: HarperCollins.

Family Management Association. (2004). *Stress line training: Manual and resource book.* Unpublished manuscript.

Gamble, T. K., & Gamble, M. (2005). *Communication works.* Boston: McGraw Hill.

Gavois, H., Paulsson, G., & Fridlund, B. (2006). Mental health professional support in families with a member suffering from severe mental illness: A grounded theory model. *Scandinavian Journal of Caring Sciences, 20,* 102–109.

Gilgun, J. F. (1992). Observations in a clinical setting: Team decision-making in family incest treatment. In J. F. Gilgun, K. Daly, & G. Handel (Eds.), *Qualitative methods in family research* (pp. 236–259). Newbury Park, CA: Sage.

Gilliard, J., Keady, J., Evers, C., & Milton, S. (1998). Telephone helplines for people with dementia. *International Journal of Geriatric Psychiatry, 13,* 734–735.

Golant, M., & Golant, S. (1996). *What to do when someone you love is depressed.* New York: Henry Holt.

Hurst, M. D. (2005). Mental-health disorders gain foothold during teenage years. *Education Week, 24*(41), 12.

Maslach, C. (1982). *Burnout: The cost of caring.* Englewood Cliffs, NJ: Prentice Hall.

Miklowitz. D.J. (2002). *The bipolar disorder guide: What you and your family need to know.* New York: Guilford.

Miller, K., Stiff, J., & Ellis, B. (1988). Communication and empathy as precursors to burnout among human service workers. *Communication Monographs, 55,* 250–265.

Mishara, B. L., Chagnon, F., Daigle, M., Balan, B., Raymond, S., Marcoux, I., et al. (2007a). Comparing models of helper behavior to actual practice in telephone crisis intervention: A silent monitoring study of calls to the U.S. 1-800-SUICIDE network. *Suicide and Life-Threatening Behavior, 37,* 297–307.

Mishara, B. L., Chagnon, F., Daigle, M., Balan, B., Raymond, S., Marcoux, I., et al. (2007b). Which helper behaviors and intervention styles are related to better short-term outcomes in telephone crisis intervention? Results from a silent monitoring study of calls to the U.S. 1-800-SUICIDE network. *Suicide and Life-Threatening Behavior, 37,* 308–321.

National Clearinghouse on Child Abuse and Neglect. (2004). *Child abuse and neglect fatalities: Statistics and intervention.* Retrieved on August 18, 2008, from http://www.nccanch.acf.hhs.gov/pubs/factsheets/fatality.cfm

O'Connor, R. (1997). *Undoing depression: What therapy doesn't teach you and medication can't give you.* New York: Berkley Books.

Partners-in-Parenting (2006). Hotlines and helplines in the U.S. Retrieved on August 8, 2008, from http://www.partners-in-arenting.com/hotlineshelplines.htm

Segrin, C., & Flora, J. (2005). *Family communication.* Mahwah, NJ: Erlbaum.

Seiler, W. J., & Beall, M. L. (2005). *Communication: Making connections.* Boston: Pearson Education.

Simon, G. (2004). Psychotherapy by telephone aids depression treatment. *Psychiatric Times, 21,* 103.

Tracy, S. (2002). When questioning turns to face threat: An interactional sensitivity in 911 call-taking. *Western Journal of Communication, 66,* 129–157.

Tracy, S. (2005). Locking up emotion: Moving beyond dissonance for understanding emotion labor discomfort. *Communication Monographs, 72,* 261–283.

Tracy, S., & Tracy, K. (1998). Emotion labor at 911: A case study and theoretical critique. *Journal of Applied Communication Research, 26,* 390–411.

Uchino, B. (2004). *Social support and physical health: Understanding the health consequences of relationships.* New Haven, CT: Yale University Press.

Vaux, A. (1985). Variations in social support associated with gender, ethnicity and age. *Journal of Social Issues, 41,* 89–110.

Wolvin, A., & Coakley, C. (1996). *Listening.* Dubuque, IA: Brown and Benchmark.

Zarit, S. H., & Zarit, J. M. (2007). *Mental disorders in older adults: Fundamentals of assessment and treatment.* New York: Guilford.

16 Commentary
Parent-Child-Societal Relationships and Media

Jennings Bryant

The three chapters in this section offer fascinating glimpses into what we know about the interface of two of our more important contemporary social institutions—family and media—and how these entities collude, catalyze, and corrupt interactions with other societal agencies and agents. Clearly, the increasingly intrusive and transparent role of diverse media technologies and message systems in the everyday lives of family members, as well as in family life more generally, are among the true revolutions in today's digital societies. How such technologically extended interpersonal and family communication affects interactions with external publics in the greater social system raises important questions that, for the most part, have yet to be addressed.

Studying any combinatorial dyad of the parent-child-societal matrix is complex. Scholarship that attempts to examine all three components simultaneously is inherently multidimensional. Adding considerations of media to the mix, thereby creating a parent-child-media-society matrix, makes for inordinately complex challenges. More than a quarter of a century ago, Anderson and Bryant (1983) delineated one simple aspect of this challenge this way:

> Television viewing cannot be fully understood apart from its relationship to the viewer's immediate socio-cultural context (family characteristics, parent-child communication style, socioeconomic status, ethnic background, and the like), or from the viewer's behavior and experiences outside of the television-viewing situation. Also, from a larger perspective, these things influence and are influenced by the television industry from which the programming originates, and they affect and are affected by the larger society as a whole. (p. 332)

Anderson and Bryant then proposed a social-systems model and presented a schematic to assist in examining these transactional processes. How much more complex the family-media-societal matrix has become today! It would be a huge challenge to construct a social-systems schematic that would enable "coders" to reliably and validly analyze today's parent-child-media-society interactions.

The authors of these three chapters should be considered pioneers approaching a vast and largely unknown wilderness, and they are to be commended for beginning to document, explore, and map such complex relationships and interactions with only limited theory and empirical generalizations as their compass. What I will attempt to do in reviewing these important chapters is to integrate a few of the similarities among the chapters, highlight special attributes of each chapter, and suggest additional avenues of research and different approaches to scholarship that are needed for a fuller and more veridical understanding of family, mediated communication, and society.

By the Numbers

It is obvious from reading these three chapters that normative data describing the presence of various and sundry media technologies in households and their usage by family members are readily available. Austin, Hust, and Kistler (chapter 13) relied heavily on Kaiser Family Foundation studies (e.g., Kunkel, Biely, Eyal, Cope-Farrar, Donnerstein, & Fandrich, 2003; Roberts, Foehr, & Rideout, 2005) to establish basic media availability and usage patterns within families, and on McNeal's (1999) and others' normative findings to document the purchasing potency of modern youth. Kendall (chapter 14) utilized results from Pew Internet and American Life surveys to establish the remarkably high degree of usage of instant messaging by today's adolescents (e.g., Lenhart, Madden, & Hitlin, 2005).

One earmark of information societies seems to be the ready availability of normative data that establish the widespread presence and usage of media technologies in both domiciles and workplaces. Indeed, in marked contrast to practices in agrarian or industrial societies, such information is now deemed newsworthy, and technology adoption rates, ratings data, circulation figures, and the like routinely find their way into the pages and screens of the popular press. The information age truly is qualitatively different from prior eras. Media industry associations now consider the regular collection and distribution of adoption and usage data for their particular medium or media to be a raison d'être, as well as an important tool for self-promotion. For example, the Entertainment Software Association has long presented normative data on diverse aspects of video game equipment sales (i.e., game platform adoptions), game unit sales, game usage patterns, and player profiles on their Web site, www.theesa.com, including evidence of how parents purchase games for children, the type of games played within families by children and parents, and numerous other findings of interest to family-communication scholars. Additionally, media research companies now routinely distribute press releases that reveal results of their formally proprietary research, which provide media adoption and usage data within families. Naturally, these press releases often suggest self-serving headlines like "Nielsen Says Video Game Penetration in U.S. TV Households Grew 18% During the Past Two Years" (Gyimesi, 2007). Such extant normative data clearly paint a picture of digital and traditional media thoroughly intertwined in the daily lives and special events of the modern family, and they suggest that these strong symbiotic relationships between media and families may have robust and important social consequences.

Unfortunately, when one attempts to move beyond media-and-family examinations to considerations of a family-media-society or parent-child-media-society matrices, normative data that would be useful in developing such triadic or quadratic profiles typically are lacking, or at least they are very difficult to find and access. For example, Penington and Baus (chapter 15) had to draw upon normative data from a helpline's annual reports to document access of this specialized service by parents with therapeutic needs. Such descriptive voids are just one of the many challenges faced by our pioneering chapter contributors.

Beyond the Numbers

Our chapter authors have gone far beyond normative data in their research to present, among many other things, patterns of using mediated communication for societal outreach. And they have been so bold as to suggest some of the ramifications of such uses of mediated communication, as well as its potential for misuse by parents, children, and external social agencies. For example, after Kendall (chapter 14) profiled the use of instant messaging (IM) by adolescents and youth pastors, she assessed user attitudes toward IM, described the assessed weaknesses of IM for optimal communication, evaluated the strengths of IM, and then provided sage advice for IM users. Penington and Baus (chapter 15) provided a systematic profile of what active listening skills entail and, more critically, how such effective listening skills and strategies can facilitate family communication, especially under conditions of emotional distress. To attain and retain psychologically healthy families requires effective therapeutic listening on occasion, so the lessons offered are beneficial for all, albeit in this instance the emphasis is on how telephone helpline volunteers can help parents undergoing emotional distress. Austin et al. (chapter 13) emphasized the role of media as strategic tools; then they turned the metaphor on itself to reveal how parents, too, can be strategic and actively utilize devices like V-chips and Internet filters as tools to enhance productive communication with their children, especially when considering issues involving consumerism.

Chapter Kudos and Criticism

Austin, Hust, and Kistler: Powerful Media Tools: Arming Parents with Strategies to Affect Children's Interactions with Commercial Interests

The authors of chapter 13 offer a very sophisticated model of parents and children interacting, and such interactions are largely devoid of the sorts of stereotypes that often characterize descriptions of parent-child communication. In other words, from an epistemological perspective, the view of the person inherent in this chapter is quite elaborate and realistic. For example, although children's potential vulnerability to media marketing is discussed, children are never reified as passive, defenseless creatures. In a world in which children, even young children, often are the true family experts in digital technologies, in which youngsters seem to develop cynical attitudes toward media messages almost as soon as they can talk, and in which parents often cannot "stump a fifth-grader" on a plethora of topics, we cannot afford to perceive children as either overly helpless or vulnerable (nor they cannot be seen as adults either), and these authors maintain a useful balance in this regard. Moreover, although in this chapter parents are sometimes envisioned as *gatekeepers* between children, media, and external societal agents, the gatekeeper concept is presented with great complexity, even with its own typology composed of multiple continua. Additionally, to balance the gatekeeper perspective, parents and children are also seen as communication *collaborators* in addressing external agents such as media marketers.

Another strength of this chapter is the manner in which the literature on parental mediation strategies is synthesized and presented. This should not be surprising, because the senior author's primary research has been among the best in the mediation arena. A recent content analysis of theory and research in mass communication revealed that mediation theory and models have been the fourth most popular type of mass communication theory in the first few years of the 21st century (Bryant & Miron, 2004). Having that literature expertly applied to the ways parents and children can and should interact with media marketers is a major coup for this volume.

In terms of criticisms of this chapter, I would offer only two comments. The first is that although the authors do take newer digital media into account, the emphasis they give such technologies would appear to be smaller than parents' concerns about such media would warrant. Having presented more than a dozen media-and-children PTA programs per year over the past three decades, I have seen 21st century parents' concerns shift markedly away from traditional media to video games, Web sites, user-generated media, and mobile media (especially text messaging). Most such digital media get relatively short shrift in this chapter, although the marketing strategies employed to reach children via such media may well require different mediation strategies than those emphasized. The second issue is closely related, and that is although the authors do mention alternative marketing strategies that are more commonly employed in digital media, those are not emphasized. Yet those alternative marketing strategies (e.g., product placement, viral marketing) are rapidly dominating the children's media marketplace (e.g., Palmer & Carpenter, 2006), and they merit enhanced attention by the authors. The strategies parents should take to effectively mediate viral marketing efforts certainly would be expected to be different than what should be employed to mediate the effects of traditional commercials and advertisements. All in all, however, this was an ideal chapter to launch this section on parent-child-societal relationships and media.

Kendall: Finding Adolescents through Cyberspace: Youth Workers, Teenagers, and Instant Messaging

In many ways, Kendall's chapter 14 is quite complementary to that by Austin et al. The latter chapter focused on one aspect of newer digital media (instant messaging, IM), emphasized adolescents as opposed to younger children, and featured a classic example of outreach via user-generated interactive media. As Kendall stated, "As technology like IM changes the way adolescents communicate with one another, it is important to ask how those changes might impact how teens communicate with parents and other adults" (p. 244). Strengths of this chapter include its sensitive incorporation of the literature and some of the more useful perspectives of computer-mediated communication (CMC) research, anchoring it in interesting theoretical contexts. It also presents the primary data from two yoked empirical investigations of outreach via mediated communication, in this case, communication between youth pastors and adolescents using IM.

My primary concerns with this chapter are how much we can generalize its fascinating findings. Most information societies are largely secular in nature, and it is likely that any sort of communication that takes place within a religious context would be somewhat different in nature from secular communication. Moreover, the sample employed is rather homogeneous—members of an evangelical sect—and those church members might well not be representative of traditional religious congregations, much less of the public at large. Finally, e-mail or Web surveys were employed, and they are notably problematic in terms of generalizability. Therefore, although I suspect that the findings of the two surveys have considerable heuristic value, it is unlikely that they represent even the penultimate word in terms of the phenomenon under investigation.

Penington and Baus: Response to Family Crisis: Mood Disorders, Supportive Listening, and the Telephone Helpline Volunteer—Analysis and Applications

Having personally dealt with family, media, and mental health on a few occasions (e.g., Bryant, Bryant, Aust, & Venugopalan, 2001), I am most appreciative of Penington and Baus's careful treatment and integration of these topics in chapter 15. They began with a brief treatment of mental health issues in the family context, transitioned to an excellent review of the literature on listening skills, discussed issues related to listening in technologically assisted applied settings, and then presented what is essentially a case study of listening in a hotline call center. Of particular interest to many will be a concluding section on implications for family members.

Penington and Baus's review of the active listening literature should be of great value to anyone interested in family communication as an area of scholarly inquiry. Moreover, their case study and its attendant evaluations have considerable utility to those who operate helplines and crisis centers, and the section examining mishandled conversations should be of special interest to such specialized publics. Finally, the authors' literature review, along with the section featuring implications for family members, also should be invaluable to those who desire for their own family to function more effectively and harmoniously—hopefully all of us. As the authors appropriately concluded, "with additional research regarding how to best use active listening and other skills associated with providing support, society will be bolstered by more effectively functioning families who set a positive pattern for families of the future" (Pennington & Baus, p. 270, this volume).

New Avenues of Research and Optional Approaches to Scholarship

Although the research represented in chapters 13–15 represents major advances in family-media-society scholarship, many challenges or opportunities for additional advancement remain. I would like to suggest three shifts that might prove productive for the next generation of family communication researchers who also have an interest in media and society issues.

Explicating the Digital Childhood

Vandewater, Rideout, Wartella, Huang, Lee, and Shim (2007) have referred to the contemporary life of infants, toddlers, and preschoolers as "digital childhood." Rideout, Vandewater, and Wartella (2003) called this time of rapid development "electronic childhood." Bryant and Bryant (2006) labeled early childhood in the information age "living in a wired family." Whatever the soubriquet used to refer to contemporary early childhood, family communication scholars need not only to describe it accurately in terms of valid normative data, they need to conceptualize the experience of growing up digital more exhaustively and design research that examines family communication and outreach within such a milieu more veridically and with more precise and exacting measures.

What are some of manifestations of this challenge? First, we need to recognize that within the same family, different media preferences may well create friction in communication styles. This is particularly true for households in which intergenerational residents may include grandparents, parents, and children in the same domicile. The older generations may restrict media consumption to traditional media, such as television, radio, newspapers, letters, phone calls, and the like, whereas the children may opt for texting, IM-ing, Web surfing, networked gaming, and use of whatever the next generation of communication technologies brings to eager young adopters. Obviously this is an extreme case, but it is happening already. And in the words of *Cool Hand Luke*, "what we (may) have here is a failure to communicate." The ramifications of barriers to communication because of differing communication technologies and media preferences within the same household have yet to be fully explored

(Bryant & Bryant, 2006), but not only would such a "disconnect" be expected to affect intrafamily communication, it would also be expected to affect interfamily communication, as well as communication with external publics.

A much simpler issue, although the remedies are no less complex, is that derived from the fact that children increasingly have their own media located independently from what used to be the "family media" center (i.e., the family television set, the family stereo, the family computer, etc.). With such dispersed media comes independent and divergent media consumption (and, with increasingly available user-generated media, production). This speaks loudly to the sorts of gatekeeping potential Austin et al. articulated so well in chapter 13. Our mediation models will have to be adjusted to this new family environment in which we no longer have a family "electronic hearth" (Bryant & Bryant, 2001). Undoubtedly such trends in family-media dispersion will ultimately affect our uses and effects models more generally.

Extending Our Research to Different Media

A natural follow-up to a focus on digital childhood and wired families is recasting our research nets to include media that have become prominent in the lives of children and adults that are often overlooked by family-communication scholars. One notable illustration would be video games. Video-game research has become rampant within communication circles during the past decade, leading to new divisions of professional associations devoted to gaming studies (e.g., Games Studies within the International Communication Association), as well as to at least one dedicated brochure promoting seven scholarly books and textbooks devoted to video game scholarship from the publisher of the present volume ("Routledge Video Games Titles," 2008). Yet, video-game researchers rarely undertake what would be considered to be family-communication research, and family-communication researchers equally rarely conduct video-game research, despite the fact that networked gaming has become a popular way for gamers to connect with external publics of all ilks. Obviously, a similar case could be made for a plethora of other digital media.

How Can We Improve How All Families Communicate with External Publics?

Stinnett, Walters, and Stinnett (1991) reported that "strong families are characterized by good communication patterns" (p. 133), both when interacting with each other and with external publics. The increasing rifts that seem likely in digital families who often fail to share technologies and public symbol systems suggest that the thrust of this volume, "Managing Relationships Outside of Home," may be made even more difficult by the sorts of mediated communication "disconnects" previously described. Penington and Baus (chapter 15) foreshadowed such potential difficulties with their thoughtful analysis of the need for supportive listening by telephone helpline volunteers, and Kendall (chapter 14) offered several revelations along these lines with her analysis of youth pastors and adolescent parishioners usage of instant messaging, but these studies merely scratch the surface of our need for better research in communication efficiencies required in gaining and maintaining help from mental health providers and the like in sustaining healthy families. Rogers (1961) emphasized the importance of effective communication with mental healthcare providers when he said, "the whole task of psychotherapy is the task of dealing with a failure in communication" (p. 330). Additional research in this arena is sorely needed.

Refining Our Fundamental Family Communication-Styles Model

When reading chapter 13's section on "General Family Communication Patterns," I was struck by just how dated the Family Communication Patterns model (McLeod & Chaffee, 1972) seemed to be, and how poorly its "socio-oriented vs. concept-oriented" typology would appear to fit the disparate communication patterns of digital families. Although many of the notions inherent in this model remain valid, the archaic terminology (e.g., the notion of laissez-faire families sounds obsolete in this "Age of Entitlement" in which the vast majority of families would qualify) makes the model suspect on its face. Certainly understanding family communication patterns or styles remains important. For example, Bryant and Rockwell (1994) found that adolescents from homes in which families had established open, discussant, participatory lines of communication between all family members (i.e., open communication) were much more resistant to the potentially negative effects of pornography than were teenagers from homes with closed, authoritarian communication styles. In that same study, whether the family used a socio-oriented vs. concept-oriented communication pattern failed to reliably mediate pornography's impact. Obviously, considerable research would need to be conducted before we scrap tried-and-true constructs, but the ostensible lack of face validity of the Family Communication Patterns model would seemingly call for such research.

New Methods and Measure

Very few attempts to integrate family systems theories into research on family and communication technology use have been undertaken (Jennings & Wartella, 2004). One potentially productive approach would be to utilize social network analysis to capture the dynamic evolution of the family system. Such an approach would permit the ready incorporation of media usage as well as outreach to other societal agents. With such a model, it is possible to create a set of attributes for each family member that characterizes his or her media usage, significant external publics, communication goals, family roles, etc., and then combine these data with family network data that focus on who communicates with whom via what channel about what. Such methods and measures permit scholars to determine how divergent roles, goals, interaction choices, and the like create relational patterns within the network (Wasserman & Faust, 1994). The promise of such theoretical and empirical perspectives would appear to match the complexity of family communication within our digital era.

References

Anderson, D. R., & Bryant, J. (1983). Research on children's television viewing: The state of the art. In J. Bryant & D. R. Anderson (Eds.), *Children's understanding of television: Research on attention and comprehension* (pp. 331–353). New York: Academic Press.

Bryant, J., & Bryant, J. A. (Eds.). (2001). *Television and the American family* (2nd ed.). Mahwah, NJ: Erlbaum.

Bryant, J., Bryant, J. A., Aust, C. F., & Venugopalan, G. (2001). How psychologically healthy are America's prime-time television families? In J. Bryant & J. A. Bryant (Eds.), *Television and the American family* (2nd ed., pp. 247–271). Mahwah, NJ: Erlbaum.

Bryant, J., & Miron, D. (2004). Theory and research in mass communication, *Journal of Communication, 54,* 662–704.

Bryant, J., & Rockwell, S. C. (1994). Effects of massive exposure to sexually oriented prime-time television programming on adolescents' moral judgment. In D. Zillmann, J. Bryant, & A. C. Huston (Eds.), *Media, children, and the family: Social scientific, psychodynamic, and clinical perspectives* (pp. 183–195). Hillsdale, NJ: Erlbaum.

Bryant, J. A., & Bryant, J. (2006). Implications of living in a wired family: New directions in family and media research. In L. H. Turner & R. West (Eds.), *The family communication sourcebook* (pp. 297–314). Thousand Oaks, CA: Sage.

Gyimesi, K. (2007, March 5). Nielsen says video game penetration in U.S. TV households grew 18% during the past two years. *Nielsen – Press Release.* Retrieved September 23, 2008, from http://www.nielsen.com/media/pr_070302.html

Jennings, N., & Wartella, E. (2004). Technology and the family. In A. L. Vangelisti (Ed.), *Handbook of family communication* (pp. 593–608). Mahwah, NJ: Erlbaum.

Kunkel, D., Biely, E., Eyal, K., Cope-Farrar, K., Donnerstein, E., & Fandrich, R. (2003). *Sex on TV 3: A biennial report of the Kaiser Family Foundation.* Menlo Park, CA: Henry J. Kaiser Family Foundation.

Lenhart, A., Madden, M., & Hitlin, P. (2005). Teens and technology: Youth are leading the transition to a fully wired and mobile nation. *Pew Internet & American life project.* Retrieved September 22, 2008, from http://www.pewinternet.org/PPF/r/162/report_display.asp

McLeod, J. M., & Chaffee, S. H. (1972). The construction of social reality. In J. Tedeschi (Ed.), *The social influence process* (pp. 50–59). Chicago: Aldine-Atherton.

McNeal, J. (1999). *The kids' market: Myths and realities.* Ithaca, NY: Paramount Market.

Palmer, E. L., & Carpenter, C. F. (2006). Food and beverage marketing to children and youth: Trends and issues. *Media Psychology, 8,* 165–190.

Rideout, V. J., Vandewater, E. A., & Wartella, E. A. (2003). *Zero to six: Electronic media in the lives of infants, toddlers and preschoolers.* Menlo Park, CA: Henry J. Kaiser Family Foundation.

Roberts, D. R., Foehr, U., & Rideout, V. (2005). *Generation M: Media in the lives of 8–18 year-olds.* Menlo Park, CA: Henry J. Kaiser Family Foundation.

Rogers, C. (1961). *On becoming a person: A therapists' view of psychotherapy.* Boston: Houghton Mifflin.

Routledge: Taylor & Francis Group. (2008). *Routledge video games titles.* [Brochure.] New York: Routledge.

Stinnett, N., Walters, J., & Stinnett, N. (1991). *Relationships in marriage and the family* (3rd ed.). New York: Macmillan.

Vandewater, E. A., Rideout, V. J., Wartella, E. A., Huang, X., Lee, J. H., & Shim, M. (2007). Digital childhood: Electronic media use among infant, toddlers, and preschoolers. *Pediatrics, 119,* 1006–1015.

Wasserman, S., & Faust, K. (1994). *Social network analysis: Methods and applications.* Cambridge, MA: Cambridge University Press.

Section IV

Evolving Caregiving Roles & Relationships

17 When the World Comes Home

Examining Internal and External Influences on Communication Exchanges Between Parents and Their Boomerang Children

Sally Vogl-Bauer

Over the last 30 years, the number of adult children returning home to live with their parents has steadily increased (Ramachandran, 2005). These adult children have been labeled "boomerang" children because, like boomerangs they leave a particular location, only to later return to their original starting points. There are many reasons why this may occur: (a) difficulty finding employment after graduation, (b) high rental rates, (c) significant debt, or (d) saving money before marrying (Clemens & Axelson, 1985; El Nasser, 2005; Gelles, 1995). Although not exhaustive, the list suggests some reason for adult children opting to return to their parents' homes to live. In fact, as of 2003, approximately 16 million families had at least one adult child over the age of 18 living at home (El Nasser, 2005). Although this phenomenon has been examined in the popular press as well as in academia (e.g., Aquilino & Supple, 1991; Clemens & Axelson, 1985; Mitchell, 2006), family communication researchers have given marginal attention to the communication exchanges in parent-adult child relationships during this unique turning point for families.

The return of adult children to their parental homes poses several interesting issues that both affect and are affected by communication. First, both parties have potentially changed a great deal. Adult children have had the opportunity to be responsible for themselves outside of immediate parental supervision. These children have not had to be held accountable for actions that may have drawn greater scrutiny if these behaviors had occurred while living under their parents' roofs. In addition, parents may have also experienced greater freedom once their children had left their parental homes. Children's spaces may have been reconfigured to meet the changing needs of parents. Furthermore, parents themselves may have taken advantage of their independence from their children, allowing them to spend time and money in ways that may not have been accessible or possible when their children were at home (Wilcox & Snow, 1992). Second, this event may not be occurring voluntarily (Gelles, 1995). As a result, the emotions experienced by both parties may impact how successfully or poorly this situation is managed (Noller & Fitzpatrick, 1993); one or both parties could feel self-conscious when adult children return home (Guerrero & Andersen, 2000). Third, this event is very visible to other family members as well as to outsiders. It is difficult, if not impossible, to disguise the return of adult children to their parents' dwelling. As a result, outsiders' perceptions of this life-stage event could significantly impact parents' and children's perceptions of themselves and each other, as well as the event (Guerrero & Andersen, 2000).

The boomerang effect poses numerous challenges for parents and adult children, however, similarities could be made to other life course events experienced by parents and adult children. For example, whenever adult children return to their parents' homes after divorce or loss of employment, parents and adult children may struggle with issues of responsibility and accountability while living under the same roof. If adult children return home with their own children, further challenges could surface (e.g., differing discipline and parenting styles). However, the psychological and emotional challenges faced by both parents and adult children when events such as divorce or unemployment occur could differ significantly from the psychological and emotional issues associated with the boomerang effect since these events are associated with lost or failed expectations held by themselves or others (Galvin, Bylund, & Brommel, 2004; Gelles, 1995). Furthermore, insiders' and outsiders' perceived judgments about these relational failures may be compounded if divorce or job loss occurs later in the lives of adult children.

This chapter explores possible ways parents and boomerang children process messages that could strongly impact their relationships. Ironically, both boomerang children and their parents may be in the unique position of embodying the roles of *both* family insider and outsider when they communicate with each other. Whether planned or unanticipated, the fact that parents and adult children are once again under the same roof, when earlier they had been apart, requires a level of readjustment by both parties since they are no longer living independent of each other. Readjustment may be further complicated if adult children also have their own children when they return to live with their parents. Mitchell (1998) noted that parents and their adult children may not necessarily perceive this life stage event negatively. However, the ability of parents and adult children to effectively communicate with each other plays a significant role in how adult children's reentry into their parents' homes will be perceived by both parties.

Golish (2000) noted that perceptions of closeness in parent-adult child relationships are impacted by times of crisis. Whether returning home to live with your parents is considered a crisis by parents or adult children is disputable. Regardless, parents and adult children face communicative challenges that may be related to (a) the internal communication occurring within the dyad, as well as (b) communicative exchanges that happen or are the result of messages occurring external to the dyad. Therefore, three primary communication issues faced by boomerang children and their parents will be briefly reviewed. Then, four different theoretical perspectives will be examined to assess the role each could play when trying to understand how parents and their adult children cope with the internal as well as external communicative influences when adult children return home.

Relevant Communication Topics When Adult Children Return Home

Based on a review of literature, three primary topics have surfaced that are key for parents and adult children to successfully discuss and manage during this particular transition period. These three areas include (a) negotiating issues of financial support, (b) managing evolving parent-adult child communication dynamics, and (c) determining household contributions and responsibilities of the adult child (Quinn, 1993). A brief overview of each of these communication topic areas is provided.

Negotiating Issues of Financial Support

The first topic, negotiations about finances, ranges from discussions about possible rent payments to conversations about health and car insurance. In addition, coverage of various living expenses, such as telephone and Internet usage may also need to be negotiated between parents and their adult children. These conversations could be difficult for one or both parties if either party is unreceptive to discussing the topic (Guerrero & Afifi, 1995), or if the expectations held for each other (and what expenses each should pay for) vary. Some believe that talking about money has surpassed sex as the topic that is most difficult for marital couples to discuss with each other (Kelley, 2007). Therefore, it would not be surprising if parents and adult children had difficulty as well discussing financially-based topics. However, the importance of clear and direct communication on these issues cannot be underscored enough (Wilcox & Snow, 1992). Financial issues may be further complicated when adult children return to live with their parents and have their own children.

Furthermore, boomerang children may be presuming that their parents are in a position to provide financial support to them (Mitchell, 1998). With today's volatile workplace, where mergers and downsizing occur with greater frequency, making long-term employment less of a certainty, this assumption could be problematic (Galvin, 2004). Compounding matters is the potential spillover effect parental perceptions of their own job insecurity and money anxiety could have for their adult children. Lim and Si Sng (2006) indicated "parental feelings of distress, concerns, and worries about money matters do cross over to affect their children, either directly or indirectly through communications or children's observations of interactions within the families" (p. 1085). Thus, beyond the day-to-day financial costs associated with returning home, boomerang children may also be impacted by financial stressors faced by other family members, which could have long term implications associated with their views about money and work.

However, the availability of financial resources may not be the best predictor of how much or what parents will be willing to give to their adult children. Holdsworth (2004) noted that levels of financial support are negotiated between parents and their adult children, and external factors could play an important role in the outcome. For example, how might the additional financial support to one family member impact others in the household? In other cases, there may be concern that offering too much financial assistance could negatively impact adult children's ability to establish independence or self-reliance from their parents (Mitchell, 1998). Today, it is not uncommon to see financial investment firms (e.g., New York Life, Thrivent Financial for Lutherans) or financial publications (e.g., Kiplinger's Personal Finance) providing information for their clients or readers on whether or how parents should financially assist their adult children, and the possible financial risks to consider if doing so.

Managing Evolving Parent-Adult Child Communication Dynamics

Parents and their adult children may not have lived together for some time. Thus, the tendency may be for either or both parties to not realize that their relational dynamics have changed. Therefore, there may need to be dialogue on such things as household rules and basic expectations that could need modification from what they were prior to adult children first moving out of their parents' households. For instance, conversations on such things as curfews (if any), guest visits, family obligations, or general privacy concerns may need to be held. In essence, rules that were once in place when children were adolescents may no longer be applicable (e.g., being home by 11:00 p.m.). Furthermore, there may be new behaviors that were not practiced when children were younger, such as having romantic interests spending the night.

Lott (1986) reported that some academic institutions were implementing programs designed to facilitate communication between parents and their adult-children for students returning home for summer after their freshmen year of college. In these programs, students' concerns, such as changing values, curfews, or friendships were identified as topics of concern; parents' concerns, such as noting their children may not want to be around them, not helping around the house, or disrupting the parents' routine were identified. The intent was to sensitize both students and parents to the changing dynamics of their relationships. Unfortunately, Lott (1986) noted that there were no clear guidelines on how to successfully facilitate these discussions between parents and their adult-children.

Martin (1986) examined a different type of parent-adult child reentry process that occurs when adult children return home after studying abroad. This study underscored the role of communication when students transitioned back into familial relationships and friendships. In particular, sojourner students reported enhanced communication with their parents upon return from their study abroad experiences. An explanation proposed by Martin (1986) was that the distance and separation that were part of the study abroad experience may have served as a catalyst for more appreciative communication exchanges between parents and their adult children once they returned home. From a developmental perspective, Martin's (1986) findings suggest that as adult children mature and return home after graduation, they may approach communication exchanges with their parents from more of an egalitarian perspective that was not initially present when students first started college.

It is important for parents and adult children to remember that as their relational roles with each other evolve and change over time, the communicative exchanges held with each other will be impacted. As a result, some adjustments by both parents and adult children may be needed. However, it is not uncommon to experience transitions in parent-adult child communication exchanges. Rather, it is normal and perhaps necessary for parent-adult child relationships to adjust to life-stage changes.

Determining Household Contributions and Responsibilities of the Adult Child

Very pragmatic conversations surrounding the types of contributions expected of adult children as well as parents need to be had. These topics may include what chores, duties, or household maintenance tasks parents and adult children will perform around the house (e.g., cooking, dishes, mowing the lawn, laundry), as well as what parents and adult children will not do. Some adult children may expect their mothers, in particular, to wait on them and take care of their needs as they might have done when they were younger (El Nasser, 2005). Furthermore, mothers, in particular, may be reluctant to ask other family members to assist in or complete certain household duties (Goodnow, Bowes, Warton, Dawes, & Taylor, 1991), potentially compounding problems associated with delegating household responsibilities to adult children when they return home.

Goodnow and Lawrence (2001) identified three factors to consider when examining family contributions: (a) describing the contributions expected or made by family members, (b) assessing the circumstances relevant to the contribution, and (c) considering the feelings expressed in regard to the contributions made by family members. The nature of the contribution, such as tasks associated with individuals' own behaviors or actions, labeled "self-care" (e.g., putting away your own clothes, cleaning up any mess individuals made) were different from tasks that would be done to benefit the family unit overall, labeled "family work" (e.g., taking out the trash, cooking a meal for the family, doing yard work). In addition, family member availability, the necessity of completing a task, and amount of effort required to complete a task were important factors linked to making family contribution requests. Furthermore, "the significance of work contributions lies in their links to ideas about family membership, family status, and family relationships" (Goodnow & Lawrence, 2001, p. 9). The changes experienced by parent-child dyads over time may serve to compound how parents and adult children negotiate what, when, or how parents and adult children solicit or make family contributions.

Conversations addressing family contributions should help to clarify expectations for both parents and adult children. This is especially important if the expectations linked to "self-care" contributions or "family care" contributions for either party have changed or were ambiguous from when the parents and adult children last lived together (Goodnow & Lawrence, 2001). It is also suggested that parents and adult children discuss the time duration of this living arrangement, so that both parties are aware of how long these roles and expectations may last. This step is also perceived to be crucial to reducing the likelihood of future "boomerang" events (Quinn, 1993; Wilcox & Snow, 1992).

It is unlikely that either parents or their adult children look forward to discussions on how each party will contribute to the household. Yet, research suggests that conversations on household contributions and responsibilities for returning adult children are necessary if this new living arrangement is to work effectively for both parents and adult children. These exchanges remove many ambiguities and clarify expectations so that both parties know what is expected of them. Taking the time to discuss and clarify fundamental living arrangement issues may make the difference in whether parents or their adult children view the new living arrangement to be a success.

Finally, multiple parent-adult child relationships can vary within the same families. It should not be assumed that parents' relationships with all of their adult children will be perceived or managed comparably by either parents or adult children (Pillemer et al., 2007). In particular, if expectations parents and adult children have for one another are incompatible, inconsistencies may be magnified when parent-adult child dyads have to renegotiate their relationships later in life. In turn, either or both parties may modify how committed they are to making their new living arrangements successful.

Application of Theoretical Perspectives for Studying the Boomerang Effect

Family interactions do not occur in a vacuum. There are events that focus on the relational dynamics present within dyads (e.g., how well parents and adult children get along), as well as communication that results from outside influences. These outside influences could (a) come from other family members, (b) come from outsiders or (c) occur as the result of global events or public policy changes. The next section highlights how four different theoretical perspectives: systems theory, relational dialectics theory, social exchange theories, and communication privacy management theory, provide insights in how boomerang children and their parents may be impacted by internal as well as external influences. These four theoretical approaches were selected based on (a) their scope and application in family scholarship (Gelles, 1995; Klein & White, 1996; Stamp, 2004) and (b) their utility to address the unique communicative features at play during the boomerang effect.

Systems Theory

Systems theory is a very popular theoretical approach taken to study family interaction (Galvin et al., 2004). Systems theories allow scholars to see how family members' behaviors could extend to others in the family unit (Peterson, 1986). In the case of boomerang children, there is the opportunity to see how the return of adult children impacts their parents, although the ramifications could extend to others presently living in family residences (e.g., other siblings). In addition, systems theory is well-suited to explore the relationships between parents, their boomerang children, and the outside world.

Theoretical Overview   Family scholars from multiple disciplines have found systems theory to offer a compelling framework for learning how families interact with one another and the outside world (Klein & White, 1996; Stamp, 2004). The fundamental premise of systems theory is that organisms must find ways to reach optimal performance levels both within themselves, as well as within the larger environment with which they are placed. In the case of families, this requires two levels of analysis: (a) examining the family unit as a collection of subsystems in order to identify how the various parts (family members) interact in attempts to maximize family interactions; and (b) examining the family unit as part of a larger suprasystem, to comprehend the family's place within a larger environment or community to learn how families contribute to as well as balance outside stimulus in order to sustain themselves, if not thrive. The majority of family communication scholarship has studied various family subsystems, such as marital relationships, parent-child relationships, or sibling relationships. With the exception of this volume, there has been significantly less family communication scholarship that has emphasized the relationship of the family system to the larger environment with which it is embedded.

There are numerous systems concepts or properties. Three, in particular, are highlighted in terms of their relevance for families with adult boomerang children. The systems components of interdependence, permeability and hierarchy play important roles in understanding how messages are exchanged and events are experienced by parents and adult children (inside and outside of home). The first systems concept, interdependence, underscores the interconnectedness of two or more system parts in order for all parts to function properly. In short, system parts rely on each other to contribute something to the dyad or collective, in order for the overall system to operate smoothly. In regard to parent-child relationships, historically the majority of the contributions or inputs came from parents (Ambert, 2001), but parents often expect children to cooperate when requests are made of them inside of the home, as well as in many venues outside of the home (e.g., when in school or at work) in terms of completing chores or following rules.

When adult children return home, a level of interdependence surfaces that may be different than what was experienced previously by both parties. First, both parties may have significantly modified their behaviors while they have been living apart. For example, new hobbies may have been undertaken and previous routines may have changed. Furthermore, these changes may not be immediately recognizable by other parties (Thompson, Acock, & Clark, 1985). Successful communication becomes imperative for these dyads to navigate through potential adjustments in roles as well as rules (Hartung & Sweeney, 1991).

Although adult children may now be dependent financially and/or otherwise upon their parents, in some ways, there may be times where parents also feel dependent on their adult children. Historically, adult children living at home provided financial support or supplemented the family household budget (Ambert, 2001; Gelles, 1995; Mitchell, 2006). While financial support may still be sought by some parents when their adult children return home, there may be other support venues that are not linked to finances, such as companionship.

Permeability is an unusual systems concept because its properties can be applied to the overall system, as well as various subsystems. Permeability refers to how receptive the system is to receiving or sending information within the system as well as outside of the system. Typically, permeability is discussed in terms of families' willingness to keep messages within the parameters of the family unit or families' willingness to receive messages from outside the family unit, such as various media messages. However, the principles of permeability could also be applied to family subsystems. For instance, parent-child relationships may be influenced by what is occurring in other parent-child relationships, such as discussing whether or not a child can get a piercing when she is thirteen, when her friends' parents have let their children get their nose pierced at that age (Montemayor, 1986). In addition, parents and children may be very protective of information shared with one another and may want to keep those discussions limited to only them, such as conversations related to fears or anxieties either may be experiencing.

Although topics change as children get older, parent-adult child dyads continue to negotiate what conversations remain exclusive to the dyad, as well as how outside factors impact decision-making efforts for parents and adult children. In some instances, topics may be avoided altogether by parents and adult children. Roloff and Ifert (2000) noted that individuals may withhold complaints if they feel powerless or believe that the information they are contemplating sharing is relatively unimportant. Aquilino and Supple (1991) found that the ability of parents and their adult children to manage conflicts is important if continued self-disclosures between the two parties are to occur. There are many issues involved in determining how parents and adult children manage their conflicts, not the least of which may be whether or not they even choose to bring up the topic in the first place.

The third systems property, hierarchy, is demonstrated several ways in family relationships. The first application of hierarchy pertains to the ideas of suprasystems and subsystems, which has been explained earlier. Another aspect of hierarchy refers to elements of influence or status. In families, the typical hierarchical structure places parents over their children. While clearly both parties have influence, their abilities and strategies to get the other to comply with their wishes vary. For many parents, influence is maintained due to their financial resources. Since many adult children return home because of their limited financial resources, parents' "purse strings" may play an important role in adult child compliance.

Issues of family influence and status may change as both parties get older (Galvin et al., 2004; Mitchell, 2006). From a life span perspective, this is demonstrated as children progress from dependent-based roles to independent-based roles. When children are younger, it is logical and accepted for children to depend on their parents to have the majority of their needs met. While children can satisfy some of the needs of their parents, for love and reciprocal affection for example, in modern society, there is not the expectation that children should be meeting the financial needs of the family. However, as children get older, and start to become more independent from their parents, changes in expectations as well as influence over one another may change. Although adult children may have established some level of independence from their parents, the act of returning home implies that adult children are still somewhat dependent on their parents. This relational dynamic may not be desired by either or both parties. In addition, the degree of perceived dependence, much less whether or not this is considered a negative event, could vary based on the dyad.

Systems Theory and Internal/External Influences Hierarchy plays an interesting role in parent-adult child relationships. Over time, issues of relational hierarchy may change (Cooney & Uhlenberg, 1992), although issues of positional hierarchy would likely remain constant. Society, or for that matter, other family members, may have expectations about when (or whether) it is appropriate for parents and adult children to see themselves as "equals," especially when adult children are still living with their parents. As the age and potentially power status of family members change, the levels of influence could also change. In the case of parents and adult children, there may be greater opportunities to mutually influence one another than had been present at earlier points in parent-child relationships (Stafford & Dainton, 1995).

Issues of permeability are especially pertinent when it comes to how parties perceive themselves and their relationships (Guerrero & Afifi, 1995), as well as how their relationships are perceived by those outside of the dyad. How successful society or outsiders perceive adult children and their parents may also create stress for family members (Ambert, 2001). For example, if adult children enter highly regarded professional positions after graduation, outsiders typically label these adult children successful. There may also be a positive sponsorship effect for other family members (e.g., siblings, grandparents) due to another member's success. In addition, the adult children's success then might be associated with the parents' effective parenting practices. Anecdotal evidence suggests that others may be negatively judgmental towards both parents as well as their adult children when adult children return home after college since this could be an indicator that either or both parties has been unsuccessful in some way. Siblings could also experience a negative backlash as others' expectations of them change as well. Outsider perceptions could also impact how parents and adult children perceive themselves, as well as each other. Furthermore, the opinions generated about the relationship, either from within or outside of parent-adult child dyads, have the potential to generate strong emotions

(Guerrero & Andersen, 2000). Therefore, members of family dyads may filter what relational messages are shared outside of the family, as well as what messages members of the dyad are open to receiving from outside sources.

Golish (2000) noted that sometimes larger events outside of the parent-child relationships serve to bring parents and their adult children closer together. Martin (1986) reported that when adult children had returned from studying abroad, their relationships with their parents actually improved and members of the dyad actually felt closer to one another as a result of the child's participation in the study abroad program. This suggests that outside events in either the parents' or adult children's lives could actually provide a catalyst for bringing both parties closer together. Furthermore, this also underscores that the events themselves do not have to be negative in nature or in response to some type of catastrophic event.

Relational Dialectics Theory

The boomerang effect may be underscored with tension for both parents and their adult children. Relational dialectics theory focuses on the bilateral tensions present in close relationships. These tensions underlie the processes as well as contradictions between opposing forces (Baxter, 1988). The challenge is for relational partners to manage these opposing forces as their relationships encounter both internal and external factors that could rock the balance presently occurring in their relationships. Three relational dialectics: autonomy-connection, openness-closedness, and predictability-novelty have been used extensively in relational dialectic scholarship (Baxter & Simon, 1993; Montgomery, 1993) and are examined in parent-adult child relationships.

Theoretical Overview   The first relational dialectic, autonomy-connection, highlights the tensions present when individuals strive to be separate from one another, while simultaneously wanting to maintain some degree of connection. In families, this dialectic may take several different forms. Typically, it has been examined from a developmental or life span perspective, with the emphasis placed on the period of adolescence. During adolescence, there tends to be regular opportunities for children to work towards establishing a level of separation from their parents. This may start with behavioral challenges, such as clothing selections, and expand to tests of family values, in an effort to disengage from the family and develop a level of autonomy from the family unit (Montemayor, 1986). The challenges facing parents and adult children when adult children return home range from issues that are acceptable for disagreement or autonomy, and where each party seeks to stay connected to the other. Unfortunately, neither parents nor children are often able to clearly articulate where they are flexible and where they are more conservative when it comes to areas of separation and areas of togetherness.

The second relational dialectic, openness-closedness pertains to what is shared between family members as well as what is revealed to others (Baxter, 1988). Typically, openness and closedness is examined in terms of self-disclosure. Individuals examine what is talked about, to whom, and the degree of intimacy of the self-disclosure. Some challenges inherent within this dialectic center on the topics discussed between parents and children. What topics does each group feel comfortable discussing? Are there any topics that would be considered taboo? In addition, topic selection will probably vary based on the age of the child. This may be due to content-related features (e.g., discussing pornography) or due to the desire to protect children against worry (e.g., discussing financial matters).

Over time, the number of topics discussed, as well as the degree of self-disclosure during conversations may vary. Taking a life span perspective, research (e.g., Guerrero & Afifi, 1995) suggests that during adolescence, the number of topics discussed between parents and adolescents tends to decline, as does the overall level of self-disclosure. However, as children get older, both the number of topics and the degree of detail present in conversations tends to increase. However, events both inside and outside the family may influence how expansive or limiting conversations are between parents and their adult children. While the dialectic of openness-closedness could be expanded to include society at large, in most instances, the focus has been on the dyad.

The final relational dialectic, predictability-novelty, focuses on the degree of routine present within relationships (Baxter, 1988). In families, this often presents itself in terms of expectations for either parents or children. In most instances, both parties want to be able to count on each other to perform certain duties on a regular basis. When this is not done, the potential for conflict in parent-child relationships increases. However, challenges may be incurred when either or both parties starts to get bored with one another. Excess routine or predictability may lead children and perhaps their parents as well, into feeling that the relationship is stagnating or dull.

Routines tend to create a sense of normalcy or comfort for people because there is no need to guess what is likely to occur on a daily basis (Kiser, Bennett, Heston, & Paavola, 2005). Patterns enable individuals to set up schedules to facilitate multitasking throughout the duties of work and home. In fact, as children get older, the need for predictability may become so strong that parents and children actually designate time to make sure they can interact on a regular basis; for fear that otherwise, in the rapid pace of daily living, this may not occur. Little is known about the type of patterns that are expected or desired from parents and their adult children. In many respects, predictability may be associated with performing predetermined roles for the household. In this instance, high predictability may be desired by both parties. Yet, spontaneity or novelty may also have to be negotiated in advance. Understanding when there is flexibility in terms of expectations or roles is important to ensure that neither party feels taken advantage of nor trapped in an excessively rule-based living situation.

Relational Dialectics and Internal/External Influences   There are numerous needs, obligations, and tensions for parents and adult children that may need to be addressed when adult children return home. When examined within the context of the three relational dialectics listed above, several internal and external factors surface when the boomerang effect occurs. Bell, Allen, Hauser, and O'Connor (1996) examined the role of autonomy during young adult transitions. These researchers found that "the opportunity to develop autonomy in a family context seems to be key for later career success" (p. 360). However, some boomerang children have not yet gained autonomy from their parents, perhaps at several levels, such as financial dependence, psychological dependence, or emotional dependence. Adult children's over-reliance on their parents could prove to be problematic for both parties. Some have referred to this phenomenon as an incomplete launching of children (Gelles, 1995). Essentially, the adult children have not yet gained enough autonomy to successfully manage on their own outside of the family.

This dialectical tension may only increase when outside influences are taken into consideration. What are society's expectations associated with adult children trying to attain financial independence, while simultaneously remaining connected to their parents? Furthermore, what happens when one or both parties do not want or desire autonomy? Is this an indication to others that there were some parenting problems? Or, are the adult children simply taking advantage of their parents (El Nasser, 2005)? Cultural influences could also impact how this dialectic is demonstrated in parent-adult child relationships. It may be normative, if not explicitly expected for adult children to move out of the family home to establish their own residences in some cultures, such as Sweden or Canada. In other cultures, the expectations may actually be reversed, with assumptions that individuals will live in the family residence much longer (e.g., Italy; Mitchell, 2006). There may also be different expectations based on family structure, the sex of the child, or the relationships adult children have with their parents (Eggebeen, 2005; Mitchell, 2006; Schwarz, Trommsdorff, Albert, & Mayer, 2005).

The dialectical tension openness-closedness may provide insights into the type of disclosures held or withheld between parents and adult children (Guerrero & Afifi, 1995). It is unclear what issues parents and their adult children feel comfortable discussing amongst themselves or with others regarding their new living arrangement. Gelles (1995) noted that the realities of today's family life are often hidden from outsiders, and sometimes between other family members as well. Would this new living arrangement be considered a private topic of conversation and be closed off to discussions with other family members or outsiders, or would their new living situation be openly accepted and discussed in front of others? Would the level of disclosure suggest the degree of comfort or conflict both parents and their adult children had with the new living arrangement? The levels of disclosure displayed by both parents and their adult children may also provide clues towards the emotions being experienced by both parties (Guerrero & Andersen, 2000) during this particular relational event.

The third relational dialectic, predictability-novelty could offer insights to the changes being experienced by both parties (Baxter, 1988). The boomerang effect may force a merging of both the past and present for parents and adult children. Both parties have a past frame of reference that could shape their behaviors. For example, when growing up, the child always mowed the lawn for the family. Therefore, it may be assumed that when the adult child returns home, he/she would automatically help with any yard work. However, while some role expectations may still be relevant for adult children and parents, changes may have occurred making previous role contributions less significant or appropriate (e.g., the adult child works hours that make it difficult to do yard work).

Finally, new patterns have had a chance to develop for both parents and their adult children since the child initially left home. How will these new patterns be able to be maintained? Or will these new behaviors be considered inconsistent, or novel, with what has been traditionally expected and will adult children as well as parents be encouraged to revert back to behaviors demonstrated when they were younger, since these patterns are more predictable (Clemens & Axelson, 1985)? Scholars have suggested including more novel activities in order to improve emotional exchanges and to keep relationships from becoming stagnant (Guerrero & Andersen, 2000). Yet, it remains to be seen if such recommendations could apply to parent–adult child relationships when adult children return home as they do to marital couples.

Social Exchange Theories

Gelles (1995) noted that the use of social exchange frameworks has been one of the fastest growing perspectives for studying families. In brief, social exchange perspectives hold several assumptions: (a) social behaviors include a series of exchanges, where individuals try to maximize the benefits they receive and minimize the costs; (b) at times, individuals will acknowledge certain costs in order to receive certain rewards; and (c) reciprocity plays an important part when individuals receive rewards from other; in short, these individuals are obligated to provide benefits back to the other party in the exchange (Gelles, 1995; Klein & White, 1996). Next, social exchange theories are examined as an overview of the communicative exchanges present between parents and adult children when the boomerang effect occurs.

Theoretical Overview   Social exchange theories emphasize perceptions of rewards and costs by relational partners (Stamp, 2004). Over time, relational partners seek to have their rewards exceed their costs. As a result, it is common to utilize a simple equation: perceived rewards minus perceived costs equals net profit or loss. While some "exchanges" may lead to immediate gains (that are short- or long-term), there are also other exchanges that could lead to immediate losses (that are short- or long-term) as well. The rewards and costs exchanged between relational partners could range from tangible goods and services, such as money or gifts, to intangible offerings, such as affection, support, or kindness (Thibaut & Kelley, 1959). It is important to remember that perceptions of rewards and costs are subjective, and may need to be negotiated between relational partners to account for perceptual discrepancies.

Assessing rewards and costs in parent-child relationships is complicated, since there are many assumptions, especially for parents, regarding the type of costs that come with the territory of being a parent. "It is taken for granted that *parents* affect their children rather than vice versa; it is also taken for granted that parents have to take care of their children ... it is not generally considered socially proper for parents to admit that they have problems with their children or that their children are affecting them negatively. Many parents, because of this ideology, do not even dare to admit this negative effect to themselves" (Ambert, 2001, p. 68). In other instances, parents may be unclear what their role should be in regard to their adult children. Therefore, parents may be hesitant in terms of how they should provide or refrain from offering support (Eggebeen, 2005). When grandchildren are added to the parent-adult child dynamic, uncertainty may be heightened for all parties. Aquilino (1999) noted that parents tend to view their relationships with their adult children in more positive terms that their adult children do. Whether this is due to parental bias, or societal expectations, is unclear.

Equity theory, a theoretical subset of social exchange theories, applies the fundamental assumptions of exchange theories, however, greater emphasis is placed on the role of reciprocity, shared comparable exchanges, and balanced rewards and costs ratios for both parties (Adams, 1965). When the ratios between relational parties are balanced, the relationship is considered equitable, when parties benefit more, these relational partners are considered to be overbenefited, and when parties endure more costs, these relational partners are considered to be underbenefited (Adams, 1965).

Researchers have applied equity theory to parent–child relationships (Vogl-Bauer, Kalbfleisch, & Beatty, 1999). Vogl-Bauer et al. (1999) hypothesized that parent-child relationships would become more equitable as children grew older and that children would contribute comparably to the relational maintenance needs of parent-child dyads. However, these researchers found that when adolescents were approximately 16–17 years old, they were still willing to be overbenefited in their relationships with their parents (Vogl-Bauer et al., 1999). Essentially, it was okay for parents to do more work and contribute more to the relational maintenance of parent-child dyads than their adolescent children. Yet, in the case of boomerang adult children, the relational dynamics may change since (a) adult children are now older, and (b) parents may be less willing to do as much for their children. As a result, these relationships could attain greater levels of equity than earlier in the life span.

Social Exchange Theories and Internal/External Influences   As noted earlier, perceptions of what are considered rewards and costs could vary for parents and their adult children. In fact, (a) both parties may view adult children returning home as very rewarding, (b) some parties may view the return as positive and rewarding, while other parties do not, or (c) both parties may consider the return home to be costly (Mitchell, 2006). In addition, outsiders may view the rewards and costs for parents and adult children differently. Some may see adult children returning home as a good thing for parents and their adult children, while others may see it in terms of some degree of failure on the part of the parents and/or children. These opinions could be expressed in the positive or negative emotional expressions exchanged within internal communications between parents and their adult children, as well as during exchanges held with individuals outside of the parent-adult child dyad (Guerrero & Andersen, 2000).

The roles that parents and children undertake may also be considered in terms of their rewards and costs. Some parents as well as adult children may find themselves unwilling to return to roles that they had once undertaken when adult children were younger (Clemens & Axelson, 1985). Conversely, some parents and children may now be more willing or able to discuss issues that were once problematic earlier in parent-child relationships (Golish, 2000). In this case, the role of equity theory may come into play, where both parties perceive their reward/cost ratios in a more comparable fashion.

Communication Privacy Management Theory

Communication privacy management theory focuses on how individuals establish and maintain boundaries between themselves and others. Petronio (2000) summarized this as "the intersection of boundary structures and rule based management systems" (p. 38). Individuals make these decisions by (a) assessing ownership rights to the information, (b) controlling the risks and responsibilities associated with disclosures, in terms of what is revealed and concealed, and then ultimately, (c) determining the level of disclosure to use during interactions (Petronio, 2000). In simplistic terms, the emphasis is placed on what is open or public between family members, as well as to society and outsiders, and what is private. Communication privacy management theory is the final theory overviewed for its potential to examine communication exchanges between parents and adult children when the boomerang effect occurs.

Theoretical Overview Communication privacy management theory emphasizes three factors in relation to privacy issues. First, disclosing and withholding information is necessary for family functioning. Deciding what information to share with other family members and what to hold back is a part of daily family functions. Disclosing information to others in your family helps maintain as well as enhance existing family bonds. Second, disclosing and/or withholding information has the potential to be beneficial as well as problematic for family members; therefore, it is important to make the appropriate choices. There may be extensive decision making done on the part of one or more family members when determining whether or not to share information. In these instances, there is clear intentionality being displayed by family members. Yet, some family disclosures could be unintentional in nature, or perhaps the consequences of the disclosure were unanticipated. Third, issues of privacy can be present within families themselves (Caughlin & Petronio,

2004). Within the realm of privacy research, there is a subarea focusing on family secrets (Vangelisti, Caughlin, & Timmerman, 2001). There are many criteria to consider when revealing family secrets; determining whether or not to disclose a secret entails numerous factors that may vary by family (Vangelisti et al., 2001). Some family secrets are messages that do not leave the boundaries of the immediate family. However, other family secrets are only intended to be shared with particular family members. Gelles noted, "We have superficial knowledge of other people's families and limited knowledge of our own" (1995, p. 4).

It becomes important for dialogue to occur between parents and their adult children so that there is a shared level of agreement on how issues are managed and communicated between themselves, other family members, and perhaps individuals outside of the family. To successfully manage communication boundaries, both parties need to feel comfortable and agree with the parameters set (Petronio, 2000). Varying degrees of negotiation may need to occur depending on whether the issues are related to the coverage of financial obligations or who does what in the family unit. Yet, as noted earlier, discussing financial issues and household responsibilities may be uncomfortable for either or both parties. Failure to talk about these matters may complicate preexisting relational issues, making it more difficult for parents and adult children to live together.

Communication Privacy Management and Internal/External Influences   There may be a range of privacy management and privacy violation issues between parents and their adult children. Topics could range from violations of physical space, violations pertaining to public versus private behaviors (Mitchell & Gee, 1996), and violations linked to the content of message exchanges (Guerrero & Afifi, 1995). At first glance, it may appear that the primary communication privacy violators in parent-adult child relationships would be parents. There have been plenty of television portrayals of the nosey parent snooping into their adult child's business. But it is equally possible that the reverse could happen: the adult child is violating the parent's boundaries. It would be unfair to assume that parents do not have information that they wish to withhold from their adult children as well.

Communication privacy management theory may also help identify the role outside influences play in the relational dynamics of parent-adult child dyads. When do parents and adult children care and respond to what others think, at the risk of violating another's wishes? When might parents and adult children care too much—or not enough? It has been noted that individuals may be more sensitive to strangers than they are to their fellow family members (Galvin et al., 2004). Communication privacy management theory offers a theoretical framework for exploring the dynamics underscoring this type of relational maintenance or transgression behavior.

Closing Remarks

In this chapter, the boomerang effect was examined as a very real event that occurs in U.S. families across the country. Mitchell (2006) noted, "... life course and living arrangement transitions are not always permanent and are highly fluid in modern society" (p. 62). Although it is known that adult children are increasingly returning to live at home after college graduation, there has only been marginal coverage given by communication scholars to the issues facing parent-adult child dyads, and the factors that could shape how successfully or problematic these events are for parents, their adult children, and offspring. Four theoretical perspectives provide different insights into the role that internal and external messages could play in parent-adult child dialogues so that the successful transition of this event could occur for both parents and their adult children.

Scholars have advocated for a bidirectional approach to parent-child communication (Stafford & Bayer, 1993). This recommendation is warranted since it is clear that adult children are impacted when they return home to their parents' residences, and that parents are equally impacted by their adult children's return as well. Learning how both parties adjust to this life stage change should be mutually beneficial. Indications are that the boomerang effect may become a more typical stage for future young adults (Ramachandran, 2005). Family communication scholars have an opportunity to enhance understanding of this life stage event and offer ways to make this adjustment positive for both parties.

References

Adams, J. S. (1965). Inequity in social exchange. In L. Berkowitz (Ed.), *Advances in experimental social psychology volume 2* (pp. 267–300). New York: Academic Press.

Ambert, A. (2001). *The effect of children on parents* (2nd ed.). New York: The Haworth Press.

Aquilino, W. S. (1999). Two views of one relationship: Comparing parents' and young adult children's reports of the quality of intergenerational relations. *Journal of Marriage and the Family, 61,* 858–870.

Aquilino, W. S., & Supple, K. R. (1991). Parent-child relations and parent's satisfaction with living arrangements when adult children live at home. *Journal of Marriage and the Family, 53,* 13–27.

Baxter, L. A. (1988). A dialectical perspective on communication strategies in relationship development. In S. Duck (Ed.), *Handbook of personal relationships: Theory, research, and interventions* (pp. 257–273). Chichester, England: Wiley.

Baxter, L. A., & Simon, E. P. (1993). Relationship maintenance strategies and dialectical contradictions in personal relationships. *Journal of Social and Personal Relationships, 10,* 225–242.

Bell, K. L., Allen, J. P., Hauser, S. T., & O'Connor, T. G. (1996). Family factors and young adult transitions: Educational attainment and occupational prestige. In J. A. Graber, J. Brooks-Gunn, & A. C. Petersen (Eds.), *Transitions through adolescence: Interpersonal domains and contexts* (pp. 345–366). Mahwah, NJ: Erlbaum.

Caughlin, J. P., & Petronio, S. (2004). Privacy in families. In A. L. Vangelisti (Ed.), *Handbook of family communication* (pp. 379–412). Mahwah, NJ: Erlbaum.

Clemens, A. W., & Axelson, L. J. (1985). The not-so-empty-nest: The return of the fledging adult. *Family Relations, 34,* 259–264.

Cooney, T. M., & Uhlenberg, P. (1992). Support from parents over the life course: The adult child's perspective. *Social Forces, 71,* 63–84.

Eggebeen, D. J. (2005). Cohabitation and exchanges of support. *Social Forces, 83,* 1097–1110.

El Nasser, H. (2005, January 11). Why grown kids come home: High rents, college loans drive 'boomerang kids' back to nest. *USA Today,* News, 1a.

Galvin, K. M. (2004). The family of the future: What do we face? In A. L. Vangelisti (Ed.), *Handbook of family communication* (pp. 675–697). Mahwah, NJ: Erlbaum.

Galvin, K. M., Bylund, C. L., & Brommel, B. J. (2004). *Family communication: Cohesion and change* (6th ed.). New York: Longman.

Gelles, R. J. (1995). *Contemporary families: A sociological view.* Thousand Oaks, CA: Sage.

Golish, T. D. (2000). Changes in closeness between adult children and their parents: A turning point analysis. *Communication Reports, 13,* 79–97.

Goodnow, J. J., Bowes, J. M., Warton, P. M., Dawes, L. J., & Taylor, A. J. (1991). Would you ask someone else to do this task?: Parents' and children's ideas about household work requests. *Developmental Psychology, 27,* 817–828.

Goodnow, J. J., & Lawrence, J. A. (2001). Work contributions to the family: Developing a conceptual and research framework. *New Directions for Child and Adolescent Development, 94,* 5–22.

Guerrero, L. K., & Afifi, W. A. (1995). What parents don't know: Topic avoidance in parent-child relationships. In T. J. Socha & G. H. Stamp (Eds.), *Parents, children, and communication: Frontiers of theory and research* (pp. 219–245). Mahwah, NJ: Erlbaum.

Guerrero, L. K., & Andersen, P. A. (2000). Emotion in close relationships. In C. Hendrick, & S. Hendrick (Eds.), *Close relationships: A sourcebook* (pp. 171–183). Thousand Oaks, CA: Sage.

Hartung, B., & Sweeney, K. (1991). Why adult children return home. *Social Science Journal, 28,* 467–480.

Holdsworth, C. (2004). Family support during the transition out of the parental home in Britain, Spain and Norway. *Sociology, 38,* 909–926.

Kelley, R. (2007, April 9). Expert advice: Love by the numbers. *Newsweek, 149*(15), 48.

Kiser, L. J., Bennett, L., Heston, J., & Paavola, M. (2005). Family ritual and routine: Comparison of clinical and non-clinical families. *Journal of Child and Family Studies, 14,* 357–372.

Klein, D. M., & White, J. M. (1996). *Family theories: An introduction.* Thousand Oaks, CA: Sage.

Lim, V. K. G., & Si Sng, Q. (2006). Does parental job insecurity matter?: Money anxiety, money motives, and work motivation. *Journal of Applied Psychology, 91,* 1078–1087.

Lott, J. K. (1986). Freshmen home reentry: Attending to a gap in student development. *Journal of Counseling and Development, 64,* 456.

Martin, J. N. (1986). Patterns of communication in three types of reentry relationships: An exploratory study. *Western Journal of Speech Communication, 50,* 183–199.

Mitchell, B. A. (1998). Too close for comfort?: Parental assessments of "boomerang kid" living arrangements. *Canadian Journal of Sociology, 23*, 21–46.

Mitchell, B. A. (2006). *The boomerang age: Transitions to adulthood in families.* New Brunswick, NJ: AldineTransaction.

Mitchell, B. A., & Gee, E. M. (1996). "Boomerang kids" and midlife parental marita lsatisfaction. *Family Relations, 45*, 442–448.

Montemayor, R. (1986). Developing autonomy: The transition of youth into adulthood. In G. K. Leigh & G. W. Peterson (Eds.), *Adolescents in families* (pp. 205–225). Cincinnati, OH: South-Western Publishing.

Montgomery, B. M. (1993). Relationship maintenance versus relationship change: A dialectical dilemma. *Journal of Social and Personal Relationships, 10*, 205–224.

Noller, P., & Fitzpatrick, M. A. (1993). *Communication in family relationships.* Englewood Cliffs, NJ: Prentice Hall.

Peterson, G. W. (1986). Family conceptual frameworks and adolescent development. In G. K. Leigh & G. W. Peterson (Eds.), *Adolescents in families* (pp. 12–36). Cincinnati, OH: South-Western Publishing.

Petronio, S. (2000). The boundaries of privacy: Praxis of everyday life. In S. Petronio (Ed.), *Balancing the secrets of private disclosures* (pp. 37–49). Mahwah, NJ: Erlbaum.

Pillemer, K., Suitor, J. J., Mock, S. E., Sabir, M., Pardo, T. B., & Sechrist, J. (2007). Capturing the complexity of intergenerational relations: Exploring ambivalence within later-life families. *Journal of Social Issues, 63*, 775–791.

Quinn, J. B. (1993, April 5). What's for dinner, mom?: Many boomerang kids have the money to support themselves, but at the moment would rather not. *Newsweek, 121*(14), 68.

Ramachandran, N. (2005, December 12). The parent trap: Boomerang kids. When 20-somethings come home, families need some frank talk about finances to stay within budget. *U.S. News & World Report, 139* (22), 64.

Roloff, M. E., & Ifert, D. E. (2000). Conflict management through avoidance: Withholding complaints, suppressing arguments, and declaring topics taboo. In S. Petronio (Ed.), *Balancing the secrets of private disclosures* (pp. 151–163). Mahwah, NJ: Erlbaum.

Schwarz, B., Trommsdorff, G., Albert, I., & Mayer, B. (2005). Adult parent-child relationships: Relationship quality, support, and reciprocity. *Applied Psychology: An International Review, 54*, 396–417.

Stafford, L., & Bayer, C. L. (1993). *Interaction between parents and children.* Newbury Park, CA: Sage.

Stafford, L., & Dainton, M. (1995). Parent-child communication within the family system. In T. J. Socha & G. H. Stamp (Eds.), *Parents, children, and communication: Frontiers of theory and research* (pp. 3–21). Mahwah, NJ: Erlbaum.

Stamp, G. H. (2004). Theories of family relationships and a family relationships theoretical model. In A. L. Vangelisti (Ed.), *Handbook of family communication* (pp. 1–30). Mahwah, NJ: Erlbaum.

Thibaut, J. W., & Kelley, H. H. (1959). *The social psychology of groups.* New York: Wiley.

Thompson, L., Acock, A. C., & Clark, K. (1985). Do parents know their children?: The ability of mothers and fathers to gauge the attitudes of their young adult children. *Family Relations, 34*, 315–320.

Vangelisti, A. L., Caughlin, J. P., & Timmerman, L. (2001). Criteria for revealing family secrets. *Communication Monographs, 68*, 1–27.

Vogl-Bauer, S., Kalbfleisch, P. J., & Beatty, M. J. (1999). Perceived equity, satisfaction, and relational maintenance strategies in parent–adolescent dyads. *Journal of Youth and Adolescence, 28,* 27–49.

Wilcox, M. D., & Snow, C. (1992, October). Boomerang kids: Just when you thought it was safe to relax … they're back. *Kiplinger's Personal Finance Magazine, 46*(10), 83–86.

18 Stepfamilies Interacting Outside the Home

Barriers to Stepparent/Stepchild Communication with Educational, Medical, and Legal Personnel

Amy Janan Johnson, Elizabeth A. Craig,
Michel M. Haigh, Eileen S. Gilchrist,
Lindsay T. Lane, and Nakia S. Welch

When considering how parents and children communicate with parties outside the home, communication with stepparents has become part of the process for many children. In half of new marriages, at least one partner has been married previously (U.S. Bureau of the Census, 2000). Sixty-five percent of these households contain children from a prior relationship, making them a stepfamily (Marano, 2000). Current estimates suggest that one third of children will live with a stepparent before they turn 18; however, this figure does not include children who may interact with stepparents while visiting a non-custodial parent (Visher, Visher, & Pasley, 2003). Even though many stepparents act as parental figures to their stepchildren (Church, 1999), there are legal and social barriers that hamper their ability to enact this role. These barriers are particularly apparent in the communication process between stepparents, stepchildren, and social entities outside the household, such as educational, medical, and legal personnel.

Composed of more than one household of former and current partners linked by children, stepfamilies have permeable boundaries (Visher & Visher, 1978). Little research has examined how these individuals communicate across these linked households (Coleman, Ganong, & Fine, 2000; for an exception see Braithwaite, McBride, & Schrodt, 2003), much less how they communicate with social entities outside the family. Communication between households further complicates the process of interacting with medical, educational, or legal personnel who may have to interact with two households in regards to one particular child.

Why is the stepparent's role important when examining parent/child communication with individuals outside the home? Many stepparents play an active role in their stepchildren's lives, although they are usually not as involved as the biological parents (Coleman et al., 2000). Stepparents provide childcare (Guisinger, Cowan, & Schuldberg, 1989), support their stepchildren financially

(Ganong, Coleman, & Mistina, 1995), and sometimes provide insurance for their stepchildren (Mason & Simon, 1995). For example, stepchildren can even receive Social Security benefits if their residential stepparent dies. By not taking the stepparent into consideration, several negative outcomes can result. It can weaken the tie between the stepparents and stepchildren if stepparents are discouraged to participate in the child's outside activities. It can cause stress for stepparents because they may feel as if their needs are not being taken into consideration (Gately, Pike, & Murphy, 2005). Not including the stepparent in this communicative process can also lead to instability in the remarriage, as remarried couples report more conflict, often related to stepchildren (Hobart, 1991).

This chapter will highlight two conflicting themes related to how stepparents and stepchildren communicate with individuals outside their household. First, through stigmatization and failure to define stepfamily roles, society encourages the stepfamily to interact and present themselves as a nuclear family with the stepparent playing a parental role (Ganong, Coleman, & Kennedy, 1990). However, the stepparent is a "legal stranger" (Mahoney, 1995) to his or her stepchildren. This lack of legal tie hinders the enactment of this parental role and limits the ability of stepparents and stepchildren to interact with individuals outside the household. To examine these barriers for stepfamilies, three contexts will be examined: the education, medical, and legal settings. Implications of these barriers for the stepparent/stepchild relationship and the health of the stepfamily will be discussed. The need for research from a communication perspective will be emphasized, and important questions in need of examination will be posited. First, two theoretical perspectives that illuminate the difficulties that stepfamilies encounter when interacting with individuals outside their household will be presented.

Theoretical Perspectives Related to Stepfamily Communication Outside the Household

Ganong and Coleman (2004) discuss two cultural views of stepfamilies: as an incomplete institution (Cherlin, 1978) and as socially stigmatized (Ganong & Coleman, 1997a). Both of these views illustrate the unique difficulties that stepparents and stepchildren encounter when communicating with social entities outside the household.

Cherlin (1978) claims that stepfamilies are incompletely institutionalized. Our society does not give these families sufficient support because it assumes that a remarried family is equivalent to a nuclear, first marriage family. This assumption is historically based: until the 1970s, most stepfamilies were formed through the death of one parent (Cherlin, 1992). Thus, the stepparent often "took the parent's place." However, the great majority of current stepfamilies (more than 80%) are formed from divorce, rendering the stepparent's role unclear (Cherlin, 1992), especially if the nonresidential biological parent remains involved.

To be "incompletely institutionalized" causes everyday life to be more difficult for stepfamilies, potentially leading to more chances for conflict. Individuals must negotiate their roles in such a manner that the family can interact successfully within the family system and with the outside environment. Many stepparents utilize the biological parental role as the basis for their role (e.g., Church, 1999), although other potential roles include "friend" or "aunt/uncle" (Fine, Coleman, & Ganong, 1998). What role is negotiated for the stepparent will affect how active the stepparent is in communicating with entities outside the home.

As there is no clearly defined stepparent role, the stepparent and his or her influence on the stepchildren are rendered invisible. One setting where the stepparent's influence is mostly ignored is the legal system. The legal relationship between stepparents and stepchildren is complicated and varies across states, but for the most part, they are considered "legal strangers" (for a review, see Mahoney, 1995). Especially at the state level, there is little to no recognition of the role that the stepparent plays in the child's life. Without this legal parental role, the stepparent does not have the right to make decisions for the stepchild in many areas. For instance, stepparents are usually not allowed to give permission for nonemergency medical treatment for their stepchildren (Berger & the Committee on Medical Liability, 2003) or even for their stepchild to go on a school fieldtrip (Stenger, 1986). Although adoption by the stepparent provides legal recognition for a parental role, this option is infeasible for many stepfamilies as the noncustodial parent must approve severing parental rights and responsibilities or must have deserted the child (Mason, Harrison-Jay, Svare, & Wolfinger, 2002). Having no clearly defined legal role limits stepparents' abilities to interact with third parties concerning their stepchildren.

A second cultural view of stepfamilies, the social stigma hypothesis, also affects how stepparents and stepchildren communicate with outside parties. This view claims "that stepparenthood is a widely known social category that triggers generally negative expectations and perceived attributes" (Coleman, Ganong, & Cable, 1996, p. 27). Individuals expect stepparents, especially stepmothers, to be "harsher" to stepchildren (Coleman et al., 1996). Third parties with whom the stepparent and stepchild are likely to interact, such as school personnel (Bryan, Ganong, Coleman, & Bryan, 1985) and nurses (Ganong & Coleman, 1997b), report negative stereotypes of stepparents and stepchildren. As individuals desire to avoid associating themselves with a stigmatized status (Jones, 2004), the family may hide that they are a stepfamily and seek to "pass" as a nuclear family (Dainton, 1993).

"Passing" as a nuclear family can lead to problems for the stepfamily. First, it denies that children may have closer ties to family members outside their residential household. It discourages a continued relationship with the noncustodial parent when contact with noncustodial parents has been linked to positive outcomes for children of divorce (Maccoby & Mnookin, 1992). Also, clinicians cite stepparents taking a parental role too early in the stepfamily's history as one main source of stepparent/stepchild conflict (Visher & Visher, 1979). Passing as a nuclear family also contributes to the societal invisibility of stepparents and reduces the ability of stepfamilies to obtain social support (Ganong & Coleman, 1997a). This invisibility reduces the perceived need for social agencies to determine how to appropriately communicate with stepparents and stepchildren. A stepfamily "passing" as a nuclear family can even lead to problems for the outside social entities. A school system can lose federal funds if it does not provide nonresidential parents with access to the child's records (Crosbie-Burnett, 1994). If a stepparent does not tell medical personnel that he or she is not the stepchild's "legal representative," the medical institution could be sued for performing nonemergency procedures with only the stepparent's permission (Berger & the Committee on Medical Liability, 2003).

In summary, these two perspectives on stepfamilies, the incomplete institution hypothesis (Cherlin, 1978) and the social stigma hypothesis (Ganong & Coleman, 1997a), illustrate two conflicting themes communicated to stepfamilies: stepparents are encouraged by society's stigmatized view of stepfamilies and lack of stepparent role definition to play a parental role and present themselves as parental figures for their stepchildren, but in many situations there are legal barriers to enacting this role. The next section of this chapter explores how these two themes are illustrated in the literature examining how stepparents and stepchildren interact with educational, medical, and legal personnel.

Interacting with Educational Personnel

Crosbie-Burnett (1994) suggested that schools are the second "most influential institution" for children after the family (p. 215). The ability of stepfamilies to successfully interact with educational personnel is important. Stepchildren perform worse than children from nuclear families on several academic factors (Nord & West, 1996), including having lower grade point averages (Coffman & Roark, 1992). Although these discrepancies are mostly explained by differences in socioeconomic status (Pong, 1997), less parental involvement of remarried couples has also been fingered as a partial explanation (Zill, 1996). Stepparents are less likely to be involved in school activities than are biological parents (Nord & West, 1996), even though stepparents have been found to play an active role in the child's education. For example, Mason et al. (2002) found "stepparents and biological parents put in a similar number of hours per week helping with homework" (p. 513). Ultimately, ignoring additional parental figures cheats stepchildren of all the support and help they could receive for their education (Crosbie-Burnett, 1994).

In seeking to encourage both parental and stepparental involvement for children of divorce, school personnel face several issues. For example, the lack of legal relationship between stepparent and stepchild affects their interaction with educational personnel. Schools are required to interact with the two legal parents. As the stepparent is not the child's legal parental representative (except in the case of adoption), stepparents do not have the legal right to give permission for the stepchild to go on fieldtrips, to sign medical emergency release forms, to sign report cards, or to view their stepchild's school records (Stenger, 1986).

A second roadblock for interaction between remarried families and schools are school policies based on the nuclear family with little leeway for more than two individuals to play a parental role (Crosbie-Burnett, 1994). A two-parent model applied to stepfamilies results in two potential outcomes: (a) the stepparent is invisible or (b) the stepparent is treated as a biological parent and the noncustodial biological parent becomes invisible (Crosbie-Burnett, 1994). Assuming that a remarried family is no different from a nuclear family leads to the assumption that no special accommodations are needed for stepfamilies (Crosbie-Burnett, 1994). However, there are issues unique to stepfamilies of which educational personnel need to be aware. For example, Midkiff and Lawler-Prince (1992) recommend that teachers determine whether parental figures of the children have the same last name as the child to avoid embarrassing mistakes caused by assuming a nuclear family form. School personnel should also be careful to use the correct terminology when referring to a stepparent, instead of assuming that any adult figure with the child is the father or mother (Pasley & Ihinger-Tallman, 1986). Stepparents may feel left out or ignored at such events as graduations and school plays (Wood & Poole, 1983), or classroom projects related to Mother's Day or Father's Day may result in uncomfortable situations for stepchildren or children from single-parent families (Coleman, Ganong, & Henry, 1984).

A third factor that inhibits communication between remarried families and schools is society's stigmatized view of stepfamilies. Some educational personnel share these stigmatized views. Certain teachers and counselors have negative stereotypes about stepfamilies and stepchildren (Guttman & Broudo, 1988–1989). For example, Bryan et al. (1985) found that counselors rated vignettes portraying stepfamilies in a more negative manner than those portraying nuclear families. A stigmatized view of stepfamilies can discourage the stepfamily from participating in the school environment. Lutz, Jacobs, and Masson (1988) found that both stepparents and nonresidential parents complained about how school personnel treated them. Stepfamilies report less face-to-face interaction with teachers compared to nuclear families or single parents (Crosbie-Burnett & Skyles, 1989). However, these studies are dated and should be replicated.

A fourth impediment to interaction between stepfamilies and school personnel relates to the structure of remarried and divorced families. A lack of understanding by the school setting that the stepchild lives in two households may lead to confusion. For example, stepfamilies may miss school notices which are sent on Fridays when the child is traveling to the noncustodial household. In addition, if the stepfamily is noncustodial, they may not automatically receive access to school records (Coleman et al., 1984), although legally, schools must provide noncustodial parents with copies of their children's records (Crosbie-Burnett, 1994).

In addition, Coffman and Roark (1992) found that members of stepfamilies were less likely to participate in extra-curricular activities because of these structural issues. Remarried spouses have time constraints which nuclear families may not, as they are more likely to both work outside the home (Coleman & Ganong, 1989) and may have other extra responsibilities such as child transportation between two households (Ganong, 1993). Visitation and custody agreements may affect stepchildren's ability to participate in extracurricular activities and may necessitate frequent absences. Stepfamilies may need to negotiate who will attend extracurricular activities and often must interact with members of the other biological parent's household at these events (Nord & West, 1996). If there is not a good relationship between the households, individuals may avoid these settings, or conflict may result (Papernow, 1993).

Ganong's (1993) examination of 4-H clubs illustrates how extracurricular educational activities are often not designed to meet the unique needs of stepfamilies. Most 4-H personnel expressed the belief that there was no need to treat stepfamilies different from others or to provide special policies for them. They were reluctant to ask children whether they were members of stepfamilies as they deemed this information too personal and not important. However, remarried families were more likely to report that they stopped participating in 4-H due to scheduling conflicts and being unable to attend required meetings.

By being aware of these circumstances that restrict stepparent/school interaction, educational personnel can more successfully address this issue. From this review of research, one method for improving interaction with stepfamilies is for educational personnel to treat the stepparent as an additional parental figure rather than a replacement for the noncustodial parental figure (Crosbie-Burnett, 1994). In addition, educational personnel may need further information regarding the unique needs of stepfamilies. Shea (1990) found that the majority of special education teachers claimed that their undergraduate education courses did not provide sufficient information about stepfamilies. All students and teachers could benefit from such information to counteract the widespread stigma associated with stepfamilies (Crosbie-Burnett & Skyles, 1989). Bronstein, Clauson, Stoll, and Abrams (1993) claim, "School systems should include family structure diversity as a regular topic in the primary and secondary school curricula, so that this hidden aspect of many children's lives can be normalized and presented as ordinary information about the world around them" (p. 275). Ignoring stepfamilies' unique concerns ignores the reality of everyday life for many school children.

Interacting with Medical Personnel

The lack of a legal relationship between stepparent and stepchild affects the stepparent's ability to interact with medical personnel concerning their stepchild. Restrictions on stepparents' ability to give permission for medical care depend on several factors, often unknown to many stepfamilies. Although many stepparents (especially stepmothers) provide childcare for their stepchildren (Church, 1999), usually stepparents cannot give permission for emergency services for stepchildren (Gorosh & Gorosh, 1982). Additionally, stepparents often lack the ability to give permission for nonemergency medical procedures (Berger & the Committee on Medical Liability, 2003). Berger et al. discuss the medical personnel's dilemma when a child is accompanied by a person who is not the legal parent. Is the situation of such seriousness that care should be given without parental consent even though legal repercussions might ensue, or should the medical personnel ask the individuals to wait until parental consent can be achieved? If there is only one member of the stepfamily (usually the biological parent) who has the ability to authorize healthcare, the flexibility of the stepfamily is limited.

One situation where stepparents can give permission for their stepchild's medical care is if the custodial parent provides a "written consent by proxy" (Berger et al., 2003, p. 1189). This document allows another individual named by the biological parent to give consent for treatment of a minor. Many stepfamilies are not aware of the need for such a document. Some physicians like this strategy; however, others are uncomfortable with such a policy (Berger et al., 2003). A written consent by proxy may also need to be provided to the noncustodial parent. Although most states allow either biological parent to consent to medical treatment, others limit this right to the custodial parent. In addition, Berger et al. state that in some cases of joint custody, *both* parents must consent to treatment of the child. If the individuals in the stepfamily are not aware of these restrictions, the children might be denied treatment while at the noncustodial home.

A situation where the stepparents' permission is actually needed for medical care occurs when the stepchildren are covered by their stepparent's medical insurance (usually only residential stepchildren, Mason & Simon, 1995). One example of this situation is if the stepparent is in the military and the stepchildren are considered his or her dependents. There is little information available concerning under what circumstances private insurance companies allow stepparents to cover their stepchildren (Mason, 2003). A lack of knowledge about these specific situational constraints can confuse the communication process for stepfamilies and medical personnel.

Besides the lack of legal relationship between stepparent and stepchild, a second factor that can confuse a stepfamily's interaction with medical personnel is the dual-household nature of the stepfamily. Having two households may also complicate stepfamilies' compliance with medical personnel. Such important issues as completing a course of antibiotics may be compromised if communication between the households is sparse or conflict-filled. If there is no open communication between the biological parents' households, information about the child's health problems may not be available to all parental figures or to medical personnel who only interact with one family in the stepfamily system. Doctors dealing with the noncustodial parent may see stepchildren on an irregular basis and may not have access to all of the information from the custodial parent's physician (Herndon & Combs, 1982). Herndon and Combs urge a custodial parent's physician to seek to improve this situation by offering to send information to the physician the noncustodial parent's family utilizes. However, the physician may not even be aware he or she is interacting with a stepfamily due to the third factor that affects stepfamily/medical interaction, the societal stigmatized view of stepfamilies.

Even medical personnel are not immune to having stigmatized views of stepfamilies. For example, Ganong and Coleman (1997b) found that nurses reported "more affectively negative" thoughts (p. 145) about a stepmother having her first baby than other types of new mothers. Nurses used the stepparent status to make assumptions about the woman's home environment and needs. They were more likely to be worried about this "homelife" (p. 145) and reported more desire to question the stepmother about an older stepchild than they were to want to question the biological mothers about their older children. Given the negative stigma of stepfamilies (Ganong & Coleman, 1997a), assumptions based on stepfamily status most likely portray the patient in a negative manner, potentially affecting the psycho-social aspects of patient care (Ganong & Coleman, 1997b). Physicians also should be aware of potential biases against stepfamilies (Wood & Poole, 1983). By having accurate knowledge about these families, physicians can instead provide them with information concerning normal stepfamily interaction patterns, potentially reducing stress and anxiety (Wood & Poole, 1983).

In summary, the lack of legal relationship between stepparents and stepchildren can limit stepparents' ability to obtain medical care for their stepchildren. Many stepparents are not aware of these restrictions, compromising their ability to communicate with medical personnel. Structural features related to a child living in two households can also limit a physician's ability to enact proper medical care. In addition, medical personnel, similar to the rest of society, have been found to make negative assumptions based on stepfamily status. All of these issues complicate interaction between stepfamilies and medical personnel.

Interacting with the Legal Community

In the legal setting, stepparents and stepfamilies are treated inconsistently, affecting the ability of the stepfamily to communicate with legal personnel effectively. This inconsistency results from stepparents being treated in two very different ways by the state and federal legal systems (Malia, 2005, provides an excellent summary of the legal status of stepparents).

State Laws

State laws often treat the stepparent as a nonentity or a "legal stranger" to the stepchild (Mahoney, 1995) because children are only allowed two legal parents (Skinner & Kohler, 2002). Stepparents have fewer rights than a foster parent

(Mason, 2003). For the stepparent to take on a legal parental role, his or her only option is adoption, which automatically terminates the other biological parent's rights (Ramsey, 1994). Few stepfamilies pursue adoption because of these restrictions (Mason et al., 2002). For most legal issues, stepparents do not have a voice in decisions that may drastically affect their everyday life (Mason, Fine, & Carnochan, 2004), such as visitation or child support (Malia, 2005). They have little influence when a judge is considering child custody, even though the "two-parent" system of the biological parent and stepparent may be seen as an advantage over a single parent household (Malia, 2005). They have little to no ability to obtain visitation or custody of their stepchild if their marriage with the biological parent breaks up or if the biological parent dies *no matter the length of time that they have helped to raise the stepchild.*

Even though state courts do not recognize a legal relationship between stepparent and stepchild, courts sometimes assume that the stepparent will take on parental and financial support responsibilities, and some states require the stepparent to support a residential stepchild (Skinner & Kohler, 2002). However, these contributions are considered an agreement between the biological spouse and stepparent which is terminated with the ending of the remarriage through divorce or death (Ramsey, 1994). Mason et al. (2002) note, "[i]f stepparents are required to accept support obligations, fairness dictates that they must also be given parental rights" (p. 520). Such a change is not considered likely by legal scholars.

Federal Laws

Although the states mostly ignore the stepparent's influence and role in the stepfamily, the federal government treats the stepparent as a provider of resources for the stepchild (Malia, 2005). Remarriage is seen as an important remedy for single-parent poverty (especially for females; Mason & Mauldon, 1996). For example, stepparent income is often taken into account for college financial aid (Crosbie-Burnett & Skyles, 1989). Some federal programs have more stringent requirements for stepchildren than biological children (Ramsey, 1986). Residential stepchildren are often covered by their stepparent's Social Security and Worker's Compensation, and some stepchildren are covered by their stepparent's medical insurance (Mason & Simon, 1995). Unless the stepchild is adopted by the stepparent, all coverage is terminated if the remarriage ends in divorce, potentially causing hardship for the child (Mason & Mauldon, 1996).

Consequences of the Stepparent's Ambiguous Legal Role

This inconsistent treatment of the stepparent greatly compromises the ability of the stepparent to communicate with legal personnel. Decisions that will greatly affect the stepparent's household, such as child custody, visitation decisions, and child support, are made with little to no acknowledgement that the stepparent's life will be affected. Gately et al. (2005) conducted one of the few studies that has examined how legal personnel and stepfamilies (fail to) communicate. They interviewed 12 stepparents whose partners had been involved in litigation in Family Court in Western Australia. These stepparents were shocked that their input was not considered in the case. This lack of acknowledgement led to a sense of unfairness and "resentment, anger, and guilt" (p. 37). The stepparents believed they were not given legitimacy as their partner's current spouse; rather, their partner's former spouse (the biological parent) was perceived as having all the power. Stepparents felt unable to defend themselves or their family if the ex-spouse provided negative or "untrue" testimony. They believed the courts were telling them that the stepchildren who they lived with and interacted with on a regular basis were "none of [their] business" (p. 42). This interaction with the legal system left the stepparent feeling out of control, and over half of the interviewees reported "significant negative emotional consequences," including taking antidepressants, a suicide attempt, and one participant having a stroke (Gately et al., 2005, p. 44). The use of a convenience sample must be noted, given that stepparents negatively affected may have been particularly likely to participate.

Although there is little research on stepparents' interaction with legal personnel, several studies have examined how stepparents feel about having no legal relationship with their stepchildren. Edwards, Gillies, and McCarthy (1999) found much ambivalence in British stepparents' attitudes. They wanted recognition for their relationship with their stepchildren. Stepparents also believed that it was important for their stepchildren to maintain a relationship with their noncustodial biological parent. This desire was contrasted with skepticism that the two households could actually cooperate well enough to co-parent the child. In addition, having two households with numerous legal parents was seen as potentially compromising the formation of at least one stable household for the children. Edwards et al. concluded that stepparents desire empowerment "but not really in the zero sum sense of disempowering someone else" (p. 101).

Mason et al. (2002) interviewed 27 residential stepfamilies (the stepchildren lived at least half the time with the family interviewed) to examine how the stepparents felt about their lack of legal ties to their stepchild. They found that the "stepparents and biological parents, even those who are lawyers, were generally unclear about the legal rights and responsibilities of stepparents, although the great majority realized there were not many" (p. 516). Many of the stepparents believed having a legal relationship with their stepchildren would aid their everyday lives. Others believed that the law had little power to improve their situation. Nearly all of the stepparents expressed a desire to continue their relationship with the stepchild if their marriage to the biological parent ended, although few seriously considered seeking custody of the stepchild. Most had thought about adoption but did not pursue it due to issues with the other biological parent. These two studies examining the beliefs of stepparents regarding their legal role do not coincide with a view of the stepparent as removed and uninvolved, as the legal system's conceptualization of the stepparent as a legal stranger seems to promote. More research is needed concerning how the lack of a legal relationship affects stepfamilies (Ramsey, 1994).

Potential Changes for the Stepparent's Role in the Legal System

Ganong and Coleman (1997a) claim, "Although this flexibility [in terms of no legal status for stepparents] can be seen as an advantage to some stepfamilies, it is likely that for many stepparents the absence of legal ties adds to their feelings of ambiguity and lack of control regarding their relationships with stepchildren" (p. 91). If stepparents desire legal support for playing an active role in their stepchildren's' lives, how might such a role be enacted? When contemplating the possibility of revising the way stepparents are perceived legally, scholars have commented that the legal system must recognize that all stepfamilies cannot be treated the same (Hans, 2002). These scholars often focus on whether the stepparent has been acting in loco parentis to the stepchild, meaning that the stepparent has been acting in a parental manner toward the child (Fine, 1997). Scholars suggest that only such stepparents should be given consideration in the legal arena (Mason & Mauldon, 1996). Some scholars suggest the implementation of a system similar to one in England where stepparents can apply for a limited amount of parental responsibility without terminating the biological parent's rights (Fine & Fine, 1992). Allowing only certain stepparents legal rights could provide children with more financial and emotional support and more closely reflect the true complexity of many stepfamilies' lives (Mason et al., 2002). It would also permit more security for certain stepparent-stepchild relationships (Skinner & Kohler, 2002). However, Fine and Fine (1992) note that this system would be hard to implement in America where states often have jurisdiction over family law and each state would have to enact its own version of the policy.

In summary, the inconsistent manner with which stepparents are treated by the legal system leads to confusion and limits stepparents' ability to communicate with many outside parties regarding their stepchildren. If individuals do not disclose that they are members of a stepfamily, communication between the stepparent, stepchild, and social entity may completely break down as each assumes that the stepparent has legal decision making privileges that they actually do not possess. A change in the legal status of stepparents could allow the stepparent more parental authority for everyday decisions regarding their stepchildren (Mason et al., 2002) and allow easier interaction with third parties. However, as this change of legal status is currently unlikely, more research is needed concerning how this lack of legal relationship affects communication with parties outside the household. Besides inconvenience, inability to communicate with social entities outside the family has several potentially serious negative outcomes for the stepfamily.

Potential Negative Results of Limited Stepfamily Communication with Third Parties

Being able to communicate with third parties is essential for all families. The system of the stepfamily must be able to interact successfully with the suprasystem in which it is embedded. Inability to do this can lead to several negative consequences for the stepfamily.

One potential aspect of stepfamily life that is compromised is the stepchildren's adjustment to remarriage. Crosbie-Burnett (1994) states the importance of outside social entities in this process: "Making this adjustment more difficult for children is the lack of understanding about, and support for, their concerns in the various microsystems in which they live: schools, religious groups, athletic teams and even the family" (Crosbie-Burnett, 1994, p. 200).

Another negative effect of not being able to easily communicate with third parties is an undermining of the relationship between the stepparent and the stepchild (Fine, 1989). This relationship is often perceived as one of the most essential in predicting the long-term viability of the stepfamily (Visher & Visher, 1978). Having third parties, such as the school system, ignore the contribution or even existence of the stepparent potentially communicates to the stepchild that he or she does not have to consider or respect the stepparent (Crosbie-Burnett & Skyles, 1989). Mason et al. (2002) found that many stepparents worried about the possibility of their relationship with their stepchild being undermined due to their invisibility to outside social entities. This lack of respect as a parental figure contradicted the views of the stepfamilies themselves, with both partners in the great majority of stepfamilies reporting that the stepparent was a parental figure to the stepchild (Mason et al., 2002).

A third negative effect of limited stepfamily communication with third parties is the potential undermining of the marital relationship itself. Visher et al. (2003) claim, "The interface between the stepfamily and the community can produce tensions that strain the couple" (p. 163). Such greater difficulties for the stepfamily may be one explanatory factor for the higher rate of divorce in remarriages with stepchildren (White & Booth, 1985). Therefore, given the serious consequences of ignoring the stepparent when considering communication with third parties, communication scholars can aid in increasing understanding about this issue in several ways.

Research Directions for Examining Communication Between Stepfamilies and Outside Entities

One of the co-authors of this chapter recently suggested that there is a "Don't ask; don't tell" attitude about stepfamilies in our culture. If stepparents do not reveal themselves as such, third parties tend to treat them as the biological parent and grant them the privileges that come with this role. This subterfuge places stepparents in an uncomfortable position, especially if they know they do not have the legal authority to make certain decisions.

Even though Visher and Visher noted back in 1978 that stepfamilies break the one household/one family barrier, research on stepfamilies has surprisingly not reflected this fact (Coleman et al., 2000). One of the few exceptions to this limitation is a study by Braithwaite et al. (2003) that examined how divorced parents and their new partners communicate when co-parenting. They found that most of the individuals were satisfied with the communication involving the other household, that it focused mainly on coordination of the children's activities, and that there was little conflict reported. In this study individuals reported several issues related to interacting with third parties. For example, one common place to communicate with members of the other household was at school events and extracurricular activities. Individuals also reported communicating with the other household about medical issues related to the children. When considering how stepfamilies actually communicate with third parties, basic questions remain unanswered and desperately need to be explored (Coleman, Ganong, & Fine, 2004). Some of these include the following: (a) How commonly do stepparents communicate with these outside entities? (b) How do stepparents introduce and represent themselves when communicating with these outside entities? (c) Does potential nuclear family bias in educational and medical settings affect stepfamily interaction (Ganong & Coleman, 1997a)? (d) Does the lack of legal relationship between stepparent and stepchild affect interaction outside the stepfamily (Ganong & Coleman, 1997a)?

Another contribution of communication research to the study of stepfamilies is a focus on impression management. Issues about face relate to the stepfamily's dilemma in terms of presenting themselves to the outside world. Several studies have found that individuals do not like to apply the term "stepfamily" to their family due to negative connotations (e.g., Edwards, 2002). Dahl, Cowgill, and Asmundsson (1987) found in their study of remarried families that: "[A]lthough more children than adults used the "step" label, it was frequently circumvented, and family members expressed uncertainty about what term to use ... most usages were felt to be awkward" (p. 43). However, there are few alternative terms for stepfamilies available (Ganong et al., 1990), except nuclear family labels. Presenting themselves as a nuclear family exacerbates difficulties in communicating with third parties.

Dainton (1993) examined impression management issues for stepmothers. Dainton discussed Goffman's (1963) distinction between two types of stigmas: discredited and discreditable. Individuals who are discredited cannot hide the fact that they belong to a stigmatized group, but discreditable people can. When a stepmother interacts in public, she is discreditable: people who do not know her cannot tell that she is a stepmother. However, her family and others may know she is a stepmother. If they reveal this fact, they may threaten the stepmother's face. Dainton calls for more research concerning how stepfamilies seek to manage their identities and avoid negative connotations of stepfamily labels and whether these strategies are effective.

Although hiding one's status as a stepfamily may avoid the potential negative attributions of others, it can cause problems for stepfamily interaction. Wood and Poole (1983) contemplate how a lack of understanding concerning how to address or introduce stepfamily members can lead to anxiety in children or hurt feelings if the members of the family buy the negative connotations of the "step" label. Members of the stepfamily are put into the uncomfortable position of having to lie about their relationships with each other (to claim a biological tie when there is not one), to "prove" their affection for one another. However, passing as a nuclear family can put the child in the awkward position of feeling disloyal to his or her other biological parent (Coleman et al., 2004). Questions related to impression management in need of research include:

1. How do stepfamilies introduce their families to others?
2. How do stepchildren feel about whether the stepparent chooses to identify themselves as a parent or stepparent?
3. How do choices about how to introduce themselves to others affect the stepparent/stepchild relationship?

A third potential contribution of communication researchers to the study of stepfamilies is the exploration of how roles are created in stepfamilies through communication. These families are a natural setting for such research. As stepfamilies are incompletely institutionalized, they must communicate more to establish roles (Ishii-Kuntz & Coltrane, 1992). Creating stepparent roles is difficult when individuals are so socialized in the desirability of nuclear family roles (Ganong & Coleman, 1997a). Couples face the additional difficulties of playing parental roles from the beginning of their marriage instead of developing these roles over time (Coleman et al., 2004). Although the different roles that stepparents take have been explored (e.g., Fine et al., 1998), the communication process by which these roles are created has not been closely examined. These questions about role development are very important because lack of role clarity is related to stress levels in stepfamilies (Fine & Schwebel, 1991). Questions in need of research include the following:

1. How do stepfamilies establish roles related to interacting with individuals outside the household?
2. Do they talk about these issues? If so, what does this communicative process look like?
3. Do stepfathers and stepmothers differ in how they handle these issues related to role communication and development?

Conclusion

Surprisingly little research has examined how stepfamilies actually interact with third parties and the impact on individual stepfamilies. Bringing a communication perspective to the issue of how stepfamilies communicate with outside entities should greatly expand our understanding of how stepfamily members interact in the spaces beyond their household. This chapter seeks to contribute to this goal by summarizing the current literature on how stepfamilies relate to educational, medical, and legal personnel and pointing out the numerous areas in need of future research. Throughout this chapter two conflicting themes are apparent. Through stigmatization and poorly defined roles for stepparents, society encourages stepfamilies to interact and present themselves as nuclear families with stepparents playing a parental role. However, the lack of legal relationship between most stepparents and stepchildren hinders the stepparents' ability to enact parental roles or to communicate with outside social entities effectively.

Another obvious conclusion from this chapter is that much of the research on stepfamilies has not taken a communication perspective. Communication scholars can contribute to this research by continuing to encourage an examination of stepfamilies across households and by detailing the actual communication processes between stepfamily members as they negotiate their everyday family roles. Communication scholars can add to the existing literature by examining the actual communication processes between stepfamilies and education, medical, and legal personnel, and exploring how these communicative encounters affect the dynamics of stepfamilies. Through interviews, diaries, and questionnaires, communication researchers can add their expertise to the important research done in this area. By examining how stepparents and stepchildren communication with those outside their households, everyday life for stepfamilies will be more thoroughly understood, and researchers and practitioners alike will understand more clearly how to help stepfamilies function effectively.

References

Berger, J. E., & the Committee on Medical Liability. (2003). Consent by proxy for nonurgent pediatric care. *Pediatrics, 112,* 1186–1195.

Braithwaite, D. O., McBride, M. C., & Schrodt, P. (2003). "Parent teams" and the everyday interactions of co-parenting in stepfamilies. *Communication Reports, 16,* 93–111.

Bronstein, P., Clauson, J., Stoll, M. F., & Abrams, C. L. (1993). Parenting behavior and children's social, psychological, and academic adjustment in diverse family structures. *Family Relations, 42,* 268–276.

Bryan, H., Ganong, L. H., Coleman, M., & Bryan, L. (1985). Counselors' perceptions of stepparents and stepchildren. *Journal of Counseling Psychology, 32,* 279–282.

Cherlin, A. J. (1978). Remarriage as an incomplete institution. *American Journal of Sociology, 84,* 634–650.

Cherlin, A. J. (1992). *Marriage, divorce, and remarriage (Revised and enlarged edition).* Cambridge, MA: Harvard University Press.

Church, E. (1999). Who are the people in your family? Stepmothers' diverse notions of kinship. *Journal of Divorce and Remarriage, 31,* 83–105.

Coffman, S. E., & Roark, A. E. (1992). A profile of adolescent anger in diverse family configurations and recommendations for intervention. *The School Counselor, 39,* 211–216.

Coleman, M., & Ganong, L. H. (1989). Financial management in stepfamilies. *Lifestyles Family and Economic Issues, 10,* 217–232.

Coleman, M., Ganong, L. H., & Cable, S. (1996). Perceptions of stepparents: An examination of the incomplete institutionalization and social stigma hypotheses. *Journal of Divorce and Remarriage, 26,* 25–48.

Coleman, M., Ganong, L. H., & Fine, M. (2000). Reinvestigating remarriage: Another decade of progress. *Journal of Marriage and the Family, 62,* 1288–1307.

Coleman, M., Ganong, L. H., & Fine M. A. (2004). Communication in stepfamilies. In A. L. Vangelisti (Ed.), *Handbook of family communication* (pp. 215–232). Mahwah, NJ: Erlbaum.

Coleman, M., Ganong, L. H., & Henry, J. (1984). What teachers should know about stepfamilies. *Childhood Education, 60,* 306–309.

Crosbie-Burnett, M. (1994). The interface between stepparent families and schools: Research, theory, policy, and practice. In K. Pasley & M. Ihinger-Tallman (Eds.), *Stepfamilies: Current issues in theory, research, and practice* (pp. 199–216). Westport, CT: Greenwood.

Crosbie-Burnett, M., & Skyles, A. (1989). Stepchildren in schools and colleges: Recommendations for educational policy changes. *Family Relations, 38,* 59–64.

Dahl, A. S., Cowgill, K. M., & Asmundsson, R. (1987). Life in remarriage families. *Social Work, 32,* 40–44.

Dainton, M. (1993). The myths and misconceptions of the stepmother identity: Descriptions and prescriptions for identity management. *Family Relations, 42,* 93–98.

Edwards, R. (2002). Creating "stability" for children in step-families: Time and substance in parenting. *Children and Society, 16,* 154–167.

Edwards, R., Gillies, V., & McCarthy, J. R. (1999). Biological parents and social families: Legal discourses and everyday understandings of the position of step-parents. *International Journal of Law, Policy and the Family, 13,* 78–105.

Fine, M. A. (1989). A social science perspective on stepfamily law: Suggestions for legal reform. *Family Relations, 38,* 53–58.

Fine, M. A. (1997). Stepfamilies from a policy perspective: Guidance from the empirical literature. *Marriage and Family Review, 26,* 249–264.

Fine, M. A., Coleman, M., & Ganong, L. H. (1998). Consistency in perceptions of the step-parent role among step-parents, parents, and stepchildren. *Journal of Social and Personal Relationships, 15,* 810–828.

Fine, M. A., & Fine, D. R. (1992). Recent changes in laws affecting stepfamilies: Suggestions for legal reform. *Family Relations, 41,* 334–340.

Fine, M. A., & Schwebel, A. I. (1991). Stepparent stress: A cognitive perspective. *Journal of Divorce and Remarriage, 17,* 1–15.

Ganong, L. H. (1993). Family diversity in a youth organization: Involvement of single-parent families and stepfamilies in 4-H. *Family Relations, 42,* 286–292.

Ganong, L. H., & Coleman, M. (1997a). How society views stepfamilies. *Marriage and Family Review, 26,* 85–106.

Ganong, L. H., & Coleman, M. (1997b). Effects of family structure information on nurses' impression formation and verbal responses. *Research in Nursing and Health, 20,* 139–151.

Ganong, L. H., & Coleman, M. (2004). *Stepfamily relationships: Development, dynamics, and interventions.* New York: Kluwer Academic/Plenum.

Ganong, L. H., Coleman, M., & Kennedy, G. (1990). The effects of using alternative labels in denoting stepparent or stepfamily status. *Journal of Social Behavior and Personality, 5*, 453–463.

Ganong, L. H., Coleman, M., & Mistina, D. (1995). Home is where they have to let you in: Normative beliefs regarding physical custody changes of children following divorce. *Journal of Family Issues, 16*, 466–487.

Gately, N. J., Pike, L. T., & Murphy, P. T. (2005). An exploration of the impact of the family court process on "invisible" stepparents. *Journal of Divorce and Remarriage, 44*, 31–52.

Goffman, E. (1963). *Stigma: Notes on the management of spoiled identity.* Englewood Cliffs, NJ: Prentice-Hall.

Gorosh, M., & Gorosh, Y. (1982). The stepfamily in the emergency department. *Emergency Medical Services, 11*, 21–24.

Guisinger, S., Cowan, P., & Schuldberg, D. (1989). Changing parent and spouse relations in the first years of remarriage of divorced fathers. *Journal of Marriage and the Family, 51*, 445–456.

Guttman, J., & Broudo, M. (1988–1989). The effect of children's family type on teachers' stereotypes. *Journal of Divorce, 12*, 315–328.

Hans, J. D. (2002). Stepparenting after divorce: Stepparents' legal position regarding custody, access, and support. *Family Relations, 51*, 301–307.

Herndon, A., & Combs, L. G. (1982). Stepfamilies as patients. *The Journal of Family Practice, 15*, 917–922.

Hobart, C. (1991). Conflict in remarriages. *Journal of Divorce and Remarriage, 15*, 69–86.

Ishii-Kuntz, M., & Coltrane, S. (1992). Remarriage, stepparenting, and household labor. *Journal of Family Issues, 13*, 215–233.

Jones, A. C. (2004). Transforming the story: Narrative applications to a stepmother support group. *Families in Society: The Journal of Contemporary Social Services, 85*, 129–138.

Lutz, E. P., Jacobs, E. E., & Masson, R. L. (1988). Stepfamily counseling: Issues and guidelines. In W. M. Walsh & N. J. Giblin (Eds.), *Family counseling in school settings* (pp. 157–165). Springfield, IL: Charles C. Thomas.

Maccoby, E. E., & Mnookin, R. H. (1992). *Dividing the child: Social and legal dilemmas of custody.* Cambridge, MA: Harvard University Press.

Mahoney, M. (1995). *Stepfamilies and the law.* Ann Arbor: University of Michigan Press.

Malia, S. E. C. (2005). Balancing family members' interests regarding stepparent rights and obligations: A social policy challenge. *Family Relations, 54*, 298–319.

Marano, H. E. (2000, Mar/Apr). Divorced? Don't even think of remarrying until you read this. *Psychology Today, 33*, 56–61.

Mason, M. A. (2003). The modern American stepfamily: Problems and possibilities. In M. A. Mason, A. Skolnick, & S. D. Sugarman (Eds.), *All our families: New policies for a new century* (2nd ed., pp. 96–116). New York: Oxford Unoversity Press.

Mason, M. A., Fine, M. A., & Carnochan, S. (2004). Gender, family structure, and social support among parents. *Journal of Marriage and the Family, 55*, 481–493.

Mason, M. A., Harrison-Jay, S., Svare, G. M., & Wolfinger, N. H. (2002). Stepparents: De facto parents or legal strangers? *Journal of Family Issues, 23*, 507–522.

Mason, M. A., & Mauldon, J. (1996). The new stepfamily requires a new public policy. *Journal of Social Issues, 52*, 11–27.

Mason, M. A., & Simon, D. (1995). The ambiguous stepparent: Federal legislation in search of a model. *Family Law Quarterly, 3*, 445–483.

Midkiff, R. B., & Lawler-Prince, D. (1992). Preparing tomorrow's teachers: Meeting the challenge of diverse family structures. *The Journal of the Association of Teacher Educators, 14*, 1–5.

Nord, C. W., & West, J. (1996). Fathers' and mothers' involvement in their children's schools by family type and resident status. *Education Statistics Quarterly, 3.* Retrieved November 30, 2005, from http://nces.ed./gov/programs/quarterly/vol_3/3_2/q2-5.asp

Papernow, P. (1993). *Becoming a stepfamily: Patterns of development in remarried families.* San Francisco: Jossey-Bass.

Pasley, K., & Ihinger-Tallman, M. (1986). Stepfamilies: New challenges for the schools. In T. N. Fairchild (Ed.), *Crisis intervention strategies for school-based helpers* (pp. 70–111). Springfield, IL: Charles C. Thomas.

Pong, S. (1997). Family structure, school context, and eighth-grade math and reading achievement. *Journal of Marriage and the Family, 59*, 734–746.

Ramsey, S. H. (1986). Stepparent support of stepchildren: The changing legal context and the need for empirical policy research. *Family Relations, 35*, 363–369.

Ramsey, S. H. (1994). Stepparents and the law: A nebulous status and a need for reform. In K. Pasley & M. Ihinger-Tallman (Eds.), *Stepparenting: Issues, research, & practice* (pp. 217–237). Westport, CT: Greenwood Press.

Shea, C. A. (1990). The 21st century family: A study of special educators' preparation. *Teacher Education and Special Education, 13*, 197–199.

Skinner, D. A., & Kohler, J. K. (2002). Parental rights in diverse family contexts: Current legal developments. *Family Relations, 51*, 293–300.

Stenger, R. L. (1986). The school counselor and the law: New developments. *Journal of Law and Education, 15*, 105–116.

U.S. Bureau of the Census. (2000). *Statistical abstract of the United States: 2000.* Washington, DC: U. S. Government Printing Office.

Visher, E. B., & Visher, J. S. (1978). Major areas of difficulty for stepparent couples. *American Journal of Family Therapy, 6*, 70–80.

Visher, E. B., & Visher, J. S. (1979). *Stepfamilies: A guide to working with stepparents and stepchildren.* New York: Brunner/Mazel.

Visher, E. B., Visher, J. S., & Pasley, K. (2003). Remarriage families and stepparenting. In F. Walsh (Ed.), *Normal family processes* (pp. 153–175). New York: Guilford.

White, L. K., & Booth, A. (1985). The quality and stability of remarriages: The role of stepchildren. *American Sociological Review, 50*, 689–698.

Wood, L. E., & Poole, S. R. (1983). Stepfamilies in family practice. *Journal of Family Practice, 16*, 739–744.

Zill, N. (1996). Family change and student achievement: What we have learned, what it means for schools. In A. Booth & J. Dunn (Eds.), *Family-school links: How do they affect educational outcomes?* (pp. 139–174). Mahwah, NJ: Erlbaum.

19 The Community Interactions of Gay and Lesbian Foster Parents

Dennis Patrick and John Palladino

It would be like being in jail. If you dropped the soap, you'd have to watch out to see if they'd get at you.... I'd rather have no father than a gay father. (A 16-year-old youth in foster care, when asked how he would feel living in a foster home with gay parents, Youth Communication, 2005, p. 12)

"She's gay—and the best foster mom I know." (The title of an article written by a 15-year-old youth in foster care, Rosario, 2003)

As the above quotations suggest, youth in foster care, like many Americans, have differing opinions on the topic of gay and lesbian parenting. No matter what one's personal beliefs, the reality is that gay men and lesbians are more likely to be parents now than in previous decades. Although it is difficult to accurately assess the number of gay and lesbian parents (National Gay and Lesbian Task Force [NGLTF], 2003), it has been estimated that there are 3 million gay fathers and 5 million lesbian mothers in the United States (Brooks & Goldberg, 2001). What is clear, however, is that there is an increase in the number of gay men and lesbians who have expressed an interest in becoming foster and adoptive parents (Drucker, 1998). As a result of their interest and a shortage of qualified foster homes, some child welfare agencies have changed their policies to make foster parenting possible for a much wider range of adults, including gay men and lesbians (American Civil Liberties Union [ACLU], 1999; Mallon, 2006). The purpose of this chapter is to examine the experience of those gay and lesbian foster parents, and the interactions they have with foster children, child welfare workers, birth families, and others in their social and professional networks.

The Need for Foster Care Providers

The family foster care system is designed to provide protection and nurturing for children who have experienced neglect and/or abuse. Although attempts have been made to reduce the number of children in care, there has been a 74% increase in the number of children in the United States who have needed care in the last 15 years (Barbell & Wright, 1999). In the year 2003, the last year for which statistics are available, there were over 500,000 children in the U.S. foster care system (Child Welfare League of America [CWLA], n.d.) and that number is continuing to increase dramatically (Mallon, 2004). Qualified adoptive families have been found for only 20,000 of the 100,000 youth in foster care who await adoption (Alexander, 2001).

While the number of children in the foster care system has *increased*, the number of available foster care families has *decreased* (Albert, 2003). This decrease is the result of several factors, including families feeling as if they have no decision making power over the foster children in their homes, the unexpected costs of fostering that are not reimbursed by the state, false accusations of child abuse made against foster parents, and the inability to find alternative care for children when foster families need a break (Albert, 2003). With more women entering the paid work force and the declining presence of two-parent families, there are also fewer available adults who can afford the commitment required to care for foster children (Testa & Rolock, 1999). Researchers who monitor the Department of Health and Human Services report that approximately 75% of foster care children receive primary services from nonkinship (nonrelative) foster parents (see Buehler, Cox, & Cuddeback, 2003; Rhodes, Orme, Cox, & Buehler, 2003). The shortage of these foster parents is now at a "critical" stage (ACLU, 1999). It is not surprising that recruiting and retaining high quality foster caregivers has been identified as a primary goal for the foster family care system in the 21st century (Barbell & Wright, 1999).

Unfortunately, a lack of research exists on the shortage of nonkinship foster parents, as well as methods for reversing the poor retention and sustainability rates among those who do obtain their foster care license: "Very little research exists concerning recruitment in general, and there is even less regarding how to recruit families willing to foster for a number of years and willing to foster children with special needs" (Cox, Buehler, & Orme, 2002, p. 152). Past research primarily focuses on successful characteristics of nonkinship foster parenting. For example, Tyebjee (2003) conducted a random poll of California residents to determine the factors and motivators that influence their attitudes toward and willingness to foster parent and/or adopt. The author concluded "the most salient reasons for a person's willingness to adopt or foster are all focused on the child, namely, to make a difference in a child's life" (p. 701). Other researchers have corroborated the notion of overall commitment to a child's well-being as the primary trait of successful foster parenting (Ackerman & Dozier, 2005; Buehler et al., 2003; Cox et al., 2002; Rhodes et al., 2003). These studies, however, have not examined the foster parent's sexual orientation as a characteristic of, or detriment to, success.

Bias Against Gay and Lesbian Foster Parents

Historically, legislation has cited gay and lesbian parents' sexual orientation as a moral concern that is incompatible with raising well-adjusted children, a view that continues to dominate the political landscape today. See Patterson and Redding (1996) for a summary of court decisions that denounce gay and lesbian parenting, and Mallon (2006) for an overview of U. S. legislation and policy relevant to gay parenting.

Despite the lack of legislative support in a number of states, gays and lesbians across the country head families as both single parents and co-parents. Of the almost 600,000 same sex couples counted in the 2000 U.S. Census, 34% of female couples and 22% of male couples reported at least one child under the age of 18 living with them (NGLTF, 2003). Brooks and Goldberg (2001) have suggested that foster parenting is a viable option for gay and lesbians willing to take in children who are often the most difficult to place, such as racial minorities, adolescents, sibling groups, and children with serious physical, emotional, and/or behavioral challenges. Openness toward children with academic and behavioral difficulties is an overall necessity in foster care, and prospective gay and lesbian parents put themselves in favorable positions when they accept placements of children with special needs. For example, in their address to the child welfare community about contemporary foster care challenges, Stokes-Chipunga and Bent-Goodley (2004) stated that "researchers estimate that 30% to 80% of children in foster care exhibit emotional and/or behavioral problems from their experiences before entering foster care or from the foster care experience itself" (p. 84). Through focus groups interviews with gay and lesbian foster and adoptive parents, Brooks and Goldberg (2001) solicited testimonies about support from state foster care agencies in need of placements for children with emotional and behavioral problems. As one participant recapped, "Overall, gay men and lesbians are more willing to consider and accept children with a broad range of difficulties" (p. 152). They further suggest that there is an informal practice of matching gay men and lesbians with the children who have the greatest number of challenges and/or special needs, while others note that adoption has become more accessible for those gay parents willing to take in children that are labeled as "hard to place" (Lewin, 2006). While this could be a compliment to their perceived parenting skills and abilities, it becomes problematic when gay and lesbian foster parents are only considered for placements of this type because it renders them as acceptable but "second best" parents (Riggs, 2007).

Challenges Faced by Gay and Lesbian Foster Parents

Despite their perceived willingness to take in children who are difficult to place, gay and lesbian foster parents, as well as gay or lesbian parents in general, still face a number of challenges. Gay and lesbian applicants for a foster care license often have to demonstrate their ability to parent far beyond what is required of heterosexual applicants (Riggs, 2007). Although studies consistently show there are no significant differences between children raised by heterosexual parents and those raised by gay and lesbian parents, there are still stigmas, stereotypes, and prejudices associated with gay and lesbian parenting (Demo, 2000). These include the belief that all children need a mother and father as male and female role models, that children raised by gay and lesbian parents are more likely to be gay or lesbians themselves, that children with gay parents will be subjected to harassment and rejection by their peers and others, and that gay men are more likely to sexually molest children (Elovitz, 1995; Hicks, 2006; Mallon, 2004; Mallon 2006). Gay men may also be perceived as lacking in maternal and/or nurturing instincts (Hicks, 2006; Lewin, 2006). Another obstacle faced by gay and lesbian foster and adoptive parents is the tendency of those in the community to see the challenges they encounter in parenting as stemming from their sexual orientation. As Alexander (2001) points out:

> attachment or psychological disturbance in adopted children of gays or lesbians will falsely conclude that it is the sexual orientation of the parents—not a biopsychological process—that is creating the difficulties.... We should avoid placing too much emphasis on the sexual orientation of the parents when what is occurring is a commonplace, adoptive family experience. (p. 94)

These prejudices could present significant obstacles for gay and lesbian foster parents or those hoping to obtain their foster care license. Ricketts (1992) outlines some of the discrimination faced by gay and lesbian parents in the United States, while Hicks and McDermottt (1999) share similar stories of foster and adoptive parents in Great Britain. More recently, Hicks (2000) found that foster and adoptive applications were denied to women who were stereotypically lesbian and perceived as threatening or militant. Stereotypically "good" lesbians were deemed safe and much more likely to receive approval, as were gay men who were not too political about their sexuality (Hicks, 2006). The eHow.com Web site titled, "How to be a Gay Foster Parent" (eHow, n.d.), advises gay and lesbian applicants to avoid volunteering their sexual orientation to the agency if they sense it might hurt their chances of becoming licensed. On the same Web site, readers are subsequently told to avoid keeping secrets from the agency, no doubt leaving potential gay and lesbian foster parents confused over the decision to reveal their sexual orientation or to conceal it from child welfare workers. Some gay and lesbian applicants ultimately decide to be open about their sexual orientation, while others hide it, fearing it will hurt their chances of getting licensed or approved for adoption (Mallon, 2006). This raises the question of how gay and lesbian foster parents reveal and talk about their sexual orientation and/or relationship, and to whom they choose to disclose this information.

Gay and Lesbian Foster Parents' Interactions with Others

With Child Welfare Workers

Previous research has suggested that the degree to which gays and lesbians are "considered, recruited, approved, and supported as adoptive and foster parents may depend greatly on a given agency's attitudes and informal practices" (Brooks & Goldberg, 2001, p. 152). Lewin (2006), in her description of the challenges faced by gay men in their quest to become parents, writes that "almost no aspect of the process is simple" (p. 132). While some agencies and workers are affirming and supportive of gay and lesbian applicants, others may be embarrassed, confused, or even hostile (Mallon, 2006). A child welfare worker's perceived comfort level with homosexuality may influence the degree to which foster parents speak openly about their orientation and/or relationship (Brooks & Goldberg, 2001). Despite the possibility of negative treatment, a number of gay men are open about their sexual orientation and/or relationship and expect to be treated fairly in the foster care and adoption process (Hicks, 2006). Additional research is needed to fully explore the interactions gay and lesbian foster parents have with the child welfare workers who ultimately place children in their home.

With Foster Children

As the quotations used to open this chapter suggest, some foster children hold positive beliefs about gay and lesbian parents while others feel negatively toward them. Since decisions about foster care placements are made on the basis of what is in the best interests of the child (Plumer, 1992), it seems reasonable to assume that competent child welfare workers would not place homophobic children with gay or lesbian foster parents. This assumption, however, rests on the belief that social workers have talked to the children they are placing about gay and lesbian parents or somehow know their feelings about it. In an auto-ethnographic like account of his experiences as a gay foster parent, Patrick (2006) describes how case workers typically do not disclose that he and his partner are a same-sex couple to the foster children placed in their home. It is left up to them to raise this issue and discuss it with their new foster children. Mallon (2006) cites similar examples of youth in foster care who were surprised to learn that their new foster parents were gay or lesbian. The failure of workers to talk with children about this issue could lead to trauma for the youth in care and the foster parents, as well as a disrupted placement. There needs to be an exploration of how workers talk to foster children about placement with gay or lesbian foster parents, and how that talk subsequently influences the foster children's perceptions of their new placement.

Some scholars have suggested that one advantage that gay and lesbian foster parents have over their heterosexual counterparts is an ability to relate to their foster children's feelings of being different. Since many gay and lesbian Americans have personally experienced discrimination, they may be particularly suited for understanding foster children who feel different from children raised in biological families (Brooks & Goldberg, 2001). The talk between foster parents and foster children about their feelings of difference, or of being teased or bullied, should be examined as well.

With the Birth Family

Some children in foster care have ongoing contact and/or visitation with birth family members, and these interactions could affect the success of their foster care placement. Birth parents may object to their child's placement on the basis of the foster parents' sexual orientation (Mallon, 2006). Hicks and McDermott (1999) tell the story of a gay male couple who were initially selected for the placement of a young boy. The placement decision was rescinded when the boy's biological mother expressed disapproval of her son being placed with gay foster parents. Patrick (2006) reports both positive and negative reactions from the birth parents of the children he and his partner have fostered. One birth mother seemed relieved there was no adult female in the foster family who could take her place or compete for her role as a mother, and she supported the placement. Other birth parents, however, attempted to have their children removed from the home, fearing having gay foster parents would make their own sons effeminate or gay. The beliefs of birth family members could impact how the foster child feels about having gay or lesbian foster parents and could ultimately facilitate or hinder the placement.

With Social and Professional Networks

Foster children who are accepting of, or neutral toward, their gay or lesbian foster parents may not know how to talk about their foster parents' sexual orientation or relationship with friends, teachers, and others in their social networks. Gay and lesbian parents who use reproductive technology or adopt a newborn have many years to educate their children on how to respond to questions and comments from strangers about their family, perhaps mirroring strategies used by African-American parents to prepare their children for discriminatory and racist questions and comments (Daniel & Daniel, 1999). It has been suggested that preparing their children, whether biological, foster, or adopted, for expressions of homophobia and discrimination is a worthwhile endeavor for gay and lesbian parents (Brooks & Goldberg, 2001). Since the average age of a child in foster care in the United States is 10 years old (CWLA, n.d.), foster parents have relatively little or no time to prepare their new foster child for the homophobia and/or heterosexism they may encounter in their social networks. Research suggests that children of gay and lesbian parents are surprisingly resilient despite the teasing and other problems they may encounter as a result of their family structure (Peplau & Beals, 2004). Many of these children have been with their parents since birth or infancy, and it is still unknown if these findings are applicable to the older children that are typically found in the foster care system. As Peplau and Beals point out (2004):

> Gay and lesbian parents have many concerns about the possible impact of sexual prejudice on the experiences of their children at school, in the neighborhood, with friends, with health care providers, and so on.

Researchers have not yet examined the strategies that gay and lesbian parents use to shelter their children from negative experiences, to help children to cope with instances of prejudice, to build resilience in their children, and to create supportive social networks. (p. 244)

Mallon (2004) provides an overview of the questions and comments that openly gay dads (biological, foster, and/or adoptive) and their children routinely get asked by neighbors, teachers, daycare providers, and physicians. Even the gay community itself may not be supportive of gay parenting (Lewin, 2006). Children of gay and lesbian foster parents are in a sense doubly stigmatized as a result of being in foster care and of having same sex parents. This potential double stigma is associated with youth who may be faced with questions they are not prepared to answer about their new placement or their new family. While these interactions can be difficult for the gay or lesbian foster parent themselves, they may be even more challenging for the children placed in their care. Research is needed that examines how children in gay and lesbian foster families respond to questions and comments from others, and to what extent, if any, gay and lesbian foster parents counsel their foster children on appropriate and/or effective responses.

As the preceding review indicates, there is a need for research on gay and lesbian foster parents (Riggs, 2007). The purpose of this study is to specifically examine communication between gay and lesbian foster parents, the children placed in their home, and the social and professional networks surrounding these families. These interactions are important since they may ultimately influence the success or failure of foster care placements with gay and lesbian parents.

Method

Participants

Given our own status as gay foster parents, it was paramount that we acknowledged our biases throughout the research process and allow the participants' insights to constitute our findings (LaSala, 2003). Yet, at the same time, our personal experiences allowed us to employ a gatekeeper participant selection (Seidman, 2006). In doing so, we interacted with other gay and lesbian parents in formal and informal settings through which we engaged potential participants in discussion about the study. We were able to rule-out parents who appeared uncomfortable about discussing the study's sensitive topic outside a perceived safe setting of gay and lesbian friends. Standards of ethical qualitative research required us to respect such hesitation and not persuade reluctant participants into disclosing sensitive information about their experiences.

After our interactions with more than 15 single and coupled gay and lesbian foster parents, we determined that 9 could offer substantial breadth and depth to our research quest. Each identified participant agreed to participate.

Our criteria were twofold. First, we wanted to weave together a story reflective of our participants' accounts that related to the experiences other gay and lesbian foster parents had shared with us throughout the formation stages of the study and who were not part of the final participant pool. Second, our aim was to position the present narrative in the literature as a stand-alone story about gay and lesbian foster parenting, as well as a foundation for other investigators to use in its continuation.

The dearth of literature about gay and lesbian parenting in general, and foster parenting in particular, warranted our specific focus. Seidman's (2006) argument about participant selection for qualitative case studies within the social sciences further validated our rationale:

> Because hypotheses are not being tested, the issue is not whether the researcher can generalize the findings of an interview study to a broader population. Instead the researcher's task is to present the experience of the people he or she interviews in compelling enough detail and in sufficient depth that those who read the study can connect to that experience, learn how it is constituted, and deepen their understanding of the issues it reflects. (p. 51)

Our final sample consisted of 4 same sex couples—3 lesbian and 1 gay male—as well as a single lesbian foster mother.

Data Collection

Each participant sat down for a face-to-face, semistructured, in-depth interview with one of the two authors. Couples were interviewed together. In order to comply with the university's human subjects review committee, informed consent was obtained from all participants and confidentiality was assured. Participants were allowed to select a site for the interview in which they felt comfortable discussing their experiences as a lesbian or gay foster parent, and all requested to be interviewed in their home. In many cases their children were in the room during the interview or were playing nearby. Interviews typically ranged from 60 to 90 minutes in length. Interviews were audio-taped and subsequently transcribed into a hard copy transcript. Data is presented in vignette or narrative form, following the flow of the participants' interviews. All individual and agency names have been changed to protect the identity of our participants.

Results and Discussion

Vignette I: Kay and Kris

When initially discussing the options available to them for becoming parents, Kay and Kris debated between adoption and artificial insemination. Plans were made with an adoption agency for them to adopt a baby girl, but the couple changed their mind when they discovered the baby was born addicted to crack. The agency did not disclose the mother's addiction during the planning stages of the adoption, and as Kris said, "That just scared us enough that we tried artificial insemination." Kay became pregnant through this method but ultimately suffered a miscarriage. During Kay's pregnancy, Kris was officiating volleyball games for her local community center and met Tina, a fellow referee who also worked at a foster care and adoption agency. She asked Kris if she ever considered becoming a foster parent. Kris told her that she was a lesbian, and Tina responded by saying that it wasn't a problem and that the agency wouldn't care. After the miscarriage, the couple made the decision to call Tina, and was invited to an all day training class at the agency. During the training, they "just sat in rows and no one really knew who was with anybody. For all they [the other applicants] knew, we were just two friends going together getting licensed." When it came time for their home study, Tina said, the agency "would not come right out and say that we were living together, but they would make it clear that we have known each other a long time and that we intend to do it [foster] together." Tina explained to Kay and Kris that the agency did not advertise itself as a "gay accepted agency," but it did not have a problem if someone else of the same sex lived in the home. Kay said, "I don't really know their reasoning. We just never questioned it.... We had to trust them to do it however they felt would be the least likely to be appealed" by the state. Within 6 weeks, the couple received their foster care license. The very next day two young boys, Marcus and Montell, were placed in their home. A few months after their first placement the couple took in Shawna, an adolescent girl.

During the interview, Kris emphasized that she and Kay wanted to be open about their relationship from the very beginning of the licensing process. What Kris and Kay discovered is that they were more open about their relationship than the agency itself was. As Kris reported, Shawna "told us the agency didn't tell her. We thought that they would. We thought it was clear, but I guess it wasn't. She [Shawna] thought one of us was a man. The agency said 'Kris and Kay' and Shawna thought that it was a man and a woman. Shawna had to put it together by herself and then I just told her right away. She said that she kind of figured that out and that she was fine with that. Her being an older kid, with knowing what it is, she was pretty cool with it."

Marcus and Montell's birth family, however, was not as understanding. Kay told us, "We made it clear that we wanted the birth parents to know up front that we were gay because we didn't want to have the kids in our home and then have them moved because somebody said something." They also thought the boys might be returned to their birth family at some point in the future, and they were hoping to maintain contact with them. Shortly after their placement, the boys' birth father petitioned the court to have Marcus and Montell removed from the foster home. In the petition the boys' father claimed he was unhappy that his boys (who are biracial) were living with a White couple in a predominantly White community. The birth mother, however, privately told Kay and Kris that the father's petition was motivated by their sexual orientation, not their race. When it came time for the judge to review the petition, Kay said, "The judge saw right through it because she had seen them do cross racial placements throughout the county and she knew that wasn't it and said that we're providing a very good home for the boys. The judge made it very clear that she was not going to discriminate."

The interactions Kay and Kris have had with their social and professional networks have been largely positive. Initially, their friends questioned their decision to become parents and were especially concerned about the couple taking in children from the foster care system. Kris said, their response was "You're gay. Why do you want to do that? I think they were afraid about fostering and that you only get really difficult kids and how bad it was going to be. They would have preferred that we tried to have our own because then at least you know that they get good prenatal care and that they are healthy kids." After meeting and getting to know Marcus and Montell, their friends had a change of heart. Kris recalled, "They all thought that the kids were so cute and that it was cool. Friends loved it." The couple reports that they have never had a problem with members of their church or teachers at their school. Kay said, "Montell's preschool we told right up front that we were lesbians and she [the pre-school teacher] was super fine with it. I don't know if it is this generation right now or what, but it doesn't seem to be an issue. We have seen more discrimination stuff racially because it is more noticeable than us being gay." Montell has a friend across the street and his friend's family "knows that we are gay and they come over all the time and are perfectly fine with it. The neighborhood hasn't been an issue. Maybe when they [the boys] get older, but we haven't experienced it yet. It has been easier than it seemed it might have been, looking back."

Vignette II: Tom and Mark

Prior to his relationship with Mark, Tom was married. Tom and his wife were foster parents who adopted four children through the foster care system. After his divorce, Tom came out as a gay man. He subsequently met Mark, moved in with him, and they celebrated their union with a commitment ceremony at their church. It was at this point that they began talking about the possibility of becoming parents. Tom called the same licensing worker that he and his wife once used. Tom told her, "Well, you know, I've come out as a gay man, and I wanted to know if being a foster parent's still an option." The worker replied, "Well, the state does not discriminate against it yet, and hopefully they never will." The worker disclosed that she had some foster parents she suspected were gay or lesbian, but Tom and Mark would be the first openly gay couple at the agency. After receiving their foster care license, Tom and Mark took in a number of foster children, and, eventually, adopted four boys who were in their care, the oldest being 8 years old at the time of his initial placement.

Tom and Mark felt the agency was "definitely" and "absolutely" supportive of them and their relationship, although they recalled one specific case manager who seemed uncomfortable whenever she was in their home. "Professional but standoffish" is how they described her. When Mark finally asked her if there was a problem, she told him, "No, you guys are good foster parents, but I have personal beliefs about gays. So that's a struggle for me, but that's my personal struggle. There's no problem, no issue with the kids, and you go above and beyond the call of duty." Although "things were strained" Mark described it as a "good conversation," and, while the case manager's discomfort continued, they never had a problem with her.

When asked what, if anything, their foster children were told about their relationship prior to being placed in their home, Mark described how one worker called to inform them of a discussion she had with Cody, an 8-year-old boy living in a homeless shelter they had agreed to take in. At the time, Tom and Mark were fostering Dustin, Cody's 4-year-old brother. Although workers apparently did not say anything to the younger children who were placed with them about their sexual orientation, this particular worker felt that Cody was old enough to be told. Tom described Cody's response: "His take on it was—two men are married? He didn't quite understand it. But before he lived at the homeless shelter, he was with a Baptist family that was making him go to church every Sunday with the tie and all this stuff. When he found out he didn't have to go church and didn't have to wear a tie he was like, [Tom laughs], "Oh, that's cool." Mark also mentioned Crystal, a 5-year-old foster daughter who one day asked them why there wasn't a mommy in the house. Mark told her, "You know, Daddy Tom and I are in a relationship and we love each other and so we're the parents. You don't have to have a mommy and you can have just a dad, just a mom, two moms, two dads, grandparents. Families all look different, and this is the way our family looks." Mark said that response "more than covered it" for her and that she was okay after that. Both Tom and Mark feel that it's important for workers to talk to children about having gay foster parents prior to placement because "they're already dealing with enough and you don't need to set them up to fail. They're already getting in a new situation and it means a new house, and if they're walking in there, you know that [having gay foster parents] just adds another layer that the kid has to cope with. They are better off knowing, this is what the deal is."

Reactions were mixed when it came to birth family members. Cody and Dustin's mom was described as "very, very grateful that her kids were in a home and being taken care of well. She hated seeing them in the shelter." Tom and Dave were also fostering a second set of brothers, Justin and Brian, and the couple would frequently run into their birth parents at the grocery store or other public places. Their birth father would then say something along the lines of "Look at the faggots over there." Tom and Mark were also the subject of several anonymous complaints to child protective services, which they suspect were initiated by Justin and Brian's birth parents, since they frequently occurred after a family visit with the boys. When a court hearing was held, and the boy's father was in front of the judge and the attorneys, he "put on his court face" and was "as nice as all get out." When they ran into him around town and no one else was around, Mark said that he had a very different attitude and would typically call them names. Eventually, the birth parents' parental rights were terminated by the court and Tom and Mark adopted Justin and Brian.

Tom and Mark describe the boys' teachers and others in their social network as supportive, although some school assignments presented a challenge. As Mark put it, if their foster children are in school and other children are talking "about their mommy and daddy, and their dog, well all of a sudden you draw a picture of your family, and if you're a foster or adoptive kid, your family does not look like what everyone else talks about, and that gets really weird for a kid." Tom feels that most of the questions other kids ask their children relate to being in foster care and being adopted, and that "having two dads, that never comes up." The couple did describe, however, many instances of going out to eat and having a server comment, "Oh, it must be mom's night off." Tom said, "Cody has looked at me funny when that's been said, and we usually just let it slide. As far as informing the general public, some people are very uncomfortable with it, and I have a tendency to just let those little comments slide rather than make that person feel uncomfortable.... You know, being a foster child in the first place, they learn pretty quickly when not to say something because they might get picked on as being a foster kid. The same thing applies for them being a child of gay parents. They have to know when to shut up."

Vignette III: Macy and Julie

Macy and Julie, both teachers, made the decision to get their foster care license when one of Julie's students, Greg, was in foster care. At the time, the plan was for Greg to return to his biological mother. Both women felt that it was not a good situation for him and wanted to get their license in case things fell apart when Greg went back home. Macy and Julie went to the agency responsible for managing Greg's case for their own training and licensing. Julie's former partner was a licensed foster parent with the same agency, so the couple was very open about their sexual orientation and felt comfortable disclosing their relationship. Both Macy and Julie described the agency as "supportive" and said their sexual orientation was essentially a nonissue. They did share, however, information they heard about a new licensing worker at the agency who was asked to participate in sensitivity training related to lesbian and gay issues. Julie described it by saying that the agency "has always been open to same sex couples fostering kids. And all of a sudden they had this licensing person coming in that isn't feeling that may be a good step for a lot of these foster kids. I think the bottom line is there's not a lot of licensing people out there [laughs] and so not a lot of people to pick from. Rather than saying, 'We don't want you on board here,' [the agency says] 'We will keep you on if you go through this training and see what these same sex couples have to offer these kids.'"

Macy and Julie were unsure what, if anything, case managers shared with their foster children prior to being placed in their home. Macy speculated that "they just sat them down and said that you're gonna be placed in a home that has two women, for, you know, heads of the household. Whether they came out and said that they were lesbian or not, I'm not sure." Julie then described what she felt agencies should be saying to foster children about potential same sex foster parents: "We have kids that have enough emotional problems, and have gone through a lot of family issues, and I think they have to be comfortable with where they are placed. If it's [having lesbian foster parents] something that they can't handle or it's gonna escalate behaviors, I think they should be given an option.... Even though there are not a lot of foster families out there that take older kids, sometimes I think they just place the kids because there's nowhere else to place them, but I think the kids should still have input.... Give them an opportunity to come beforehand and meet us." Even though the six children Macy and Julie have fostered did not have the chance to meet them prior to placement, the couple did not encounter any significant problems specifically related to their sexual orientation.

Macy and Julie also reported "no problem whatsoever" with the birth families of the children placed in their home. Although they never discussed their relationship specifically with these families, they believed the families knew about it. As Julie said, "When you have kids visiting their biological families and one time Macy takes them or one time I take them, it's just something that comes out of that. I'm not sure it always has to be something that's verbally said. It just obviously is awareness of the situation."

The response from the community has been "great" according to the couple. Macy gave the following example of their foster daughter Rose, who is in high school: "Some of her friends at school have asked, 'I hear you talking about your foster moms,'" and she just right out said, "Well, they're a gay couple,'" and the reaction of her friends is, "Oh, that's cool.'" Teachers have also been supportive. The couple did have a complaint, however, with some of the forms at the school. Macy said, "As odd as it sounds, I think it's very ironic that you fill out these forms, or you fill out an emergency form on the kids, and it says 'father.'... And it's adding 'mother' again or 'mom' again and crossing out the 'father.' Everything's more of the traditional heterosexual, all the forms. It's just automatic, you know." Despite this frustration, the couple believes they have "been very supported in the community."

Vignette IV: Marsha and Sue

Marsha and Sue were interested in adoption but did not want to wait months for a potential placement. They made the decision to become foster parents because they were told it was the quickest way for children to be placed in their home. They called a number of different agencies and eventually chose one that was recommended to them by lesbian friends. They went through the training together, introducing themselves as a couple to the other potential foster parents. Sue said, "Marsha is more talkative to people in general, and I would be much more likely to be the person that would just let it go until something came up. And Marsha is much more like, I'm a lesbian you know." Both Marsha and Sue laughed. Marsha, still laughing, added, "It's usually the third or fourth sentence." Since the agency they selected to work with was recommended to them by another lesbian couple, they felt comfortable disclosing their sexual orientation during the foster parent training.

The couple was unsure if the agency discussed their relationship with the children placed in their home. Sue said, "I'm guessing they don't give them that kind of information. I feel like they probably don't feel like they need to. Monique was the oldest [foster child] we have done, and she was 6. I did wonder if anybody talked to her about our house, or who we were, and I really don't think so." They felt Monique really didn't care about their sexual orientation as long as she was taken care of and allowed to have fun. Marsha and Sue strongly believe case managers should have those conversations with foster children, especially older children who might be homophobic. They admitted, though, that they could not imagine anyone at their agency actually having that kind of conversation with a foster child. Marsha said, "I just can't fathom [laughing] these workers doing it.... I can't see the agency being the people to do that.... I have very low expectations for them. I feel like they're undereducated, underpaid, they're bouncin' around all over the place cause they have mountains of paperwork and all of these things to deal with, and it's hard and it's stressful, and they're young so they leave and they go do something else.... Most of these people are 23 years old, and it's a different person every time, and they know nothing about parenting and next to nothing about how to interact with people." Marsha and Sue, however, discuss their relationship with both their foster and adoptive children once they feel they are old enough to understand. Marsha claimed that "We're very open about things. I'm a speech and language pathologist that focuses on language, and I see language as a huge tool and asset, and I don't know how much Gabrielle [foster/adopted daughter] understands about things that we have said to her, but I know she says them, and I know she has the words so she uses them.... You have to give her those words, because she's gonna walk into a room full of other people, that are gonna be like, 'Where's your dad?' I want her to have an answer. So if there were [foster] kids in our home, I feel like they would need some of those things."

Marsha and Sue reported a highly positive relationship with the one birth family with whom they have worked closely. When they anticipated that their foster daughter, Sidney, would be returning to her birth family, they did what they could to facilitate the move so it would be a positive experience for her. As Marsha described it, they went "probably way beyond what some people would do." This included inviting the birth parents to their home for dinner, sending them pictures and videotapes of Sidney, loaning them a camera and developing their photos for them, and giving them a baby crib and a high chair. Marsha described the reaction of Sidney's birth father when she returned home: "Here's this older black man, saying to us how grateful he was that Sidney lived with us, and how thankful and how we did such a good job with Sidney. And that there should be more people like us, doing those kinds of things. And he said he didn't once worry when she was with us. Pretty amazing from somebody whose child was taken away from them and placed with two White gay women [laughs]."

Marsha and Sue's interactions with the community, based on their experience with daycares and schools, have been positive. The couple has lived in their current house for less than 1 year, and prior to moving they researched schools and daycares to find ones that were racially diverse (while they are White, their foster and adoptive children have been African-American) and to see if there were any other families headed by same sex couples in the area. Marsha said, "The hugest thing for me is the racial issue. I think about that a thousand times more than I do that we're gay parents." Sue added, "Yes, cause most people in the end don't care that we're gay. They, oddly enough, if they like you, they could care less.... The racial things I think are gonna be more of an issue to overcome than the sexual orientation issues for us."

Vignette V: Joan

Joan and her former partner of 23 years were attempting to have a child through artificial insemination and in-vitro fertilization. They were unable to conceive and their relationship ultimately ended. Joan considered the open adoption of an infant but felt there was not much of an opportunity for her to be selected by a birth parent because of her age, the fact that she was single, and that she was a lesbian. After talking with a gay male couple who were long-term foster parents, she made the decision to get her foster care license. When asked if she ever considered concealing her sexual orientation from the state agency, Joan responded, "I personally would not ever feel comfortable going into a situation where I was asking to be entrusted with the care of a child without revealing that. I think it would be dishonest because some people do have strong feelings. I also don't think it's anything to be ashamed of. And if I were to conceal that fact, and have it be discovered later, I think that it would look like I was ashamed of it, and that maybe there was a reason that somebody should be more suspicious." Joan went on to describe the agency's response to her disclosure: "I was anticipating and completely ready for a negative response. And I was absolutely wonderfully surprised. I'm sorry if I tear up a little bit.... The licensing worker didn't bat an eye. She welcomed the information and the history about the relationship with my former partner. She reassured me I would not have any trouble with anybody at their agency. She did caution me that the judge that was in the county would not look upon it favorably, and suggested that wouldn't be something we would want to openly discuss at an adoption hearing, but that it would be part of my file and part of my home study. So I was pleasantly surprised."

Since the three foster children placed in Joan's home have all been under the age of 3, they were too young for a discussion of her sexual orientation.

If the children were older at the time of their placement, Joan was unsure of how she would start the conversation or what she would say. She does believe, though, that it is "important to be open and honest, and not act as if this is something to be ashamed or concealed." She also feels that foster children need to know that other people "have some discriminatory views against people who are gay or lesbian. And that the child will have to learn how and when to talk to people about it and.... other people might bring up the subject to them. And let the child know that you're open to them coming to talk to you about what somebody may have said or what they may have heard."

Joan has never discussed her sexual orientation with the birth families of her foster children. As she put it, "It's not come up between me and any of the birth parents or the birth parents' aides for that matter.... You know they might suspect, but it's never come up as an issue.... I haven't revealed it, not because I'm hiding it.... but because I don't share much of anything personally about my life with any of the birth parents.... I don't think it's appropriate for them to know that."

Joan has been equally reticent to openly reveal or discuss her sexual orientation in her community because, as she describes it, it is "a very conservative, rural county, and it's heavily Christian based. And I have not felt comfortable being open in that environment. I've not had an opportunity where I've been called on to have to reveal that kind of information about myself. It's more, 'I go, I sit, I listen, I go home.'" Joan went on to describe an annual camping weekend sponsored by a local group of foster and adoptive parents. While she and her foster children attended this past year, she camped on the fringes of the main camping area and did not actively take on any leadership or volunteer roles. She believes that her sexual orientation does limit her involvement in the greater community support system to a certain extent.

Discussion

The vignettes presented above illustrate the interactions foster parents typically have with a range of individuals, including agency workers, foster children, birth family members, other foster and adoptive parents, teachers, day care workers, and judges. Many of these conversations focus on the decision to reveal or conceal their sexual orientation. This struggle exemplifies a central concept of Petronio's (2007) communication privacy management (CPM) theory, which is the tension that individuals experience between revealing and concealing private information. When the foster parents we talked to opted to disclose their sexual orientation and/or relationship to others, the response was often positive or neutral. This is perhaps not surprising, since the parents often self-selected foster care agencies, schools, and other environments they believed would support and value their relationships and families. In a communication study of gay dads, Galvin and Patrick (2008) found that while gay fathers sometimes experienced difficult conversations with others, they more often reported multiple positive experiences with extended family members, teachers, neighbors and others. Galvin and Patrick claim that these normative experiences serve to reduce the overall image of these families as unconventional. The foster children placed in the home of the lesbian and gay foster parents in this study were either too young to comprehend the nature of their sexual orientation or relationship, viewed it positively or neutrally, or were more concerned with having fun or enjoying house rules like not having to attend church. There was an awareness among these parents, however, that some older children may have problems being placed in a lesbian or gay family, which could add another layer of complexity above and beyond being separated from their birth family. The parents believed that these foster children should have a voice in where they are placed, and/or should have an opportunity to meet the potential family prior to a final placement decision being made.

Surprisingly, gay and lesbian foster parents often had no idea if case managers said anything about their relationship to foster children being placed in their home. While they felt workers were responsible for disclosing the information on their behalf and monitoring the children's responses to the disclosure, their experience as foster parents suggested this was not routinely done. This finding adds an interesting twist to CPM theory. The theory posits that people disclose to each other with the expectation that recipients, who are now "co-owners" of the information, will keep the information confidential (Petronio, 2004; Petronio 2000). Gay and lesbian foster parents had the expectation that information on their sexual orientation would and should be shared with foster children who may potentially be placed in their home. The failure of workers to do so constitutes what the theory calls "turbulence," a disruption in the coordination of privacy rules (Petronio, 2007). In this case, however, the turbulence is not a result of sharing information that was meant to be private, but stems from the failure to *not share* information with specific targets, namely potential foster children. Foster parents made it clear they did not expect or necessarily want the information shared with any other targets, including birth families or other members of the communities.

The most difficult and negative interactions gay and lesbian foster parents reported having were with the birth families of their foster children. While these conversations were sometimes difficult, they were offset by the support they received from agency workers, friends, and teachers. Looking into the future, lesbian and gay foster parents anticipated more challenges related to the interracial nature of their foster care placements and adoptions than difficulties related to their sexual orientation. Galvin (2006) refers to the process through which nonnormative families label, explain, and legitimize their families as "discourse dependency." Interracial families that consist of foster children and gay or lesbian parents have the challenge of developing and defending multiple identities. This research shows that the very nature of any one of these identities can be called into question at any time, in the most unexpected and public of places, such as a grocery store or in a restaurant. Gay and lesbian parents use these interactions as opportunities to teach their foster children if and how they should respond to questions about or challenges to their family identity.

With the exception of disclosing or confirming their sexual orientation, the foster parents we talked to reported few, if any, specific conversations with their foster children about same-sex relationships. Likewise, there were no reported interactions that were designed to prepare youth for questions or challenges to family identity that may occur in the absence of one or both parents. The families with interracial placements seemed much more concerned about race than they were about sexual orientation. Since the surrounding community was generally accepting or unaware of the parents' sexual orientation, these kinds of conversations were not necessary. That, of course, could quickly change if questions were asked or challenges were raised, forcing gay or lesbian parents to address the issue with their foster children.

By sharing their experiences and insights, the gay and lesbian foster parents profiled in this chapter revealed both the rewards and the difficulties of community interactions. They represent instances of successful parenting and successful placements, both short- and long-term. We hope we have fulfilled our goal of representing the lives of our participants in enough detail to increase and deepen understanding of what gay and lesbian foster parents experience. What is missing, however, are the voices of case managers, birth families, other community members, and the foster children themselves. Their narratives could provide an alternative view to the ones expressed by the parents. The lives of gay parents who are not as open, of foster children who are not as accepting, and of agencies and communities that are not as supportive, need to be explored as well.

The families presented in this chapter have survived and even thrived in their respective communities, often with the assistance of social service agencies, friends, teachers, and others. We would like to end with a quote from Julie, one of the lesbian foster moms we talked to for this research. Her comments reflect a belief of how gay and lesbian foster parents can help the children in their care navigate through and successfully integrate into the surrounding community.

> I think in a lot of ways that maybe we are more understanding of a lot of kids that come into foster care, because we are the minority and we have had to really learn to respect ourselves, and respect ourselves to a certain level where we can reach out to the community and say, "You know what, I'm not ashamed of who I am, and I'm proud of who I am." They come into care and they are the minority and they don't have good self-esteem, and you really have to build that in them so they can go out and be a positive part of our society and community.

References

Ackerman, J., & Dozier, M. (2005). The influence of foster parent investment on children's representations of self and attachment figures. *Applied Developmental Psychology, 26,* 507–520.

Albert, T. (2003, May/June). Why become a foster parent? *Children's Voice,* Article 0305. Retrieved February 1, 2006, from htpp://www.cwla.org/articles/cv0305foster.htm

Alexander, C. (2001). Developmental attachment and gay and lesbian adoptions. *Journal of Gay and Lesbian Social Services, 13,* 93–97.

American Civil Liberties Union. (1999, April 6). *Overview of lesbian and gay parenting, adoption, and foster care.* Retrieved October 10, 2000, from http://www.aclu.org/issues/gay/parent.html

Barbell, K., & Wright, L. (1999). Family foster care in the next century. *Child Welfare, 78,* 3–14.

Brooks, D., & Goldberg, S. (2001). Gay and lesbian adoptive and foster care placements: Can they meet the needs of waiting children? *Social Work, 46,* 147–157.

Buehler, C., Cox, M., & Cuddeback, G. (2003). Foster parents' perceptions of factors that promote or inhibit successful fostering. *Qualitative Social Work, 2,* 61–83.

Child Welfare League of America. (n.d.). *Quick facts about foster care.* Retrieved February 1, 2006, from http://www.cwla.org/programs/fostercare/factsheet.htm

Cox, M., Buehler, C., & Orme, J. (2002). Recruitment and foster family service. *Journal of Sociology and Social Welfare, 28,* 151–177.

Daniel, J. L., & Daniel, J. E. (1999). African-American childrearing: The context of a hot stove. In T. J. Socha & R. C. Diggs (Eds.), *Communication, race, and family: Exploring communication in black, white, and biracial families* (pp. 25–43). Mahwah, NJ: Erlbaum.

Demo, D. H. (2000). Children's experience of family diversity. *National Forum, 80,* 16–20.

Drucker, J. (1998). *Families of value.* New York: Plenum Press.

eHow (n.d.). *How to be a gay foster parent.* Retrieved January 27, 2006, from http://www.ehow.com/how_17539-be-gay-foster.html

Elovitz, M. E. (1995). Adoption by gay and lesbian people—The use and mis-use of social science research [Electronic version]. *Duke Journal of Gender Law and Policy, 2,* 207–217.

Galvin, K. M. (2006). Diversity's impact on defining the family. In L. H. Turner & R. West (Eds.) *The family communication sourcebook* (pp. 3–19). Thousand Oaks, CA: Sage.

Galvin, K. M., & Patrick, D. (2008). *When having two daddies is just one more way to be a family.* Unpublished manuscript.

Hicks, S. (2000). 'Good lesbian, bad lesbian…': Regulating heterosexuality in fostering and adoption assessments. *Child and Family Social Work, 5,* 157–168.

Hicks, S. (2006). Maternal men—perverts and deviants? Making sense of gay men as foster carers and adopters. *Journal of GLBT Family Studies, 2,* 93–114.

Hicks, S., & McDermott, J. (Eds.). (1999). *Lesbian and gay fostering and adoption.* London: Jessica Kingsley Publishers.

LaSala, M. C. (2003). When interviewing "family": Maximizing the insider advantage in the qualitative study of lesbians and gay men. In W. Meezan & J. I. Martin

(Eds.), *Research methods with gay, lesbian, bisexual, and transgendered populations* (pp. 15–30). New York: Haworth Press.

Lewin, E. (2006). Family values: Gay men and adoption in America. In K. Wegar (Ed.), *Adoptive families in a diverse society* (pp. 129–145). New Brunswick, NJ: Rutgers University Press.

Mallon, G. P. (2004). *Gay men choosing parenthood.* New York: Columbia University Press.

Mallon, G. P. (2006). *Lesbian and gay foster and adoptive parents.* Washington, DC: Child Welfare League of America.

National Gay and Lesbian Task Force. (2003). *Lesbian, gay, bisexual and transgender (LGBT) parents and their children.* Retrieved March 2, 2007, from http//www.Freedomtomarry.org/images/pdfs/LGBTParentsChildren.pdf

Patrick, D. (2006). The story of a gay foster parent. *Child Welfare, 85,* 123–132.

Patterson, C., & Redding, R. (1996). Lesbian and gay families with children: Implications of social science research for policy. *Journal of Social Issues, 52,* 29–50.

Peplau, L. A., & Beals, K. P. (2004). The family lives of lesbians and gay men. In A. L. Vangelisti (Ed.), *Handbook of family communication* (pp. 233–248). Mahwah, NJ: Erlbaum.

Petronio, S. (2000). The boundaries of privacy: Praxis of everyday life. In S. Petronio (Ed.), *Balancing the secrets of private disclosures* (pp. 37–50). Mahwah, NJ: Erlbaum.

Petronio, S. (2004). Road to developing communication privacy management theory: Narrative in progress, please stand by. *The Journal of Family Communication, 4,* 193–207.

Petronio, S. (2007). Translational research endeavors and the practices of communication privacy management. *Journal of Applied Communication Research, 35,* 218–222.

Plumer, E. H. (1992). *When you place a child.* Springfield, IL: Thomas Books.

Rhodes, K. W., Orme, J. G., Cox, M. E., & Buehler, C. (2003). Foster family resources, psychosocial functioning, and retention. *Social Work Research, 27,* 135–150.

Ricketts, W. (1992). *Lesbians and gay men as foster parents.* Portland, ME: National Child Welfare Resource Center.

Riggs, D. W. (2007). Reassessing the foster-care system: Examining the impact of heterosexism on lesbian and gay applicants. *Hypatia, 22,* 132–148.

Rosario, A. (2003). She's gay—And the best foster mom I know. In A. Desetta (Ed.), *In the system and in the life: A guide for teens and staff to the gay experience in foster care* (pp. 62–63). New York: Youth Communication.

Seidman, I. (2006). *Interviewing as qualitative research: A guide for researchers in education and the social sciences.* New York: Teacher College Press.

Stokes-Chipunga, S., & Bent-Goodley, T. (2004). Meeting the challenges of contemporary foster care. *The Future of Children, 14,* 75–93.

Testa, M. F., & Rolock, N. (1999). Professional foster care: A future worth pursuing? *Child Welfare, 78,* 108–124.

Tyebjee, T. (2003). Attitude, interest, and motivation for adoption and foster care. *Child Welfare, 82,* 685–706.

Youth Communication. (2005). *What we think: Teens in care talk about gay foster parents.* Retrieved January 27, 2006, from http://www.youthcomm.org/FCYU-Features/NovDec2005/FCYU-2005-11-08.htm

20 Research Commentary

Evolving Caregiving Roles and Relationships

Dawn O. Braithwaite and Jordan Soliz

As we come to the end of this volume, we cycle back around to the editors' goals for the book—understanding the interaction of parents and children both inside and outside of the family home, zeroing in on the latter. The various authors in this volume have written about the communication of parents and children as they interact with and within different systems, for example, childcare, medicine, sports, education, workplace, media, and technology. The chapters in this final section of the book converge to remind us that parent-child communication also occurs in other than what might be thought of as "traditional" families. The three chapters focus on parent and child interaction in later life as "boomerang" children return home, in stepfamilies, and in foster care with gay and lesbian parents.

The authors in this last section join others, including the co-authors of this commentary, who are studying family forms and relationships that fall wide of traditional vision of the American family. Even though these nontraditional family forms are prevalent, a scan of media images, popular writing, and research about parents and children lead us to remember what Braithwaite and colleagues (2008) stressed, "heterosexual, two-biological parent, first-marriage households do not represent the only, or even the predominant, family relationships at the start of the 21st century. Families come in different forms, many outside of the bonds of heterosexual first marriage" (p. 2). The chapters in this final section of the book are but a small representation of the large variety of family types and parenting interactions that occur.

Summary of the Chapters

In her chapter, "When the World Comes Home: Examining Internal and External Influences on Communication Exchanges between Parents and Their Boomerang Children," Sally Vogl-Bauer focused on parent-child communication in a stage of life that is underexamined in the literature, that is when adult children return to live at home with their parents. Vogl-Bauer examined the communication challenges faced within the parent-child dyad and with those eternal to the dyad. Within the dyad, parents and adult "boomerang" children must negotiate finances, communication dynamics, and household responsibilities. She then employed four communication theories, systems, relational dialectics, social exchange, and communication privacy management to better understand the internal and external dynamics in play. Vogl-Bauer identified the importance of communication that can influence success of this living arrangement.

Amy Johnson, Elizabeth Craig, Michel Haigh, Eileen Gilchrist, Lindsay Lane, and Nakia Welch addressed issues concerning, "Stepfamilies Interfacing Outside the Home: Barriers to Stepparent/Stepchild Communication with Educational, Medical, and Legal Personnel." While most of the extant stepfamily literature focuses on communication within the stepfamily household or with other members of the extended family, these scholars centered on how stepchildren and stepparents interact with those in educational, medical, and legal systems. They argue the importance of examining this communication as the lack of legal standing may limit the role of the stepparent outside of the home. In the course of the chapter, Johnson and colleagues examine stepfamilies as an incomplete institution and the social stigma hypothesis to shed light on their external communication challenges. The scholars stress the importance of looking at the interaction of stepparents with third parties.

Finally, Dennis Patrick and John Palladino explored "The Community Interactions of Gay and Lesbian Foster Parents," focusing specifically on communication of gay and lesbian foster parents and their foster children, child welfare workers, birth families, and other members of their informal and formal networks. Patrick and Palladino reported the results of a study in the form of a series of vignettes that represented the interaction of gay and lesbian foster parents with the different players in the foster children's lives. They employed Petronio's Communication Privacy Management theory to enlighten foster parents' choices to conceal or reveal their own sexual orientation and the implications for their foster children and the foster parent's interaction with others, including boundary turbulence resulting from this information.

While these three articles are diverse in many ways, they share a similar focus on the importance of understanding parent-child communication as occurring in other contexts than within the family home and in other than traditional family structures or temporalities. The authors share a commitment that a communication focus is important to navigating the waters in which these families swim. In the remainder of this commentary, we will address the contributions of a communication perspective on family types that face external challenges to their family identity. We conclude with a discussion of additional family types that have parallel experiences to the families highlighted in these final three chapters and a call for translating our scholarship into practice to improve the experiences of all families.

The Contributions of Communication

It is not uncommon for scholars to conceptualize families that fall outside of traditional conceptions by what they are *not*, defining them by the ways they *diverge* from conventional understandings of family. This approach is centered in what Ganong and Coleman (1994) referred to as a deficit comparison model, identifying these families as an "incomplete institution" (Cherlin, 1978), as authors in this section recognized. The deficit model is highlighted when "alternative" family types (e.g., GLBT families or stepfamilies) are compared against traditional nuclear families and found wanting due to differences or lack of a common bloodline (Furstenberg & Cherlin, 1991).

When families exist outside of what is expected in a given culture, how are these families composed and understood? Adopting the perspective that communication constitutes relationships (Baxter, 2004), we understand all families as a discursive construction (Bourdieu, 1996). In the case of families that fall outside of traditional boundaries, Galvin (2006) argued that the identity of these families is "highly discourse dependent" (p. 3). This means that the structure and expectations of these families are more equivocal and necessitate negotiation. For example, in our own work we have seen that for stepfamilies this means developing and negotiating expectations that are different than first-marriage families (e.g., Baxter, Braithwaite, & Nicholson, 1999).

The social constructionist view of family is centered in how families negotiate identities and expectations within the family walls and without (Berger & Luckmann, 1966; Gergen, 2000; Leeds-Hurwitz, 2006). This perspective helps explain why the authors in this section of the book called for taking a communication focus on their family contexts of interest. Rather than viewing identity as fixed, identities are ever-changing within social relationships and contexts (Eisenberg, 2001; Gergen, 2000). Likewise, given the extent to which our individual and social identities (e.g., age, race/ethnicity, religion, sexual identity, gender) can influence our interactions and relations with others (Harwood, 2006; Hecht, Warren, Jung & Krieger, 2005), families are a social context in which communication reflects and shapes both the collective familial identity and the divergent identities of individual family members (Harwood, Soliz, & Lin, 2006). Thus, we come to understand family identity in the communication of family members, as well as in and to those outside the family (Bergen & Braithwaite, in press).

From this perspective, nontraditional family forms "bear a heavier legitimation burden" (Braithwaite et al., 2008, p. 7) than do families accepted as natural or normal, as the chapters in this section exemplify. As the authors point out, these families must work harder at negotiating their place in the world, and often encounter suspicion and misunderstanding to those external to the family. For instance, Bergen, Suter, and Daas (2006) identified various strategies employed by lesbian couples to legitimize their parental identity of nonbiological lesbian parents as this identity is often challenged due to social disapproval and lack of legal recognition of the nonbiological parent. These strategies include reliance on maternal address terms, giving the last name of the nonbiological mother to the child, and a series of "legal moves" (e.g., wills, power of attorney) meant to take advantage of legal routes to legitimizing the parental role.

As families provide a central site for developing and enacting identity, families outside of the norm are sites of "contested identity," lacking the dominant cultural template that traditional families enjoy. Both within the family, and especially outside of it, these families are often misunderstood and may face social disapproval. As a result, others may not know, or even consider how, to interact with them and treat them. For example, Bergen (2006) interviewed commuter wives and examined their interactions with those outside of their family who often questioned their marital status or practices in a culture where men are more often the commuters. In the three present chapters, there are no clear norms guiding interaction of parents and their adult "boomerang" children, with stepparents intersecting with the educational and medical systems, and for gay and lesbian foster parents interacting with the foster care system. This necessitates communication on the part of the family members and others in their networks to establish appropriate ways for family members to legitimize their family identity to others as well as maintain their identity and roles with each other.

Reflecting this, Galvin (2006) discusses the discourse practices family members engage in when responding to external challenges to the family identity. Labels and names are used to identify perceptions of the family members (e.g., stepsister vs. sister, Tony vs. Dad) and serve to demonstrate inclusiveness and expectations of family roles and closeness to those inside and outside of the family. In a similar fashion, family members may perceive the need to account for and explain family circumstances to each other and to outsiders or to actively defend more hostile challenges to their family form. For instance, individuals in transracially adopted families may be questioned about the physical (i.e., racial/ethnic) differences in the family and thus the authenticity of the parent-child relationship ("Is she a real daughter?"). In her study, Harrigan (in press) found that parents of visibly different adoptive children perceived the need to manage both differences and similarities to biologically related families as they interacted with those outside the family, as well as within the family. Oswald (2000) discussed how GLBT family members perceived of and participated in heterosexual weddings, for example, how they handled questions about "when are you going to get married" from those who do know their status as a gay person, or how they coped with gendered parts of the ritual like throwing the bridal bouquet to single female guests at the wedding. Likewise, although there is no evidence for negative psychological effects, children of gay and lesbian parents may be confronted with inquiries about their families ranging from questions of parental identity ("Why do you have two mommies?") to more prejudicial challenges stemming from the social stigma still present in certain social realms (Stacey & Biblarz, 2001). Because these nontraditional family types are often challenged by persons or organizations external to the family, internal communication practices among family members such as active discussions about origin of the family, stories meant to bring family members together, and rituals symbolizing important experiences and events all function to discursively create, manage, or solidify family identity.

Implications and Future Directions

The three chapters in this final section of the book bring to the forefront examples of family types that often must legitimize their family identity both internally, with the social network, and, as the chapters highlight, to external social institutions. It is important to recognize that these three chapters represent but a sample of the diversity of family forms that face considerable challenges in terms of managing their family identity. Thus, we take this opportunity to briefly describe four additional family types where we believe the study of communication would benefit from further attention from family scholars and practitioners: custodial grandparents, extended family relationships, fictive kin, and multiethnic families.

Custodial Grandparents

Nearly half of the 3.9 million multigenerational households are headed by a grandparent as the primary caregiver and households with custodial grandparents are becoming more common (Pruchno, 1999; Simmons & Dye, 2003). Although not always the case, these families experience a unique set of circumstances that can add additional stressors in the family such as role ambiguity resulting from parental absence, financial and time constraints associated with caregiving, and the unexpected caregiving role of the grandparent. Similar to Vogl-Bauer's discussion of conflict between parents and their "boomerang" children, custodial grandparents and their grandchildren often experience role ambiguity (Emick & Hayslip, 1999) and many of the internal dynamics center on managing expectations of roles and responsibilities. Further, although custodial grandparents often face a unique set of challenges stemming from the circumstances surrounding their caregiving role, there are limited formal resources and programs available to these grandparents stemming from lack of recognition of this nontraditional caregiving role (Hayslip & Kaminski, 2005; Jendrek, 1994). Compounding this is the fact that, similar to Johnson and colleagues' discussion of the stepparent as a "legal stranger," many grandparents do not have a formal, legal custody of the grandchild and are often hesitant to take that right away from a parent (Goodman, Potts, Pasztor, & Scorzo, 2004). In short, custodial grandparents and their families can face unique challenges as they communicatively manage roles and family identity within and outside of the family.

Fictive (voluntary) Kin

Relatively little attention has been directed toward those families formed outside of blood and legal kinship (Johnson, 2000). Communication scholars and others are turning their attention to those people perceived to be family, but who are not related by blood or law. These people have been referred to as fictive kin, chosen kin, or voluntary kin. As we discussed earlier, the deficit model is often applied to these voluntary family members, which draw attention to how they are different from blood and legal family (what they lack) rather than focusing on what voluntary families are and what they bring to persons in these relationships. While fictive kin have been present for a long time and across cultures, today they are prevalent in American culture due to longer lifespan, an escalating divorce rate, and the fact that many people do not live near their blood and legal families. Braithwaite and her colleagues (2008) studied voluntary families and found that they are important to the family members and provide important sources of identity, social support, and belonging. The researchers identified different types of voluntary kin, focusing on how voluntary kin may (a) take the place of departed or estranged family members, (b) meet needs that blood and legal family cannot or will not provide due to differing values, interests, or distance, (c) meet needs in a certain context or stage of life, or (d) knit two unrelated families together.

Extended Family Relationships

Family communication researchers have tended to focus their inquiry into the enactment of family and parent-child communication within the walls of a single "nuclear" family household. However, interaction within the household is very much influenced by extended kin, and Floyd and Morman (2006) pointed to these relationships as among those understudied and not well understood. For example, Milardo (2005) studied the relationship of uncles and nephews, finding that nephews may go to their uncles for advice rather to their parents. Other scholars have examined the role of extended family in the stepfamily. DiVerniero (2007) examined some of the challenges that relationships with extended family members presented to parents and children in the stepfamily, finding that members of stepfamilies struggled with how to maintain these relationships post-divorce and how to talk about the "old" extended family with their new stepfamily members. Recognizing the influence of multiple marriages, Lambert (2006) explored challenges of what she termed "post-affinial relationships," referring to relationships between members of stepfamilies that divorce. She explored how these parents and children identify and interact post-divorce and into the formation of another stepfamily(ies).

Multiethnic Families

The 1967 U. S. Supreme Court's decision in *Loving v. Virginia*, which abolished legal sanctions against interethnic marriages, coupled with more accepting attitudes toward these unions, has led to an increase in multiethnic families over the last four decades. However, given the monoethnic norm evident in traditional conceptualizations of families, multiethnic families face similar challenges as the family types discussed in the three preceding chapters. Similar to the stigma attached to gay and lesbian parents discussed in Patrick and Palladino's chapter, multiethnic families still face disapproval and prejudicial attitudes from society at large and, in some cases, the extended family (Killian, 2001; Negy & Snyder, 2000). Within the family, parent-child communication may often involve messages aimed at creating or managing ethnic identity for the children (Rosenblatt, 1999) as establishing a sense of identity is important for the well-being of the children both in relationships with family members and in their interactions in a society in which monoethnicity is the norm (Root, 1998; Vivero & Jenkins, 1999). Actively addressing these social challenges as a couple or family while, at the same time, managing the different social identities in the relationship, is a key function of communication in multiethnic families (Socha & Diggs, 1999; Soliz, 2008).

It should be evident that we, along with many family communication scholars, advocate a more inclusive definition of family; one that moves beyond current legally recognized relationships or more socially approved family forms. In doing so, we emphasize Floyd, Mikkelson, and Judd 's (2006) point that scholars should be proactive in arguing for more inclusive, self-definitions of family while simultaneously considering the "conceptual uniqueness" of family because "excessively broad definitions of the family paradoxically make family a less and less important concept" (p. 37). With this recognition and value placed upon the constitutive nature of families comes a responsibility to move beyond identifying and understanding communication associated with legitimizing family externally and among family members and consider ways to translate this research into practice. One way to do this is to bring our findings to the very people who need them—the families. Developing programs or materials to educate families on discursive practices that differentiate positive and negative functioning within the family as well as those that are successful in legitimizing family identity outside of the home is an obligation family communication should embrace. Similarly, we should develop ways to educate legal and government institutions on the importance of diversity of family forms. In doing so, we must also address the important question of how to balance this more inclusive definition of family with the need for public policies that, by their nature and purpose, differentiate family relationships from other types of relationships (e.g., child benefits, health care benefits).

References

Baxter, L. A. (2004). Relationships as dialogue. *Personal Relationships, 11,* 1–22.

Baxter L. A., Braithwaite, D. O., & Nicholson, J. (1999). Turning points in the development of blended family relationships. *Journal of Social and Personal Relationships, 16,* 291–313.

Bergen, K. M. (2006, November). *"Your husband lets you do that?": "Commuter wife" as a contested identity.* Paper presented at the annual meeting of the National Communication Association, Boston, MA.

Bergen, K. M., & Braithwaite, D. O. (in press). Identity as constituted in communication. In W. F. Eadie (Ed.), *21st Century Communication.* Thousand Oaks, CA: Sage.

Bergen, K. M., Suter, E. A., & Daas, K. L. (2006). "About as solid as a fishnet": Symbolic construction of a legitimate parental identity for nonbiological lesbian mothers. *Journal of Family Communication, 6,* 201–220.

Berger, P. L., & Luckmann, T. (1966). *The social construction of reality: A treatise in the sociology of knowledge.* New York: Anchor Books.

Bourdieu, P. (1996). On the family as a realized category. *Theory, Culture, & Society, 13,* 19–26.

Braithwaite, D. O., Bach B. W., Baxter, L. A., Hammonds, J., Nunziata, A., Willer, E., et al. (2008, November). *Constructing family: A typology of voluntary kin.* Paper presented at the annual meeting of the National Communication Association, San Diego CA.

Cherlin, A. J. (1978). Remarriage as an incomplete institution. *American Journal of Sociology, 84,* 634–650.

DiVerniero, R. A. (2007, November). *Stepchildren's communication to manage uncertainty in stepfamilies.* Paper presented at the meeting of the National Communication Association, Chicago.

Eisenberg, E. E. (2001). Building a mystery: Toward a new theory of communication and identity. *Journal of Communication, 51,* 534–552.

Emick, M. A., & Hayslip, B. (1999). Custodial grandparenting: Stresses, coping skills, and relationships with grandchildren. *International Journal of Aging and Human Development, 48,* 35–61.

Floyd, K., Mikkelson, A. C., & Judd, J. (2006). Defining the family through relationships. In L.H. Turner and R. West (Eds.), *The family communication sourcebook* (pp. 21–42). Thousand Oaks, CA: Sage.

Floyd, K., & Morman, M. T. (2006). Introduction: On the breadth of the family experience. In K. Floyd & M. T. Morman (Eds.), *Widening the family circle: New research on family communication* (pp. xi–xvi). Thousand Oaks, CA: Sage.

Furstenberg, F. F., & Cherlin, A. J. (1991). *Divided families: What happens to children when parents part.* Cambridge, MA: Harvard University Press.

Galvin, K. (2006). Diversity's impact on defining the family: Discourse-dependence and identity. In L. H. Turner & R. West (Eds.), *The family communication sourcebook* (pp. 3–19). Thousand Oaks, CA: Sage.

Ganong, L. H., & Coleman, M. (1994). *Remarried family relationships.* Thousand Oaks, CA: Sage.

Gergen, K. (2000). *The saturated self: Dilemmas of identity in contemporary life.* New York: Basic Books.

Goodman, C. C., Potts, M., Pasztor, E. M., & Scorzo, D. (2004). Grandmothers as kinship caregivers: Private arrangements compared to public child welfare oversight. *Children & Youth Services Review, 26,* 287–305.

Harrigan, M. M. (in press). The contradictions of identity-work for parents of visibly adopted children. *Journal of Social and Personal Relationships.*

Harwood, J. (2006). Social identity. In G. Shepherd, J. St. John, & T. Striphas (Eds.), *Communication as...: Perspectives on theory* (pp. 84–90). Thousand Oaks, CA: Sage.

Harwood, J., Soliz, J., & Lin, M.C. (2006). Communication accommodation theory. In D. O. Braithwaite & L. A. Baxter (Eds.), *Engaging theories of family communication* (pp. 19–34). Thousand Oaks, CA: Sage.

Hayslip, B., & Kaminski, P. L. (2005). Grandparents raising their grandchildren: A review of literature and suggestions for practice. *The Gerontologist, 2,* 262–269.

Hecht, M. L., Warren, J. R., Jung, E., & Krieger, J. L. (2005). The communication theory of identity: Development, Theoretical Perspective, and Future Directions. In W. B. Gudykunst (Ed.), *Theorizing about intercultural communication* (pp. 257–278). Thousand Oaks, CA: Sage.

Jendrek, M. P. (1994). Grandparents who parent their grandchildren: Circumstances and decisions. *The Gerontologist, 34,* 206–216.

Johnson, C. L. (2000). Perspective on American kinship in the late 1990s. *Journal of Marriage and the Family, 62,* 623–639.

Killian, K. D. (2001). Reconstituting racial histories and identities: The narratives of interracial couples. *Journal of Marital and Family Therapy, 27,* 27–42.

Lambert, A. (2006, February). *Post-affinal kinships in multiple divorce families.* Paper presented at the annual meeting of the Western States Communication Association, Seattle, WA.

Leeds-Hurwitz, W. (2006). Social theories: Social constructionism and symbolic interactionism. In D. O. Braithwaite & L. A. Baxter (Eds.), *Family theories in communication* (pp. 229–242). Thousand Oaks, CA: Sage.

Milardo, R. M. (2005). Generative uncle and nephew relationships. *Journal of Marriage and Family, 67*(5), 1226–1236.

Negy, C., & Snyder, D. K. (2000). Relationship satisfaction of Mexican-American and Non-Hispanic White interethnic couples: Issues of acculturation and clinical intervention. *Journal of Marital and Family Therapy, 26,* 293–304.

Oswald, R. F. (2000). A member of the wedding? Heterosexism and family ritual. *Journal of Social and Personal Relationships, 17,* 349–368.

Pruchno, R. (1999). Raising grandchildren: The experiences of black and white grandmothers. *The Gerontologist, 39,* 209–221.

Root, M. P. P. (1998). Experiences and processes affecting racial identity development: Preliminary results from the biracial sibling project. *Cultural Diversity and Mental Health, 4,* 237–247.

Rosenblatt, P. C. (1999). Multiracial families. In M. E. Lamb (Ed.), *Parenting and child development in "nontraditional" families* (pp. 263–278). Mahwah, NJ: Erlbaum.

Simmons, T., & Dye, J. L. (2003, October). *Grandparents living with grandchildren: 2000.* Census 2000 Brief. Retrieved April 9, 2004, from http://www.census.gov/prod/2003pubs/c2kbr-31.pdf

Socha, T. J., & Diggs, R. C. (1999). *Communication, race, and family: Exploring communication in black, white, and biracial families.* Mahwah. NJ: Erlbaum.

Soliz, J. (2008). Interethnic relationships in families. In W. Donsbach (Ed.), *International Encyclopedia of Communication, Volume 6* (pp. 2358–2362). Oxford, England: Wiley-Blackwell.

Stacey, J., & Biblarz, T. J. (2001). (How) does the sexual orientation of parents matter? *American Sociological Review, 66,* 159–183.

Vivero, J. J., & Jenkins, S. R. (1999). Existential hazards of the multicultural individual: Defining and understanding *cultural homelessness. Cultural Diversity and Ethnic Minority Psychology, 5,* 6–26.

Epilogue
Circulation and Coordination
Managing Child-Parent-Societal Interfaces

Kathleen M. Galvin

Family systems exist within a network of community and institutional systems. Raising well-functioning children necessitates effective communication between and among members of these networks. Family communication research on children has focused intensively on parent-child and sibling relationships; few studies have focused sustained attention on child-oriented communication among family members and representatives of the larger society. When families and institutions intersect, messages circulate unpredictably among all parties as they attempt to coordinate and manage their boundaries. Communication scholars have paid limited attention to the intersections of the family and schools (Cooper 2006), healthcare and recreation (Pecchioni, Thompson, & Anderson, 2006), and media (Bryant & Bryant, 2006). There is a great need for systematic research addressing interactions among family members and representatives of educational, health/recreation, and mediated societal systems of care relevant to children's lives.

Parents and Children Communicating with Society extends the mission advanced in the editors' breakthrough text, *Parents, Children, and Communication* (Socha & Stamp, 1995). This edited collection expands the conversation by exploring the interactions involving children and parents and institutional members as they attempt to: manage privacy boundaries, address family-society communication problems, confront social status inequalities, adapt to differing communication standards, and coordinate shared systems of care. Specifically, the authors address the challenges faced by families with children as they interact with representatives of educational, health, and media institutions, as well as the unique challenges faced by members of understudied family forms as they relate with society.

In contrast to earlier times when such institutions were less complex, advances in media technology, healthcare, and psychological and educational practices serve to problematize even seemingly simple interactions. Parental figures and institutional representatives find themselves caught in an ongoing circulation of messages and meanings that impacts discussion and shared decision making on complex child-related issues. These include decisions regarding screenings and interventions for physical and/or psychological disorders, addressing a child's instructional options, or monitoring a child's use of complex technologies. Lines of responsibility blur as institutional representatives enter homes to evaluate foster parenting skills or parents attend educational programs in home schooling practices or home-based medical intervention practices.

Communicative Praxis: Circulation and Boundary Coordination

This volume addresses the communicative processes integral to creating productive intersections among family and societal systems. Many family scholars reference a systems perspective (Galvin, Dickson & Marrow, 2006) or ecological systems perspective (Bronfenbrenner, 1986, 1989) when addressing the interactions of families and societal organizations. According to this perspective, when separated entities engage each other individuals and environments begin to interact as totalities, eventually creating changes within these totalities (Magnusson, 1995). Whereas a systems perspective offers an overarching frame for viewing these chapters, message circulation and boundary coordination serve as overarching themes.

The research chapters effectively depict the complexity of coordinating shifting family-institutional boundaries. The authors' discussions range from descriptions of boundary interactions between two discrete systems to the complex boundary shifting inherent in multisystem interactions. When addressing the interface of two specific systems—family and a societal organization—the issues are less complex but no less intriguing. For example, Kendall's (chapter 14) examination of using computer mediated communication (CMC) within a pastoral context, and the comparative evaluations by youth pastors and adolescents reveal assessments that reflect a dialectic tension of connection and intrusion. Similarly, an analysis of the interactions between parental stress helpline volunteers and callers underscores the difficulty of implementing appropriate therapeutic skills when confronted with highly stressed callers affected by mood disorders (Pennington & Baus, chapter 15). These chapters provide nuanced and insightful analyses of interactions between families and members of mediated helping environments. In addition, although it is common to assume similarity among persons within each bounded area, Wingard's (chapter 5) research on triangulation of homework depicts moments when parents and children struggle with each other as they attempt to coordinate their responses to institutional expectations.

Given the growing need for multiple institutional responses to complex family stresses, it is no longer sufficient to consider message transmission across singular boundaries. Instead, the focus must incorporate message circulation as members of all relevant systems attempt to coordinate their efforts. Boundary management increasingly involves the intersection of multiple complex systems as increasingly sophisticated knowledge and technological capabilities provide distinctive options for family members who find themselves in roles of consumers, supplicants or combatants. Conversely, professionals may play roles of informants, negotiators, or problem solvers. Many chapters depict the challenges of boundary management when complex institutional networks are activated to serve a family's needs. For example, when responding to the expectations of groups in surrounding communities, state foster care representatives, birth family members, and same-sex foster parents engage in highly-charged interactions across multiple boundaries (Patrick & Palladino, chapter 19). Similarly, stepfamily members must be aware of multiple institutions' regulations (e.g., legal and medical) for invoking legitimate service claims and must recognize the need for representatives of varied institutions to interact with each other as well as with family members (Johnson, Craig, Haigh, Gilchrist, Lane, & Welch, chapter 18). By depicting the ever expanding range of institutions' representatives who interact with parents and children, the research chapter authors engage issues traditionally ignored or understudied in family communication literature. These chapters demonstrate the great need for future research addressing multi-systemic communication.

Communicative Praxis: Coordinating Message Circulation

As scholars address communicative situations involving multiple institutional and family systems, they will need to understand the complexity of family/institutional interfaces as well as communicative practices for coordinating movement across shifting borders. Sue Clark's Work/Family Border theory (2000) describes the experiences of moving between work lives and family lives, revealing multiple complexities. Her research shows that "people were largely proactive or enactive—they moved back and forth between their work and family lives, shaping each as they went by negotiating and communicating" (p. 751). Border crossers impact multiple personal and institutional systems; they shape each system they enter, mold the borders between them, and determine their own relationship to these systems and their members. Her theory presents a dynamic model for exploring family/institutional interfaces.

Clark (2000) depicts borders as physical, temporal, or psychological, the third involving "rules created by individuals that dictate when thinking patterns, behavior patterns and emotions are appropriate for one domain but not the other" (p. 756). Each border type comes into play as individuals attempt to coordinate these domains. Clark depicts the following border characteristics that are exemplified by selected research chapters: (a) *Permeability* implies the degree to which elements from one domain may enter other ones. In their nuanced and theoretically driven piece, Duggan and Petronio (chapter 7) reveal how parents of children with serious medical conditions and their care team interact, depicting the multiple subsystems that come into play as parents and medical team members struggle to manage the flow of information, often under highly regulated and stressful conditions. (b) *Flexibility* refers to the extent to which a border may contract or expand depending on the demands of other domains. For example, case managers, birth family members, and foster children themselves affect a foster family's borders through regulation and requests (Patrick & Palladino, chapter 19). In their discussion of care-oriented principles and practices in a children's mental health system, Davis, Dollard, and Vergon (chapter 8) underscore the complexities and benefits of a team based approach involving communication among support persons such as parents/caregivers, formal supports (e.g., therapists), and informal supports (e.g., neighbors). (c) *Blending* implies that, when the area around a presupposed barrier is not longer exclusive to one domain, a borderland emerges that is not exclusive to either domain. In examining circumstances in which parents coach their own children, Littlefield and Larson-Casselton (chapter 11) describe periods of equality and mixed roles, such as a parent-child dyad co-owning athletic information that is not shared with other members of the family or the team. (d) *Border Strength* is determined by a combination of permeability, flexibility, and blending. High impermeability (strength), inflexibility, and resistance to blending create strong borders; the opposite is also the case. In situations when Early Intervention is forced on certain parents who are assigned tasks to perform at home, these parents may exhibit resistance or increase border strength to avoid doing the onerous or overwhelming intervention tasks (Mills & Walker, chapter 9).

To further develop her theory, Clark (2000) relies on the work of Lave and Wegner (1991) that identified border-crossers as central and peripheral participants in the domains. Central participants are characterized as internalizing the domain's culture, competent in related responsibilities, connected with central members and personally identifying with the domain's responsibilities. Imagine a "helicopter parent" who gains power by buttering up the child's basketball coach, volunteering to help with team activities, and talking about professional basketball with the coach (Turman, Zimmerman, & Dobesh, chapter 10). Peripheral participants are characterized by ignorance or disdain for a domain's culture, lacking full competence to perform their responsibilities, loosely connected with central members, and exhibiting limited identification with domain responsibilities. For example, Miller-Day and McManus (chapter 4) reveal how poverty, and its attendant negative outcomes such as depression, mental health problems, and stress, contributes to creating low societal status and peripheral participants. The authors make a compelling case for the need to develop efficacy in order to reverse the helplessness and/ or hopelessness moving across generations of working-poor families. Yet, given variations in competencies and knowledge, roles will shift and require ongoing coordination.

In addition to serving as exemplars of border-crossing complexities, the research chapters illustrate parents and children whose success in boundary coordination is affected by position and privilege, characteristics inextricably linked to communication competence. Just as power regulates access to resources, power confers increased capacity to negotiate borders through a linguistic proficiency that facilitates talk among multiple constituencies. Many communities represent social and economic divides that influence the availability of communication resources needed to engage institutional involvement with local children. Power accrues to a parental figure whose education and/or workplace experience provides the communication competencies that make her an effective advocate for her child's medical resources. Conversely, a principal who cannot communicate effectively with students and their family members in a low-income neighborhood reduces the school's access to valuable community resources.

Future Research Directions

By depicting the complicated issues of message circulation and boundary coordination within these chapters, this volume paves the way for related studies. These model chapters should motivate other communication scholars to consider involvement in joint research programs with scholars from related academic areas. The research commentaries clearly identify important future research directions. Communication scholarship is only beginning to address critical child/family/institutional issues such as community responses to child abuse (Wilson, 2006), shared medical decision making involving parents, children, and health professionals (Clayman, Galvin, & Arntson 2007), family members and health professionals' interactions regarding genetic disease (Gaff & Bylund, in press), and the communicative interfaces created among adoption professionals, prospective parents, and mediated resources (Wahl, McBride, & Schrodt, 2005).

Some of these chapters model the creation of research teams to address macro level communication problems that necessitate interactions among multiple knowledge systems. For example, the research by Miller-Day and McManus (chapter 4), Wingard (chapter 5) and Davis, Dollard, and Vergon (chapter 8) demonstrates the impact of large interdisciplinary research teams in addressing the complex communicative issues resulting from family and multi-institutional interactions. As more family-oriented communication scholars address societal issues, it will be necessary to collaborate with scholars in other areas and to seek funding to support large scale projects. Certain problems will be addressed fully only through applied research that contributes to systematic second-order change that alters the nature of the system itself (Watzlawick, Weakland, & Fisch, 1974). For example, Wilson (2006) depicted the impact of a community's efforts to respond to the death of a child by implementing first and second order changes that involved new interaction patterns for parents and community members. Finally, such research must be inclusive of the range of family forms and the parental roles assumed by multiple caring persons (Braithwaite & Soliz, chapter 20, this volume; Galvin, 2006).

In the preface to this volume, Anita Vangelisti asserts that *Parents and Children Communicating with Society: Managing Relationships Outside of Home* "maps out territory for research on parent-child communication that is both influential and mostly unexplored by those who study communication" (p. xiii). It is imperative that communication scholars join together to confront challenges faced by parents and children representing multiple family forms, as they interact with institutional representatives within interactive societal contexts characterized by ongoing message circulation and boundary coordination. This new frontier represents a major scholarly challenge for the 21st century.

References

Bronfenbrenner, U. (1986). Ecology of the family as a context for human development: Research perspectives. *Developmental Psychology, 22,* 723–742.

Bronfenbrenner, U. (1989). Ecological systems theory. In R. Vasta, (Ed.), *Annals of child development* (6th ed., pp. 187–250), Greenwich. CT: JAI Press.

Bryant, J. A., & Bryant, J. (2006). Implications of living in a wired family: New directions in family and media research. In L. H. Turner & R. West (Eds.), *The family communication sourcebook* (pp. 297–314). Thousand Oaks, CA: Sage.

Clark, S. C. (2000). Work/family border theory: A new theory of work/family balance. *Human Relations, 53*(6) 747–770.

Clayman, M. L., Galvin, K. M., & Arntson, P. H. (2007). Shared decision making: Fertility and pediatric cancers. In T. K. Woodruff & K. A. Snyder (Eds.), *Oncofertility: Fertility preservation for cancer servivors* (pp. 149–160). New York: Springer.

Cooper, P. J. (2006). Family – school relationships: Theoretical perspectives and concerns. In L. H. Turner & R. West (Eds.), *The family communication sourcebook* (pp. 405–424). Thousand Oaks, CA: Sage.

Gaff, C., & Bylund, C. L. (Eds.). (in press). *Talking about genetics: A family affair.* New York: Oxford University Press.

Galvin, K. M. (2006). Diversity's impact on defining the family: Discourse-dependence and identity. In L. H. Turner & R. West (Eds.), *The family communication sourcebook* (pp. 3–19). Thousand Oaks, CA: Sage.

Galvin, K. M., Dickson, F. C., & Marrow, S. R. (2006). Systems theory: Patterns and (W)holes in family communication. In *Engaging theories in family communication* (pp. 309–324). Thousand Oaks, CA: Sage.

Lave, J., & Wegner, E. (1991). *Situated learning: Legitimate peripheral participation.* Cambridge, England: Cambridge University Press.

Magnusson, D. (1995). Individual development: A holistic, integrated model. In P. Moen, G. H. Elder, Jr., & K. Luscher (Eds.), *Examining lives in context: Perspectives on the ecology of human development* (pp 19–60). Washington, DC: American Psychological Association.

Pecchioni, L. L., Thompson, T. L., & Anderson, D. J. (2006). Interrrelations between family communication and health communication. In L. H. Turner & R. West (Eds.), *The family communication sourcebook* (pp. 447–468). Thousand Oaks, CA: Sage.

Socha, T. J., & Stamp, G. H. (Eds.). (1995). *Parents, children and communication: Frontiers of theory and research.* Mahwah, NJ: Erlbaum.

Wahl, S. T., McBride, M. C., & Schrodt, P. (2005). Becoming "point and click" parents: A case study of communication and online adoption. *Journal of Family Communication, 5,* 279–294.

Watzlawick, P., Weakland, J., & Fisch, R. (1974). *Change: Principles of problem formation and problem resolution.* New York: W. W. Norton.

Wilson, S. R. (2006). First and second-order changes in a community's response to a child abuse fatality. *Communication Monographs, 73*(4) 481–487.

Author Index

Subject Index